From Development to Dictatorship

A VOLUME IN THE SERIES

THE UNITED STATES IN THE WORLD

edited by Mark Philip Bradley, David C. Engerman, and Paul A. Kramer

A list of titles in this series is available at www.cornellpress.cornell.edu.

From Development to Dictatorship

Bolivia and the Alliance for Progress
in the Kennedy Era

Thomas C. Field Jr.

Cornell University Press
Ithaca and London

Publication of this book was supported by grants from the Scouloudi Foundation, in association with the University of London's Institute of Historical Research, and from Embry-Riddle Aeronautical University.

First published 2014 by Cornell University Press

Printed in the United States of America

Library of Congress Cataloging-in-Publication Data

Field, Thomas C., Jr., author.
   From development to dictatorship : Bolivia and the alliance for progress in the Kennedy era / Thomas C. Field Jr.
       pages cm
   Includes bibliographical references and index.
   ISBN 978-0-8014-5260-4 (cloth : alk. paper)
   1. Bolivia—Politics and government—1952–1982.   2. Bolivia—History—1952–1982.   3. Bolivia—Social conditions—1952–1982.
4. United States—Foreign relations—Bolivia.   5. Bolivia—Foreign relations—United States.   6. Alliance for Progress.   I. Title.
   F3326.F48   2014
   984.05'2—dc23   2013038571

Cloth printing   10   9   8   7   6   5   4   3   2   1

To Milena

Contents

Preface

During a six-month jaunt around South America in early 1963, American journalist Hunter S. Thompson became fixated on what he called "Baffling Bolivia: A Never-Never Land High above the Sea." Swigging bourbon whiskey on the couch of a US Embassy official as armed workers and peasants patrolled the streets, Thompson was enthralled by the "manic atmosphere" he found in revolutionary Bolivia's capital city, La Paz, "compared to the gray formality of Lima and the tomb-like dullness of Quito." Summing up his experiences in typical tongue-in-cheek fashion, Thompson wrote that "Bolivia is a land of excesses, exaggerations, quirks, contradictions, and every manner of oddity and abuse."[1] US officials in Bolivia rivaled Thompson's prose. Ambassador Ben Stephansky noted in 1962 that he had been assigned to a "complicated and perplexing country." Two years later, his successor Douglas Henderson likewise complained that Bolivia had an "Arab-like political world" with "byzantine complexity." In May 1963, Central Intelligence Agency (CIA) operative General Edward Lansdale—himself no literary slouch—lamented that Bolivia "is a land of vexing paradox for the US."[2]

Little has changed in fifty years. Since I began work on this book, Bolivia has experienced violent civilian uprisings, at least one peasant massacre, the declaration of a US ambassador persona non grata, the expulsion of the Drug Enforcement Agency, a weeklong strike by mutinous national police, and most recently the ejection of the United States Agency for International Development (USAID). Over the past seven years, I have been intrigued by the Bolivian riddle. In the process, I have incurred many debts.

My conversations with historian Luis Antezana Ergueta significantly contributed to my Bolivian orientation. His book on the 1964 coup is passionate and provocative, and I sometimes think I would have never understood anything in this country's political life without our early conversations. Several people shared contacts and helped me feel at home in Bolivia, personally and intellectually. These include Evan Abramson, Hervé do Alto, Guido Antezana, Ricardo Calla, Jorge Calvimontes, José Luis Cueto, Emilse Escóbar, Alex Fernández, Ingrid Fernández, Loyola Guzmán, Bill Lofstrom, Juan Molina, Nancy Nallar, Uvaldo Nallar, Lola Paredes, Phil Parkerson, Luis Pozo, Pablo Quisbert, René Rocabado, Andrés Santana, Carlos Serrate, Carlos Soria, and Eduardo Trigo. Thierry Noel kept me company—often against his wishes—as I typed through endless drafts. His unparalleled knowledge of the Bolivian armed forces, and his excellent espressos and araks, significantly contributed to this book's completion.

In my reconstruction of the narrative of US development assistance to revolutionary Bolivia in the years leading up to the 1964 coup, government records have proven especially useful. This book benefited greatly from documentation at the Biblioteca y Archivo Nacional de Bolivia in Sucre, where a massive collection of papers from Víctor Paz Estenssoro's second presidency (1960–1964) was made available to scholars in the early 2000s. Long hidden in the rafters above the presidential palace, these documents demonstrate the centralized manner by which Paz ruled, depict his government intentionally utilizing the communist threat to secure ever-increasing levels of US assistance, and reveal the extent to which Bolivia's revolutionary leaders viewed economic development as their only path to national liberation. Archive Director Marcela Inch offered me an informative introduction, and archivists Álvaro López, Óscar Hurtado, and Corina Garcia provided patient professionalism during my many visits. This book also benefited from the expert archival assistance of Rossana Barragán at the Archivo de La Paz, Marta Paredes at the Foreign Ministry Archive, and Edgar Ramírez at the archive of the state-run mine company, the Corporación Minera de Bolivia. Each repository provides its own perspective on the intensity with which the Bolivian government sought rapid modernization in the early 1960s, even at the occasional expense of democratic liberties. Vlasta Měšťánková at the Archiv Národní in Prague sent digital scans from the archives of the Czechoslovak Communist Party, which contain numerous memoranda of private conversations with Bolivian officials and Communist Party members. The archive of Paz Estenssoro's Movimiento Nacionalista Revolucionario (MNR; Revolutionary Nationalist Movement) and the records of the Central Obrera Boliviana

(COB; Bolivian Workers' Central), both located at the Bibliothèque de Documentation Internationale Contemporaine in Nanterre, France, bring into stark relief a bitter feud between Paz's technocratic, modernizing approach and the Bolivian labor movement's stubborn refusal to be depoliticized.

During my extensive sojourn in Bolivia, I also identified dozens of memoirs by key political figures. Former Paz government officials blame the 1964 military coup squarely on the CIA, while labor leaders concede their central role in destabilizing Paz's government. Rank-and-file mine workers express little guilt for agitating against Paz's MNR, given the party's submission to the United States during the presidency of John F. Kennedy (1961–1963). Meanwhile, military conspirators proudly recount their decision to lead a popular revolt against what had become an increasingly repressive regime. Political pamphlets, dozens of which were generously provided by Luis Antezana Ergueta, have been especially helpful in tracing the ideological trajectory of Bolivia's cornucopia of political movements. As Antezana put it, "the history of Bolivia is written on pamphlets."

On the US side, recent declassification projects, ably facilitated by Stephen Plotkin and Sharon Kelly at the John F. Kennedy Presidential Library and by Regina Greenwell and Jennifer Cuddeback at the Lyndon Baines Johnson Presidential Library, shed extensive light on the doggedness of US liberal support for Paz Estenssoro's modernizing approach. Documents from the State and Defense departments and the CIA, as well as oral histories and personal papers, demonstrate that US support for the MNR never wavered, and they reveal the way technocratic ideologies of development were prisms through which both administrations waged war on the Bolivian labor movement. Embassy post files, USAID records, and additional State Department documents, all located at the National Archives and Records Administration (NARA) in College Park, Maryland, substantially complemented the presidential library collections and filled in numerous gaps regarding the process by which US officials offered unstinting support to Paz's government.[3]

US aid to revolutionary Bolivia was controversial, and the debate in the American press illuminates a sharp divide between liberal developmentalists, who aggressively defended Paz's MNR, and American conservatives, who characterized the regime as "candy-coated despotism."[4] With the help of ProQuest's historical newspaper database, I analyzed all articles on Bolivia between 1961 and 1964 in nine US newspapers, including the *New York Times*, the *Boston Globe*, the *Christian Science Monitor*, the *Chicago Tribune*, and the *Washington Post*. *Time* magazine offers online access to its historical archive, providing a disturbing view of the extent to which American liberals excused Paz Estenssoro's authoritarianism in the name of Third World development. In an attempt to trace Cuba's growing disenchantment with the MNR, I read Havana's weekly newspaper *Bohemia*,[5] which is available at the Library of Congress, and transcripts of Cuban radio broadcasts, housed in the Cuban Heritage Collection at the University of Miami. Finally, I conducted a systematic survey of Bolivia's newspaper of record, *El Diario*, which adopted a strong anti-Paz bias in the early 1960s under the direction of Julio Sanjinés Goytia and Mario Rolón Anaya, both of whom were close friends of General René Barrientos, leader of the 1964 coup. I also read selected months of the independent communist weekly, *El Pueblo*, and Cochabamba's Marxist daily, *El Mundo*, which gave extensive pro-Barrientos coverage during this period under the direction of Víctor Zannier, another friend of the general.

Many of the key players in this narrative were still alive when the research was conducted. Through extensive interviews on both sides of the US-Bolivian relationship, I was able to identify sentiments and trends not often reflected in the documentary records. Ambassador Douglas Henderson, CIA station chief Larry Sternfield, and embassy air attaché Edward Fox all spent hours discussing the details of US policy toward Bolivia in those tense years. Their stories built on what the documents suggest: that the Kennedy and Johnson administrations were convinced that Paz Estenssoro was the only person who could shepherd Bolivia along the path of anticommunist modernization and that US officials—begrudgingly in the case of Sternfield and Fox— were forced to stand by while General Barrientos carried out his revolt. In Bolivia, I interviewed members of Paz Estenssoro's family and several former cabinet officials, all of whom blame the CIA, and Colonel Fox in particular, for Paz's downfall. General Barrientos's civilian friends and family scoff at any suggestion that the United States orchestrated the coup, a sentiment shared by retired military officers who supported the uprising from its inception. I also interviewed important figures on the Bolivian Left—Communist, nationalist, and Trotskyist, including former mine union leaders, student activists, and urban intellectuals, who concede—sometimes with a poignant sense of regret—the central role they played in Paz's downfall. Finally, I conducted several interviews with adherents of the MNR's eternal right-wing enemy, the Falange Socialista Boliviana (FSB; Bolivian Socialist Falange), including former student leaders and young militants who launched a guerrilla struggle against the Paz government in the jungles of Santa Cruz in 1964.

Many friends and colleagues read and commented on sections of the manuscript. These include Onur Erdem, Piero Gleijeses, Molly Giedel, James Hershberg, Jeremy Kuzmarov, Alvise Marino, Ramiro Paz, David Schmitz, Maria del Carmen Soliz, Bill Walker, Joel Wolfe, Marilyn Young, and anonymous readers for *Diplomatic History* and Cornell University Press. A few individuals read the entire manuscript, including James Dunkerley, Mark Gilderhus, Robert Karl, Kenneth Lehman, David Painter, Stephen Rabe, Bradley Simpson, Larry Sternfield, and Jeffrey Taffet. In each case, this initiated a scholarly collaboration that I hope will extend years into the future. Several others shared information, contacts, or documents, including Elizabeth Burgos, Glenn Dorn, James Dunkerley, José Gordillo, Apple Igrek, Robert Kirkland, Erick Langer, Guy Laron, Rory and Mariela Martin, Monsignor David Ratermann, James Siekmeier, the Fox family, the Barrientos family, Joseph Barry at the Air Force Academy, Angélica Pérez at the Inter-American Development Bank, Padre Roberto at Radio Pio XII, Michael Fouch at the Hall County Library in north Georgia, and Alex Bakir, who spent a morning wading through Spanish-language documents for me at the Hoover Institution. Juan Molina of Radio Pio XII spent an entire day interpreting Quechua for me in the village of Irupata; Eleanor Joyner (codename HONEYBEE), of the American Cryptogram Association, made quick work of some hard-to-decrypt coded telegrams, originally drafted by Bolivia's secret police; and the late Melvin Burke, who worked for USAID-Bolivia in the 1960s, extended warm friendship at one of this book's turning points. In addition to Professor Burke, several other collaborators have since passed away, including Ambassador Henderson, Colonel Fox, and Communist leaders José Luís Cueto, Simón Reyes, Daniel Ordóñez, Rosendo Osorio, and Domitila Barrios de Chungara. I extend my condolences to all their families.

I traveled extensively during most of my research for this book, and I owe a great debt to those who offered me a place to stay: Artemy Kalinovsky, Dayna Barnes, Gokhan Sahin, and Teoman Ayas in London; David Ward in Boston; Giacomo Boati in Paris; Martin Ditto in Washington, D.C.; the Magarzo family in Tarija and Santa Cruz; and Alvise Marino and David Ward in New York City. Edward Anderson in D.C. and Alex Bakir in London shared their homes for weeks (was it months?) on end, never asking for a penny. Finally, on three occasions the family of Colonel Edward Fox shared their hospitality and the enduring affection they feel for their adopted *patria*, Bolivia.

During her stint as a visiting professor at the Johns Hopkins School of Advanced International Study (SAIS)-Bologna, Marilyn Young first prompted me to look deeper into US relations with revolutionary Bolivia, and she has been an unstinting supporter of this book since then. John Harper inspired me to write, and to write often. At SAIS-DC, Piero Gleijeses showed me how to conduct historical research, and he continues to offer frank academic direction and criticism. Francisco González brought Latin American history to life, and Kelly Kornell provided generous administrative support for years after I left. At the London School of Economics, Tiha Franulovic and Demetra Frini were patient, understanding, and helpful as I finished my research abroad. Steven Casey and Kristina Spohr provided needed direction during my first years in London, and Nigel Ashton encouraged me to find my own academic voice. Arne Westad read numerous troublesome drafts, always prompting me to push my conclusions further and never losing faith in the book. At New York University's Tamiment Library, Marilyn Young and the late Michael Nash extended the warmest possible hospitality to me and my family, and both shared their extensive knowledge of twentieth-century Cold War and labor history. At Embry-Riddle University, Frank Ayers, Archie Dickey, Richard Bloom, and Philip Jones provided my research with generous financial and moral support. Deborah Faupel has been a wonderful addition to the research institute, and Leanne Harworth never failed to obtain obscure interlibrary loan material from around the country. At Cornell University Press, Michael McGandy guided the manuscript forward with deftness, insight, and a keen eye for detail, and Sarah Grossman patiently walked me through the process. David Engerman, coeditor of the United States in the World series, offered wise and creative suggestions on earlier drafts, cartographer William Keegan incorporated countless suggestions into the book's maps, and production editor Pamela Nelson provided innumerable (and invaluable) stylistic suggestions.

Financial support was provided by the George C. Marshall Foundation, the Society for Historians of American Foreign Relations, the John F. Kennedy Library Foundation, the Lyndon Baines Johnson Library, the University of London, the London School of Economics, and Embry-Riddle University. Without the support of these institutions, I would have never been able to concentrate on this book for the time it required, much less travel to so many archives to reconstruct the narrative. I am also grateful to the journal *Diplomatic History* and its editor Thomas Zeiler for granting permission to republish portions of my 2012 article "Ideology as Strategy: Military-led Modernization and the Origins of the Alliance for Progress in Bolivia," from volume 36 (1): 147–183, in chapter 1 of this book.

Families undergo a unique sacrifice when someone takes up a project of this magnitude. My parents never lost faith that I would finish, and they doggedly stood by me as only parents know how, stepping in with loving support at several crucial junctures. My daughter Eleanor was born just as I began writing this book. Many of these pages were drafted with her sleeping in my arms, and I cannot imagine having finished without the inspiration she unknowingly provided. Finally, over the past six years, my spouse Milena showed constant love and unremitting stoicism as I toiled away in libraries across the world and typed through the night in La Paz coffee shops. With calm and steadfast support, she also helped guide the manuscript through unexpected turns and the occasional dead end. To her, this book is dedicated.

Abbreviations

CAS	CIA Station
ABNB	Archivo y Biblioteca Nacional de Bolivia
ALP	Archivo de La Paz
CIA	Central Intelligence Agency
CIWS	Central Intelligence Weekly Summary
COB	Central Obrera Boliviana (Bolivian Workers' Central)
COMIBOL	Corporación Minera de Bolivia (Mining Corporation of Bolivia)
CREST	CIA Records Search Tool
DCM	deputy chief of mission (US Embassy)
DIA	Defense Intelligence Agency
FOIA	Freedom of Information Act
FRUS	*Foreign Relations of the United States*
FSB	Falange Socialista Boliviana (Bolivian Socialist Falange)
FSTMB	Federación Sindical de Trabajadores Mineros de Bolivia (Union Federation of Bolivian Mine Workers)
GOB	Government of Bolivia
IDB	Inter-American Development Bank
IDP	internal defense plan
INR	State Department Bureau of Intelligence and Research
JCB	Juvenil Comunista Boliviana (Bolivian Communist Youth)

JFKL	John F. Kennedy Presidential Library
KSČ-NA	Komunistická strana Československa (Communist Party of Czechoslovakia), Národní archiv (National Archive)
LBJL	Lyndon Baines Johnson Presidential Library
MEMCON	Memorandum of Conversation
MNR	Movimiento Nacionalista Revolucionario (Revolutionary Nationalist Movement)
NARA	National Archives and Records Administration, College Park, Maryland
NSA	national security adviser
NSAM	national security action memorandum
NSC	National Security Council
NSF-CO	National Security Files, Country File
OAS	Organization of American States
OPS	Office of Public Safety
PCB	Partido Comunista de Bolivia (Communist Party of Bolivia)
PCML	Partido Comunista Marxista-Leninista (Marxist-Leninist Communist Party)
PIR	Partido de la Izquierda Revolucionaria (Party of the Revolutionary Left)
POF	Presidential Office Files
POR	Partido Obrero Revolucionario (Revolutionary Workers' Party [Trotskyist])
PR	Presidencia de la República (Presidency of the Republic)
PRA	Partido Revolucionario Auténtico (Authentic Revolutionary Party)
PRIN	Partido Revolucionario de la Izquierda Nacionalista (Revolutionary Party of the Nationalist Left)
PURS	Partido de la Unión Republicana Socialista (Party of the Socialist Republican Union)
RG	Record Group (NARA)
RREE	Ministry of Foreign Relations (Bolivia)
SDANF	State Department Alpha-Numeric Files (NARA)
SDDF	State Department Decimal Files (NARA)
SDLF	State Department Lot Files (NARA)
SOUTHCOM	US Southern Command

USAID   United States Agency for International Development
USAIRA   US Embassy air force attaché
USARMA   US Embassy army attaché
USIS   United States Information Service
WGA   Wálter Guevara Arze Papers

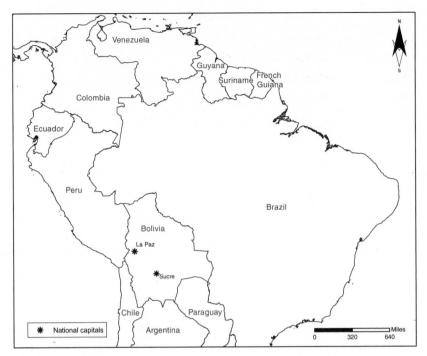

Map 1. South America, early 1960s

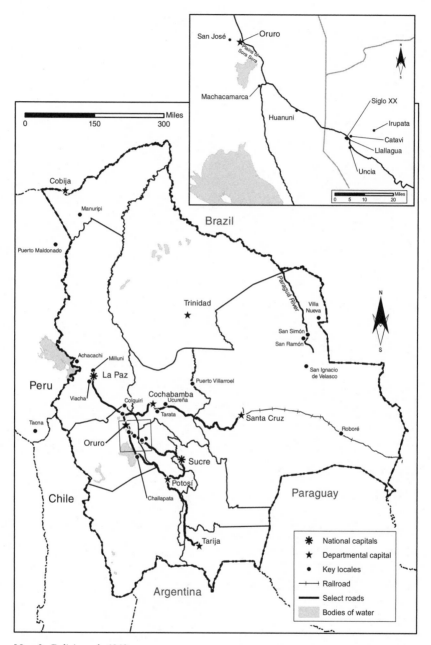

Map 2. Bolivia, early 1960s

From Development to Dictatorship

Introduction

Ideology as Strategy

Military forces can contribute substantially to economic and social development, and we should make such a contribution a major function of these forces.
—President John F. Kennedy, 18 December 1961

On 1 May 2013, Bolivian president Evo Morales announced that his government was expelling the United States Agency for International Development (USAID). "The times have passed," Morales declared, when the United States could use "charity" as a fig leaf for "manipulation . . . domination . . . [and] subjugation."[1] USAID rejected these "baseless accusations," lamenting an abrupt end to Washington's seventy-year effort to "promote human, economic, social, and cultural development" in Bolivia.[2] Such passionate rejections of development are rare, but this is hardly the first time the United States has been accused of intervening in Bolivia under the cover of promoting economic development. In July 1963, USAID sent $100,000 of military hardware to equip an Indian peasant militia charged with "eliminating" two left-wing union leaders, Federico Escóbar and Irineo Pimentel, depicted by the development economists as obstacles to Bolivia's modernization. When Escóbar and Pimentel were arrested four months later, Communist miners retaliated by taking four US development officials hostage and holding them for nine tense days in their dynamite-laden union hall.[3]

To fully grasp the origins of Bolivia's long, tumultuous relationship with US development programs, this book returns to Washington's largest aid effort in Latin America, the Alliance for Progress. Launched by President John F. Kennedy shortly after his 1961 inauguration, the Alliance for Progress was a product of heady times. Later that year, Kennedy boldly predicted that the world was on the verge of a "Decade of Development," and he vowed to approach development as a "cooperative and not a competitive enterprise."[4] Privately, President Kennedy was more prosaic, informing his staff that "military forces can contribute substantially to economic development," particularly in Latin America, where the "military occupy an extremely important strategic position."[5]

President Kennedy's interest in Third World development arose from his realization that the world was rapidly changing. In the late 1950s and early 1960s, dozens of nations were in the process of gaining independence from Western European imperialism, and many were resisting submission to the bipolar world order. Insisting instead that they would follow a third path between capitalism and socialism, Asian and African nationalists—soon joined by their Latin American counterparts—shifted the international debate away from the Cold War and toward the struggle for economic and political independence. In the process, these "third way" nationalists called for greater attention to their populations' desires for rapid modernization, forcing the United States and the Soviet Union to reorient their foreign policies in a direction more sympathetic to Third World development.

By the early 1960s, both superpowers had gotten the message, and the bipolar Cold War devolved into a ground-level struggle—rhetorical and ideological—"over the very meaning of European modernity."[6] To be sure, Latin American nationalists did not lead the charge, but their decades-long struggle against North American "neocolonialism" nonetheless found resonance within the largely Afro-Asian Third World movement. Particularly for radicals and Latin American communist parties, the emergence of a nonaligned, tricontinental identity offered the tempting prospect of receiving development aid from both sides of the Cold War divide.

With nonalignment blurring Cold War battle lines, US liberals like President Kennedy argued that Washington's reticence to engage the Third World amounted to a strategic liability. The Soviet Union was in a process of loosening its Marxist orthodoxy, and its previous disparagement of bourgeois nationalism was giving way to a fruitful policy of "peaceful coexistence," including economic agreements with countless noncommunist Third World regimes, including nationalist Bolivia. Forced by strategic necessity to adopt a more creative approach, US policymakers increasingly warmed to theories of modernization, which offered a useful schema within which to carry out politically meaningful action in the global south. By adopting a development-oriented approach, the incoming Kennedy administration (1961–1963) sought to guide the uncommitted Third World toward Washington's vision of middle-class modernity, preventing the region's descent into worker-and-peasant socialism. USAID's development ideology was therefore constructed within a geopolitical milieu, with theory and strategy fully intertwined.

In analyzing ideology as strategy, this book seeks to resolve a frustrating paradox. How did the decade of development, the 1960s, so quickly descend into the decade of the military coup d'état? For several reasons, Bolivia is a useful case in exploring this dilemma. First, in 1952, Bolivia lived through Latin America's second social revolution, after Mexico's, in which the country's landed oligarchy was destroyed.[7] Second, despite their historical antagonism toward Moscow, Bolivia's revolutionary nationalists increasingly saw themselves as adherents of the international "third way," prompting the Soviet Union to offer $150 million in development aid in late 1960.[8] Third, Washington was also generous to revolutionary Bolivia, and by 1964 the country was the second highest per capita recipient of US aid in the world, with the Alliance for Progress development program providing roughly 20 percent of Bolivia's gross domestic product (GDP).[9] Finally, like so many other Third World nationalist regimes, Bolivia began two decades of military rule in 1964, making the country an ideal case study of developmentalism *and* militarization, the dual hallmarks of the global 1960s.

This book is not the first to demonstrate that technocratic programs meant to better societies can be co-opted by states seeking to depoliticize resistance movements. In the 1970s, Edward Said lambasted oriental studies in late nineteenth-century Western Europe for providing a supposedly objective scientific rationale for imperial expansion. In Said's view, French and British orientalism was resurrected after World War II by American social scientists who constructed technocratic development theories and " 'applie[d]' [their] science to the Orient, or anywhere else" that the United States sought to intervene. More recently, James Ferguson deconstructed World Bank programs in tiny Lesotho, finding the presence of strategic concerns at every level of what he calls the "development enterprise." For both Ferguson and Peter Uvin, who considered aid agencies in pre-genocide Rwanda, "development" is a useful intellectual construct for states thirsty for bureaucratic power with which to control and administer complex and potentially rebellious populations, "to make society legible," in the words of James C. Scott.[10]

International historians have become increasingly sensitive to the relationship between foreign policy strategies and ideologies of development,[11] particularly with regard to the heavy-handedness of US-backed military-led modernization programs in Cold War Asia.[12] Much of the modernization literature retains a distinctly top-down focus, but this new wave of scholarship has nonetheless challenged long-held orthodoxies regarding development and its role in international politics, and it has gone a long way toward resolving the paradoxical intimacy between authoritarianism and modernization in the twentieth-century Third World.

By connecting the high politics of modernization theory with the bottom-up effects of development programs on the ground, this book contends that development ideology has a tendency to justify authoritarianism and encourage the rise of Third World armed forces. In the narrative that follows, development was not a foreign import. It was rather a decades-long imperative of Bolivia's nationalist revolutionaries who sought to organize, modernize, and administer what they saw as a chaotic society. US liberal strategists received and largely adopted Bolivians' linkage of political authority with ideological development, and they resolved to help guide the country's modernization along a path that was tolerable to Washington's broader anticommunist agenda. With Washington providing expert technocrats armed with economic theories and tens of millions of dollars, Bolivia's modernizing nationalists set about creating a development-oriented authoritarian state. By 1964, the shift to military rule was ideologically effortless.[13] There is no theoretical dilemma after all; the development trope is perfectly compatible with that of the military coup d'état.

Revolutionary Bolivia before 1961

In order to understand the implications of Washington's large-scale development intervention in Bolivia in the early 1960s, it is necessary to consider the country's previous three decades of revolutionary upheavals. In the wake of Bolivia's disastrous Chaco War with Paraguay (1932–1935), domestic radicals coalesced into three competing revolutionary parties: the communist Partido de la Izquierda Revolucionaria (PIR; Party of the Revolutionary Left), the Trotskyist Partido Obrero Revolucionario (POR; Revolutionary Workers' Party), and the nationalist Movimiento Nacionalista Revolucionario (MNR; Revolutionary Nationalist Party). All three of these upstart parties called for the nationalization of Bolivia's booming mining sector, and they vowed to return land to the country's indigenous majority. During its first hundred years of independence, Bolivia's liberal modernizers had largely succeeded in destroying the pre-1850 system of traditional Indian communal lands, and by 1950, most indigenous Bolivians had been subjected to semi-serfdom (*pongaeje*), with 615 wealthy families (0.7 percent of the population) controlling half of the arable land and the poorest 83 percent scratching about on a mere 1 percent.[14]

International politics ensnared all three of Bolivia's revolutionary parties during World War II, with the communist PIR adhering loyally to the Soviet party line, the POR affiliated with the Trotskyist Fourth International, and the nationalist MNR "deeply committed to the German war effort."[15] During the war, Bolivia's mines supplied Moscow's allies in Washington, severely curtailing the Communist Party's enthusiasm for radical political action or salary strikes. The POR and the MNR capitalized on this fact, and during the 1940s their popularity skyrocketed among Bolivia's multitude of mine workers, particularly after the PIR joined an "antifascist" front with Liberals and Republicans. This culminated in the gruesome 1946 overthrow of the nationalist military regime of Gualberto Villarroel, who was dragged by demonstrators from the presidential palace, beaten to death à la Mussolini, and hanged from a lamppost in the central plaza. For the next six years (the *sexenio*, in nationalist memory), MNR and POR members suffered fierce repression and forced exile, eventually reaching a revolutionary nationalist-Trotskyist accord that served as the ideological forerunner of the 1952 insurrection. Once again, the clarion call was "the land to the Indians, and the mines to the state." With the revolutionary winds taken from its sails, the communist PIR disbanded in 1950, only to be resurrected the following year as the Communist Party of Bolivia, still too weak to play a meaningful role in the coming revolt.[16]

Bolivia's April 1952 revolution began as a coup d'état organized by officers sympathetic to the nationalist MNR, whose leader, Víctor Paz Estenssoro, had emerged victorious in presidential elections the year before, only to be denied the office by the military. When loyalist forces rallied to the government's side on 9 April, the MNR coup was spontaneously converted into a popular insurrection under the leadership of party second-in-command Hernán Siles Zuazo. Nationalist and Trotskyist miners flooded into the city armed with Mauser rifles dating from the Chaco War, and police opened their armories to local civilians, including labor unionists affiliated with the MNR, the POR, or both. After three days of fierce fighting, the army had been routed, and Víctor Paz was called back from exile in Buenos Aires to take up his rightful place as president. Acceding to demands from the armed miners and Indian peasants, the regime granted universal suffrage (April 1952), nationalized the country's enormous tin-mining companies (October 1952), and signed into law a program of radical and thoroughgoing agrarian reform (August 1953).[17]

Despite their willingness to oust the country's tin magnates and destroy its landed oligarchy, Bolivia's nationalists averted a break with Washington. This was facilitated by US officials' recognition that the MNR was a hodgepodge coalition of former Trotskyists and radical nationalists, joined as much by their antipathy toward the Soviet Union as they were by their hatred of Bolivia's oligarchy. Recognizing revolutionary Bolivia's instability and seeing the MNR as a useful bulwark against communist inroads, the incoming administration of Dwight D. Eisenhower (1953–1961) proceeded to dole out tens of millions of dollars in foreign aid, a uniquely generous gesture during the austere 1950s.[18]

Aside from ensuring that nationalist Bolivia would retain its official noncommunist character, Eisenhower's largesse secured the MNR's commitment to compensate the former owners of the nationalized mines, and Paz Estenssoro agreed to open up Bolivia's burgeoning petroleum sector to foreign investors. Moreover, in 1956, Paz invited the International Monetary Fund (IMF) to oversee—conveniently during the incoming Siles administration (1956–1960)—the implementation of an anti-inflationary austerity plan.[19] Finally, there was a marked uptick in US military aid after 1958, which President Siles employed in order to lessen his reliance on Paz Estenssoro's notoriously repressive civilian militias.[20] Despite the appearance of submission, all of these measures dovetailed nicely with the MNR's own ideology of development and capitalist modernization, and nationalists retained important trappings of revolutionary idealism despite their intimacy with the United States. Presidents Paz and Siles might have been awash in development aid from Washington, but their wholesale agrarian reform marched apace. Moreover, Bolivia's tin mines remained in the hands of the state, with US dollars indirectly compensating their former owners.

As Moscow turned its gaze toward the Third World in the late 1950s, the MNR moderated its fierce anti-Stalinism, securing in the process a closer identification with the international nonaligned movement. In late 1960, Moscow offered Bolivia a long-coveted tin smelter, along with $150 million in development aid.[21] Paz Estenssoro also cultivated ties with Czechoslovakia and Yugoslavia during his ambassadorship in London (1956–1960), and he returned to office in 1960 promising to revitalize the revolution.[22] When he invited legendary labor icon Juan Lechín to be his running mate and received an endorsement from the now-strengthened Communist Party, Bolivian leftists began to believe that "a revolution within the Revolution" was possible.[23]

US president John F. Kennedy had no intention of abandoning the struggle for the global south, however, and less than two months after his January 1961 inauguration, he announced the Alliance for Progress for Latin America, a "vast cooperative effort, unparalleled in magnitude," which would "transform the American Continent into a vast crucible of revolutionary ideas and efforts" and ensure "an ever-broadening base of material advance."[24] These words were meant for Latin American modernizers like Víctor Paz Estenssoro, whose nationalist regime had implemented Alliance-style redistributive reforms nine years earlier. One of Kennedy's first acts was to dispatch a "Special Presidential Economic Mission" to La Paz, in order to find out just what Víctor Paz wanted. Kennedy's developmentalists were unanimous in their response: "We would regard it as a tragic error to abandon Bolivia under the current circumstances. . . . In all possibility, we will never have a better chance to achieve a turn-about and a take-off in Bolivia.[25] . . . To resign from combat now, or to take the road that leads to chaos in the hope that a bright phoenix will somehow rise from the ashes, is a choice prudence will not allow."[26] Kennedy never shied away from development as "combat," and the way in which the resulting adventure played out on the ground is the subject of the pages that follow.

Structure

Chapter 1 of this book traces President Kennedy's initial encounter with revolutionary Bolivia in 1961. Kennedy saw in President Paz a kindred spirit, a young, fellow modernizer heading up what one Kennedy scholar calls a "regime in motion."[27] With the Soviet Union offering to provide Bolivia with a long-coveted tin smelter and $150 million in low-interest credits,[28] Kennedy and his development-minded aides frantically sought ways to reorient Bolivian development through the nascent Alliance for Progress. In practice, Kennedy's liberal appointees sought to accentuate the MNR's newfound enthusiasm for incorporating the armed forces within the development process, resulting in a military-led development paradigm similar to that depicted in Bradley Simpson's study of US-Indonesian relations in the 1960s.[29] In Bolivia, development's principal points of entry were the Indian peasant countryside and the highland mining camps, particularly the country's largest tin mine at Siglo XX, where the armed, communist-led mine workers fiercely resisted MNR attempts to achieve political hegemony. Alliance for Progress reforms targeted these recalcitrant unions as "obstacles to development," vividly demonstrating the program's strategic foundation.[30]

Chapter 2 follows the Alliance for Progress in Bolivia through its first two years, as perennial political crises drove an increasingly authoritarian approach to economic development. Chief defenders of President Paz's repressive response to unrest, particularly in the leftist mining camps, were Kennedy's liberal appointees, Ambassador Ben Stephansky, a high-profile labor economist, and Alliance for Progress administrator Teodoro Moscoso. Washington's larger ambivalence toward Bolivia's development was laid bare when the US Treasury Department, under strong congressional pressure, launched a program in mid-1962 to sell off enormous quantities of tin from its strategic mineral stockpile. With the only direct motor of Bolivian development, tin prices, sputtering downward, officials in La Paz once again threatened to take their country down the path of Soviet-leaning international neutrality. In September 1962, President Paz canceled his trip to Washington and removed Bolivia from the Organization of American States, and Ambassador Stephansky warned his superiors that "a crisis in Bolivia's political orientation is near at hand."[31]

Despite Washington's fears, Paz Estenssoro was not prepared to cleave his country from the inter-American system. Chapter 3 demonstrates the dual process by which Kennedy's Alliance for Progress bolstered Paz's efforts to maintain Bolivia's noncommunist orientation. First, civic action programs of the Alliance for Progress fueled a rapid militarization of development in the countryside, with many projects receiving the enthusiastic endorsement of future coup leader General René Barrientos. Second, Kennedy's Special Group on Counterinsurgency allocated $100,000 through USAID to equip a pro-Paz Indian peasant militia that planned to attack the left-wing miners of Siglo XX, who were mounting a fierce campaign to block mass firings and other labor reforms required by Alliance for Progress development programs. The resulting bloodshed in the village of Irupata between armed miners on the one hand and Indian peasants and undercover soldiers from Paz's presidential guard regiment on the other led US officials to conclude that President Paz was "for the first time taking decisive steps to end labor indiscipline in the mines and assure the basis for orderly economic development."[32]

Violent battles between the miners and Paz's US-backed modernizing regime did not end at Irupata. In December 1963, Paz Estenssoro's secret police arrested Siglo XX union leaders Federico Escóbar and Irineo Pimentel, prompting rank-and-file miners to take two dozen hostages, including four US development officials. Chapter 4 narrates the resulting standoff, which nearly descended into civil war. Despite President Paz's desire to use the hostages as a cause célèbre to take the mines by military force, the incoming administration of Lyndon Johnson (1963–1969) vetoed a full-scale attack while US officials remained in the line of fire. The miners eventually capitulated in the face of vague threats by Washington, a massive Bolivian military mobilization, and rumors that thousands of armed, pro-Paz Indian peasants were set to march on the mining camp. The release of the American hostages a few days before Christmas did little, however, to resolve the battle of attrition that had emerged between Paz's development-oriented government and the rebellious miners, who subsequently declared their camp as "Free Territory of Siglo XX."

Chapter 5 traces General Barrientos's meteoric rise from air force chief to vice president during the first half of 1964, during which time he suffered a mysterious assassination attempt hours before he was set to depart for London as embassy air attaché. With public opinion mobilized behind Barrientos's vice presidential candidacy, President Paz reluctantly chose the young general as his running mate. Bolivian sources, written and oral, agree that Barrientos was loyal to Paz in early 1964, bragging widely that he had copiloted the plane that brought Paz back from Buenos Aires in the days following the 1952 revolution. Paz's dismissal of Barrientos as an uncultured jock, however, gradually pushed the general into the eager embrace of civilians opposed to the MNR regime. As the presidential elections approached, Barrientos was briefly drawn into a conspiracy that received the combined support of the Bolivian Right and Left. Strident US opposition to the coup, and the wavering of Armed Forces Commanding General Alfredo Ovando, convinced Barrientos to abandon his civilian co-conspirators. In May 1964, the Paz-Barrientos ticket emerged victorious in an election marred by mass abstention.

After a string of student and miner martyrs in late October anti-Paz demonstrations, two La Paz regiments declared themselves in rebellion on the morning of 3 November 1964. General Barrientos had already retired to his home province of Cochabamba, from which he led units into a full-scale revolt. Rather than risk civil war, Paz Estenssoro escaped to Lima on a Bolivian air force plane the following day. General Ovando negotiated the peaceful transfer of power, feigning loyalty until Paz had safely departed. Twelve years of MNR rule had come to an end, and US officials were forced to deal directly with the development-oriented military they helped create. The Bolivian revolution, and the Alliance for Progress, had been fully militarized.

Chapter 1

Modernization's Heavy Hand

The Triangular Plan for Bolivia

If ideologies of development are intellectual tools capable of being wielded by states for political ends, their strategic nature should be evident from the very inception of any development-oriented intervention. Indeed, the communist threat was midwife to the extensive foreign aid program launched by the Kennedy administration in Bolivia in early 1961.[1] President Víctor Paz's pesky nationalism, and his continuing toleration of domestic communism, motivated US policymakers to redouble their efforts to shore up his government and direct its process of development. Bolivia had already implemented thoroughgoing redistributive reforms, and according to Kennedy officials, the country's experience within the Alliance for Progress would be a test case of their thesis that social reform was a precursor for rapid modernization. What Bolivia needed, in their view, was an extensive program of economic aid, large enough to convince Paz Estenssoro to wage war against domestic leftists, depicted by liberal economists as the principal obstacles to development. This confluence of ideology and strategy, laid bare in the earliest months of the Kennedy administration, explains the highly politicized nature of the apparently technocratic development project that was being launched. Far from abandoning ideology in favor of authoritarianism, the Kennedy administration's approach was authoritarian from the beginning. Paz Estenssoro, never relinquishing his dream of exercising total political control, was this project's willing accomplice.

Víctor Paz Estenssoro and Authoritarian Nationalism

In their adoption of authoritarian development as foreign policy, Kennedy officials were largely responding to an existing paradigm of authoritarian nationalism in Bolivia. President Paz had demonstrated that he was willing to accept foreign aid from any source, Western or communist, in his unrelenting drive to "turn Bolivia into a real Nation."[2] The Bolivian leader had also begun to display a more favorable view toward the armed forces, which he hoped to employ in the service of national development. Finally, Víctor Paz ruled with an iron fist, directed at Bolivian conservatives during his first term (1952–1956), and he revived this repressive machinery when he resumed power in 1960.[3] Kennedy officials were alarmed by the extent to which Paz was courting the communist world and repressing the domestic right wing, but they were also confident in their capacity to woo the Bolivian leader back into the Western camp. In early 1961, US officials sought to bolster Paz's reliance on the armed forces as harbingers of development while simultaneously convincing him to turn his repressive apparatus against the Bolivian Left.

A nationalist, Víctor Paz sought to maintain neutrality in foreign affairs. "His points of reference," according to his son Ramiro, were leaders of the nonalignment movement, such as Indonesian president Sukarno, India's Jawaharlal Nehru, and Ghana's Kwame Nkrumah.[4] According to a journalist for the Movimiento Nacionalista Revolucionario (MNR; Revolutionary Nationalist Movement), Paz also "loved [Yugoslav prime minister Josip Broz] Tito. He wanted to be a Latin American Tito, to play both sides of the Cold War."[5] Aside from fellow Latin Americans, the only foreign leaders to visit Bolivia during the early 1960s—Sukarno, Tito, and France's Charles de Gaulle—shared Paz Estenssoro's worldview.[6] For Paz, this neutralist tendency was nothing new. During World War II, the MNR party chief scored large propaganda victories by criticizing the Bolivian government's overt alliance with the Allied powers, claiming that it prevented the country from taking full advantage of global tensions to procure higher prices for Bolivian tin.[7]

Paz believed the Cold War was no different, and his government was well-represented at meetings of the nonalignment movement, including the 1961 Belgrade conference and the 1962 and 1964 gatherings at Cairo.[8] Building on a trip to Prague during his late 1950s ambassadorship in London, Paz also sent an official envoy to Czechoslovakia in 1960, culminating in a cultural agreement on 23 January 1961.[9] Days earlier, Prague's vice minister of foreign affairs, Jiří Hájek, visited Bolivia to discuss a high-profile antimony smelter offer.[10] Meanwhile, the Central Intelligence Agency (CIA) worried that the Paz government was "under heavy domestic pressure" to accept a standing Soviet offer, first made in October 1960, to provide Bolivia with a long-coveted tin smelter and $150 million in economic and technical assistance.[11] In early February, Paz scandalized outgoing US ambassador Carl Strom with his view that "acceptance of Soviet bloc economic aid will not endanger the U.S. grant-aid program." When informed that such aid might enable the Soviets to "score politically in Latin America," Paz precociously stated that he felt "no obligation to impede such a development."[12]

These Communist bloc "economic overtures," in the words of the State Department Bureau of Intelligence and Research (INR), had introduced a "disturbing political issue." INR also noted that the Czechs were permitting $2 million of their exports to be paid for in local currency to their embassy in La Paz, money that was pumped freely into "known Czech political and propaganda activities in Bolivia."[13] Assistant Secretary of State for Latin America Thomas Mann worried that Washington's failure to provide extensive economic aid would "create a vacuum into which the Communists would move," since the "Soviets are genuinely interested in establishing a foothold in Latin America."[14]

Paz's nationalist ideology also reserved a special, albeit complicated, role for the armed forces. Military officials bitterly recall that the MNR temporarily closed the officers' academy in the aftermath of the 1952 revolution, purged the officer corps of 150 to 200 suspected "counterrevolutionaries," forced remaining officers to swear loyalty to the party, and mandated that the new academy admit children from the "middle class, workers, and Indian peasants." Despite opposition from his party's left wing, however, Paz reconstituted the armed forces in mid-1953 as "an instrument that contributes to the economic development of the country thereby achieving the welfare of the Bolivian people."[15] Officers who survived the purges latched onto the military's newfound role as a force for development. Indeed, they had little choice. As one expert on the Bolivian armed forces notes, the MNR's early suspicion of the military forced enterprising officers to "develop the idea that the army should move forward toward self-sufficiency and play an active role in development."[16]

When Paz Estenssoro prepared to return to the presidency, he made it clear that "the armed forces would be called upon to perform work of first magnitude," with Bolivia entering its "revolutionary constructive development phase." Meeting with the High Command in 1959, Paz repeatedly referred to officers as *compañeros* of the MNR, anointing them the party's "Military

Cell" and thanking them for providing "new evidence of the unity that exists in the revolutionary ranks." Citing ongoing military-led development experiments in Indonesia, India, Iraq, and Egypt, Paz Estenssoro argued that it was "fallacy" to think that the military could not serve as an armed wing of the governing party.[17] The 1960 MNR platform formalized this relationship, calling for extensive military involvement in the revolution's "fundamentally constructive phase." The armed forces were "few in number, but well gifted and instructed with professional cadres," the platform read, stressing the need for technical expertise in the modernization process.[18] In his August 1960 inaugural address, President Paz confidently declared that "after eight years of a revolutionary regime, it is safe to say that the armed forces have truly been returned to the people."[19]

Aside from expressing a desire for international neutrality and seeking warmer relations with the Bolivian armed forces, Paz revived his previous reliance on police repression in his drive for political power.[20] On 21 February 1961, President Paz responded to a nationwide teachers' strike by declaring a ninety-day state of siege and rounding up dozens of right-wing opposition leaders—and one token Communist, Oruro University Rector Felipe Iñiguez—unceremoniously airlifting the majority into Paraguayan exile.[21] This modified version of martial law meant that "public manifestations and political meetings" were "absolutely prohibited," bars and cafés were forced to close at midnight, and after 12:30 a.m., no two individuals could be seen together in public.[22] Citing "permanent subversive activity by certain Far Right and Far Left groups, who view liberty as an environment in which to hone their coup intentions," pro-MNR colonel Eduardo Rivas Ugalde, then serving as Paz's government minister, accused "petty bourgeois elements . . . and communist agitators" of "exploiting" the teachers' economic demands. Rivas vowed to "maintain public order, prevent bloodshed, and defend [the] conquests" achieved by the 1952 revolution.[23]

The following day, Kennedy's top aide for Latin America, Arthur Schlesinger, arrived in La Paz for a three-day leg of his six-country regional tour. Ostensibly taking part in a fact-finding mission for Washington's Food for Peace program, Schlesinger was also seeking to identify political leaders who were dedicated to the "modernization of Latin American society." The White House aide believed that the "chief obstacle to modernization" was precisely the "agrarian, semi-feudal economic structure" that had been destroyed by the Bolivian revolution nine years hence. Seeking a "middle-class class revolution . . . as speedily as possible," Schlesinger warned that the Soviet Union, "in association with Cuba . . . [was] exploiting the situation and providing the

US with unprecedented serious competition." He characterized the situation as requiring an "extremely high degree of urgency," since the middle classes were the only barrier to the "workers-and-peasants," who would soon take matters into their own hands.[24]

Víctor Paz would eventually epitomize the middle-class revolutionary Schlesinger so eagerly sought. Nonetheless, in their first meeting, Arthur Schlesinger referred to the previous day's roundup of right-wing opposition leaders, preaching to Paz at length that "it was not only necessary to protect the revolution from the oligarchy of the right; it was also necessary to protect it from the conspiracy and sabotage of the left." Schlesinger drew Paz's attention to the Cuban revolution, which "may have begun as a national revolution, but . . . has now been clearly seized by forces from outside the hemisphere intent on destroying free institutions and establishing a Communist state." President Paz responded confidently that the Cuban system "puts land in the hands of the state," whereas the Bolivian revolution "puts land into the hands of the peasants," adding for good measure that Cuban president Fidel Castro "must be eliminated."[25]

At the time, Paz's attempt to demonstrate unswerving anticommunism left Schlesinger unconvinced. Citing Bolivia's burgeoning relations with the Communist bloc, Schlesinger characterized the meeting as "a typical Paz performance. . . . His words are excellent, but his actions belie his words."[26] In his report to President Kennedy, Schlesinger warned that Bolivia was "on the brink of a serious political convulsion. . . . Bolivia might well go the way of Cuba. . . . After Cuba, we simply cannot let another Latin American nation go Communist; if we should do so, the game would be up through a good deal of Latin America. . . . One can already imagine the speeches in Congress on the theme, 'Who lost Bolivia?' . . . The loss of Bolivia would be a catastrophe." According to Schlesinger, the Kennedy administration needed to launch a "serious effort at economic development" alongside a "shrewd and tough politico-diplomatic offensive" that would "create the conditions which would drive Paz to take an anticommunist line." Schlesinger enthusiastically endorsed Kennedy's ambassadorial appointee, Russian émigré labor economist Ben Stephansky, who was a "liberal opponent of communists and fellow travelers" who could "talk to Paz in Paz's own language and help nerve him into bolder action." This "adroit and aggressive ambassador" would be well placed to implement a development program accompanied by "explicit economic conditions and implicit political conditions, reinforced by a stern and resourceful diplomatic determination." Schlesinger also concluded that a fortified Bolivian military would "strengthen the government against the possibility of a revolt by the armed miners . . . [and] help Paz to recover his freedom of action." Schlesinger ended his report by reiterating that "Bolivia must be saved," adding that the new administration must "think through with care and precision the requirements of salvation."[27]

Prior to Stephansky's arrival, US Embassy Deputy Chief of Mission (DCM) William Williams seconded Schlesinger's analysis, agreeing that "another Cuba in Bolivia would obviously be disastrous." Williams wrote that if Bolivia went the way of Cuba, a "purely national revolution would be superseded by one managed by International Communism, thus discouraging nationalists in neighboring countries who think it is possible to bring about thoroughgoing reforms under a non-Communist system." US aid to the Bolivian MNR since 1953 had had "an important and favorable influence on the thinking of South American revolutionaries," Williams explained, adding that "we still have the chance to turn the Bolivian revolution to our advantage and make it the most potent counterweight to the Castro revolution in Latin America." Success would require the "wit and will . . . [to] liberate" Paz from the "left majority in his own party," Williams continued, recommending that the Kennedy administration "dole the money out bit-by-bit depending on [Paz's] performance" on key issues such as "Communism in the country, labor indiscipline, [and] relations with the Bloc countries."[28]

With the teachers' strike and state of siege entering their ninth day on 1 March, newly appointed Inter-American Development Bank (IDB) president Felipe Herrera began a five-day tour of Bolivia. If Herrera was bothered by the lack of political liberties or the recent roundup of politicians, he made little fuss. On the contrary, the IDB president announced the tentative approval of a US-backed $10 million economic development program, conditioned on harsh labor reforms in Bolivia's state-run mining sector.[29] Albeit preliminary, Herrera's dramatic aid offer was just the sort of development-oriented impetus President Paz needed. One day after signing the 4 March IDB loan agreement, the Bolivian president told outgoing ambassador Carl Strom that he was preparing to "take decisive action [to] end [the] teachers' strike," including the "arrest [of] Communist trade union leaders [in] all sectors with [the] exception of mining," where he would need "at least another month to strengthen [the] party position in [the] mines before attempting [to] arrest Communist leaders there."[30]

President Paz further revealed that he would order the Bolivian army to occupy major rail centers during the crackdown and that he was fully committed to "defend [the] Bolivian revolution against [a] communist attempt [to] sabotage economic recovery." Ambassador Strom reported to Washington that this would be the "first use [of] uniformed forces to impose GOB [Government of Bolivia] policy" since the revolution began and that the United States would have "much to gain" if Paz followed through. Strom forwarded a list of military equipment Paz requested in connection with the operation, including hundreds of rockets (2.25 inch, 3.5 inch, and 5 inch), 1,450 bombs (fragmentary, chemical, incendiary, and pyrotechnical), 300 boxes of airplane ammunition, 20 airplane machine guns, and 5,000 tear gas grenades. Secretary of State Dean Rusk immediately approved the shipment, and two days later, 28,400 pounds of weaponry landed in La Paz.[31] The teachers promptly gave up their grievances.[32]

Later that day, President Kennedy announced that he was dispatching his first special economic mission, which would depart immediately for La Paz to "review the status and effectiveness" of US aid programs and provide recommendations that would "give strength and viability to the Bolivian economy . . . keeping [the] country in [a] friendly posture toward [the] US."[33] Incoming ambassador Stephansky later explained that Kennedy dispatched the mission to see "whether or not Bolivia was really over the brink."[34]

Five days later, Kennedy unveiled his heralded Alliance for Progress program of extensive development assistance to Latin American reformers. It was not a coincidence that his speech waxed lyrical on the benefits of rapid social and economic progress while giving very short shrift to the importance of political democracy.[35] Indeed, the Kennedy administration's early commitment to Bolivia demonstrated that the development ideology of the Alliance for Progress had little to do with democratic liberties. It did, however, have everything to do with anticommunist development, and Bolivia was well poised to play a central role in this emerging program.

President Paz was a sincere nationalist who sought to take advantage of global tensions to increase foreign development assistance to Bolivia. Moreover, the governing party was slowly warming to the armed forces, and the repressive state apparatus Paz controlled could be deployed at will against political enemies. Authoritarian development predated the Alliance for Progress in Bolivia, but there is no evidence that liberals in Washington were bothered by it. On the contrary, they viewed Paz's strong-armed rule as well suited for a large-scale, politicized development intervention. With Paz continuing to court the Communist bloc, however, it remained to be seen whether or not he would live up to his promises, thus fulfilling Schlesinger's dream of saving Bolivia from the scourge of communism.

The Triangular Plan

From its inception, the Alliance for Progress in Bolivia was an experiment in authoritarian development, and it was in the country's massive tin mines that US aid was most clearly wielded for political ends. Development economists employed by the Kennedy administration pointed to Bolivia's rebellious miners as the principal obstacles to economic progress, and these liberal intellectuals readily served Washington's anticommunist crusade. In technocratic language, they called for the depoliticization of the Bolivian labor movement, providing an elegant theoretical basis for what was an unmistakably political project. With US development funding firmly secured by mid-May 1961, President Paz unleashed his long-promised crackdown on the Left. In so doing, he enjoyed no shortage of repressive weaponry from the United States.

After eleven days in Bolivia, President Kennedy's special economic mission reported back on 24 March that the country "offers substantial opportunities for economic development," despite its "unfavorable trend." Headed by Marshall Plan economist and former assistant secretary of state for economic affairs Willard Thorpe, the mission condemned Eisenhower-era aid programs to Bolivia for having given Washington "no control over the secondary use of aid funds," a leverage that these economists believed should be used to require harsh economic reforms. Recommending that the Kennedy administration incorporate future aid within an "integrated plan for development," the Thorpe mission honed its sights on what it called "labor-coddling" in the nationalized mining sector. Noting that President Paz had intimated a willingness to crack down on the miners' unions, the mission estimated that he would do so only with "proper encouragement and assistance" from the United States. Because of the uncertainty of Paz's political will, the economic mission conceded that a large-scale program would be a "gamble, possibly against odds." They nonetheless argued, employing the unmistakable rhetoric of modernization theory, that Washington would "never have a better chance of achieving turn-about and take-off in Bolivia." The mission concluded that it would be a "tragic error to abandon Bolivia under the current circumstances."[36]

In its formal recommendations, the Thorpe mission reiterated the importance of cracking down on the miners' unions, where the "hard and tough core of the labor movement is to be found." The mission went on to estimate that Bolivia's state-run mining company, Corporación Minera de Bolivia (COMIBOL; Mining Corporation of Bolivia), was employing "four to five thousand more workers than are necessary for the efficient functioning of the mines." The economists recommended that these miners be laid off as soon as possible to test Paz's willingness and capacity to "introduce increased labor discipline in the economy." The Thorpe mission believed that the "principal roadblock" to this "rationalization" effort would be Vice President Juan Lechín, executive secretary of the Federación Sindical de Trabajadores Mineros de Bolivia (FSTMB; Union Federation of Bolivian Mine Workers), whose "strongly leftwing or communist influenced . . . anti-American" sector of the governing MNR would resist any action against the "known communist leaders" in the mines. The Lechín threat was aggravated, according to the economic mission, by the fact that the miners were organized into armed militias, and thus able to impose their will on COMIBOL's management rather than the other way around. The mission, therefore, recommended strengthening the "morale of the army," both by supporting military-led "economic development through construction and other engineering works" and by providing increased "internal security" equipment to counterbalance the armed miners.[37]

In a separate letter to the White House, mission member Seymour Rubin, who had been appointed legal counsel for the United States Agency for International Development (USAID), stressed that the proposed program would surely fail unless "labor leaders whose actions are dictated by pro-Communist and pro-Castro sentiment . . . [are] removed." Rubin warned, "If Bolivia turns the way of Castro, the failure of United States support to bring benefits to a country will be publicized throughout the continent." Conceding that the "hazards and difficulties . . . are admittedly great," Rubin concluded that "to resign from combat now, or to take the road that leads to chaos in the hope that a bright phoenix will somehow rise from the ashes, is a choice which prudence will not allow."[38]

The Thorpe mission report made quite a wave in Washington. *Time* magazine hailed "Kennedy's fact-finders" for recognizing that under the Eisenhower administration, "the US [had] been acting too much like an indulgent uncle." An unnamed Kennedy official told *Time* that Washington would no longer just "dump $50 million in there, or $10 million, and say, 'Here you are, fellows, have a ball.'" Instead, the Kennedy administration would ensure that future aid went toward "businesslike development." *Time* cleverly titled its article "After the Ball."[39]

Meanwhile, Secretary of State Rusk's top aide, Theodore Achilles, reported to Alliance for Progress architects Lincoln Gordon and Adolf Berle that the Thorpe mission had recommended "not so much an increase in American assistance as its reorientation" toward development. Despite the fact that this would be "a gamble" and would be "dependent on the Bolivian Government taking the necessary measures to make our aid effective," Achilles concluded that it was "difficult to see any alternative. . . . Clearly we cannot abandon Bolivia."[40]

The State Department's INR agreed with this approach, and it had previously argued that economic development would be "unlikely to succeed . . . unless President Paz can impose certain reforms in the mines over the probable objections of opposition mine union leaders." INR concurred, therefore, with the Thorpe mission's view that Washington should fully support the IDB's demands that Paz apply the harshest labor reforms "as soon as possible, to determine whether the MNR has sufficient power to enforce them." Because of the country's "labor and political anarchy," INR believed that the Alliance for Progress would fail in Bolivia "unless Paz has the intent or power to act against the social and labor ills in the mines."[41]

Incorporating the Thorpe mission findings, the State Department released a "Proposed New Program for Bolivia" on 30 March. Since the mission had been the "first that President Kennedy has sent specifically to any single country in Latin America," the State Department noted that "both the friends and enemies of the United States will be keenly awaiting the first news of any New Program." The State Department believed that the "greatest difficulty in achieving the objectives of our program . . . [is] Bolivia's dearth of adequate human resources," and it therefore proposed working closely with IDB economists, who were already conditioning development programs on tough COMIBOL labor reforms. Recognizing the difficulties of taking on armed miners, the State Department concluded by recommending that the United States provide the Bolivian military with "sufficient hardware to meet any internal threat."[42]

Several days later, the head of US Southern Command, General Andrew O'Meara, arrived in Bolivia to begin preparations to reinforce the Bolivian military's capacity to repel an attack by the miners. Since his visit coincided with Kennedy's CIA-sponsored invasion of Cuba, General O'Meara was greeted by violent student and worker riots. US flags were burned, the US and Guatemalan embassies were stoned, and hundreds of leftists queued up to give blood for Cuban army casualties.[43] Earlier that month, President Kennedy warned British prime minister Macmillan that "Bolivia is on the verge of being taken over by Communist elements favorable to Señor Castro."[44]

In its impending battle with the Bolivian Left, Washington would count heavily on an important ally: Guillermo Bedregal, COMIBOL's young, headstrong president. A fervent modernizing nationalist, Bedregal actively sought to leverage foreign investment in his spirited drive to wrest control of the mining camps from leftist union leaders, whom he referred to as "feudal lords," whose "hatred of the State" was a "type of suicidal and anti-historical anarcho-syndicalism" that had to be destroyed. Bedregal writes in his memoirs that the miners "viewed and treated COMIBOL as if it were any other boss, as opposed to a company that had been recovered for the nation." It comes as little surprise that Bedregal enthusiastically supported the US-backed IDB proposal to condition foreign aid on harsh labor reforms.[45] Bedregal had accompanied IDB President Herrera on his 6 March return flight to Washington, where he held two months of "truly satisfactory" meetings with State Department officials. In a letter back to President Paz in April, Bedregal boasted that his conversations had resulted in the "COMIBOL program constituting the nucleus around which all other [US aid] programs will function."[46]

In his memoirs, Bedregal recalled that Herrera's personal interest in COMIBOL put IDB economists in a position of exercising "leadership over the entire project." When the West Germans signed on in late April, the Triangular Plan mine rehabilitation program was born.[47] All three of the Triangular Plan's partners—the United States, the IDB, and West Germany—shared the view that armed, organized labor was fully responsible for COMIBOL's problems, and the German participants wrote to Bedregal to stress the need for a "considerable reduction in the number of workers," a reform that would require "strict administration" in the face of "opposition by the armed miners and especially their leaders."[48] No participant was more intransigent than the IDB, however, prompting embassy DCM Williams to worry that the development bank's economists were being "unrealistic" to insist that the Bolivian government proceed with "stripping labor leaders of their control in the mines" as a *precondition* for foreign aid.[49]

There was no doubt that Triangular's labor reforms would be fiercely opposed by Bolivia's mine workers. Yet as stipulated in the Control Obrero[50] section of the 1952 nationalization decree, any change to COMIBOL's structure would require FSTMB approval. To overcome this obstacle, Paz asked Vice President Lechín to pass through Washington in April, on his way back from a five-month trip abroad. Ambassador Strom was concerned that the leftist firebrand would create the "impression . . . [that] he successfully negotiated increased aid during [his] US visit," but Paz explained that Lechín's cooperation would be necessary if the Triangular Plan were to pass through the FSTMB Control Obrero hurdle.[51] In a letter to his son the following month, President Paz defended his ongoing alliance with Lechín as necessary to ensure that "the very adroit communists" do not gain "total control of the unions."[52]

In his memoirs, Lechín claimed that he was unaware of the harsh conditions attached to the Triangular Plan money, and when he arrived back in Bolivia, he boasted widely that he alone had "secured the Triangular Operation." Lechín went directly to the Eleventh FSTMB Congress on 7 May to defend the Triangular Plan by explaining that "countries that have not won economic independence" were justified in "doing a series of [foreign policy] zigzags until we obtain objectives in the interests of the workers." Despite attempting to couch his position as analogous to Stalin's 1939 pact with Hitler, Lechín was forced to rebuke charges that he had become an agent of US imperialism. "I am an agent only of the Bolivian people," Lechín responded magnanimously.[53] The Communist-led delegation from Bolivia's largest mine, Siglo XX, had already walked out of the congress, however, issuing a statement that it would "reject the Triangular Plan because it understands that it is an imperialist plan."[54]

In mid-May, the Kennedy administration officially announced the Triangular Plan, which included $13.5 million in technical assistance to COMIBOL, the first tranche of three.[55] Hidden from public view was a confidential set of conditions known as the "Accepted Points of View," which committed the Bolivian government to implement a "state of emergency in the mining industry," sharply restrict Control Obrero, lay off 20 percent of the mine labor force—approximately five thousand workers—and remove Communist union leaders from their posts.[56] Despite boasting the tepid support of Lechín's MNR Left Sector, Paz realized he would have trouble with leftists outside the governing party, who were already planning a hunger march against the plan.[57] In conversations with the US Embassy, the president vowed to "crack down on communist elements" hell-bent on "sabotaging Bolivia's economic recovery." Paz's military High Command subsequently informed US officials that the government was preparing to arrest dozens of "Communist trade union leaders, university rectors, and many teachers," adding that army units would be deployed around Siglo XX to prevent its miners from marching to La Paz or from mobilizing its militia in opposition to the crackdown.[58]

On the afternoon of 6 June, fifty arrests were carried out without bloodshed. To facilitate one roundup, Bedregal called union leaders to La Paz under the pretense of discussing their complaints regarding Triangular. When they arrived, Bedregal never appeared. Instead, agents from Paz's Control Político arrived, permitted MNR union leaders to go free, and flew the Communists and Trotskyists to Puerto Villarroel, a makeshift detention camp in the Amazon jungle.[59] One Communist union leader, Simón Reyes, was fortunate enough to have missed the meeting. When he heard of what had happened, he immediately called Bedregal, explaining that there was going to be a "terrible reaction in the mines." The COMIBOL president feigned sympathy with Reyes's point of view and asked the union leader to come immediately to the presidential palace to formulate a plan. When Reyes arrived, he too was arrested and put on a plane with a score of university students and professors. This second group, all Communist Party members, was flown away to internal exile in the Amazon village of San Ignacio de Velasco.[60]

Anticipating a violent reaction by sympathetic unions, the following morning President Paz announced the existence of a "communist plot" and declared yet another ninety-day state of siege, his February siege having expired seventeen days earlier.[61] Flaunting Paz's decree, four thousand factory workers and students marched through the streets of La Paz on 8 June, chanting slogans against the Bolivian government and the United States. The urban unions declared belligerently that they were "not afraid of repression because they are accustomed to defeating armies," and the student federation erected barricades and declared a "state of emergency" throughout the country's universities.[62] After dispersing these protests with copious amounts of US-supplied tear gas, Paz's MNR organized a counterdemonstration that evening by loyalist Indian peasant groups. In front of ten thousand Indian peasants chanting "Death to Communism!" President Paz proudly announced that his government was holding fifty Bolivian leftists incommunicado in Amazon detention camps. The crowd responded boisterously, "To the firing squad!"[63] Meanwhile, MNR-affiliated Indian peasant communities around the nation sent cables to President Paz expressing their "unconditional support for the government," thanking Paz for once again invoking a state of siege to "defend the government, the homeland, and the Catholic religion."[64]

Washington did not delay in showing its gratitude for Paz's decision to round up dozens of Bolivian leftists under the pretext of what the CIA conceded was a "government-fabricated coup."[65] In response to Paz's "favorable actions," the State Department authorized its embassy to "release [USAID] cash grant payments for April, May, and June," expressing satisfaction that "for the first time after ten months in office," President Paz had taken "positive action toward controlling the communist movement within Bolivia and to re-establish the authority of the Bolivian government over labor."[66]

Meanwhile, Paz followed through on his plan to send a military regiment to the mining region, and Bolivia's High Command requested US assistance to create a "modified battle group" that would be "highly mobile with heavy power," designed to contain the "latent danger for Bolivia inherent in communism," especially in the highland mining camps. On 8 June, Army Commanding General Alfredo Ovando "urgently" requested $650,000 in "emergency materiel . . . to be airlifted . . . for use [by the] Bolivian army in strengthening GOB to meet [the] current political crisis."[67] The request received an enthusiastic endorsement from Kennedy's recently arrived ambassadorial appointee, Ben Stephansky, who reported to Secretary Rusk that a mobile artillery battalion "would strengthen anti–Commie forces in [the] present situation," since the "army is loyal to Paz and is [the] force most likely [to] resist [a] further shift . . . [in the] government apparatus to [the] extreme MNR left."[68] President Kennedy signed the request on 30 June, and military airlifts began arriving on 16 July.[69]

Nine days after Paz invoked his second state of siege and rounded up Bolivian leftists opposed to the Triangular Plan, Washington's UN ambassador Adlai Stevenson arrived in La Paz for a two-day leg of his regional tour. The liberal icon offered strong support for President Paz's actions, expressing confidence to members of the press welcoming him at the airport that the Alliance for Progress would "make Bolivia a leading example of free world development cooperation." Echoing other US modernizers, Stevenson declared that "rapid economic and social advance is urgently needed," despite the fact that this would "be difficult and require painful sacrifices." Nonetheless, Ambassador Stevenson was confident that "progress is certain if free men join together in a spirit of responsibility and discipline." He closed his first speech in La Paz by proclaiming that "the Bolivian revolution will demonstrate to peoples of this continent that social and economic progress can be achieved under free institutions and Western Christian traditions."[70]

Unfortunately for Ambassador Stevenson, fatal street riots on 15 June prevented him from seeing much of the city. Instead, he spent three hours discussing economic and social development with President Paz at the latter's suburban home, while students and workers battled throughout the day with police and pro-MNR Indian militias, clashes that resulted in at least four deaths.[71] A student delegation was dispatched to Stevenson's hotel, where the delegates pled for Washington to end aid to Bolivia, as it "just enrich[es] the governing party." They complained that the Triangular Plan was "an attack on national sovereignty, because its conditions require the firing of workers and the imprisonment of union leaders."[72]

Stevenson was unfazed by what he witnessed in "that embattled city on top of the world," telling US Embassy officials a few days later that he "found the whole thing fascinating—in spite of the altitude—and left full of anxieties and admiration."[73] A day after he returned to Washington, Stevenson wrote to President Paz that his trip had given him a "better understanding of the frustrating conditions you confront, and great hope for the way you are coming to grip with the political challenge."[74] The following day, Paz notified the US Embassy that his police services had "seriously depleted" their tear gas supplies battling the students and workers. Secretary Rusk responded by authorizing an emergency shipment of 3,500 additional tear gas grenades from US Southern Command in Panama and existing embassy supplies in Quito, Ecuador.[75]

Since this violence was directly related to the newly minted Alliance for Progress, President Kennedy could not remain a passive observer. In addition to personally approving the creation of a mobile artillery battalion to enforce implementation of the Triangular Plan, Kennedy authorized $3 million to reimburse an expensive settlement President Paz made with urban factory workers in late June, an agreement that stymied a unified anti-Triangular front. When the payment was made four months later, President Kennedy notified Paz Estenssoro that he was "impressed by the courage and determination with which your government has undertaken measures to achieve social progress and embark upon a long-range development program."[76] On 22 June, Kennedy took advantage of a sick day to pen a personal letter to Paz, in which he reiterated that his administration "regards the economic and social development of Bolivia as one of the principal goals of the Alliance for Progress." Kennedy further expressed his "deep admiration for your courage and vision in confronting the difficulties which your nation is now undergoing, and to wish you every success."[77]

Thus began Kennedy's foreign policy toward Bolivia, a program of politicized, authoritarian development that took dead aim at the country's leftist miners. Ambassador Stephansky later recalled that there had been a "sense of real anxiety and . . . unease about Bolivia" during the first half of 1961. Many US officials believed the country was "half way over the brink to chaos," worrying that "it could slide down and be the second Cuba."[78] With Kennedy's economists providing technocratic language regarding the importance of labor discipline for economic and social progress, US policymakers waged an anticommunist crusade under the unabashed auspices of the Alliance for Progress. The enterprise was enthusiastically supported by President Paz, whom Stephansky called "a real egghead, which is awfully nice . . . a man with an extraordinary breadth of intelligence."[79] Yet Paz was an egghead with guns,[80] which he was decisively turning against the miners.

A View from the Mines

The Alliance for Progress in Bolivia faced no greater enemy than the Communist-led union at the country's largest tin mine, Siglo XX. Armed and organized, these miners brazenly rejected the Triangular Plan conditions, and they refused to give in without a fight. Recognizing that US aid programs were being used to carry out an aggressive political project, the Communists called for all-out war against the Paz government. Still enjoying support from the MNR Left, however, Paz Estenssoro would emerge victorious in his first offensive against the Bolivian labor movement.

Although the United States supported the MNR since 1953, Bolivia's popular militias remained a thorn in Washington's side. Far outnumbering the armed forces, which barely outfitted 7,500 soldiers in 1961, Bolivia's Indian peasant and worker militias boasted 16,000 men. The CIA reported that the militias had "enjoyed a privileged position in Bolivia because [they] are credited with playing the major role in the MNR defeat of the army in the 1952 revolution," adding that the miners' militia was the "most effective paramilitary element . . . in part because of their access to explosives." According to the CIA, the Communist-led militia at Siglo XX represented the "single greatest threat to the stability of the country."[81] A Pentagon handbook agreed that while the miners' militias were "not the largest forces," they were still "considered the most effective because they are better organized, trained, disciplined, and equipped."[82]

Despite having been officially disbanded when the MNR reorganized the armed forces in 1953, the miners' militia at Siglo XX continued to operate under the command of respected MNR leftist Octavio Torrico. Poorly armed in anything but dynamite, Torrico's militia relied heavily on the cooperation of the two leftist militias, affiliated with the Partido Comunista de Bolivia (PCB; Communist Party of Bolivia) and the Trotskyist Partido Obrero Revolucionario (POR; Revolutionary Workers' Party), which organized late-night gangs of mineral-robbing *jukus* and used the proceeds to buy arms from soldiers, police officers, and members of the legal MNR-affiliated Indian peasant militias. The POR *juku* was especially efficient, and by 1964 the Trotskyists collected nearly one hundred weapons, including two US-made M-1 carbine machine guns. Nevertheless, the miners' most effective weapons were homemade grenades, coffee cans filled with dynamite plastique and metal screws, which they launched using Indian-style slingshots or rigged underneath planks of wood as land mines to stymie the advance of military vehicles that dared approach the mining camps.[83]

Overcoming traditional Trotskyist strength in Siglo XX, the PCB had made large strides during the late 1950s, and by 1961 Communists controlled the entire union leadership.[84] The party boasted hundreds of nonaffiliated supporters who, motivated by sympathies for the 1959 Cuban revolution, filled the ranks of the party's youth front organization, the Lincoln-Castro-Murillo Brigade.[85] According to Arturo Crespo, a powerful MNR leftist at the adjacent camp of Catavi, the PCB used Siglo XX as a base from which it "played a very important role in Bolivia in its fight against US imperialism and the MNR governments." PCB members, according to Crespo, "were organized into cadres [and] observed an internal discipline and solidarity comparable only to the Trotskyist organizations."[86] The PCB was especially impressive in organizing security for the raucous visit of a Soviet parliamentary delegation to Siglo XX in December 1960, a necessary precaution as Trotskyist leaders responded to the visit with a spirited anti-Moscow protest.[87] A US diplomat later recalled that Siglo XX "was politically volatile territory. . . . I used to think when I traveled to the district that they should put a big red star up over the mine entrance. . . . It was like traveling to North Korea or something like that. For me, it was just a Commie land of 25 different varieties."[88]

The Communist Party cadre in Siglo XX was headed by Control Obrero Federico Escóbar Zapata, a loose-tongued orator and rough-and-tumble miner who was loved and despised in equal measure. Affectionately called Macho Moreno by his followers, Escóbar—who had visited Havana in December 1960—"was an incredible administrator; he defended the workers tirelessly."[89] As one rank-and-file miner recalled, "He was always seen solving problems for the benefit of his class, for his comrades and also for those who were not in the Party." Another miner recounted that Escóbar "treated everybody equally, be it a woman or a man, a *campesino* or a miner. He made no distinctions. . . . Someone like Federico Escóbar had never been seen around here."[90] Escóbar's children recall that their mother Alicia would complain that her husband was never home, nagging him to "just marry the union and go live there!"[91] According to another miner's wife, when Escóbar was at home, there was a line of "twenty fellow miners and miners' wives with twenty different calamities waiting their turn."[92] The US Embassy shared these views, writing in 1963 that Escóbar was a "romantic Marxist and a hero to his people. . . . He regards the interests of his miners as paramount." The embassy added that Escóbar had "spent twenty-one years in the mines [and] knows as much

Figure 1. For Bolivia's development-oriented nationalists and their liberal allies in the United States, the armed militia at the Siglo XX mining camp represented "the single greatest threat to the stability of the country." Having pegged these miners as obstacles to development, in 1962 the Kennedy administration dispatched Labor Information Officer Thomas Martin on intelligence-gathering missions to Siglo XX. Despite striking up a demonstrably warm friendship with the workers, Martin was taken hostage the following year. For more on Martin's tumultuous tenure as a "pioneer in reaching out to the miners," see chapter 4. Photograph courtesy of the Martin family.

about mining and mining conditions as most COMIBOL engineers," a quality proudly confirmed by his family and comrades.[93]

The wife of one Siglo XX miner, Domitila Barrios de Chungara, recalled that she first met Escóbar after COMIBOL forced her out of the company house where she was living with her family. According to Domitila, she was nine months pregnant at the time, and her husband was away attending his mother's funeral. When the company guards left her crying on the street, surrounded by her children and the family belongings, neighbors took her to see Escóbar. "I had never seen a man like him, so simple, so good," Domitila recalled. "He took my hand as if he had known me for years." After serving Domitila dinner, Escóbar drove her to COMIBOL's local headquarters, where he "chewed out the guards" for having evicted her. He then drove them all back to the house, where he forced the company guards to put everything back in its place, scolding them that "a lady lives here, and ladies don't have their things thrown about like this." Four days later, Domitila gave birth to a son, Rodolfo, at which point she received a letter from Escóbar, along with the official COMIBOL order authorizing her to live in the house. He wrote: "Look madam, this is the order that permits you to live here. No one has the right to put you out of this house." Shortly afterward, Domitila joined the Communist Party.[94]

Fully aware that Kennedy's Alliance for Progress had targeted them for extinction, these leftists prepared for battle. Siglo XX Trotskyist Filemón Escóbar (no relation to Federico) writes that the Triangular Plan was "much more sinister" than anything that had come before, since it "sought nothing less than the liquidation of the revolutionary workers' movement . . . the liquidation of all union interference, and the sweeping out of the mines all workers considered 'extremist.'" Filemón concludes that US aid funds were nothing more than a "price paid to destroy the workers' movement."[95] Federico Escóbar's PCB comrade Víctor Reinaga agrees that "the Plan's foreign technicians saw only one problem with COMIBOL: the workers' so-called 'high salaries.'"[96]

Melvin Burke, a USAID economist working on the Triangular Plan in the late 1960s, eventually came around to the miners' point of view, telling his superiors on his resignation that "AID [has] nothing to do with economics or the development of Bolivia." For Burke, the plan was a "Trojan Horse," which "had no economic basis except to destroy . . . the communist union," and he praised the miners for having "fought against the so-called 'rationalization' (elimination) of 'redundant' mine workers."[97] In academic work published years later, Burke provided extensive evidence that COMIBOL was using "creative accounting, . . . [and] overstated and understated actual profits and losses at will" in order "create a pretext to 'rationalize' (reduce) the labor force." According to Burke, the Triangular Plan was a fig leaf that hid its "covert political" goal, which was to "destroy the workers' union and denationalize the mining industry of Bolivia."[98]

Despite the fact that Vice President Lechín was apparently "seduced" by the prospect of US aid to COMIBOL,[99] the FSTMB's disparate factions closed ranks in June by declaring a nationwide strike in the wake of President Paz's anticommunist crackdown. COMIBOL responded by closing the company commissaries and pharmacies, "paralyzing the sale of meat, medicine, and other supplies." According to Catavi Control Obrero Crespo, it was clear that the Bolivian government "had carefully prepared for this strike" by cutting back on recent shipments to the mining camps and that President Paz sought to "obtain the surrender of the workers and their families by way of hunger." Miners' wives traveled to nearby Indian peasant communities to trade personal effects for produce, and the unions organized a commando column that planned to hijack a cargo train carrying grain from Argentina to the Bolivian capital. Crespo concedes that the plan "appeared crazy, but we had to try it. There was no other alternative, as we could not let our children die of hunger." He recalls that "we imagined seeing the faces of COMIBOL's administrators when they learned the workers had enough flour to make bread for a month."[100]

In mid-June, COMIBOL offered to lift the blockade and release the majority of the leftist detainees but refused to grant liberty to Siglo XX union leaders Federico Escóbar and Irineo Pimentel. The FSTMB leadership rejected any deal that did not include the two popular union leaders, forcing the Paz government to turn to more sinister methods of strike busting. Bribing the MNR-affiliated union leaders at San José, on the outskirts of Oruro, with "400 American coats and 500,000 pesos," the government convinced them to go back to work. Alarmed, the FSTMB strike committee rushed to San José, where it was greeted by an angry mob chanting, "Our children are hungry. Down with the Strike! . . . Get out of the camp, communist traitors!" The strike committee was then chased out of San José under a "shower of hurled rocks." As he fled for his life, committee member Crespo thought to himself that "the sacrifices of thousands of workers and their families in a strike that had lasted over fifteen days . . . had been futile. The sharks had won."[101]

With the general strike broken by San José, whose leaders the FSTMB disparaged as "traffickers of unionism,"[102] the government blockade closed in on Siglo XX, where the union refused to resume work until its leaders were released from their Amazonian detainment. COMIBOL President Bedregal railed against this "illegal strike," claiming that it "demonstrates the level of indiscipline and repudiation of obligation on the part of the workers."[103] President Paz once again turned to the United States, pleading with UN Ambassador Adlai Stevenson for a $12 million emergency credit "to cover Bolivia's critical needs pending the re-establishment of social peace."[104] On his return to the United States, Stevenson testified to Congress in support of Paz's measures, calling the Triangular Plan impasse "the most explosive situation in South America."[105]

With Ambassador Ben Stephansky's arrival in La Paz in late June, Paz Estenssoro boasted a powerful new ally. Stephansky carried with him a personal note from President Kennedy, stressing Washington's desire to "bring to fruition" the Triangular Plan,[106] and the ambassador did not hesitate to lend support for Paz's $12 million request. Stephansky explained that the Bolivian government was on a "dead-end street" and would likely resort to "inflationary spending" without an immediate credit.[107] The State Department agreed that "we are faced with an immediate emergency. . . . Soviet pressure is strong, the Bolivian Government is in a precarious situation, [and] the immediate economic problems are severe. . . . Despite strong Communist infiltration in the labor movement . . . the Bolivian government is basically still oriented toward the free world. . . . We cannot regard Bolivia as a loss." Once again, however, the economists at USAID and the IDB were the most intransigent, demanding that labor reforms be enforced before another dollar was released.[108] Embassy DCM Williams renewed his complaint that the economists were being "unrealistic," but the developmentalists would not budge.[109]

Fortunately for President Paz, the Bolivian government benefited from a secret weapon in Siglo XX: a group of Canadian priests who had gone into the mining camp on a mission to ensure "the defeat of communism in Bolivia." The Oblate priests of the Order of Mary Immaculate warned their superiors throughout the year that "communism had infiltrated the region like never before," and they solicited financial support, without which they said it would be impossible "not only to resist the avalanche of atheistic materialism that seeks to defeat us, but also to chalk up a huge triumph for our Holy Cause." With generous donations from the Canadian faithful, the Oblates erected Bolivia's most powerful radio transmitter, aptly named Pío XII, from which they broadcast vitriolic anticommunist screeds and called for Federico Escóbar's permanent expulsion from Siglo XX.[110]

The Oblate mission leader, Father Lino Grenier, refused even to baptize Escóbar's children, prompting the union leader to later take to the miners' radio, Voz del Minero (Voice of the Miner), and declare that "if there is a God who takes into account the human race, he will see that the majority is made up of the poor." Escóbar added, "I am sure that Karl Marx up there in Heaven, with our Lord Jesus Christ, has more influence than the mercenaries who have wagered on the Church." Condemning those "who say we need priests to teach us how to pray," Escóbar explained that "we have already prayed plenty, and the more the poor pray, the poorer they stay." The Communist leader concluded his diatribe by proclaiming, "Fellow workers: what our country needs is to liberate itself. Let us say with our fists raised to the air, 'Liberty for our People!'"[111]

When Paz Estenssoro's Control Político rounded up leftists in early June, Father Lino provided COMIBOL with lists of Siglo XX "troublemakers" and sent a constant stream of cables to La Paz vowing to "cooperate completely" with the government's anticommunist crackdown.[112] One miner later recalled that the Oblates "shamelessly supported the Triangular Plan. . . . They only saw communism in our demands." When Pio XII began handing out food to miners who agreed to go back to work, union members declared, "If the priests want to bust our strike, we'll bust them first!" On 4 July, Communist miners attacked the Catholic radio station, first clashing with a group of nuns and then with members of the Catholic Workers' League who rushed to defend Pio. When one of the union miners launched a dynamite stick onto the roof of the station, all hell broke loose. A Catholic miner inside Pio at the time recalls that "it was all rocks, pistol shots. . . . They wanted to destroy the transmitter and drag Father Lino outside, eliminate him."[113]

Amid the chaos, Pio XII transmitted a nationwide call for help, declaring that "now is the time to put an end to communism in Bolivia!" Warning the population "not to be tricked by the miserable and disgusting communists," the Catholic station declared, "Women of Bolivia: it would be preferable for you to kill your children this moment if you are not capable of defending the Catholic religion!" From inside the building, Father Lino, a black belt in karate, told his followers, "God says you have to let yourself take punches, but we cannot tolerate this outrage! We must defend ourselves!"[114] Local pro-MNR Indian peasant communities cabled their unwavering support to President Paz, assuring him that they were "ready to march on Catavi [Siglo XX]" should he give the word.[115]

Early the following day, the bishop of Oruro arrived at Siglo XX with a government commission. The highest Catholic official in the region scolded the Oblates and the Catholic workers, reminding them that they were called to love all human beings, even communists. The bishop suggested that capitalism was just as evil, and even claimed he was "prepared to kiss the hand of the miner who is about to throw dynamite against my breast." One by one, union miners told the commission that they were devout Catholics but that they despised Father Lino, whom they accused of being an agent of the CIA. Meanwhile, thousands of miners marched through the camp, carrying signs that read, "Foreign Priests get out of Siglo XX!" and "Death to Lino!" Giving Lino forty-eight hours to leave the mining camp, the demonstrators then proceeded to burn his effigy in the central plaza. Several months later, Father Lino slipped away in the middle of the night in the company of six armed guards. A Catholic miner recalls, somewhat bitterly, "He just disappeared. He didn't bid farewell to anyone." Shortly afterward, Lino left the priesthood, married, and became a successful businessman in Brazil.[116]

If the situation in Siglo XX gravely endangered the Triangular Plan, the Bolivian government's attitude at the August 1961 meeting of the Organization of American States (OAS) meeting at Punta del Este, Uruguay, threatened to drive the final nail into the coffin. US Treasury Secretary Douglas Dillon, who headed the US delegation, complained to President Kennedy that Bolivia "followed [a] straight communist line throughout the conference, taking clear guidance from the Cubans." Dillon reported that many Cuban amendments meant to undermine the Alliance for Progress "were voted down unanimously, except for Bolivia," and he characterized the conference as a "remarkable show of solidarity on the part of all except Cuba and Bolivia."[117] Secretary Rusk asked Stephansky to warn President Paz of the "difficulty such action causes the US in carrying out our aid programs in Bolivia," since it was "most disturbing to [the] highest levels in [the] US government."[118]

Bolivia's High Command was also growing anxious. The US-built Max Toledo First Motorized Battalion had just been festively inaugurated in Viacha, outside La Paz, and the generals were feeling bold.[119] On 18 August, three of Bolivia's top generals informed embassy officials that Paz had "lost control of the situation and could not remain in office much longer." Commander-in-chief General Ovando and Air Force Commanding General René Barrientos explained that "within the next six months it would be necessary to establish a military junta," adding that they planned to "eliminate the MNR party and get rid of the gangsters." Vowing to establish a "completely pro-Western civilian government," the generals acknowledged that "they could not do this unless they had the support and backing of the US government."[120]

Ambassador Stephansky conceded that Paz's "failure to take decisive action on [the] political-labor front," and his inability to "provide some assurance [of the] successful implementation . . . [of] the Triangular Operation," meant that his government was "politically weak and growing weaker." Nonetheless, Stephansky believed that the United States should leverage the generals' threat, coupled with the intransigence of economists at the IDB and USAID, in order to "apply all available pressure [on] Paz to obtain [a] GOB decision [to] take genuinely decisive action" in the form of an "all-out win or lose battle" against the miners at Siglo XX.[121]

The pressure worked. In "tense meetings" with IDB economists, Vice President Lechín finally agreed to accept significant restrictions on Control Obrero veto power, paving the way for COMIBOL to make administrative decisions, including mass firings and the removal of individual union leaders, without labor interference.[122] Late on 28 August, Lechín addressed a special FSTMB session in Oruro, with dozens of his leftist colleagues still sweltering in the Amazon jungle. The only voice to oppose the Triangular Plan was Siglo XX Trotskyist César Lora. Filling in for Escóbar and Pimentel, Lora angrily denounced the plan as "submissive" to the United States. Lechín responded that they were dealing with "an issue of food," and accused Lora of turning the session "into a place to defend political positions . . . [and] put[ting] us where the reactionaries want, so that due to a lack of money they can denationalize the mines. They want to drown us in division." Under the combined pressure of President Paz, the IDB, USAID, and the Bolivian High Command, Lechín delivered the unanimous votes of his MNR Left Sector, and the Triangular Plan was "half-heartedly approved."[123]

Having forced the FSTMB to capitulate, President Paz signed a supreme decree on 31 August, stipulating that Control Obrero "would not be recognized if [its] veto will prejudice production," and he privately committed his government to "make use of all power available to it in preventing strikes."[124] It was a time of jubilation for US officials. Ambassador Stephansky gave special credit to the IDB economists, "without whose push it is probable [that the] decree, if issued at all, would have been watered down." Stephansky also stressed the importance of providing US support for an "intensive propaganda campaign," including stuffing miners' pay envelopes with pro-Triangular literature and bringing "selected groups of workers" to La Paz for "indoctrination as propaganda agents [in] support [of the] mine rehabilitation program."[125]

The White House thanked Paz two weeks later with a $7 million credit to cover losses during the strike and authorized $750,000 in USAID funds and $260,000 in "Presidential Funds" to organize two new Bolivian army engineering battalions for development programs in the countryside.[126] Stephansky was optimistic that "if we carry out [the Alliance for Progress] program with [a] sense of urgency before year's end, we could possibly channel GOB thinking into [a] constructive development approach."[127]

Despite publicly rejecting charges that US aid programs were conditioned on harsh labor reforms, Ambassador Stephansky and IDB economists were the very individuals driving the toughest line.[128] Technocrats who sincerely believed their development theories, they served as ideologically motivated foot soldiers in the Kennedy administration's anticommunist crusade. The Bolivian miners refused to be depoliticized, however, and their organized resistance to the Alliance for Progress would continue to cause headaches in La Paz and Washington. Political strategists and liberal economists were firmly wed, however, in their eager desire to use development as a tool to drive communism out of the Bolivian mining camps.

Development and Its Discontents

In order to obtain approval for the Triangular Plan and "begin tidying up the trade union sector,"[129] President Paz suspended constitutional liberties for almost the entire year. Yet his second ninety-day state of siege was set to expire on 7 September, and fifty leftist leaders still remained incommunicado in Amazonian detention camps. Bolivian leftists, especially Communist miners from Siglo XX, agitated for their colleagues' release, and Paz Estenssoro finally relented once Triangular had been safely approved. It was clear that the Alliance for Progress in Bolivia was meeting with fierce resistance in the mines and that it would continue to be used to justify growing military strength and unceasing shipments of tear gas and riot gear.

Aside from battling Oblate priests and nuns, Siglo XX's Communist miners took advantage of the long strike in mid-1961 to organize fresh cadres, especially among the women of the mining camp. One miner's wife recalls that the Triangular Plan, and its accompanying repression, "awoke the indignation of the entire mining population." Wives of those arrested had gone to La Paz one by one to demand their husbands' release, but the government "turned a deaf ear" to their pleas. When they returned to the camp, several of the women met with Communist Party members, who agreed to help them organize the Comité de Amas de Casa de Siglo XX (Siglo XX Housewives Committee).[130]

In late July, the committee, which its founders later admitted had been "chiefly aligned with the PCB," sent a delegation to the capital, where they declared themselves on a hunger strike pending the union leaders' release. The women lost one hunger striker, Manuela de Cejas, to death before President Paz finally agreed to release the prisoners. A poem written in homage to Manuela vividly demonstrates the level of anger among the Siglo XX miners and their families regarding Triangular and its US backers:

> You went to the La Paz hunger strikes,
> arriving at the doors of COMIBOL,
> tear gas surrounded your children,
> launched by agents paid by the Yankee dollar.
> Manuela de Cejas,

valiant woman without equal,
you offered your life for the working class,
fighting alongside your husband
against the Triangular Plan,
opposing the White Massacre . . .

. . . Onward, women!
Toward the liberation of a people
oppressed by American capitalists,
tyrants, wagers of massacres, murdering dogs.
One day they will fall
into a disgusting, endless abyss.[131]

Hours after Paz Estenssoro signed the antilabor decrees on 31 August, he released Escóbar and Pimentel.[132] When the two union leaders arrived in La Paz that afternoon, they told the Amas de Casa that they would be unable to return to the mining camp immediately, explaining that "we have many commitments to take care of here." The women were furious. "How are you going to say this to us after we have been in La Paz for so many days on your behalf?" The women decided to trick Escóbar and Pimentel onto their bus, promising them that when they arrived in the suburb of El Alto, high on the altiplano, the two men could return to the city. When they reached El Alto, however, three of the women positioned themselves in front of the doorway. "No, *compañeros*, you are coming with us! We came here to fight, we sacrificed, we carried out the hunger strike to bring you back. So you are coming with us!" Escóbar and Pimentel were livid, but the women held their ground. When the two flustered union leaders retook their seats, Escóbar's wife, Alicia, broke out in tears, saying, "We have fought so much and still now they say this, that they don't want to return with us. I really don't know what to say. All of these women, not just your wives, have sacrificed so much, and they receive this in return? No, you two are badly mistaken. You have no idea how you are making these women feel right now. But you better pay attention. You ignore us, but you better pay attention to these women." As the bus approached Bolivia's mining region, the women began to see masses of workers who came out to celebrate Escóbar and Pimentel's release, with marching bands greeting them in each village. When they reached the outskirts of Siglo XX, the freshly liberated union leaders were lifted onto the shoulders of their fellow miners and carried the rest of the way to the Plaza del Minero. During a celebratory feast the following day, Escóbar turned to one of the women and said, "You were right to say that we should be here. I now feel prouder, happier, because I know that I have support." The women were not so lucky. One of them notes that "afterward came the fights in each home. We hunger strikers won the fight in La Paz only to end up in fights with our husbands."[133]

With Paz's decision to release the leftists, the CIA fretted that "Bolivia's most effective Communist agitators" were back at their posts, a development that "enhanced the possibility of disorders."[134] Meanwhile, the State Department worried that Bolivia remained the "weakest of all the countries on the continent" and that it was still the "prime Soviet target in South America." US officials compared Bolivia to an "under-nourished, ill-clad, ill-housed individual who is exposed to tuberculosis," and they believed the only way to immunize the patient from the disease—communism—was to do "everything we can to prevent Soviet access to the internal affairs of Bolivia." The State Department warned that, if permitted, Moscow would have more success at rapid modernization since it would have the "assistance of a Castro-type government which, being less responsive to public pressure than is the present government, might well engage in sufficiently repressive measures to bring about by force the reforms we have been maintaining are necessary."[135]

If by "Castro-type government" the State Department meant authoritarian, US policy was rapidly moving in that direction. On 5 September, President Kennedy signed National Security Action Memorandum (NSAM) 88, in which he ordered his administration to take additional steps to "train the Armed Forces of Latin America in controlling mobs, guerrillas, etc." Explaining his view that the "military occupy an extremely important strategic position in Latin America," Kennedy—who days later heralded to the United Nations the "Decade of Development"—called on his government to "increase the intimacy between our Armed Forces and the military of Latin America."[136] The following month, Kennedy met with Pentagon officials at Fort Bragg, North Carolina, where he reiterated his desire that the US armed forces work "in conjunction with indigenous military forces toward the attainment of US national objectives in Latin America." The Defense Department responded enthusiastically with a list of ways it could support "existing US political, economic, and social measures" in Latin America and contribute directly to the "implementation of the Alliance for Progress."[137]

Nowhere was President Kennedy's interest in "controlling mobs, guerrillas, etc." more evident than in Paz Estenssoro's Bolivia. One month after Kennedy issued NSAM 88, the Paz government announced yet another fabricated coup, its third such ruse that year, and rounded up what the CIA called a "heterogeneous group of rightists and leftists." Two days later, on 21

October, President Paz declared his third ninety-day state of siege in eight months, and proceeded to implement a reform long sought by US officials, the raising of fuel prices.[138] These dual measures sparked violent riots by thousands of students, who destroyed a gas station; the offices of the government newspaper, *La Nación*; and two police stations. Paz responded by closing schools for the remainder of the year, imposing press censorship, and ordering his security services to brutally repress the demonstration.[139]

A Bolivian general told the US Embassy that the death toll was five times what the government had admitted, meaning as many as twenty students lay dead. Far from being moved to reproach, Ambassador Stephansky requested an immediate shipment of 3,000 tear gas grenades, explaining that the Bolivian police were using them up at a rate of 200 per day. Two days later, a CIA-contractor plane delivered 3,300 grenades to USAID's mission director in La Paz. Secretary Rusk asked Stephansky to stress to President Paz that this shipment was "clear-cut evidence of support for his government," which should completely quash any thought . . . that elements [in] this government [are] sitting by waiting for Paz to fall."[140]

After three more years, however, and tens of millions of dollars in US assistance, Paz did fall. In the meantime, development-minded US policymakers interpreted Paz's repressive machinery as providing the necessary "authority . . . [and] discipline . . . [to] bring [Bolivia's] illiterate, unskilled population into the modern world."[141] Celebrations would have been premature, however, and Stephansky noted that "the real test [of the] government's determination to live up to [its] commitments . . . will of course come when labor troubles develop" during the application period of Triangular's mass firings.[142] With Escóbar and Pimentel back at the crucial Siglo XX mine, the Alliance for Progress in Bolivia was certain to meet with fierce resistance. It would continue to reveal a strongly authoritarian face.

It seems that the closer historians study President Kennedy's foreign policy in individual countries, the more heavy handed it appears.[143] Political goals drove the Alliance for Progress from its very inception, and the administration's fierce ideological bent merely exaggerated and radicalized the level to which Washington intervened. In Bolivia, Kennedy's much-heralded program brought with it deep involvement by the United States in nearly every aspect of the country's social, political, and economic life. Building on President Paz's long-standing paradigm of authoritarian development, US liberals took the nationalized mines as their logical starting point and adopted a heavy-handed mine rehabilitation plan drafted largely by the Bolivians themselves. Resistance by the non-MNR miners was swift and fierce, however, forcing the Alliance for Progress to rest squarely on political repression. Bolstered by Paz's apparent resolve, US developmentalists showered the Bolivian government with police, military, and economic assistance, willingly serving Washington's strategic battle against communism in the heart of South America.

Within eight months of taking office, the Kennedy administration had successfully pulled Bolivia back from the brink of Cold War neutrality. Basking in the new administration's development orientation, Paz Estenssoro had warmed to the Alliance for Progress as the most promising path forward for his revolutionary regime. Communism had not yet been defeated in Bolivia, however, and as the Alliance for Progress moved along, liberal developmentalists would be called on to justify ever-growing levels of repression against leftist opponents of the Triangular Plan labor reforms. For US and Bolivian officials seeking political hegemony in these regions, economists' anticommunist theories were a godsend, as was their tendency to justify the rise of the Bolivian armed forces.

Chapter 2

Development as Anticommunism

The Targeting of Bolivian Labor

Before the ink could dry on Bolivia's Alliance for Progress agreement, internal tensions began to emerge in Washington and La Paz. US conservatives, viewing the Paz regime as repressive and socialist, were the first to question the wisdom of large-scale assistance to the Movimiento Nacionalista Revolucionario (MNR; Revolutionary Nationalist Movement). Meanwhile, Paz's domestic opposition on the right and left fiercely resisted his authoritarian measures, creating an environment of perennial political crisis. From the mines to the cities, supposed beneficiaries of US aid rejected the harsh Alliance for Progress conditions and the Paz government's accompanying repression. The Kennedy administration had initially adopted development as a tool to combat political unrest, and anti-Paz disturbances only strengthened US liberals' resolve to deepen Washington's commitment. For the Alliance for Progress, these crises gave rise to an increasingly authoritarian program, demonstrating clearly the strategic component of development ideology as a form of intervention.

The Debate in Washington

Despite the enthusiasm with which the Kennedy administration viewed economic and military assistance to the MNR, there was significant resistance in conservative US circles. Viewing revolutionary Bolivia as a leftist authoritarian state, some foreign policy bureaucrats and conservative US press outlets decried the White House's rapid incorporation of Bolivia within the nascent Alliance for Progress. The debate between these "realists" and Kennedy's liberal developmentalists delayed the approval of additional aid money until mid-1962, and it revealed the strategic nature of both sides of the US foreign policy debate. The underlying question, for conservatives and liberals alike, was how best to ensure that Bolivia remained a loyal ally safely beyond the reach of international communism.

Almost as soon as the Kennedy administration adopted Bolivia within its Alliance for Progress, the White House asked Congress to authorize the sale of fifty thousand tons of tin from US strategic stockpiles, one-quarter of total world production.[1] This affront prompted President Paz to pen a frantic letter to Kennedy, noting that the stockpile sale "does not coincide . . . with the plans of the Alliance for Progress." Guillermo Bedregal, the president of the Corporación Minera de Bolivia (COMIBOL; Mining Corporation of Bolivia), told White House aide Richard Goodwin that the sell-off was "in flagrant contradiction" to the Kennedy administration's developmental goals, adding that he considered it to be "an act of real economic aggression."[2]

In a lengthy response on 6 October, which received widespread coverage in the Bolivian press, Kennedy wrote Paz Estenssoro that the Bolivian president should "be assured that my Government retains a deep interest and concern in the rapid development of the Bolivian nation and the economic and social program of the Bolivian people." Dramatically, Kennedy assured Paz Estenssoro that "we will not take any action—in tin or in any other matter— which will tend to frustrate our mutual goal of a better life for the people of Bolivia" and that Washington would "sell no tin from our stockpile without first consulting with your government." President Kennedy explained that he was merely seeking congressional authorization for stockpile sales that he would consider only "at a time of world-wide shortage" with the purpose of "discouraging tin consumers from substituting other materials for their normal tin consumption." Kennedy reiterated to Paz his commitment to "protect the long-term stability and continued prosperity of the tin market."[3]

Days before receiving this bold statement of support, Paz wrote two additional letters to President Kennedy. One was private and referred to the June anticommunist crackdown Paz Estenssoro launched in order to gain approval of the Triangular Plan over the strong objections of leftist miners. In order to pass the mine rehabilitation program, Paz revealed that it had been "necessary to seize the communist labor union leaders," whose opposition threatened to thrust Bolivia "into a period of disorder and anarchy, with the government unable any longer to maintain itself." Paz wrote that the resulting general strike had made it "essential . . . to break up the unity of the labor unions and to separate the masses of workers from the leaders in the service of International Communism." The Bolivian president explained that he had engaged in "direct negotiations" with urban unions, promising raises for those who broke the general strike, a tactic that bore fruit and occurred with the "full cooperation" of US Embassy officials. The government's inability to come up with the money was "giving rise to a reactivation of the social demands, again under the direction of pro-Communist leaders." The situation was becoming critical, Paz explained, since the end of October had been "fixed as the last date for meeting the demands." The Bolivian president implored Kennedy to consider providing his government with "a minimum of $3 million immediately in order to meet the just demands of the workers."[4] In early November, Kennedy sent word through Fowler Hamilton, director of the United States Agency for International Development (USAID), that Paz's request had been approved and that Kennedy was "impressed by the courage and determination with which your Government has undertaken measures to achieve social progress and embark upon a long-range development program."[5]

Finally, a third letter from President Paz publicly reminded Kennedy that at the August 1961 meeting of the Organization of American States (OAS), Bolivia had been one of the first Latin American nations to submit a ten-year "National Economic and Social Development Plan" as called for by the Alliance for Progress. Since Paz's government had been so quick to fulfill the requirement, Paz hoped President Kennedy would look favorably on a $45 million request to fund an "emergency program" that would permit the "immediate commencement of the execution" of the development plan. Much to the chagrin of the White House officials, this letter remained unanswered until early 1962, partly because of growing doubts in the State Department regarding the wisdom of continued aid to revolutionary Bolivia.[6]

Supporting the $45 million request was Kennedy's "Special Economic Representative" to Bolivia, University of Virginia development economist Rowland Egger. Sent to Bolivia in the wake of Washington's adoption of the anticommunist Triangular Plan mine rehabilitation program, Egger was a consistent pro-Paz voice in the US foreign policy apparatus. After several weeks in La Paz, the economist praised President Kennedy's "profoundly perceptive" decision to "stay with the Bolivians." Acknowledging that the Bolivian Revolution had been "messy" and conceding that it had "skidded dangerously close to communism," Egger felt sure that President Paz was "now moving—perhaps less rapidly than some of the more impatient among us desire—to consolidate the revolution . . . [and] slowly beginning to turn in favor of a firm alignment with the democratic forces of world politics." Given Paz's favorable political disposition, the economist recommended that Kennedy approve the $45 million request, which would alleviate the "short-term stresses and dislocations" caused by the Triangular Plan's labor reforms, especially if a portion of the aid were set aside for local development projects "along the lines of the TVA [the Depression-era Tennessee Valley Authority]." It is impossible to know if Egger was bothered by Paz's repression; it merited no mention in his first letter back to the White House. On the contrary, the economist closed his letter: "In short, I am having a wonderful time."[7]

Conservatives in Washington were less sanguine. Almost three months after Paz's October request, Kennedy aide Arthur Schlesinger threatened to "file some sort of protest" against USAID's failure to move forward on the $45 million request. White House Assistant Budget Director Kenneth Hansen answered combatively the following week, accusing the modernization crowd of advocating that Washington "blindly accept the burdensome support of Bolivia's development on the basis of a rather esoteric plan and great faith in a dramatic turn-around in the political orientation and administrative efficiency throughout many levels in that society." Rather than generously funding Bolivia's ten-year development plan, which he disparaged as an "attempt at hasty pump-priming," Hansen recommended the administration restrict its development efforts to Triangular and its accompanying anticommunist labor reforms. Hansen admitted that his proposal was harsh, but he offered that "the realities of development and social and economic growth are also harsh." He concluded that it would be better to invest "time, money, and manpower" into strictly controlled programs like Triangular than to make a "precipitate and headlong plunge into an adventure which, in my judgment, could prove to be exceedingly disappointing and which may result in considerable damage to the Alliance for Progress."[8]

Conservative criticism of Kennedy's aid programs in Bolivia also appeared in the US press. In the Los Angeles Times, political scientist William S. Stokes criticized Kennedy's generosity toward Paz Estenssoro, writing that "even in the face of the most overwhelming evidence that the government of the MNR is authoritarian and that its economic system of socialism is a colossal failure, the United States has almost literally leaped to extend financial aid and support." Stokes warned that "it seems fair to say that there is a good chance that Bolivia will continue its leftist path and might move into the Communist or Cuban orbit," adding that "it is questionable that American interests are advanced by using foreign aid to support political authoritarianism and economic socialism." The *Chicago Tribune's* Jules Debois agreed, writing in early 1962 that "Paz Estenssoro only allows fragmentary political parties, including the Communists," keeping anticommunist Bolivians like former president Enrique Hertzog in "enforced exile." Dubois condemned the Paz government for leaving the "easily mobilized . . . Indian masses . . . vulnerable to exploitation by the Communists."[9]

Liberals answered these criticisms with their own opinion pieces. British academic John Halcro Ferguson wrote in the *Washington Post* that the MNR was "perhaps the most stable regime Bolivia has ever known," adding that despite "calamitous" economic conditions, there was hope that the "carefully worked out" mine rehabilitation program would encourage Bolivian development. The *New York Times* praised President Kennedy for responding favorably to Paz's requests for economic assistance, a move that had convinced the Bolivian leader to spurn Moscow's more generous aid offers. The newspaper also expressed its enthusiastic support for the Triangular Plan, including its labor reforms requiring the Bolivian government to "discharge . . . some 7,000 surplus workers."[10]

The Bolivian government provided fuel for its conservative enemies in early 1962 by once again demonstrating reluctance to go along with Washington's attempts to sanction Fidel Castro's Cuba at the January 1962 OAS meeting. *Washington Post* columnist Drew Pearson complained about the "six abstaining nations . . . [whose] pussyfooting position" undermined hemispheric unity.[11] Meanwhile in La Paz, deadly street battles broke out between Cuba's supporters and detractors, each side pressuring the government position at the OAS.[12] US officials pressured Paz relentlessly to come out against Cuba, and Secretary Rusk recruited a bipartisan US Senate delegation to lean on Latin American holdouts at the meeting.[13] Nonetheless, Bolivia's left-leaning foreign minister, José Fellman Velarde, remained immune to US arguments that communist Cuba's continued participation in the regional organization would represent an "unfortunate precedent."[14]

Realist doubts notwithstanding, Kennedy's economists and top aides believed Bolivia's MNR was a model regime for economic development. It repressed its right and left opposition with equal vigor, defended previously enacted redistributive reforms, and looked unswervingly toward the United States for political direction and economic support. Where liberals saw an authoritarian reformer, however, US conservatives saw only Marxist-inspired dictatorship. Kennedy's detractors despised the MNR's state-led growth model and sympathized with Bolivia's long-suffering right-wing opposition. Through 1962, these contesting ideologies were negotiated within a

US government bureaucracy dominated by strategic considerations. Neither conservative anticommunists nor liberal developmentalists would win the day without convincing policymakers that their approach would best protect US geopolitical interests in the heart of South America. The persistence of political crisis in Bolivia would play directly into the liberals' hands, as they had consistently advocated for Washington to make a full-scale commitment to authoritarian development under Paz Estenssoro's modernizing regime.

Political Crisis and Economic Development

The strategic debate in Washington pitted conservative realists against liberal interventionists, each side arguing that its ideology would better shore up Bolivia within the US sphere of influence. Had the Paz government governed a more stable country, it is likely the conservatives would have won. As political crises snowballed, however, liberals gained the upper hand. Kennedy and his economists offered an aggressively militarized version of economic development, and they capitalized on Bolivian crises to earn the reluctant approval of the foreign policy establishment.

Ambassador Ben Stephansky, who later complained that "Bolivia was a place that was being shat on" by conservative bureaucrats,[15] warned the State Department in late 1961 that the Bolivian Left was mobilizing to "frustrate not only the Triangular Plan, but also [the] expanded US aid program under [the] President's Special Program for Bolivia and [the] Alliance for Progress." Stephansky was "encouraged by [the] Bolivian government's alertness [to] the problem" but believed that Washington "may have to help [the] GOB [Government of Bolivia] when it comes really firm to grips with the communists." For the economist-turned-ambassador, development would require a one-year supply of riot gear, thus avoiding repeated emergency shipments of the sort provided in support of Paz Estenssoro's state of siege decrees in February, June, and October. Stephansky's request included 60 tear gas guns, 200 US Army helmets, 500 gas masks, 13,000 tear gas projectiles, 250 12-gauge riot guns, 15,000 rounds of 12-gauge ammunition, 400 .38 Special revolvers, and 15,000 rounds of .38 Special ammunition.[16]

In mid-January 1962, Stephansky was the only Latin American ambassador to participate in the "Working Group on Problems of the Alliance for Progress," which also included Kennedy aide Richard Goodwin, Alliance for Progress administrator Teodoro Moscoso, and military-led modernizer extraordinaire Walt Rostow, at the time serving as the State Department's chief of policy planning. Working-group participants acknowledged that Bolivia posed "profoundly difficult problems," but they felt confident that the country's ten-year development program had "passed through the Punta del Este barrier." Recommending that Washington push forward with new development programs, the working group concluded, with typical Rostow flair, that "the country's leaders are well-endowed with that indispensable precondition for development—the will to modernize—and this may be the most important ingredient of all."[17]

Advocates for military-led modernization received yet another boost in January, when President Kennedy's multiagency Assessment Team on the Internal Security Situation in South America revealed that Bolivia and Colombia were two countries that "require urgent attention." Composed of officials from the State and Defense departments, USAID, the FBI, and the CIA, the assessment team reported that both countries suffered from "critical problems in internal security accompanied by violence." The "principal problem" was the need for "recognition of the urgency to do something now," especially to contain "disorders developing from economic and social pressures," which were precisely where "much of the communist threat is based." In Bolivia, ongoing authoritarian anticommunist programs provided a ready-made answer.[18]

A week after Kennedy's assessment team pegged Bolivia as needing urgent attention, the State Department Bureau of Intelligence and Research (INR) praised Bolivia's employment of military-led development in a report titled "Creating Allies for Socio-Economic Progress with Political Stability in Latin America." Already, "one-third of its small army . . . is engaged in colonization and road-building in eastern Bolivia," INR explained, adding that "another one-third is working on agricultural projects on the altiplano." The report waxed lyrical on the benefits of Bolivia's civic action projects, which were bringing about an "improvement of living standards at the same time that they involved the military in the Alliance for Progress, increased popular respect for the military and indoctrinated the military in the benefits of widespread socio-economic progress." Recognizing that not all Latin American militaries would be as "eager to participate" in the Alliance for Progress, INR nonetheless recommended a "large-scale expansion of the present limited civil [sic: civic] action programs" into neighboring countries.[19]

Despite his frequent skepticism of the development program in Bolivia, Secretary Rusk found INR's ideas regarding military civic action to be "provocative and stimulating." Rusk authorized Stephansky to visit US Southern Command in Panama on his way back to La Paz to discuss "military matters related to Bolivia," noting that the Alliance for Progress was "primarily political in nature, ultimately designed to encourage the growth of reasonably stable governments capable of absorbing reform and change, secure from both the extreme Left and the extreme Right." Concerned that "Bolivia, Ecuador, and one or two others could well become Cubas," Rusk was warming to military-led modernization, which might permit Washington to break the communists' "monopoly of sympathy toward change."[20]

Back in La Paz, Ambassador Stephansky continued beating the drums of authoritarian development. "Past training of the *carabineros* [police] has been eminently successful," the ambassador reported in March, "with notable success in quelling riots." By bolstering President Paz's security services, Stephansky was sure that the Bolivian government would discontinue its "toleration of communists within the party," move to "curb labor anarchy," and resolve to shepherd the country down the "long, difficult road of development." Conceding, however, that there existed "cabinet-level criticism" of the Alliance for Progress in Bolivia, Stephansky believed it was wise to hold off on new projects until Washington could work out its differences. Bolivian political crises, of which Paz Estenssoro had no shortage, were the key to convincing holdouts.[21]

On 20 March 1962, Ambassador Stephansky hosted a meeting with President Paz and several cabinet ministers. The Bolivian president expressed frustration that, despite the fact that his government had submitted a development plan back in August 1961, Chile and Argentina had received privileged treatment. Ongoing negotiations with Washington had begun to make his government "look absurd," Paz complained, characterizing delays as a "violation [of] US word with respect [to an] emergency interim program until [the] Alliance got started." His regime was at a crisis point, Paz warned, threatening to consider "desperate measures in order [to] save his country." Intimating that he would give the Kennedy administration one more chance, President Paz informed Stephansky that he was dispatching two of his most trusted ministers to Washington to achieve a "breakthrough."[22]

With Paz providing the crisis, White House aides brought pressure to bear on the foreign policy establishment. Richard Goodwin complained to Secretary Rusk in early April that "considering the amount of emphasis we have placed on Bolivian development, this record is very, very poor." Goodwin was concerned that Washington's "lack of vigorous action" was prompting "severe criticism of the Alliance for Progress by important figures of the noncommunist left" and warned that "we are headed for possible disaster" if a major development program were not approved "within the next four months."

Pointing to a recent Soviet offer to establish a "permanent trade mission" in La Paz, Goodwin predicted that if the United States did not "make good on [the] Alliance for Progress," Moscow would "make Bolivia a showpiece of Socialist development, just as it was helping Cuba become a Socialist showpiece in the Caribbean."[23]

Hoping to rally support for Paz's MNR, President Kennedy sent USAID General Counsel Seymour Rubin as his "personal representative" to Bolivia's tenth-anniversary celebrations of the 9 April 1952 revolution. Rubin, who had served on Kennedy's economic mission in 1961, reported back that President Paz had gone "out of his way to excoriate communism and the local communists, largely on the ground of their disservice to the Bolivian national interest." In a long report to the White House, Rubin warned that within Bolivia there "exists considerable pressure to accept aid from the Soviet bloc," attributable in large part to "dissatisfaction with progress made so far under the Alliance." Rubin expressed confidence, nonetheless, that "Paz is for the present and foreseeable future firmly in control and . . . his policy will be firmly pro-Alliance." Arguing against those who questioned continued aid, Rubin wrote that "a base has been formed in Bolivia for a breakthrough on economic progress." He concluded that "continued assistance to Bolivia is in the best interests of the US and presents substantially fewer risks than a 'hard' line which would terminate aid unless and until basic reforms, political and economic, are made."[24]

Despite White House pressure, bureaucratic doubts persisted, and the State Department's 20 April "Guidelines for Policy and Operations" represented its harshest anti-Paz position to date. Proposing that the United States begin seeking alternatives to the "dictatorship of the Marxist-oriented MNR party," the State Department recommended encouraging a "greater influence of the military in Bolivian politics," which would exert a "moderating influence" on the Bolivian government. The report also suggested the need to begin working closer with Paz's right-wing opposition and prepare for the possibility that "the violent overthrow of the present Bolivian government" could occur.[25]

Stephansky issued a passionate retort to this latest attack on Paz's MNR. Explaining that the MNR had merely "adopted . . . [the] repressive political system that existed before the revolution," the economist argued that authoritarianism "would probably be adopted in greater or lesser degree by any other political group that assumed power while Bolivia remains in its present state of political and economic underdevelopment." The US ambassador roundly rejected the State Department's view that "opposition parties could and would do a better job of developing Bolivia economically and along more democratic lines." Stephansky added that a political role for the military was not ipso facto desirable, but he conceded that "qualified individual military officers in many cases could exercise a moderating influence." Instead of encouraging the right-wing opposition to "replace the present party by the only means presently at their command—violent revolution," Stephansky urged "toleran[ce], in the short run, of a good deal of the non-Bolshevik Marxism of the socialist brand that has such wide currency in the intellectual life of the country." By "resigning ourselves to working with those who think they are Marxists," Washington could shore up the Paz regime against the most likely alternative, "a communist takeover by non-violent means."[26]

Once again, crisis played into the hands of liberal interventionists. In mid-April 1962, the Chilean government announced that it would begin unilaterally diverting the rivers of the border-skirting Lauca River for a hydroelectric project, prompting tens of thousands of Bolivians to take to the streets. The unrest was seized on by Paz's left and right opposition, and massive riots quickly moved from the Chilean Embassy to Bolivian government buildings. The headquarters of the MNR newspaper, La Nación, was bombed and sacked; several government ministries were stoned; vehicles were overturned and burned; and dynamite, Molotov cocktails, and firearms were used against riot police.[27] At least three fatalities resulted, and Stephansky reported that "large numbers on both sides [were] injured." Predictably, he requested an immediate weapons shipment, and at 2:30 a.m. on 29 April, a CIA charter plane carrying 4,400 tear gas grenades left Miami destined for La Paz. Paid for by USAID's Office of Public Safety (OPS) and approved by Secretary Rusk, the shipment was followed by another charter flight the following day, filled with 1,600 tear gas grenades, 500 .38 Special revolvers, 250 12-gauge shotguns, 50,000 rounds of .38 Special ammunition, and 12,500 shotgun shells.[28]

During the rebellion, Air Force Commanding General René Barrientos explained to US officials that Paz was "not demonstrating his former force in controlling the MNR party." Barrientos believed the Bolivian leader was therefore "losing political strength" and failing to prevent the left wing of his party from "being used by the communists . . . [and] doing all they could to destroy" the Alliance for Progress. Barrientos assured the embassy that he had no plans to intervene, saying that "because of tradition, the armed forces would never successfully govern Bolivia." He nevertheless requested Washington to "send more people" to training schools in the Panama Canal Zone and military facilities in the United States and to continue providing material support and training to the Bolivian armed forces.[29]

The following day, the White House approved dispatch of a sixteen-man "Counterinsurgency Training Team" for a forty-day mission in La Paz. The team included experts in Special Forces, psychological warfare, civil affairs, and intelligence, and it was charged with training fifty-two army officers and ten air force officers in "counterinsurgency/counterguerrilla methods and practice." Two weeks later, the Bolivian armed forces announced plans for series of maneuvers near the Chilean border, prompting the State Department to fret that such action with "US-equipped forces would be particularly embarrassing." State ordered embassy officials to try to "head them off," but when approached, Bolivian officers answered innocently that they had received vast amounts of US equipment but had "no experience using it in the field."[30]

Bolivia was receiving so much military aid under the aegis of the Alliance for Progress that Paraguay lodged a "detailed and worried" complaint with Washington in early April 1962. Asunción was principally concerned that a "Castro-Communist takeover in Bolivia would lead to a new war with Paraguay," and it accused the United States of "effectively disrupting the military and political balance now in existence among the American states." Secretary Rusk responded to Paraguayan concerns by explaining that the "Bolivian armed forces have been subordinated to the discipline of the MNR party and have been under rigid control by the government." Rusk wrote that Washington was merely assisting in the "restoration of the military establishment as a force needed to maintain internal security against Communist subversion . . . and to assist in the economic development of Bolivia." Military hardware had nothing to do with disturbing the regional balance of power, Rusk stressed, reiterating that US military aid was meant to "counter internal communist threats, as well as to contribute to certain economic and social projects in which the Bolivian army is engaged."[31]

Kennedy's appointment of a development-minded liberal, Edwin Martin, as assistant secretary of state for Latin America brought another pro-Paz voice to the State Department. In late April, Martin requested that State Department analysts draft a thorough accounting of US attempts to undercut communism's appeal in Bolivia, especially among the unions, students, and teachers. The department reported back that the United States Information Service (USIS) had recently sent labor officer Thomas Martin to Bolivia to work in "close coordination" with embassy labor attaché Emmanuel Boggs "in an effort to reach the rank-and-file of mine and factory workers through various information media." Meanwhile, the State Department was sending "150 to 200 Bolivian students and university teachers" to the United States each year, and USAID was training Bolivian labor leaders in Puerto Rico. A key goal of these programs was to create a "more independent labor movement . . . [and] an intellectual class with a healthy skepticism of out-dated socio-political theories such as theoretical Marxism."[32]

The State Department also believed it was important to aid in the "creation of a Bolivian national culture" relying especially on the "important culturalization role of the armed forces in this primitive, multiracial, multilingual society." The military's "moderate political orientation" convinced the department that Washington should provide "early tangible support to existing army literacy programs, looking toward greater use of army facilities and personnel in a national program" that could "make use of the Peace Corps" to develop a "Bolivian Youth Corps." US officials viewed Mexico's revolutionary experience as a model, in which a national identity was adopted that "included folkloric tradition based upon indigenous cultures, a revolutionary tradition, and people skilled in handicrafts." US information programs should "encourage Bolivian pride in the contribution to the nation's culture by its indigenous people," the State Department recommended, adding that it should try to create an "appreciation of Bolivian culture by other Latin American and European countries."[33]

Having fully come around to the liberal interventionist point of view, the State Department reported in mid-May that "increased political stability in Bolivia will depend on getting economic development projects under way." Despite acknowledging that the country's capacity to absorb large quantities of aid was "unquestionably limited," State's INR wrote that "substantial progress can be registered with modest programs." The department began to echo Kennedy's economists, pointing out that "President Paz is under strong pressure from the left to establish diplomatic relations with [the] Soviet bloc, accept bloc development aid, scrap the monetary stabilization effort, and cease close cooperation with the United States." For the time being, pro-Paz voices were on the rise in Washington.[34]

The US debate over economic assistance to the Paz regime was long and drawn out. Conservative skeptics of development ideology believed that US support for Bolivia's revolutionary regime went against democratic, capitalist values. Fortunately for the development-minded economists and diplomats appointed by the Kennedy White House, Bolivia suffered from constant political crises, and the military-led modernization paradigm provided a ready-made solution. Rather than encourage the abandonment of authoritarian development, political unrest justified its adoption.

Triangular in Trouble

The centerpiece of the Alliance for Progress in Bolivia was the Triangular Plan mine rehabilitation program, conditioned on harsh labor reforms in the state-owned mining company, COMIBOL. From a technocratic standpoint, the program was adopted to increase COMIBOL's profitability and therefore improve the Bolivian government's fiscal position. Economic theories notwithstanding, the program's convenient political side effect, the de-communization of the miners' unions, was the central reason why it was adopted. Once again, technocratic ideologies of authoritarian development fueled a strategic intervention. For their part, Communist miners refused to give up without a fight.

The fiercest resisters of the US-backed Triangular Plan were the Communists at Bolivia's largest tin mine, Siglo XX. Both the union's general secretary, Irineo Pimentel, and Control Obrero Federico Escóbar boasted legendary followings among the miners for their insubordination toward COMIBOL's administration and their tireless advocacy on behalf of rank-and-file workers.[35] In early January 1962, COMIBOL's Advisory Group, a selection of foreign experts sent to ensure implementation of the Triangular conditions, wrote to President Paz that the "real cause of the deterioration in COMIBOL's mines . . . is the total lack of respect by union members for management's authority." The technicians explained that the "correction of this lack of authority was and is one of the major points considered when the Triangular Plan was formulated," adding that it was precisely "the commitment of the Bolivian government to give back to management the rights to manage" that had convinced Triangular's partners to participate. The experts warned Paz that a "failure to restore the rights of management . . . will seriously endanger the Plan."[36]

In late April, COMIBOL management began a Triangular-required tour of the mines. COMIBOL president Bedregal later wrote that his colleagues "thought it was crazy to go to Siglo XX, especially in circumstances of such severe social unrest." Other technicians warned Bedregal "that the unions are armed, that the MNR command units had practically disappeared from the region, and that no state authority existed at all that could respond to emergency situations." Nonetheless, Bedregal recalled, "I was stubborn and decided to go."[37] Indeed, he had no choice.

When the delegation arrived at the outskirts of Siglo XX, Bedregal "immediately recognized the corpulent figure of Federico Escóbar Zapata from the distance." The union leader approached the managers' car and said, "Good afternoon, Mr. President. . . . I can see that you have no bodyguards." Bedregal responded immediately, "Look here, Escóbar, what need do I have for bodyguards or 'security' as you call it? I need neither to watch my back nor be afraid. I have come to this mine to talk with my countrymen, the mine workers, in the name of the National Revolution. The rest is nonsense. Where shall we go?"[38]

Escóbar escorted the company executives to the mining camp's theater, accompanied by "three men armed with rifles, who flaunted cartridges across their entire chest." Bedregal felt a cold chill, "possibly from the irrational fear that any human being would perceive when he more or less intuits what could possibly occur in that immediate future where the seconds seem days, the minutes hours, weeks, and months." Bedregal's chill quickly warmed, however, when he entered Siglo XX's theater to face thousands of miners "who began to shout aggressive and stereotypical slogans." The stage was surrounded by images of Lenin and Marx, and enormous red flags, many including the hammer and sickle, "overwhelmed a small national flag that waved modestly in the corner."[39]

Feeling rather out of place, the COMIBOL president later recalled that he "immediately called up in the depths of my spirit the presence of Jesus and the Virgin Mary, his Divine Mother," and he proposed that the assembly start with the singing of the Bolivian national anthem. "The melody and the lyrics of our Anthem contain a bit of magic, a bit of fancifulness, and a great deal of symbolism," Bedregal recounts, lamenting, however, that the miners appeared to stumble over the words. Once the halfhearted show of patriotism reached its final line, the theater full of workers broke out into more slogans: "Long live the Bolivian proletariat!" "Down with Yankee imperialism!" "Death to COMIBOL!" "Death to the president of COMIBOL!" Bedregal was haunted by the distinct feeling that he "had not a single friend in the room." When Escóbar rose to open the meeting, the COMIBOL president silently began praying the rosary. Once Siglo XX's leaders had presented their speeches, the meeting was adjourned until the following day, and Bedregal's commission retired to the company sleeping quarters. Bedregal writes that his "brain worked feverishly, possibly incited by a fear that would not go away and would certainly increase when I faced the hostility of masses of workers and their families the following day." After another round of prayer, the corporation president drifted off to sleep.[40]

Bedregal writes that the following morning, 30 April, "I could not hide my discomfort toward the arrogant attitudes and rude manners of the union leaders," whom he called a "union aristocracy." The tense meeting lasted five hours, at which point several members of the Comité de Amas de Casa served Bedregal a bowl of sardine soup. A "silence fell over the room," at which time Bedregal realized that the women had used rotten sardines. He tried to complain, but it was no use. "The masses wanted to see me humiliated, eating this rank swill." Bedregal writes, "I do not know where I found the indispensable patience to take the affront, but I grabbed the plate with my left hand and with the right I raised the spoon and declared, 'I am going to eat this poison that you have prepared, in order to demonstrate that I reject your provocation.'" Bedregal then "took a deep breath of air . . . and in less than three minutes, I engulfed the noodle soup mixed with rotten sardines." Upon finishing, Bedregal immediately felt ill. The woman who had served him the soup "took pity on me," Bedregal writes, and advised him to "withdraw to the balcony, stick a finger in your throat, and vomit." Despite following her recommendation, Bedregal's state did not improve, and he was taken to the hospital to have his stomach pumped. "For the ten years that followed," Bedregal writes, "I suffered from almost constant gastric problems."[41]

Once he was released from the hospital, Bedregal slipped out of the mining camp without a word, prompting the miners' federation to "angrily protest" on 2 May, accusing Bedregal of having "abandoned the area without fulfilling his commitment to remain until various outstanding issues were resolved." The COMIBOL president responded that he could not negotiate in the face of such "belligerence" or subject the corporation's foreign technicians to the "threatening" atmosphere at Siglo XX.[42] In early June, dozens of miners from neighboring Huanuni declared themselves on a hunger strike, occupying the corporation headquarters in La Paz, and several unions threatened to strike unless Bedregal resumed his tour of the mines. Government officials in the region cabled President Paz to ask that COMIBOL "make whatever effort is necessary to resume his visit and thus avoid serious conflict." On 25 June, Bedregal began his second foray into the mines.[43]

Bedregal began with the Huanuni mine, where miners once again "attempted to serve Bedregal a dish of obviously decomposed food." The COMIBOL president protested that he "didn't come here to be tortured!" and the miners responded by letting loose a vitriolic series of complaints regarding poor pay and working conditions. Matters took a turn for the worse when Federico Escóbar arrived with a contingent from nearby Siglo XX, announcing that they had come to take the commission back to their mine. "This time

Bedregal is not going to run away," the Siglo XX leader declared. That is just what the mine corporation president did, however, driving through the night in a rented jeep and arriving back in La Paz at 7:00 a.m.[44]

For the next leg of his mine tour in late July, Bedregal picked the less radical mines of San José and Colquiri. The first went off without a hitch, but during the commission's visit to Colquiri, the miners presented COMIBOL with a list of 250 requests, including a "Westclox watch for each worker, one aviator type uniform per worker per year, a library in the mine, new lunch pails every six months," and other items Bedregal found to be "ridiculous." After looking over the list, he "excused himself from the meeting, climbed into a car with four other members of the commission . . . fled the community, and came to La Paz."[45]

Profoundly rattled, the COMIBOL president promptly drafted a letter of resignation. President Paz would hear nothing of it, however, and the letter was never made public.[46] Washington's embassy was frustrated by COMIBOL's lack of seriousness, writing that the "ludicrous situation" surrounding Bedregal's trips demonstrated the "serious need for education in labor-management relations," on the part of both COMIBOL's administration and the unions.[47] The foreign experts in charge of implementing the mine rehabilitation program warned Bedregal that unless COMIBOL was able to bring Siglo XX under control, "we will see ourselves obliged to recommend the suspension of the Triangular Plan's financial aid."[48]

Just as they had for months, the development economists who designed and carried out Kennedy's Alliance for Progress in Bolivia were unwavering in their opinion that harsh labor reforms should precede additional foreign aid. In the process, they received unwavering cooperation from Bolivia's nationalist leaders, who had long sought to establish political authority in the rebellious mining regions. Given fierce resistance to the Triangular Plan among the Bolivian miners, however, it was clear that the Alliance for Progress would eventually require some form of armed force. US liberals and their Bolivian allies never flinched. Instead, they deepened their ideological commitment to authoritarian development, its antidemocratic tendencies being laid barer with each passing month.

Development versus Democracy

By mid-1962, conservative US opposition to the Alliance for Progress in Bolivia had been silenced by crisis. Ongoing anarchy, especially in the mine region, only strengthened the Kennedy administration's resolve to remain deeply involved in Bolivian affairs. When the Paz administration presided over obviously rigged congressional elections in 1962, conservatives once again raised their voices in doubt, but liberals felt vindicated. Paz was an authoritarian modernizer, and he was in favor of anticommunist development. What more could Washington want? Political democracy was a luxury only advanced countries deserved; for Bolivia, authoritarianism was the only path to progress.

Just prior to the May 1962 congressional election, US Embassy officials hosted a meeting with conservative politician Hugo Roberts Barragán, an anti-Paz "conspirator and revolutionary" who expressed confidence that the Bolivian president was "certain to fall, possibly shortly after the elections." The MNR leader had "nurtured communism in Bolivia," Roberts explained, condemning US support of Paz for "only help[ing] to build up communist strength." Given embassy officials' "significant confidence in [the] accuracy [of] Roberts' analysis," Deputy Chief of Mission (DCM) William Williams predicted that "significant political changes could occur in the next few months."[49]

The US Embassy acknowledged that the MNR exercised control over "all phases of electoral campaigns and balloting" during the June elections, including the "physical intimidation of opposition candidates and their activities." Embassy analysts concurred that the poll was marred by "widespread fraud . . . harassment and often violent repression . . . by the MNR and Government agents," adding that "public apathy" and a general "disorganization" made it clear to all observers that the "official results do not reflect the relative popularity of the competing parties nor the actual votes cast." It appeared to the embassy that Paz had "decided [the] contest in advance and arranged [the] election and tally to come out that way." The rightist opposition returns were "so low it is absurd," the embassy reported, adding that the only opposition party to receive favorable treatment was the Communist Party, which issued a press statement "congratulating the successful work" of the electoral commission. Paradoxically, the US Embassy believed that the rigged poll was good news for the Alliance for Progress, since Paz would be now able to "proceed with [the] economic development plan." Embassy officials worried nonetheless that the governing party's "poor showing" could not be papered over by the "obvious manipulation [of the] tabulation."[50]

Secretary of State Rusk had never been comfortable with the unrelenting pro-Paz enthusiasm of Kennedy's developmental economists and top aides.[51] On receiving news of the fraudulent poll, Rusk was livid, and he strongly condemned the Paz government's "rigging" of the parliamentary election and the MNR's decision to "intensify persecution [of the] non-communist opposition." Referring to ongoing negotiations between USAID and Bolivian ministers, and rumors that Kennedy was preparing to invite President Paz to Washington, Rusk worried that the White House's "seeming endorsement of [the election] by possible early announcement of [a] new aid package and [a] Presidential guest visit incurs hostility toward [the] US of non-communist opposition leaders and groups presently suppressed or victimized who might one day succeed [the] MNR in government." Rusk warned that Paz's growing authoritarianism "encourages violence, with all its political and economic disadvantages, as [the] only means by which [the] non-communist opposition can effectively give expression [to] its views," adding gravely that the Bolivian government's "intentional and calculated inflation of [the] PCB vote creates the appearance of growth which enhances their attractiveness to non-communist leaders as allies." Rusk concluded that Paz's selective repression would "increasingly push dissidents into [the] arms [of the] extreme left," and he characterized the election as an embarrassment to the Alliance for Progress.[52]

Ambassador Stephansky responded that while it was "evident [the] MNR has slipped . . . there is no viable alternative as yet to its leadership and none will be available for some time."[53] After "pondering the problem of democratic processes in underdeveloped countries," the development-minded ambassador issued a dogged defense of MNR authoritarianism in a nine-page treatise titled "Bolivia and Democratic Processes." Stephansky conceded that "by any standard tests of democratic processes derived from maturely operating democratic systems, the elections were not democratic." Rather than apply "such standard tests," however, which "disclose glaring weaknesses," the US ambassador recommended asking what were the "appropriate tests" that apply to Bolivia, "one of the most backward countries." Stephansky explained that the right wing harbored a "fanatical hatred of the MNR," leading it to "cling grimly to the hope of [its] violent defeat." He explained that there were "constant rumors of possible coups" in the lead-up to elections, and he warned that the Right, in alliance with the anti-Paz Left, was attempting to "make their strongest effort to undermine the MNR" before USAID announced a new aid package. For Ambassador Stephansky, approval of this package was the "last hope for [the] Alliance."[54]

Stephansky then turned to the issue of the Bolivian armed forces. "The MNR destroyed an oligarchic army," he explained, "and created in its place (mostly under Paz) a popular army strongly oriented to civic action." For Stephansky, this "interesting 'nationalizing' institution" was the key to the

Alliance for Progress in Bolivia, since it "takes the Indian recruits from all parts of the country, often provides the beginnings of literacy, a craft, and hygiene . . . assimilating a kind of 'internal immigrant' from many scattered cultures and regions in Bolivia." The armed forces are "overwhelmingly anticommunist and actively campaigning against communist influence here," Stephansky explained, adding that they were also "committed to social and economic reforms," including the "aims and objectives of [the] 1952 revolution." With funds from the Alliance for Progress, the Bolivian air force was "flying food, building materials, jeeps and other equipment to areas not served by commercial airlines," Stephansky continued, and "80 percent [of the] GOB military budget is spent for civic action programs." The ambassador stressed that these programs to "help . . . identify [the military] with the common people" were a bedrock of US policy in Bolivia, and that they were "in keeping with the theory of guerrilla warfare that gives advantages to the side that has the support of the local populace." Stephansky was adamant that a "failure [to] continue military assistance would play into communist hands and nullify [the] aid program designed [to] restore order and economic progress to Bolivia."[55] Moreover, Stephansky conceded that, in the event that Communists seriously threatened to take power, "US interests would be served by a military-assisted takeover against communism," acknowledging that "doctrinaire attitudes toward [the] military in politics can play into communist hands." He believed that "the time could come in Bolivia when we could be forced with [the] alternatives of [a] Castro-type state or [a] military-backed government," proposing that the development-oriented military remain a central aspect of US aid programs.[56]

Stephansky concluded his epic cable by discouraging US officials from becoming overly concerned with political democracy. Instead, Washington should have been asking how the MNR could "win in the fight against communist efforts to take over the revolution" and how "sufficient order and discipline" could be "evoked in order to achieve economic development." He argued that "economic development . . . provides the possibility of reducing the communist threat," after which "political development could proceed." He pointed to rising young leaders like "Bedregal, [Economy Minister Alfonso] Gumucio, [and] Barrientos," who would be able to accede to power in 1968. Stephansky stressed that "only Paz can hold the country together" and urged the State Department to "recognize that Bolivia is a backward place, with a rudimentary democracy." If Washington could "refine our analysis in these terms," Stephansky concluded, "we might perhaps enter the fray with greater skill to move this country our way, insofar as our feeble perspectives permit us to see what our way is in this complicated and perplexing country."[57]

Assistant Secretary Martin believed that Stephansky had done a "masterly job." The ambassador's defense of President Paz was a "more sophisticated and penetrating analysis of a complex political and economic situation than any I have seen since I came into the bureau or for a long time before that." Martin was nonetheless concerned that Stephansky's recommendations were "tying the United States too closely to one political party," and he wondered if there were "ways to moderate the degree of repression exercised by the MNR" toward Bolivia's right-wing opposition, "without making it a major or obvious objective." Martin was concerned that US support for the "exceedingly fragile" MNR was akin to backing a "losing horse" and recommended against Washington "committing itself politically one way or another." Noting that he was battling strong Paz skepticism in the department, Martin urged Stephansky to concede that the "MNR's virtues are not overly numerous."[58]

In late July, the State Department Policy Planning Council weighed in on the debate. Led by one of Washington's foremost proponents of military-led modernization, economic historian Walt Rostow, the council lamented that "dealing with Bolivia seems to generate an exceptional amount of emotional heat among the majority of American officials involved." On the one hand were those who "frequently take a stand which might be summarized as a conviction that the United States has committed or promised financial and technical aid, and therefore we must give it to Bolivia regardless of the soundness or completeness of the proposed project, and with little consideration of political developments in Bolivia." The council warned that this view "drifts into the personality cult when it maintains that we must support President Paz at all costs—that only he can control the situation and work well with us." On the "other extreme," Rostow's group noted that some US officials believed the Bolivians were "opportunistic liars, corrupt, with interests concentrated on self-enrichment, and somewhat second-rate and undeserving of help because they are lacking in skills." Both these approaches were "inaccurate and disappointing," the council argued, adding that an "objective, dispassionate approach . . . is scarce both in Washington and in the field." The group fretted that "all of the senior members of the staff of our Embassy in La Paz are disturbed about the presentation which the Ambassador makes of the Bolivian situation," which was "more delicate and explosive than he indicates." According to these officials, Stephansky was obscuring the fact that "disorder and violence are always just beneath the surface, that the MNR is now paying only lip service to the ideal of political freedom of expression, and that the leftist extremists are in greater control of the government." The council warned that Paz skeptics in La Paz and Washington meanwhile believed that "we didn't really mean our commitment to assist Bolivia, and that if things are prolonged it may go away." The group concluded that a more technocratic approach coupled with "a convincing presentation and forceful action" would overcome the doubts of US officials who lacked the "desired drive and determination" to continue economic aid to Bolivia.[59]

As this debate dragged on throughout the summer of 1962, two members of Paz's cabinet remained bogged down in negotiations with USAID and IDB officials in Washington.[60] Hoping to apply maximum pressure for a proposed $80 million Alliance for Progress development program, in May the Bolivian president had dispatched Economy Minister Gumucio, who had threatened to resign the previous month as a "blast" against the Alliance for Progress, and Peasant Affairs Minister Roberto Jordán, who announced to attendees at an April IDB meeting in Buenos Aires that he sought to determine "whether the Alliance is fact or fiction." The State Department initially expressed confidence that negotiations would conclude by 31 May, with USAID and IDB economists "moving ahead with engineering studies to fill in the outlines by the generalized and impatient expectations of the Bolivians." The State Department wrote to White House National Security Adviser (NSA) McGeorge Bundy that "given [Kennedy's] personal interest in Bolivian development as publicly expressed to President Paz, and the still extremely precarious political situation in Bolivia, we consider it important that the Ministers be received by the President."[61]

In late June, with the IDB stalling negotiations because of persistent Communist sabotage in Bolivia's mines, USAID Director Fowler Hamilton warned Kennedy aide Richard Goodwin that despite the fact that "Bolivia lacks an adequate development plan," the "urgent political and economic problems of Bolivia require an immediate program." The situation "continues to be extremely precarious," he explained, with the Paz government under "intense pressure" to accept large-scale Soviet bloc assistance. Denying the $80 million aid request would lead to repercussions that "would be serious indeed," Hamilton added, since forcing Gumucio and Jordán to "return home empty-handed would be exploited by the Communists to claim the Alliance is long on words but short on deeds." Hamilton stressed to the White House that further delays would represent a "serious political blow to Paz."[62]

A week later, Paz expressed frustration over the now two-month delay, asking Stephansky impatiently if he could expect his ministers to return home anytime soon. Publicly denying the existence of any stalemate, Stephansky warned the State Department that the impasse was "embarrassing to [Paz] from [a] local political point [of] view with increasing public speculation" regarding Washington's position.[63] Gumucio visited the White House on 18 July to share what Arthur Schlesinger called "his anguished tale." Schlesinger wrote that the economy minister "bears all the aspects of a man tried beyond endurance until his spirit is substantially broken," adding that Gumucio had spent every day for two and a half months suffering "unexampled confusion and frustration," principally in his negotiations with the IDB. Schlesinger asked his colleague Ralph Dungan to receive Gumucio immediately "for the sake of our future relations with Bolivia," urging him to find some way to obtain approval and avoid forcing Gumucio to "return to Bolivia a most irritated and discouraged man at the end of the week."[64]

White House pressure broke the stalemate. The following day, Bolivia won approval of an $80 million Alliance for Progress package, the first large-scale program approved since the May 1961 mine rehabilitation plan was launched. Thanks to President Kennedy's development-minded aides, Washington resolved to provide Paz Estenssoro with its "full backing" in his drive to "maintain effective government while getting on with some of the important tasks of development." Stephansky's passionate defense of the MNR helped convince a hesitant foreign policy apparatus that "there is no preferable alternative presently available" to Paz, and in its 19 July "Experimental Policy Paper for Bolivia," the State Department stressed the importance of demonstrating results in economic development "without delay."[65]

MNR skepticism had been muted, but conservative realists continued to advise a cautious approach. After the new program was approved, Assistant Budget Director Hansen urged the White House consider it a "test" of whether or not the Paz government was "capable of effectively utilizing a higher level of grant and loan funds." The "hard facts" of the Bolivian situation "indicate that this commitment is a high-risk undertaking," he wrote, explaining that Washington would soon see if it could "reasonably commit itself and invest its funds in Bolivia without making a mockery of the development concepts in the Alliance for Progress." If Paz failed to "gain sufficient party control and general political initiative to move toward the realignments and reforms he professes to seek," Hansen warned that the new round of US aid would "do nothing but finance the status quo."[66]

MNR partisans in Washington were not swayed by these words of caution. After months of debate, a clear policy had emerged in favor of Paz as precisely the development-oriented leader for which the Alliance for Progress was created. The State Department wrote in late July that the Bolivian government had "already made major land reforms and moved decisively toward greater social equality," adding that the country's 1952 revolution had "brought more rapid and fundamental changes than those experienced by any other country on the continent." For this very reason, the Kennedy administration had come to believe that its aid program to Bolivia was a "test case of the thesis that social and political reforms are essential for development." The State Department stressed that "should the effort fail in Bolivia, it will bring in doubt the underlying concept of the Alliance."[67]

Throughout the better part of 1962, Kennedy's liberal appointees battled back bureaucratic skepticism regarding the wisdom of US support for revolutionary Bolivia. Their argument was that the Paz regime was sufficiently authoritarian to promote modernization without permitting Bolivia to fall into communist hands, a rubric into which the rigged congressional elections neatly fit.[68] Despite outbreaks of conservative resistance, liberal developmentalists continued to emerge victorious. With strong support from the Kennedy White House, it seemed that Paz Estenssoro would remain a centerpiece of Kennedy's development policy in Latin America.

Tin Dumping and Counterinsurgency

For a country whose main export is tin, nothing is more damaging than a fall in mineral prices. Unfortunately for Bolivia, as one former ambassador put it, "Washington doesn't pay too much attention to what's going on there until you're in trouble."[69] Under strong pressure from Congress in 1962, the Treasury Department began an extensive, and extended, sell-off of tin from the US strategic stockpile. Citing a growing balance of payments deficit, the White House had previously requested such authority, brutally demonstrating that the economic well-being of the United States trumps that of weaker countries.[70] Despite the fact that US tin dumping raised the ire of Kennedy's economists who were so invested in Bolivia's economic development, the crisis paradoxically supported their position. Without a deeper commitment to the country under the Alliance for Progress, Bolivia would now surely be lost to communism.

Before the ink had dried on the new $80 million Alliance for Progress package, the State Department announced that Washington would immediately begin selling two hundred tons of stockpile tin each week for the foreseeable future. Tin prices had already been moving downward, prompting

Stephansky to warn that the sell-off would "probably be construed here as 'dumping.'" Undersecretary of State George Ball responded that tin prices were still "well above [the] 1953–1960 average," but Stephansky explained that this argument "means nothing to a country which suffered extreme depression during this period precisely because of [the] abrupt and large drop in tin prices following the Korean War." Ball was unmoved. Instead, he suggested that lower tin prices would put more pressure on the Bolivian government to implement the Triangular Plan's labor reforms and "reduce costs through rationalization [of the] mining industry." Stephansky retorted that the tin sell-off "seriously undermines propaganda benefits to be derived from [the] $80 million," adding that, "so far as Bolivia [is] concerned, [it] will damage the Alliance for Progress itself." Stephansky predicted that the sell-off would appear to many Bolivians as an "example of US hypocrisy" and would lead to a situation in which President Paz "could fall or be forced [to] take [a] strongly antagonistic attitude toward [the] US Alliance."[71]

In late July, Assistant Secretary Martin joined Stephansky in questioning why Washington was considering a tin sell-off in spite of the fact that such a move "conflicts with our commitments to Bolivia" and "hands the communists a made-to-order propaganda issue." Martin expressed concern that the sell-off threatened to derail the Triangular Plan, which "has as one of its important political objectives the weakening of communist hold on mine labor by demonstrating that the best hope for the miners' welfare lies in a cooperative effort by Free-World capital supplies and Bolivian labor." The stockpile sales would "permit the communists to appear as the defenders of the miners and will thereby favor their efforts . . . to frustrate the Triangular operation." Martin echoed Stephansky's view that the sell-off had neutralized the "psychological impact of the recent joint announcement of US-IDB financing of an $80 million interim development program," complicating President Paz's attempts to resist Soviet bloc economic aid. Tin dumping also made it "more difficult for us to insist that the GOB effectively implement" labor reforms in the mines, and it would probably lead to a cancellation of Paz's upcoming trip to Washington.[72]

As the crisis mushroomed, the Bolivian press reprinted sections of Kennedy's October 1961 letter, in which he vowed that the United States would do nothing to harm the tin market.[73] In conversations with the US Embassy, Foreign Minister Fellman Velarde demanded $9 million in order to "compensate Bolivia for loss [of] income resulting from [the] fall in tin prices" caused by sell-off. Stephansky believed that $4 or $5 million would probably satisfy the Bolivians, adding that a failure to respond favorably would put Paz's "head in [a] political noose." In this context, Kennedy's White House invitation was "extremely embarrassing," Stephansky wrote, warning that Paz would certainly decline unless he could "receive advanced assurance that talks on tin will result in some measure [on] our part" to compensate Bolivia. Anything less, Stephansky concluded, would be "political suicide."[74]

Secretary Rusk was in no mood to humor the Bolivians. Long a voice of skepticism toward Paz, Rusk wrote to his ambassador that he did "not wish to negotiate with him as to terms on which [Paz is] willing to accept [the] President's invitation and need [to] know soonest whether there is to be [a] visit." Deeply angered, Paz issued a press release hours later that he had "decided to postpone his visit to the United States in view of the situation created on the tin market by the sales from the American strategic reserve," adding that it had not been possible "to achieve assurance regarding the special consideration due Bolivia."[75] For good measure, Paz pulled Bolivia out of the OAS later that afternoon.[76]

US tin dumping and Paz Estenssoro's subsequent decision to cancel his White House trip to and boycott the OAS sent shock waves through Bolivia's body politic. Members of Parliament raked Washington over the coals for having broken written commitments regarding tin price stabilization, and they wondered aloud if funding from the Alliance had been conditioned on the rejection of Soviet bloc aid offers. Bolivian legislators asked President Paz "how you can explain that the offer made by Nikita Khrushchev in 1960 to provide a tin smelter and a $150 million credit has not yet been accepted. . . . What powerful forces have prevented, and apparently continue to prevent, the dispatch of a Commercial Mission to the Soviet Union?" Another group of parliamentarians demanded that President Paz explain the "antinational and antirevolutionary agreements with foreign signatories and with the IDB." Condemning the Bolivian president's "vacillating policy toward US tin dumping," members of Parliament demanded that he immediately send a mission to Moscow to "arrange and finalize the $150 million credit."[77] In Washington, Bolivia's anticommunist ambassador pinned the blame squarely on Paz Estenssoro, lamenting his government's tendency to "give hell periodically to Uncle Sam."[78]

Ambassador Stephansky, who would later refer to an "unseen diabolical hand whose special purpose is to perturb relations between Bolivia and ourselves on the question of tin,"[79] reported to Secretary Rusk that the United States was receiving a "severe trouncing" in the Bolivian Parliament. Warning that the Communists were "mounting a vigorous campaign [for] Bolivia [to] accept Soviet aid," Stephansky lamented that US government agencies "do not have [a] common approach to this country," and he requested that he be recalled for "immediate consultation in Washington."[80]

When Secretary Rusk received Ambassador Stephansky's "alarming telegram," Rusk quickly telephoned Undersecretary George Ball to share the news. Ball agreed to speak with State Department analyst Herb May in order to discern if the situation was "nearing a critical stage." May responded that things in Bolivia "have been critical for a long time," and he told Ball that they should "get Ben [Stephansky] back as soon as possible."[81]

The day after Paz declined his White House invitation, President Kennedy issued National Security Action Memorandum (NSAM) 184, assigning Bolivia to the Special Group on Counterinsurgency (CI), along with a declaration that the country was "sufficiently threatened by Communist-inspired insurgency to warrant . . . specific interest."[82] Created by the president in January 1962, the Special Group (CI) aimed to use "all available resources with maximum effectiveness in preventing and resisting subversive insurgency and related forms of indirect aggression in friendly countries." The group, which included Attorney General Robert Kennedy, Deputy Secretary of Defense Roswell Gilpatric, USAID Director Hamilton, NSA Bundy, and Director of Central Intelligence John McCone, recognized that "subversive insurgency ('wars of liberation') is a major form of politico-military conflict equal in importance to conventional warfare," and it sought to ensure that this was "reflected in the organization, training, equipment, and doctrine of the US armed forces and other US agencies abroad and in the political, economic, intelligence, military aid, and informational programs conducted by the State Department, Defense Department, USAID, USIA, and CIA."[83]

When the Special Group (CI) first met on Bolivia in mid-September, it considered an embassy-drafted internal defense plan (IDP). The plan warned that the Paz government "does not adequately recognize the seriousness of the communist threat either to itself or the hemisphere" and that Communists were "working hard to subvert the government and turn Bolivia into a worker-peasant state." According to the report, the Communists' "salami tactics" sought to take advantage of the "illiterate, poverty-stricken Indians who . . . lack the knowledge and means to improve their lot." The IDP explained that Communists "operate so freely and openly in their efforts to proselytize labor and peasant segments of the population" that they were unlikely to resort to armed revolution "until they are certain they can succeed." Communists "already dominate the majority of the larger labor unions and at least some of the major peasant syndicates as well as primary and secondary teachers' organizations," the IDP lamented, adding that they had also "deeply penetrated the government," leaving "few, if any agencies . . . free of communist influence." Noting that the Kennedy administration had "consciously taken" a risk by trying to "provide the country with a degree of prosperity and to put it on the road to social, political, and economic development," the IDP nevertheless warned that it "may not be possible to achieve this in time to be effective against the communist threat."[84]

Before leaving for emergency consultation in Washington in late September, Stephansky filed a string of alarming cables. Since the cancellation of Paz's White House visit, the "situation has gravely deteriorated," Stephansky wrote, warning that President Paz had "given up and evidence [is] piling up that we may well be in the process [of a] complete [MNR] Left Sector takeover with large-scale Soviet aid." Ambassador Stephansky declared that a "crisis in Bolivia's political orientation is near at hand," since the MNR Left Sector was pushing for "advanced stage socialism with greater ties to [the] Soviet Union and at least partial collaboration with the Communist Party." Stephansky advised Washington to be "flexible [in] this situation to permit support of Paz so long as he appears able and willing [to] take firm steps in [the] face [of the] Communist threat, but to seek another alternative should Paz prove too weak or unwilling to do so." It was high time, Stephansky concluded, to begin "serious consideration [of] contingency alternatives."[85]

Assistant Secretary Martin agreed that recent events demonstrated the "continuing threat that the extremist and communist-infiltrated MNR Left Sector would take over control of the badly divided MNR party and the apparatus of government." President Paz appeared to have "neither the ability nor the will to oppose the growing influence of the MNR party's left wing or to rid it of its pro-Castro, pro-Communist elements." Martin wrote ominously that the White House's "optimistic expectation that Paz would impose internal discipline in carrying out the conditions for the $80 million is fast on the wane," and cited "growing evidence that a complete takeover by the MNR Left Sector, accompanied by large-scale Soviet aid, may be in process."[86]

Despite President Kennedy's strong commitment to the Alliance for Progress in Bolivia, the highland nation remained small in the eyes of the larger US government apparatus. The need to alleviate Washington's balance of payments problem far exceeded any importance Bolivian economic development might have held for the United States. By aggravating political crises, however, the Treasury Department's tin sales provided yet another reason to deepen US involvement in Bolivia. Ideological developmentalism had initially been

adopted as a form of political intervention; a heightened threat only strengthened liberal commitment to carry it out via political repression.

Ideologies of authoritarian modernization meld technocratic, economic
language with hard-nosed political interventionism. Yet Third World development programs are much easier to approve than implement. In Bolivia,
crises fueled development-oriented repression and conservative resistance redoubled liberal resolve. The Alliance for Progress was riddled with political
problems from the beginning, but its ideologists were never swayed. Armed
with theories of rapid modernization, they proceeded to offer unflinching
diplomatic and material support to an authoritarian Third World regime.
Democracy did not belong in Bolivia; economic development did. Paz's repression, facilitated by USAID weapons shipments, was just what the Bolivian
people needed to rapidly modernize. Convinced that it was "necessary to put
all emphasis on economic development," Ambassador Stephansky was un-
concerned with political liberty. With enough dollars, tear gas, and riot gear,
progress would eventually come, and "the Bolivians will show a kind of discipline and ability that they are not generally credited for."[87] The Bolivian Communist Party put it another way, quipping in October 1962 that the Alliance
for Progress was bringing "nothing but tears to the eyes of Bolivians."[88]

The Kennedy administration labored to defend its development policy in
revolutionary Bolivia, and the country's repeated crises encouraged the policy's persistent reliance on authoritarian solutions. When US tin dumping
made a mockery of Washington's commitment to Bolivian economic development in mid-1962, the Paz government once again threatened to veer
sharply leftward. If the Alliance for Progress was initially approved as an anticommunist strategy, the growing communist threat crystallized liberal resolve
to intervene extensively and aggressively. It was not hard to see that this experiment was reeling toward a tragic apogee, one whose suffering would be
borne entirely by the Bolivians themselves, the Alliance for Progress's supposed beneficiaries.

Chapter 3

"Bitter Medicine"

Military Civic Action and the Battle of Irupata

As crises continued to threaten Bolivia's political orientation in the early 1960s, US liberals sought to reassure President Paz and deepen their commitment to his repressive, modernizing regime. Communism in Bolivia, both domestic and international, drove an increasingly heavy-handed policy of thoroughgoing intervention in Bolivia's internal affairs, elegantly articulated through a development discourse. While Cuban-sponsored guerrilla activity unnerved Washington, US policymakers were more immediately concerned by the possibility of a political takeover by the semiautonomous Movimiento Nacionalista Revolucionario (MNR; Revolutionary Nationalist Movement) Left Sector, headed by Vice President and miners' federation leader Juan Lechín. To face down this threat, US officials would rely extensively on the Bolivian armed forces to carry out the development enterprise. In mid-1963, the CIA also entered the country in full force, charged with shoring up MNR moderates under President Paz and ridding leftism from Bolivian society. These policies took the form of military-led development in the countryside and militarized development in the mining camps. Given the aggressive nature by which US liberals intervened and the sheer quantity of military hardware the Kennedy administration was sending, it was only a matter of time before Bolivian blood would be shed in the name of the Alliance for Progress.

Communism in Revolutionary Bolivia

The Kennedy administration supported authoritarian development in Bolivia in order to wage war against communism, but the battle lines in the country's revolutionary environment were far from clear. The heterogeneous governing party, which the State Department occasionally referred to as the "Marxist-oriented MNR,"[1] displayed a troubling toleration of communism, both domestic and international, and members of the Communist Party and the MNR Left Sector were given free rein to cooperate with Cuban-backed guerrilla movements targeting neighboring Peru and Argentina. Indeed, in the early 1960s the Cuban Embassy operated with nearly total impunity in La Paz, and Havana returned the favor by muting its disagreements with the MNR regime. Meanwhile, alternating between double-dealing and thinly veiled blackmail, President Paz employed the communist threat to secure ever-higher levels of US support.

The phenomenon of communism in revolutionary Bolivia is complex.[2] In exchange for Communist Party endorsements in his 1951 and 1960 presidential contests, Paz Estenssoro had generally eschewed political repression against the Partido Comunista de Bolivia (PCB; Communist Party of Bolivia).[3] In return, the Communist Party forswore insurgent activity against his government. According to Central Committee member Ramiro Otero, the PCB's decision in 1960 to offer Paz "conditional support" reflected its position of "employing only *political* pressure toward his government" as long as Paz respected the party's legal status. José Luis Cueto, editor of the PCB weekly *Unidad*, also stresses the importance of maintaining their freedom of operation. "Above all, we had to protect the Party's legality," Cueto recalls, conceding that this fixation led PCB leadership to accept a "cynically complicit coexistence with the MNR."[4]

Moreover, Marxism was hardly restricted to the PCB and Trotskyist Partido Obrero Revolucionario (POR; Revolutionary Workers' Party). The MNR Youth faction represented one of Bolivia's strongest pro-Cuba organizations, and there were many Leftists in the governing party, including Vice President Lechín, a former POR member; Marxist political scientist René Zavaleta; ex-PCB intellectual Sergio Almaraz; and former POR labor activist Edwin Möller.

President Paz sought to neutralize domestic communism through mutual toleration and, in the case of the MNR Left, through co-optation.[5] Unfortunately for Paz, one of the earliest effects of the Alliance for Progress was the radicalization of the Bolivian Left, both inside and outside the governing party, which began to distance itself from his regime. In mid-1961, a large group of MNR Youth leaders condemned Paz for rounding up Bolivian Communists in order to ram the Triangular Plan through the miners' federation. The crackdown "fills us with shame," they wrote, adding that Paz's actions "bring dishonor to the party, and not just that, they also bring dishonor to the country." Explaining that they were officially resigning from the governing party, the MNR Youth declared that "communism is in the just demand of the workers who cannot live on starvation wages; it is in the demands for better social conditions; it is in the condemnation of the wicked sale of our mines to the Almighty Power of the North, the desire to preserve jobs, rejecting the Triangular Plan conditions . . . [which] will plunge the country into a constant wave of strikes and could bring us to the verge of civil war." Calling for a "revolution that is not betrayed," the dissidents asked rhetorically, "When will the true revolution arrive?"[6] Meanwhile, MNR leftists in Parliament asked incredulously "why the Executive Branch signed the so-called Triangular Plan if its application . . . will result in a serious impact on national dignity and a damaging precedent that will weaken the sovereignty of the Homeland."[7]

As Bolivian leftists distanced themselves from Paz's MNR, they also grew noticeably closer to the Cuban Embassy. The CIA reported in April 1963 that "the militantly leftist youth organization of the [MNR] . . . has been receiving funds for propaganda purposes from the Cuban Embassy in La Paz." The agency added that MNR Youth were "present at a 19 April [1963] party at the Cuban Embassy commemorating the second anniversary of the Bay of Pigs invasion," where several "boasted that they were responsible for covering La Paz with pro-Cuban posters and for an illuminated sign on a hillside overlooking the capital declaring that Bolivia supports Cuba."[8] Despite denying having received funds from Havana, MNR Youth leader Dulfredo Rúa concedes that they were "very close" to Cuban ambassador Ramón Aja Castro and that they "held many meetings during this period with the Communist Youth in our strategy to defend the Cuban revolution." Rúa's former colleague Alberto Muñoz agrees that "it probably appeared to many that we were receiving money from the Cubans, because we were very publicly identified with their Embassy. We were strongly pro-Cuba, and our contacts with the Embassy were very close. We attended huge parties at the Embassy, and the Ambassador was a good friend of ours."[9] In mid-1961, a Cuban Embassy employee informed the Bolivian government that Havana was indeed providing financial support to several groups of domestic leftists, adding that "an enormous quantity of individuals from every social class came by" the Cuban mission. Most troubling was the employee's claim that Siglo XX's union leaders Escóbar and Pimentel appeared to "enjoy the full confidence of Embassy personnel, such that they would be received at any hour of the day or night."[10]

In an attempt to deflect growing leftist dissent, Paz continued to tolerate Communist activity in Bolivia. Doggedly resisting US pressure to break diplomatic relations with Cuba and Czechoslovakia, the Paz government stood aside while the Czech government, according to the US Embassy, "shipped 15,124 pieces of propaganda directly into Bolivia in 1962."[11] Paz also considered acceptance of economic aid programs generously offered by Communist bloc countries. Czechoslovakia eased the terms of a 1961 antimony smelter offer, seeking to "actively take advantage of every opportunity to deepen divisions between Bolivia and the capitalist states headed by the US."[12] According to Ambassador Stephansky, the deal was "irresistible . . . and it is difficult to see how [the] GOB [Government of Bolivia] can refuse to accept it."[13] The CIA agreed, adding that it would be "just as hard to turn down Yugoslavia's offer of a $5 million loan."[14]

According to the State Department, Havana was meanwhile "making a concerted effort to fish in Bolivia's troubled waters," and the hundreds of MNR leftists and PCB members who traveled to Cuba and the Soviet bloc represented the "largest number from any one Latin American nation."[15] *Time* magazine reported that "Bolivia is an extreme" case, where Marxism had infiltrated nearly every aspect of the country's revolutionary environment.[16]

It would be an error, nonetheless, to interpret Cuban activity as having been directed against the Paz government. On the contrary, Havana's intervention was principally aimed at maintaining local support for its continued diplomatic presence in Bolivia. MNR Youth leaders who studied in Cuba in the early 1960s were told repeatedly that "a guerrilla effort against Paz Estenssoro does not suit us."[17] One of those present recalled that "the Cuban line was that Paz was a revolutionary, but with some obvious differences. They expressed a moderated sympathy for his government."[18] In its occasional articles on Bolivia prior to 1964, the Cuban weekly, *Bohemia*, praised Paz Estenssoro for standing up to the United States on the issue of diplomatic relations and pointed to the miner-dominated MNR Left Sector as the "vanguard" of the Bolivian revolution.[19] In this way, Havana and La Paz engaged in an intricate minuet that amounted to a tacit agreement of mutual toleration, one that paralleled Paz Estenssoro's similar arrangement with the PCB.

The extent to which Cuba was using its embassy in La Paz to organize regional subversion was partially revealed in mid-March 1963, when a civilian

DC-6 airliner operated by Bolivia's Lloyd Aéreo Boliviano crashed high in the Andean mountains on its way from Arica, Chile, to La Paz. A Cuban courier and a Czech officer were aboard, but US officials were not overly suspicious until receiving reports that Cuban ambassador Ramón Aja Castro was "frantic." Ambassador Stephansky immediately dispatched three military teams to climb up to the snowy crash site from nearby villages, and at 4:00 a.m. on 18 March, Embassy Army Attaché Paul Wimert was the first to reach the wreckage, having climbed overnight from Tacna, Peru. Working for "almost [a] full hour undisturbed," Wimert was able to "take possession [of] all [the] papers on or near [the] body" of the Cuban courier, who he noted had a "machine pistol . . . clutched" in his arms. When Peruvian authorities arrived and sought to obtain from Wimert "any papers he may have picked up . . . he passed them secretly to the other US team." For their part, the Peruvians were more forthcoming and promptly handed over a second pouch of Cuban papers to US officials in La Paz, bragging all the while how they had barred entry to Cuban officials who had also sought to reach the crash site.[20] Meanwhile, Washington's ambassador to Chile complained that Aja Castro was well known as "the center and coordinating figure in [the] entire Cuban intelligence operations set-up in South America."[21]

Days after the crash, a handful of Peruvian leftists were arrested by local police in Cochabamba, reportedly with a "considerable sum of money on their person." Rather than informing US officials, Paz Estenssoro had his secret police escort two of the detainees, Alcides Rivas Paredes and Genaro Arze Pineda, to an "unnamed border point," where they were quietly handed over to Peruvian military authorities. Weeks later, Lima reported that Rivas and Arze confessed to having been part of a large-scale, Cuban-sponsored guerrilla operation termed Operation Matraca that was planning to enter Peru via Puerto Maldonado, an isolated Amazonian military outpost just across the border with Bolivia. The would-be guerrillas also admitted to having been sent by Havana "to spread Castro-Communist propaganda among [the] Bolivian working class."[22]

The Cochabamba arrests were potentially explosive. The Peruvians had been holed up in the family home of one of President Paz's close friends and associates, Víctor Zannier, an independent Marxist and MNR collaborator who was also director of El Mundo, one of the city's two daily newspapers. When diligent local police searched Zannier's house, they found "200 Castro-Communist books and pamphlets and some arms," information the Paz government also chose to withhold from US officials.[23] There is no doubt that, in helping the Cuban-trained Peruvians prepare for Operation Matraca, Zannier believed he enjoyed Paz's protection. Indeed, one of the Peruvian guerrilla leaders, Héctor Béjar, later declared assuredly that "Paz Estenssoro and the head of Bolivian Political Police, Colonel [Claudio] San Román, were aware of the operation and supported it."[24] One of Matraca's Cuban organizers shares the belief that President Paz colluded with the operation, chalking this up to "good relations between the Bolivian and Cuban governments."[25] This is also confirmed in interviews with Paz's private secretary, Carlos Serrate, who concedes that "Paz looked the other way, hoping to maintain a nationalist image on the domestic scene."[26]

It is possible that President Paz's support for Operation Matraca went even further. Mario Monje, first secretary of the Bolivian Communist Party, revealed to Czech officials in May that "Paz Estenssoro financially supported the entire thing" to the tune of $20,000, apparently provided to Zannier.[27] Monje had recruited Zannier personally, and he boasted to fellow Communists that this provided Matraca with "a direct contact to the Presidency."[28] According to PCB leader Otero, collaborating with the guerrillas was "Monje's thing, and Monje grabbed anyone inside or outside the Party, dubious people like Zannier," in his goal to "placate Paz, to make sure things didn't blow up here in Bolivia."[29] Looking back, PCB Central Committee member José Luis Cueto laments that "Monje trusted Paz, a faith that appeared in hindsight to have been erroneous."[30] Two months after the Cochabamba arrests, Monje conceded to Czech officials that his decision to include President Paz "very likely did not sufficiently ensure [Matraca's] confidentiality." Specifically, he worried if "the American Embassy has already been informed."[31]

Monje may have had reasons for concern. "The Americans knew everything," recalls Paz's private secretary Serrate, and Ambassador Stephansky "was informed at every step of the way. He knew Paz was cooperating with [the guerrillas], and he understood this as Paz's domestic game."[32] Yet not a word regarding Matraca appears in US diplomatic cables until *after* the attack. Even then, there is no evidence that US officials grasped the connection between Zannier and President Paz. If Stephansky was aware that Paz was colluding with a Cuban-sponsored guerrilla operation against Peru, he apparently withheld this information from Washington.[33]

Whether or not President Paz leaked Matraca to a tight-lipped US ambassador, Paz certainly did not betray Bolivian leftists who helped organize the operation. According to his private secretary, Paz "avoided publicizing" the Cochabamba arrests, so as to respect his delicate modi vivendi with Cuba and the Bolivian Communist Party.[34] PCB Central Committee member Otero appreciates that "Paz revealed nothing" regarding their participation, which "had the capacity to become an enormous scandal."[35] Cueto agrees that "Paz Estenssoro showed us quite a lot of flexibility as we carried out the preparation and escort of the guerrillas to Peru."[36] The Peruvian leftists were less fortunate. Thanks to Paz's double-dealing, Lima quietly reinforced the border, waiting for the remainder of the guerrilla band to attack.

Meanwhile, Washington stumbled around for intelligence. In April, an employee of the United States Agency for International Development (US-AID) ran into a Venezuelan friend in Lima, who casually informed her that "he had recently completed guerrilla warfare training in Cuba and was on his way into [the] hills of Peru to engage in guerrilla activities there." The loose-lipped guerrilla did not reveal that preparations were being made in Bolivia, however,[37] and US officials apparently did not connect the dots until mid-May, when a dozen guerrillas were ambushed by Peruvian authorities just after they arrived in Puerto Maldonado.[38] On reports that members of one group had retreated back into Bolivian territory, the Paz government agreed to seek their arrest, asking US officials that this be held in "strict confidence" to avoid political recriminations among the Bolivian Left.[39]

On 30 May, eleven Peruvian leftists were arrested in Manuripi, just on the Bolivian side of the border from Puerto Maldonado. CIA Station Chief Tom Flores "worked out [a] basic plan" for the ensuing interrogation, but much to Washington's chagrin, not one of them "deviated from [the] group story that they are no more than leftwing *Apristas* trying to seek political asylum in Bolivia."[40] The Paz government agreed to submit the group to civilian courts, where judges accepted their story, and all eleven were granted asylum and released five weeks later.[41] The Peruvians spent the following months in hiding, some in La Paz, others in Bolivian mining camps, where Communist Party members helped them organize their next attack on Peru.[42]

Seeking to avoid a similar fate for its impending guerrilla attack on Argentina, termed Operation Sombra,[43] Havana dispatched a highly respected intelligence agent, José María Martínez Tamayo (a.k.a. "Papi"), who entered Bolivia in 1963 on a fake Colombian passport under the name Ricardo Aspurú.[44] According to one of Papi's contacts in Cochabamba, "Sombra was much better organized, respecting total confidentiality."[45] PCB leader Otero agrees that "no one found out about Sombra." Crucially, Zannier was kept far away, and not a word regarding the operation was said to President Paz.[46]

Despite having fully incorporated his country within the Alliance for Progress, President Paz remained a sincere, if flawed, nationalist. Seduced by the prospect of massive US aid, Paz might have "sacrificed a portion of his nationalism," in the words of his private secretary,[47] but Paz confided to his family that a time would come when he would "have more room for [international] maneuver."[48] In late April 1963, Paz dispatched his first ambassador to communist Yugoslavia, along with a personal note praising Marshal Tito for following, along with India and the United Arab Republic, "the line of international neutralism," which advocated for "the coexistence of the community of nations, known as the Third Way." Two weeks later, Paz assigned an ambassador to independent Algeria, with a note hailing Ahmed Ben Bella's "policies of anti-colonialism and the defense of the principle of self-determination."[49]

Paz Estenssoro's neutralist pretensions, and his modi vivendi with the PCB and the Cuban government, earned him few accolades among his enemies on the Bolivian Right, who had long pointed to this mutual tolerance as proof positive that the MNR was a covert communist government.[50] Liberals in Washington were unconvinced. The United States was heavily invested in Paz's modernizing regime, and Bolivia's leftward shift only increased their resolve to help guide its economic development. Recognizing that the greatest threat to Paz's government lay not in the Communist Party but in the Bolivian labor movement headed by Vice President Juan Lechín, Kennedy officials set out on a political mission to destroy the MNR Left.

The Lechín Threat

With communist activity fueling Washington's perceptions of a growing threat, the stage was set for a full-scale intervention. Central to US concerns was Vice President Lechín, whose MNR Left Sector advocated for acceptance of Soviet bloc economic aid and a strengthening of Bolivia's ties with Cuba. The key to defeating Lechín rested in the mining camps, where the Alliance for Progress's Triangular Plan called for a series of harsh, anticommunist labor reforms. With Ambassador Ben Stephansky taking the lead, US policymakers finalized an "Internal Defense Plan for Bolivia" in early 1963, which recommended implementation of these labor measures without delay.

Bolivia's leftward turn in the wake of 1962 US tin dumping and the September cancellation of Paz's White House trip left US liberals deeply depressed. That same month, Kennedy's Special Group on Counterinsurgency (CI) placed Bolivia on its watch list, asking Ambassador Stephansky to draft an internal defense plan (IDP) that would shore up Paz's regime along anticommunist lines. The State Department called for an abandonment of the "'normal' program in Bolivia," expressing concern that, "unless we move immediately," Lechín's Left Sector would come to power, and "Bolivia will enter the Soviet camp." According to State Department officials, Bolivia had to be "taken by the hand, guided and trained every step of the way, with the energetic, continuous, and extensive injection of most of the skills required for development."[51] According to Ambassador Stephansky, anticommunist development required that "Paz . . . be persuaded to split with Lechín" and convinced "to run again for the presidency in 1964."[52]

Stephansky's spirits were buoyed by the October 1962 Cuban Missile Crisis, an event that he characterized as a "most fortunate coincidence" for US-Bolivian relations. Throughout the year, Stephansky explained, Lechín's MNR Left Sector had been "openly taking major steps to consolidate its organization and move into contention for victory in [the] 1964 elections" on a platform that was "strongly pro-Cuban, and advocating trade, aid, and diplomatic relations with Soviet Russia." The Missile Crisis "caught [the] Left Sector with its ideological pants down," Stephansky reported, adding that Paz's supporters in the MNR had "visibly stiffened resistance to [the] Left Sector's penetration and consolidation activities." Citing a gushing letter Paz wrote to Kennedy in support of Washington's handling of the crisis, Stephansky reported that anticommunists in the governing party were finally pushing for a "stronger wedge between Paz and Lechín." Stephansky warned that the "Castro-Commie machine [is] not yet defeated," but he believed that Alliance for Progress aid money, "complemented by programs attacking areas [of] Commie influence," would ensure that a Paz-Lechín break would occur.[53]

In its anti-Lechín crusade, Washington boasted powerful allies in the Bolivian armed forces. In late October 1962, Generals Barrientos and Ovando visited the US Embassy to explain that while "time [is] not ripe for [an] open break [between] Paz and Lechín," the military was firmly in the Paz camp and was planning to promptly make these sympathies known. They also asked for a fresh shipment of hardware. Stephansky did not delay, cabling Secretary Rusk hours later a request for 14,000 tear gas canisters, 400 M-1 carbine machine guns, 400,000 rounds of machine gun ammunition, 50,000 rounds of .38 Special ammunition, and 25,000 shotgun shells. A perennial MNR skeptic, Rusk hesitated, referring to reports that Paz's security services were using these weapons to crack down principally on Bolivian conservatives and that they had engaged in an "apparently unprovoked attack on school children" during the most recent state of siege. Stephansky was unshaken, replying promptly that the "appearance of carbines in [the] hands [of the] *carabineros* [police] . . . might have avoided bloodshed," because the students "might have fled earlier."[54]

Ironically, Stephansky harbored a latent personal affection for Juan Lechín. As he later explained, "[Lechín] was one of the most charming and loveable people you'll ever meet, charmed the pants off you." Stephansky would argue tirelessly with Vice President Lechín that there was "nothing incompatible between modernization and efficiency" called for in the Alliance for Progress and "your type of socialism, whatever it may be." Lechín was immune to this line of argument, however, responding that "this present revolution is the bourgeois revolution. We're going to have the real revolution one day." Stephansky later scoffed, "This is the kind of crap I'd get from him. . . . He was one of the most capriciously irresponsible guys . . . [who] never really worked in the directions I felt would pull along with what was happening constructively."[55]

Lechín might have believed the real revolution was coming, but Ambassador Stephansky's push for "modernization and efficiency" was backed up by the dollars and the political weight of the United States. In his late 1962 IDP, Stephansky coldly detailed how to "precipitate a conflict between Lechín and Paz, or between the left and moderate wings of the MNR." White House aide Goodwin loved the program, explaining on 2 November that it was the best hope of "keeping the extremists out." According to Goodwin, for the plan to succeed, "someone has to be given the authority to commit and spend a decent-sized chunk of aid money with permission to deviate from normal criteria." Within three weeks, many of the covert operations had "already broke[n] loose for signatures."[56]

USAID's new administrator, David Bell, joined the chorus shortly after his appointment, explaining to the White House in early February 1963 that "Bolivia has become the target of increased penetration by the Soviet bloc." The only way to ensure that the country did not fall "into the hands of communism" was to "demonstrate to the Western Hemisphere and the world that a national revolution which profoundly altered the social and political life of a feudal country can, with US assistance, gradually became a viable, free, mixed society." It was clear that he had thoroughly adopted the pro-Paz line set out by his fellow Kennedy appointees, as he wrote that US aid should be used as a leverage to convince Paz to reduce the influence of the leftist-dominated miners' unions, meanwhile seeing to it that the armed forces were "quietly strengthened" through engagement in road building, land clearing, and school building. Bell was certain that a stronger military would permit Paz to "better cope with the armed miners and *campesinos*."[57]

Even Paz skeptics at the White House Bureau of the Budget were tenuously willing to go along. Warning that the Alliance for Progress in Bolivia was a "classic example of US development assistance in form and not substance," the bureau conceded nonetheless that an expanded program would have a chance if it were used to "exert maximum leverage" to ensure that the Bolivian government moved forward to "rationalize employment" in the mining camps, through the firing of five thousand "surplus" miners.[58]

President Paz initially planned to visit Washington in May 1963, at which point Stephansky stressed that the "most important feature" of the upcoming trip was Paz's candidacy for the 1964 elections. Having changed the constitution during his June 1961 state of siege to permit reelection, Paz was demonstrating a "stronger interest in running again," thereby blocking Lechín's candidacy. On this topic, Stephansky was unequivocal: "the best chance for political moderation and for the Alliance to succeed is [for] Paz to repeat [in] 1964." In fact, Stephansky believed that "the success of the Paz visit will be measured by our ability to work out the basis for his candidacy in 1964," and he urged Kennedy to "be as flexible as necessary to get him to run again." In return for US support, Stephansky explained that Paz would offer "commitments on a harder line on Cuba, a harder line on the internal Communist problem . . . a harder line on Soviet bloc aid . . . and increasingly better performance for economic development." Aware of the potential criticism that Paz was becoming a dictator, Stephansky recommended that Washington cultivate a new generation of MNR leaders, like General Barrientos and Guillermo Bedregal, president of the Corporación Minera de Bolivia (COMIBOL; Mining Corporation of Bolivia), who could take over in 1968.[59] The State Department agreed wholeheartedly that Paz should be "induced to run for a third presidential term."

Once again, however, Paz's White House trip was postponed.[60] He surprised US officials on 10 April with news that a visit would be "impossible at this time," since Lechín planned to return home from his ambassadorship in Rome to coincide with Paz's trip abroad.[61] According to Paz, Lechín planned to use his absence to "force cabinet resignation," attempt to divide the armed forces, and "push through [the] Czech smelter project" long delayed by MNR anticommunists. Paz's decision to postpone his trip put Lechín "on the spot," since Lechín would have to either return to Rome or continue on to Bolivia and "end up in [an] open fight." Paz was sure Lechín "would lose," even if the coming months would prove a "rugged time." He assured Stephansky that he had the "upper hand" and that by September or October, Lechín would be "licked." Paz wanted to visit the White House with his reelection "lined up," and he coquettishly revealed that he was mulling over tapping General Barrientos as his running mate.[62]

Lechín did return to Bolivia in May. One of his first actions was to visit General Barrientos, who lived just across Avenida 6 de Agosto, and he asked Barrientos to be his running mate in 1964. Lechín then proceeded to share with Barrientos the details of his plan to "embarrass the government," which Barrientos later spilled to US Embassy Air Attaché Edward Fox. By encouraging dissident Communists at the Siglo XX mining camp to organize a series of "strikes and slow-downs," Lechín would force Paz to "come to terms with him." In their intransigent opposition to the Paz government, Siglo XX leaders Federico Escóbar and Irineo Pimentel found themselves squarely at odds with the PCB leadership, something Lechín believed he could exploit in order to "regain his lost strength before the 1964 elections." Barrientos disappointed Lechín, explaining that he was firmly in the Paz camp and would remain there. Lechín then set out on a countrywide campaign tour, falsely claiming to his supporters that "the American Government favored his candidacy and US aid funds would continue" if he were elected.[63]

General Barrientos visited the US Embassy on 24 April, just before he was to depart to Washington for the Inter-American Air Force Chiefs Conference. Accompanied by Colonel Fox, Barrientos explained that the armed forces were preparing to declare themselves in support of Paz's reelection, with Barrientos as running mate. Stephansky responded that it was "too early" to discuss vice presidential candidates but assured the general that the United States "would not look upon his nomination with disfavor."[64] Three days later, General Barrientos accepted the military's official proclamation in favor of the Paz–Barrientos ticket and promptly departed for Washington. He expressed concern to Fox, however, that the armed forces had jumped the gun, and he revealed that he planned to stay in the United States for a few extra weeks, "ostensibly to have some dental work done, but actually to let the public interest in his candidacy die down." The wily general was perfecting the art of a reluctant leader, confidently telling Colonel Fox that his political career would extend "twenty years or more into the future."[65]

On 16 May 1963, one week after General Barrientos shook hands with President Kennedy in the White House Rose Garden, the Special Group (CI) approved a final draft of Stephansky's IDP. It began:

> Bolivia is threatened by an extreme left wing takeover that would place in power a sector of the governing . . . MNR . . . which is heavily infiltrated by communists. Such a takeover would be likely to result in a government of the Castro-communist mold, antagonistic toward the United States and having

close ties with the communist world. The MNR Left Sector . . . is headed by Vice President Juan Lechín, an opportunist with extreme leftist, if not communistic, ideas, who has distinguished himself mainly for his political rabble rousing and oppositionist activities. The loss of Bolivia to Castro-communism would signify a serious failure by the United States, despite more than a decade of assistance, in its effort to channel a genuine national revolution into the course of stable economic and democratic development.

The IDP added that only Paz was "strong enough to prevent" a Lechín victory in 1964, but the president's "present lack of will . . . to resist communist and extreme leftwing infiltration and activities . . . [was] the single greatest threat to internal security." The plan called for using Alliance for Progress funds as a "powerful instrument . . . [toward] obtaining . . . many of our political goals," including the "elimination of the basis of power of [the] MNR Left Sector, especially in the mining unions," the "development of alternatives to the MNR," the creation of a "more disciplined and responsible free labor movement," and the "prevention of Sino-Soviet bloc penetration." Also central to the IDP was an increased reliance on the Bolivian armed forces, "identified with the aspirations of the people" through civic action programs backed by the Alliance for Progress, which received Paz's unqualified support. The plan stressed the "urgency" of moving forward, since the 1964 elections represented the culmination of the "struggle between extremist followers of Vice President Lechín and the more moderate supporters of President Paz."[66]

As a result of Washington's enormous financial commitment to Bolivia's economic development programs, Kennedy officials felt supremely confident in their ability to serve as key arbiters in the country's internal affairs. Within this ideologically charged environment, Ambassador Stephansky—a labor economist by trade, lest we forget—sought to convince President Paz that his vice president, labor leader Juan Lechín, was the chief obstacle to Bolivia's modernization. Meanwhile, the militarization of US development programs continued apace, with the countryside as its first target.

Military Civic Action

One of the most important aspects of the Alliance for Progress in Bolivia was a program of military civic action in the countryside, which aimed to put USAID funds to work in rural development projects carried out by Bolivian Army engineering battalions created with US training and equipment.[67]

Civic action had a long history in Bolivia,[68] and it had been seized on by military officers in order to survive the aftermath of the 1952 revolution. The approach was received enthusiastically by Kennedy's development-oriented appointees, and it received high marks from the Pentagon and the CIA, bureaucracies seeking a rubric within which they could collaborate meaningfully within Washington's newfound interest in Third World development.

A key asset in Washington's program of military-led development was Air Force Commanding General René Barrientos. A fervent supporter of the 1952 revolution, Barrientos never tired of reminding Bolivians that he had copiloted the plane that brought Paz Estenssoro back from Buenos Aires in the days following the insurrection.[69] In the early 1960s, Barrientos had become a visible public figure, thanks to his role inaugurating these civic action programs, his legendary bravado, a fluency in Quechua, and friendships with the leftist directors of two major newspapers, *El Diario* in La Paz and *El Mundo* in Cochabamba.[70] Throughout 1962, the general's speeches, elegant but utterly vacuous,[71] received wide play in the Bolivian press. Barrientos declared that "the armed forces will never divest themselves of the beautiful treasure of constitutionality, nor will they permit Bolivia to lose this amazing reward won by blood and agony."[72] In March 1962, Barrientos explained that the "participation of the nation's entire armed forces in this present process of the National Revolution has always been selfless, silent, and decisive." By putting down numerous right-wing conspiracies since 1952, the armed forces "has sealed with valor, loyalty, and bloodshed its definitive membership in the cause of the Bolivian people, of the *campesinos*, of the workers in the mines and cities, in the cause of the men who struggle and work to mobilize Bolivians' most audacious, dignified, and decisive efforts against illiteracy, exploitation, and the indignity that had denigrated the Republic and aggravated our backwardness." Continuing with this arousing language, Barrientos assured the Bolivian people that the process of "raising the banner of economic independence and social justice . . . has awoken the unanimous fervor and profound conviction of the components of the armed forces."[73]

Although Barrientos considered himself a loyal *movimientista*, his rustic vigor did not square with the bureaucratic schisms that were overtaking his beloved revolutionary party. He warned that "it is unjustifiable for the [MNR] sectors to bring about the distraction of the essence of the nationalist revolution, to bring about the ignoring of its authority or to weaken its unity." Expounding at length on the "dangers of the struggle between sectors," Barrientos stressed that a "member of the armed forces has the obligation to help overcome these negative conditions, providing an example of authority, order, and discipline, living up to his conciliatory role and his mission as guardian," and ensuring that the "enemies of the Revolution" could not take advantage of divisions in the revolutionary family. The general continued: "Authority is the fundamental basis of all human organization, and it is the great force employed by mankind as an indispensable and decisive instrument to overcome primitivism and all the dangers and obstacles that oppose the ordering of societies in their methodical pursuit of advanced stages of civilization and progress." Barrientos concluded his lengthy communiqué by once more stressing that the "new military" had become "an instrument in defense of the National Revolution, an armed, productive organization at the service of the overwhelming majority, with a firm conscience in the struggle for the liberation of the *campesinos* and the workers who will later make up a prosperous and content Homeland."[74]

It is not difficult to see that this approach dovetailed nicely with President Kennedy's, articulated in National Security Action Memorandum 119, whereby Third World militaries were to be called on to play a central role in national development.[75] Kennedy built on this idea at a July 1962 gathering of Latin American military officers in Panama, where he declared that "armies can play constructive roles in defending the aims of the Alliance for Progress by striking at the roots of economic and social distress."[76] Kennedy's Alliance for Progress administrator, Teodoro Moscoso, echoed his boss at another meeting of Latin American officers in mid-1963, explaining that economic development "has a great deal to do with the military," because even a "few isolated clashes of violence . . . [could] scare investors, domestic as well as foreign, from risking their capital." In Moscoso's view, one country's military was especially worthy of praise:

> I was in Bolivia several months ago, and what I saw the armed forces doing in the name of the betterment of their country and the lives of their people was something truly incredible. Roads are being built and repaired, virgin lands are being colonized, maps of the country are being drawn up, rural schools are being built, potable water is being provided to tiny communities, and medical services are being given to people who live in remote areas. And all of this and more is being realized through the resources, the energy, and the dedication of the Bolivian armed forces.[77]

One of the areas where General Barrientos was most interested in making an authoritative impact was his native Cochabamba Valley, where tensions between followers of Paz and Lechín were fueling violent clashes. MNR

infighting had become the target of intense criticism "for its permissive attitude toward these acts of violence," according to José Gordillo, who has written extensively on Cochabamba peasant experiences during the revolutionary
period. Gordillo writes, "In contrast to these violent political events, there
began to circulate a series of news stories and images of soldiers' benevolent
attitudes toward the peasant sectors of the Valley, to whom they periodically
gifted school buildings and health centers." These civic action programs were
often inaugurated by General Barrientos himself, who informed the Indian
peasants that the funds came from Kennedy's Alliance for Progress. This process led to the emergence of a "military developmentalist discourse," according to Gordillo, "which—while maintaining itself within the framework of
the discourse of revolutionary nationalism—implicitly challenged the MNR
project and signaled a viable political alternative." Barrientos went to great
lengths to spread his message, telling members of the press in early 1963 that
rural development "is our revolutionary language."[78]

In order to facilitate his political ascent, General Barrientos called the Pentagon in early 1962, requesting the presence of his old friend Colonel Edward
Fox, with whom he had "played cards and done bachelor things" in Cochabamba during Fox's 1952–1955 stint as aviation adviser to Washington's military group.[79] Colonel Fox, whom a former CIA station chief refers to as
"practically the Godfather of the Bolivian air force,"[80] eventually brought his
fiancée, Evelyn, to Cochabamba, and the two started a family in tight quarters with their Bolivian friends. A genteel but fiery Texan, Evelyn Fox recalls
that when one attempted coup d'état broke out in 1954, her husband handed
her a grenade and said, "If anyone comes in the house, you know what to
do." She later said, "I had no *idea* what to do! But that was the kind of adventure that was commonplace during our time in Bolivia."[81] Antonio Arguedas,
a close Barrientos associate, recalls that "the difference between Fox and the
other [Americans] was that he was more a man of the people, which agreed
with Barrientos's nature." Arguedas adds that Colonel Fox "was not a self-
absorbed American who thought he was the center of the universe . . . in a
word, he was not the kind of *gringo* who went around saying, 'America is the
best in the world.' "[82] Colonel Fox reflected this humility in interviews with
this author: "So many of our people went in there trying to change their way
of life, their beliefs, their religions. I shouldn't really speak for the Indians, but
I would imagine they liked any leader—Paz or Barrientos—who would improve their way of life and not treat them like animals. They weren't political
people. They supported anyone who gave them support and recognition.
Recognition of their way of life. . . . I got along very well with them. I didn't

try to tell them how to live. The only time you should ever tell them anything is if they ask."[83] Colonel Fox recalls that in early 1962, "somebody important must have pulled some strings, because René made one call and within two days two C-130s were sent to pick up our whole family."[84]

Once Colonel Fox was back in his adopted country, as embassy air attaché and undercover agent for the Defense Intelligence Agency (DIA),[85] he requested Stephansky's permission to visit his old friend in Cochabamba. According to Fox's subsequent report, Barrientos was "surprised [and] thrilled to have me there and provided me with a car and driver which is a rare treat in Cochabamba." On his first evening back in town on 6 October 1962, Fox received Barrientos in his hotel room, where the two caught up over the course of several "meaty" hours. The general revealed to his friend that he was considering entering politics as Paz's running mate in 1964, and he spoke confidently of his stellar working relationship with Army Commander Ovando. He also assured Colonel Fox that the military was firmly "behind Paz and not Lechín," adding that any officer who allied with Lechín would be fired. They would carry out a coup, Barrientos stressed, before permitting Lechín to succeed Paz in 1964.[86] Fox's response, which did not make its way into the official report, was, "You do what you have to do, René, and I will try to support you when I can. But we can't bullshit each other."[87]

When the two arrived in the countryside the following day, it quickly became clear to Colonel Fox that "the General had won the love and confidence of the Indians in this area." Amid hugs and confetti, Barrientos praised US economic assistance in front of a gathering of at least a thousand Indian peasants. Speaking in their native Quechua, Barrientos explained that schools "were being constructed throughout the country under a joint United States and Bolivian effort," detailing the civic action programs and the "part that the military was to play." He then told the peasants that the food and milk the children would receive at the schools came from the United States, stressing that "they should be grateful for the help that is coming from the North Americans." During the massive *chicha*[88]-fueled lunch that followed, eight Indian peasant leaders from nearby communities approached the general, asking him to "visit their sections as soon as possible." In a neighboring village, Barrientos "once again . . . praised the United States and explained the civic action program to the people."[89]

Interestingly, the entourage also included several leftists, including *El Mundo* editor Víctor Zannier and Barrientos's hometown mayor and lifelong friend from Tarata, Alberto Iriarte.[90] When General Barrientos revealed their ideological inclinations to Colonel Fox, he assured the air attaché that these

"Reds . . . are weak people who can do nothing concerning my efforts in this Valley" as long as he had the Indian peasants on his side. Fox did not seem bothered by these acquaintances, reporting back to the embassy that "the entire week of activities was most successful and General Barrientos put on the show that I had expected to see."[91] Fox later revealed to this author his view that " 'Communist' is just a word. It doesn't mean anything in that country. They might be leftists or they might not be, but there weren't any real communists down there. There, you have to take things on a person-by-person basis." Fox explained that Cochabamba Communists were like Southern Democrats in the United States, adding that many Communists were opposed to Paz, which almost endeared them to the colonel.[92] Former CIA station chief Sternfield agrees that "there was always a sense that the people in Cochabamba—even the nominal Communists—were 'part of the family,' and better than those guys" in the MNR.[93]

In Bolivia, Alliance for Progress civic action programs would soon gain a powerful ally in the Pentagon. Once Ambassador Stephansky's IDP had been approved by the White House, the deputy undersecretary of defense for special operations, General Edward Lansdale, visited Bolivia accompanied by the head of US Southern Command, General Andrew O'Meara.[94] Lansdale, a CIA agent who headed US covert operations in the Philippines and Indochina in the late 1940s and 1950s, was now in charge of Operation Mongoose, the Kennedy administration's program of sabotage against Castro's Cuba. Lansdale's interest in Bolivia arose primarily from the country's politically mobilized peasantry, a similar demographic he experienced in Southeast Asia. He later recalled that although the Kennedy administration was "highly sensitive about my showing up in foreign countries," he had "begged to be permitted to go down and take a look" at Bolivia and Venezuela.[95]

In his report back to the Special Group (CI), Lansdale wrote that Bolivia was a "land of vexing paradox for the US." Its people were "warmly friendly toward us (the smiles and waved hands of the children reminded me of the Philippines) yet it has fallen in love with Marxism (of both the Lenin and Trotsky version)." He noted that the country could be summed up by "the basic paradox: a land of wide-open spaces, Bolivia has hidden its capital city down in a crevice, almost as though it wanted its leaders to become moles." Military-led development was central to Lansdale's narrative, and he offered effusive praise for Bolivian colonel Julio Sanjinés Goytia, at the time serving as director of USAID's Military Civic Action program, whose "fire and enthusiasm" for civic action were catching on in the junior officer corps. According to Lansdale, Sanjinés represented the "beginning of a path off towards objectives more in harmony with US beliefs" and away from the "left fork of the political road," which Washington had followed since the 1952 revolution.[96]

General Lansdale was so impressed with Sanjinés—a scion of one of Bolivia's founding families whose anti-MNR attitude was only thinly veiled by the colonel's resignation to the revolution's irreversibility[97]—that he recounted at length how Sanjinés had put Alliance for Progress funds to use in the leftist Indian peasant stronghold of Achacachi:

> Achacachi is a dry and dusty place, noted for its shortage of water. It was picked for a Civic Action well-drilling project. Rather than announcing this early, as a *politico* would be tempted to do, Sanjinés moved into Achacachi with a crew of engineers, including Army men in civilian clothes, and made a quietly unobtrusive survey for potential water sources; the survey showed promising sites. The well-drilling crews and equipment were readied and put on a standby basis in La Paz, alert to move on signal. Sanjinés then had a leading La Paz newspaper (owned by Sanjinés . . .) send reporters to Achacachi to ask the people how they would like a Civic Action project to provide free water in the city. The people interviewed replied, "All the government ever does is talk, not act," "The Army is worthless and would never do anything for us," and similar comments. Sanjinés met with town officials, told them of the proposed project, and was invited to give it a try. He signaled to La Paz, the Army engineers (in uniform), and equipment showed up promptly and went to work, completing the new water works in record time. The La Paz newspaper then publicized the Civic Action project complete with earlier scoffing interviews. It made quite a convincing story.[98]

In his report to the Special Group, Lansdale praised Kennedy's Alliance for Progress for "back[ing] civic action projects aggressively with plans, funds, advice, materiel, and other help." These "imaginative" projects were "making a dramatic change in the psychological climate" by stressing a "public service role" for the armed forces and changing the "vividly brutal portrayal of the military as monsters inflicting pain and suffering on the lowly Indian." For Lansdale, the most important aspect of the civic action program was the colonization of Bolivia's Amazonian lowlands, where many of the displaced miners were to be settled. The whole enterprise was analogous to the "opening of our own West," he wrote, where military battalions act as "pathfinders, engineers, and guardians." Lansdale warned, however, that since Bolivia "serves the Communists as a Switzerland—a transit area to other Latin American places for people, funds, and materiel," there was a danger that the civic action colonies would become hotbeds of Communist influence. "It would be a macabre joke," he wrote, "if the US and Bolivian governments helped these people get a fresh start in life—and the Communists then taught them how to live it, the Communist way."[99]

Washington's struggle to win the propaganda battle in Bolivia reminded Lansdale of the situation in Laos in 1958, where a "technically beautiful psychological operation" was defeated by the Communists, who "just kept going for the jugular." He sought ways to "put some effective bare-knuckles into our psychological operations," adding that he was especially concerned with "invitations to the Communists among the Bolivian military." Civic action could be "just the right political touch to help carry the fight for us," he wrote, stressing its "psychological appeal," which could help to pave the way for a "strong Vice Presidential candidate" in 1964, namely, "Air Force Chief General Barrientos."[100]

Lansdale concluded his report by noting that Government Minister José Antonio Arze Murillo had recently asked CIA Station Chief Tom Flores for greater covert cooperation with Bolivia's nascent anticommunist efforts. In Lansdale's view, Washington "would profit if CIA were to go into a huddle with [US Southern Command] soonest on how best to go all the way in, now that an opening has been made."[101] When Flores departed three months later, his successor as station chief, Larry Sternfield, was explicitly charged with working closely with Arze Murillo and with Paz's feared Control Político in destroying all threats to the MNR regime.[102]

In a Pentagon-endorsed study of military-led development in Bolivia, William Brill praised Washington's military mission in La Paz for being a "forward-looking, civic action-oriented group." Brill gives credit for this attitude to an "enlightened Mission Chief," Colonel Truman Cook, "one of those model officers one often hears about . . . [who] fully grasped the importance of civic action for Bolivia."[103] Cook attended the water treatment inauguration in Achacachi and later contributed the prologue to Sanjinés's Alliance-funded book on civic action, in which the military mission chief wrote that although the "absorbing task of nation building is both intricately complex and challenging," civic action provides the "blend of military assistance with indigenous self-help" that best fits the "needs of underdeveloped nations." The armed forces, according to Cook, "can be a creative institution in the dynamic process of economic and social development," and it was important to guard against "negative reasoning" by military skeptics, who argued that "the involvement of the military in . . . development irrevocably leads to the assumption of power by the military."[104]

Colonel Cook was technically correct that civic action would not necessarily produce a coup d'état. Nonetheless, military-led development helped create an environment in which the armed forces began to be seen as indispensable forces for rapid modernization, free from the sectarianism and partisanship that threatened to overwhelm the national revolution. As Brill notes, US-built engineering battalions were the "best fed, best equipped, trained and paid branch within the Bolivian army." Moreover, the engineers had an "independent air," and their "emphasis on professionalism was invariably accompanied by an anti-MNR position."[105] Most important, General Barrientos, who would eventually launch his 1964 revolt from Cochabamba, "evidenced an unquestioned enthusiasm for civic action," and the Indian peasants who were benefiting from these projects were nearly unanimous in crediting Barrientos for US-provided largesse: "It is because of him that we have this school. He is a great man and he is a Cochabambino."[106]

The Battle of Irupata

Despite the high-profile nature of civic action in the countryside, the labor reforms called for by the Alliance for Progress's Triangular Plan remained USAID's "number one priority."[107] The program conditioned development assistance on a Bolivian government commitment to "support with the entire wherewithal in its power" a decisive crackdown on the miners' unions, "making use of all its power to prohibit strikes and other activities that prejudice mining production."[108] In mid-1963, the economists' demands dovetailed with the growing militarization of Washington's larger aid program, as well as a burgeoning CIA role in support of President Paz's repressive apparatus. This culminated in a covert, US-funded Indian militia operation against the Siglo XX mining camp, approved by the Kennedy White House under the official aegis of the Alliance for Progress.

COMIBOL President Bedregal later conceded that the application of Triangular's conditions was "hard work, and at the same time inhumane." In his memoirs, he writes that "the restructuring was grueling, especially when one imagines what it means to a family of mine workers to lose their job. . . . The human problem was heart-wrenching." He remains unrepentant, however, characterizing the Triangular Plan as his brainchild, a " 'major surgery' that thankfully brought us out of the red ink." Bedregal remains convinced that Paz's government was the "most gallant in Bolivian history" for its revolutionary vision in building a "True Nation" in the face of fierce resistance by the "feudal lords" in the miners' union at Siglo XX.[109]

In late June 1963, President Paz gave assurances to a correspondent for *Time* magazine that a "breakthrough" in the mining situation was expected within the "next three months." The journalist told US officials that Paz "seemed to convey a genuine concern about communist potential within the trade unions," adding that he appeared "visibly proud of the army," reserving "particular praise [for] the civic action program."[110] Days later, General Barrientos told US Embassy officials that Paz would implement the Triangular conditions by September. When asked why this date had been chosen, Barrientos said that "it was no magic number but a time when the Government would be well prepared to handle any leftist uprising in the mine areas." The general was confident that the armed forces would be called on to "participate actively in the September crisis."[111]

The Kennedy administration also sought ways to participate in the impending mine showdown. From late May until mid-July, Ambassador Stephansky held meetings with USAID and IDB officials in Washington, seeking to convince them of the "necessity of using all our pending loan applications as incentives to [*sic*: for] Paz to carry out the COMIBOL reforms." By "holding back on disbursements and programs," Stephansky was confident that "Paz's will to carry out the reforms will remain strong." USAID officials agreed that "we should use our entire AID program as an instrument to obtain GOB performance in COMIBOL," but they wondered "how Paz could exert pressure on the miners if they resist." The meeting ended with Stephansky vaguely explaining that "the government would have to engage in rough tactics."[112]

In his meetings with midlevel USAID and IDB economists, Stephansky did not elaborate on these "rough tactics," but on 9 July, Alliance for Progress Administrator Teodoro Moscoso approved the ambassador's "Contingency Plan," which authorized USAID's Office of Public Safety (OPS) to "force a show-down, . . . provoke" a strike by the miners at Siglo XX, and arm an Indian paramilitary force to attack the mining camp. The contingency plan, which received State Department approval later that day, also recommended that the Bolivian government "cut off food shipments" so that "the miners will begin to suffer."[113] Despite approving of the general plan, US embassy Deputy Chief of Mission Stutesman, a hard-boiled realist who later called developmentalists like Moscoso and Stephansky "poor saps" for believing so strongly in the Alliance for Progress,[114] warned that while "drastic and effective action [is] needed," withholding food could have "violent consequences." Instead, Stutesman recommended that Washington work closely with the Bolivian government to ensure that the miners' food supplies were "maintained at reasonably low levels" for the duration of the crisis. The Paz skeptic reminded his superiors that "our focus here should be political, not economic," adding that he had reasons to doubt "President Paz's willingness to employ military forces" against Siglo XX.[115]

Throughout early July, Siglo XX and neighboring Catavi were on partial strike in opposition to the Triangular Plan conditions. Bedregal referred to this strike as "unparalleled criminality," and he imposed a total lockout, freezing salaries and halting shipments of food and medicine. The Federación Sindical de Trabajadores Mineros de Bolivia (Union Federation of Bolivian Mine Workers) responded by calling a rolling strike throughout the mines, and President Paz, just back from the second anniversary celebration of the US-built Max Toledo First Motorized Battalion, declared, "Now is the time to crush anarchy in the unions."[116]

In addition to imposing a lockout, President Paz mobilized what his private secretary refers to as "Paz Estenssoro's very well paid and very well armed rural brigades," under the command of Wilge Nery, an anticommunist Indian peasant leader and national MNR deputy.[117] According to then–Catavi union leader Crespo, the mobilization of Nery's militia "created a general upheaval in the nationalized mining centers, particularly in Catavi-Siglo XX."[118] MNR Left Sector officials in nearby Uncía warned President Paz on 1 July that the belligerence of Nery's force led to a situation in which "violent acts could occur at any moment, as party members are determined to defend themselves, rifle in hand."[119] Siglo XX union leader Pimentel advised COMIBOL officials that the "arms trafficker" Nery was "continually provoking workers . . . [who] have no arms but they do have other means" to defend themselves.[120] Local leftists decried Paz's move to "contract mercenaries headed by Wilge Nery," declaring that "the workers will not tolerate a policy of repression."[121] Even some Indian peasant communities cabled that they were "watching with puzzlement as authorities give ear to the mercenary and traitor to the *campesino* class, Wilge Nery," expressing their "complete solidarity with the miners."[122]

Paz's alliance with loyalist Indian peasant leaders like Wilge Nery had a long history in the countryside surrounding the mines of northern Potosí. Anthropologists Olivia Harris and Xavier Albó write that beginning in the late 1950s, Nery "created divisions between miners and *campesinos* to prevent a possible alliance, saying that the miners were 'communists,' and that communists sought to rob the *campesinos*' land and make it community property." Harris and Albó write that Nery "took advantage" of the ancient rivalry between two Indian peasant communities, the Jucumani and the Laime, "obtaining arms for the former." The Laime were "obliged to seek aid from other sources," they explain, "in this case the miners' union of Siglo XX." In late 1962, Siglo XX union leader Federico Escóbar "struck up an agreement in which the miners would obtain arms for the Laime and would send cadres to Laime ranches to educate the *campesinos* in literacy and political awareness." In exchange, "the Laime would come to the miners' defense in case of labor conflicts."[123]

In December 1962, Nery sent an alarming cable to President Paz to warn that Escóbar was providing clothes, housing, and education to the Laime, stressing that "we are not able to act because cooperation from superior authorities does not exist." Nery asked the Bolivian president to furnish him with a "rural police force" whose purpose it would be to halt Communist-miner influence among the Laime.[124] Harris and Albó write that the region's tension increased to the point at which mining-town leftists would capture Indian peasants in the streets and ask them if they were Laime or Jucumani: "if they were the former, they would let them pass; but if they ended up being Jucumani, they would beat them and expel them."[125]

Into this ideological and ethnic battle waltzed a supremely confident Ben Stephansky. After six weeks in Washington, the ambassador returned to La Paz on 15 July and rushed directly to Paz Estenssoro's suburban home. There, he produced a harsh letter from Alliance for Progress Administrator Moscoso, threatening to freeze aid funds until the Triangular conditions were met. Realizing this could occur only through armed force, President Paz became "deeply depressed and discouraged," complaining that Washington was "not responsive to [the] requirements of an electoral year." Expressing frustration at "being compelled to adopt the most rigorous measures" six months prior to the MNR convention, where party "infighting would be [the] toughest," Paz warned that Washington's demands would cause him to "lose total labor support as well as partisans [to] their cause."[126] Warned by Stephansky that he was about to "kiss millions of dollars goodbye,"[127] President Paz finally relented, promising to follow through "to [the] bitter end even if [a] national crisis results." Paz hinted that he might pull out of the presidential race in order to apply the conditions "with no concern as to the political consequences." At the mere mention that he would not run for reelection, Stephansky flinched, stressing that "it was too early to throw in the sponge." He explained that Washington was prepared to approve a laundry list of development projects once the reforms were applied, including "public works . . . IDB housing . . . rural schools . . . warehouse . . . loan agreements . . . roads . . . [and] power projects." Stephansky then sweetened the deal with a personal White House invitation from President Kennedy, and Paz melted, assuring Stephansky that the crisis would soon be brought to a head.[128]

In a separate cable sent only to Secretary of State Rusk, Assistant Secretary Martin, and Alliance for Progress Administrator Moscoso,[129] Stephansky elaborated on his meeting with President Paz. "After my pep talk on not throwing in the sponge, I informed Paz [that] we are prepared to support him to assure victory" in the mine operation. Paz replied that he would need $4 million to cover foreign currency losses for one month. Additionally, he said he would need access to military funding to cover "outlays for internal measures which could conceivably in an acute crisis come to $1 million." Paz added that "these estimates [are] not . . . applicable" if the crisis lasted over one month, in which case "civil war would be [a] real possibility." Having just returned from Washington, where the Kennedy administration had earmarked these precise amounts, Stephansky did not hesitate to assure Paz that the United States was "prepared to support him within the levels he indicated." President Paz was "encouraged [by] my expression [of] our support," Stephansky reported, adding that Paz appeared to be "standing firm in Catavi."[130]

Three days later, President Paz met in "secret session" with General Barrientos, Armed Forces Commanding General Luis Rodríguez, and Army Commanding General Hugo Suárez. Paz assured his generals that "he was not repeat not backing off COMIBOL situation but that on the contrary he was prepared to go all the way in fighting troublesome leftist and communist mining groups." The generals likewise "assured [the] president that their forces will support him completely."[131] Barrientos later provided the details of Paz's plan to the US Air Attaché Fox: "Colonel Claudio San Román, head of . . . the government's covert action arm . . . has organized a 200-man battalion of civilians armed with 170 rifles and 30 machine guns and disguised as Indians for deployment in the Catavi area. This battalion will descend on Catavi . . . kill as many of the extremist leaders as possible, and force the miners into a defensive situation."[132]

The following night, Paz's government minister Arze Murillo, since May a close CIA contact, explained to Stephansky that this paramilitary operation would "virtually certain[ly] bring on [a] general miners' strike" and that the ensuing bloodshed would create the pretext for the military to "move into the mine areas to restore order . . . [and] eliminate commie and leftist mine leadership."[133] Meanwhile, Barrientos told Fox that a "state of siege would probably be declared tonight and that it is highly possible civil war may break out soon." He then "specifically asked that General O'Meara be informed of this impending situation and that if open conflict should break out the Bolivian Government may find it necessary to request Special Forces assistance in backing up the Bolivian Armed Forces in maintenance of internal security."[134] Stephansky poignantly declared that "the crunch is on in Catavi."[135]

The prospect of direct US military intervention prompted President Kennedy to request an immediate report on the Bolivian situation. Hours later, Assistant Secretary of State Martin replied to the White House: "In anticipation of what might happen as [a] result of Bolivian President Paz's decision to enforce labor discipline in the mines, a US contingency fund of [$4,000,000] was set up. In response to an emergency request received yesterday, [$325,000] was authorized for two projects [to assist in the mining areas] based on a program discussed with President Paz. We will make available [overt and covert] financial assistance and appropriate equipment for use in Bolivia, upon request." Martin added that Ambassador Stephansky would ask President Paz "today whether he thinks non–Bolivian units will be required to deal with the situation." If so, Martin explained that "we would consider any request he might make in the OAS [Organization of American States] framework," reserving the right to intervene unilaterally only if OAS members displayed a "reluctance . . . to 'interfere' in affairs of a neighboring state."[136]

Three days later, on 23 July, Stephansky sent another limited distribution cable to Rusk, Martin, and Moscoso, requesting $110,000 of military equipment, to be drawn on the $4 million contingency fund, partly for use in equipping Nery's Indian militia. The proposed shipment included 4,500 tear gas grenades, 200 semiautomatic M-1 carbine machine guns, 200,000 rounds of machine-gun ammunition, 50,000 rounds of .38 Special ammunition, and 12,500 shotgun shells. The following day, the US military mission chief in La Paz submitted an "urgent" request for 408 3.5-inch high-explosive rockets. Ambassador Stephansky recommended that the entire shipment be "airlifted immediately to support [the] anticipated internal security action."[137] Meanwhile, the ambassador pondered an unprecedented evacuation of US citizens, writing that while the embassy's "emergency burn facilities . . . [are] adequate," he was forced to "balance [the] catastrophic political consequences of any mass evacuation of American families from La Paz against [the] dangers of keeping the American community in pawn by delaying [an] evacuation movement." He decided that it would be best to send a helicopter and crew to La Paz immediately, "ostensibly . . . to conduct high altitude performance tests."[138] On

24 July, Secretary Rusk approved the helicopter and the entire weapons shipment, imploring Stephansky to "ensure that [the] Special Fund [is] actually used for purposes approved." At 11:05 a.m. on 26 July, the Alliance for Progress weaponry arrived at USAID's OPS office in La Paz.[139]

Hours later, Government Minister Arze Murillo dispatched a presidential guard contingent to deliver the US weapons to Nery's militia,[140] and President Paz sent a handwritten note to regional authorities, ordering them to "offer their cooperation to Wilge Nery." Secret police chief San Román likewise ordered transit police to "grant free circulation throughout the Republic" for Nery's vehicles.[141] The CIA reported that Paz planned to employ this paramilitary force in order "to avoid using the army as a repressive force against the miners, to create a climate for [an] army occupation to pacify the area, and to create a climate for [the] elimination of extremist labor leaders."[142]

Indian peasant leader Fabián Portugal recalls the day soldiers from Paz's presidential guard arrived to reinforce Nery's militia, which had set up camp in the village of Irupata, thirty-six kilometers east of Siglo XX. "One truck arrived, full of arms, and then another full of ammunition," Portugal recounted, and the local villagers were then driven en masse to Llallagua and ordered to "stock up on rations: alcohol, coca, food."[143] The group made quite a commotion. Siglo XX union official Cirilo Jiménez recalls that "they practically informed on themselves, buying up food" at the local marketplace. "That is how we learned they were to attack," Jiménez explains, "and we mobilized immediately."[144]

Tipped off that Nery's militia was set to attack the mining camp, in the early morning hours of 29 July, several dozen armed miners departed for Irupata under the command Octavio Torrico, a tall, lanky, and beloved MNR leftist who served as the unofficial head of the Siglo XX mine workers militia. Once they were in position at around 4:00 a.m., Torrico spoke up, ordering Nery's men to give up their weapons. Half drunk from a night of revelry, the Indian peasant leader awoke and responded, "If you want these weapons, come and get them, you fucking communists." Torrico then ordered his men to throw live dynamite around Nery's safehouse as a noisy show of force. Nery immediately announced his surrender, and his pregnant wife emerged frantically from the hut with a white flag, inviting Torrico to come collect the armament.[145]

As Torrico and two of his fellow miners approached Wilge Nery's safehouse, however, they were cut down in a sudden barrage of paramilitary machine-gun fire. Enraged, the remaining miners launched an immediate counterattack with homemade dynamite grenades and the few rifles they had.

Figure 2. Technocrats who designed Kennedy-era development programs in Bolivia conditioned aid money on the physical removal of Communist union leaders from the mining camps. To carry out this mission, USAID provided weaponry in mid-1963 to equip an Indian peasant militia charged with "eliminating" Siglo XX union leaders Federico Escóbar and Irineo Pimentel. The miners militia, armed with a few rifles and dozens of homemade dynamite grenades, headed off the peasant paramilitary force at the village of Irupata on 29 July. Here, Siglo XX miner Lucio Otalora poses with his handiwork. Photograph by Dmitri Kessel/Time & Life Pictures/Getty Images.

In the melee, Nery's wife was fatally wounded, as were two undercover soldiers from Paz Estenssoro's presidential guard. Local villagers were more fortunate, as they knew the terrain well and were able to escape. From the surrounding hills, they gazed down nervously throughout the day as the workers held Nery hostage and dozens of miner reinforcements arrived from Siglo XX and Catavi. For hours, the workers tensely debated what they should do with Nery. Finally, at around 4:00 p.m., the decision was made to execute him, and minutes later two shots rang out.[146] As anthropologists Harris and Albó write, "thus died Nery, the culprit of the exacerbation of the feud between the Laime and Jucumani, and of miner-*campesino* tensions."[147]

US officials had a large stake in the fate of Nery's militia, and they followed these events very closely. Embassy Air Attaché Fox reported through Defense Intelligence Agency (DIA) channels that the "communists struck the first blow in the final confrontation between the Paz moderate forces and the leftists," adding that "a large number of arms was seized by the miners." According to Colonel Fox, General Barrientos was "concerned over the violence . . . and the government's failure to use sufficient force in the fight against the Communists." Barrientos told him that "if Paz tried to back out, the Armed Forces would take over," leading Fox to conclude that "the possibility of civil war is coming closer."[148] The CIA was more optimistic, characterizing the battle of Irupata as evidence of President Paz's "determination to win the issue in the tin mines, even at the cost of violence."[149] Ambassador Stephansky agreed, and he fired off an urgent cable, through CIA channels, to Secretary Rusk, Assistant Secretary Martin, and Alliance for Progress Administrator Moscoso, asking for a fresh shipment of military hardware for the "immediate support [of] militia operations [in the] Uncía area." Stephansky warned that a "failure to reply promptly" would mean the "failure [of] GOB will and capability [to] confront [the] mine situation."[150]

The State Department relayed each of these cables directly to the White House Special Group (CI), and to Attorney General Robert Kennedy in particular, conceding that "this showdown was brought about by our insistence that the Bolivian Government carry out these mine reform programs, which will weaken the mining unions that form Lechín's major base of support." Reporting that the contingency funds had been provided "to aid Bolivian military [*sic:* militia] movements in the mining area," the State Department explained that the "fast breaking situation affords the Group a unique opportunity to determine the adequacy of our counterinsurgency efforts."[151] In its talking points for the Special Group, the State Department elaborated in alarming tones: "We are not averse to seeing a violent confrontation between Paz and Lechín forces since this will tend to place them in irreconcilable positions from which they will find it difficult to retreat, and we believe that Lechín's political standing will suffer in the event of such clashes. . . . Were the situation to indicate the desirability of sending Special Forces, this would require a decision at the highest level of government."[152]

It is surprising to note how much the US press was aware of these events. Henry Lee of the *Chicago Tribune* acknowledged that the tension resulted from the Alliance for Progress Triangular Plan, framing the battle as a clash between the free world and communism. If the miners were defeated, Lee wrote, "communism in this country will be crippled if not destroyed." Juan de Onís of the *New York Times* reported that the conflict marked a "turning point in the Bolivian Revolution," adding that it was a "decisive test of the will and ability of the central authorities to maintain a national development policy." De Onís wrote assuredly that the Kennedy administration was "right behind Dr. Paz on the mining question" before he outlined in remarkable detail the Triangular Plan conditions.[153]

In the *Washington Post*, Dan Kurzman wrote that a "major Latin American test between communism and democracy was heading toward a possibly violent climax in Bolivia," where President Paz was battling leftist miners over "labor reforms recommended by American and West German technicians." Kurzman added that the Kennedy administration's resolute support for the Bolivian president "could set Bolivia on the road to prosperity," since "President Paz is in no mood to let the Communists stand in the way." George Natanson of the *Los Angeles Times* wrote, "Bolivia survives thanks to Paz Estenssoro who refuses to accept the dictates of the far left." [154]

Finally, *Time* magazine misreported that "a gang of miners with a vague and perhaps imaginary grievance dragged a member of the legislature from his home, strapped a stick of dynamite to his body, and blasted him to bits. When his pregnant wife came running out of the house waving a white handkerchief, a miner shot her to death." One wonders how *Time* could have characterized the miners' grievance as imaginary when, two paragraphs later, the article conceded that the Bolivian government was preparing to "put into effect an announced plan to cut the workforce at the Catavi mine by 30%," representing approximately four thousand miners. Without flinching, however, *Time* reported, "If [Paz] succeeds, it will be an important victory for him and for Bolivia."[155]

There is no doubt that the fiercest advocates for, and organizers of, armed action against the Siglo XX miners were Kennedy's development-minded appointees: White House aides Goodwin and Schlesinger, Assistant Secretary Martin, Alliance for Progress Administrator Moscoso, and Ambassador Stephansky. To be sure, MNR skeptics in Washington were not doves; they were busy trying to convince the White House to cut off economic assistance and channel support to Bolivia's right-wing opposition. This narrative clearly suggests, however, that authoritarianism was far from Kennedy's track two. It was Alliance for Progress development in action, an aggressive modernization project implemented through armed force. Days after the bloodshed at Irupata, the State Department rallied, reporting, "United States policy toward

Bolivia for the last ten years . . . will have been largely justified if our current efforts succeed. . . . The MNR government for the first time is taking decisive steps to end labor indiscipline and assure the basis for orderly economic development. . . . In oversimplified terms, President Paz is now committed to the economic development of Bolivia under the Alliance for Progress."[156]

When asked later about the Alliance for Progress's rapid militarization in Bolivia, Ben Stephansky responded, "I don't think it was counterinsurgency so much as it was a major effort to improve communications."[157] This is a shocking reply, given that Ambassador Stephansky was a central proponent of the Irupata operation and of military-led development in general. Privately, he hailed the Bolivian government for "staking its all on . . . economic development," adding, "To do so, it [is] prepared [to] prescribe some bitter medicine [to] the mining sector."[158] Senator Gale McGee, a close Kennedy ally, was more forthcoming. In a public relations video released shortly after the bloodshed, the liberal senator declared that "inefficiency threatened the country," making "harsh measures necessary to break the communist influence" in the mines. Senator McGee concluded optimistically that the families of those "dead in the violence of politics can hopefully forget the scars of hate and waste if the Alliance-supported program is fulfilled in Bolivia's mines."[159]

According to US liberals, the Alliance for Progress in Bolivia was designed to counter backwardness and foster anticommunist progress. President Paz's tolerance of domestic and international communism, coupled with rising dissent in the MNR Left, heightened their sense that a deeper intervention was necessary. Never abandoning the development-oriented rubric with which they began, Kennedy officials accelerated and accentuated their support for the Paz regime. This took two forms: military-led development in the countryside and authoritarian development in the mines. Armed with the technocratic language of economic and social progress, Alliance for Progress officials waged a geostrategic struggle against communism in the heart of South America. Unfortunately for Washington, Siglo XX leaders Escóbar and Pimentel survived the initial showdown. As Paz prepared for his triumphant White House visit, there was no escaping the prognosis that as an authoritarian project, the alliance's toughest battles lay ahead. For their part, the miners had just seized two hundred US-made weapons, and they anxiously awaited the next confrontation.

Chapter 4

Development's Detractors

Miners, Housewives, and the Hostage Crisis at Siglo XX

Central to the Alliance for Progress in Bolivia was the idea that order and authority were necessary ingredients for economic and social development. Throughout the program's implementation, political crises strengthened US liberal resolve to redouble efforts in support of President Paz's modernizing regime. Indian and miner blood was shed at Irupata in the name of rapid modernization, and Kennedy officials consistently viewed these types of clashes as showdowns between ordered progress and chaotic backwardness. The latter paved the way for communism, the developmentalists argued, and they provided neat, theoretical formulas within Washington's larger strategic milieu. Meanwhile, Bolivian popular forces continued to resist Alliance for Progress reforms. When Siglo XX miners took four US officials hostage in December 1963, the incoming Johnson administration was put to the test. It would answer with resounding certainty: even without President Kennedy, Paz Estenssoro's authoritarian approach to development would continue to receive Washington's full support.

After Irupata

The Kennedy administration had long pressured President Paz to move forward with the Alliance for Progress Triangular Plan, which required tough, anticommunist labor reforms in the nationalized mining sector. The Indian militia at Irupata equipped by the United States Agency for International Development (USAID) was meant to break miner resistance to Triangular, and in the aftermath of the July battle, US officials anxiously awaited Paz Estenssoro's next move. For liberal developmentalists like Ambassador Stephansky, Bolivia had reached a movement of decision, with President Paz set to depart for Washington in October. Paz did not disappoint, and he moved rapidly to implement the long-awaited labor reforms, firing hundreds of leftist miners and issuing warrants for the arrest of their Communist union leaders.

Having taken a stand against the leftist miners at Irupata, on 3 August President Paz suspended Control Obrero by supreme decree, and a few days later the first one hundred retirement notices were issued.[1] US Embassy officials performed "spot-checks" to ensure that "Commie-liners" were the first to be released, including Siglo XX union leaders Escóbar and Pimentel.[2] Siglo XX responded by once again going on strike, a "desperation move" according to Ambassador Stephansky.[3] Guillermo Bedregal, president of the Corporación Minera de Bolivia (COMIBOL; Mining Corporation of Bolivia), condemned the miners for their "ethical and mental underdevelopment" and for having been "lulled to sleep by the Marxist drug."[4] USAID's mission director in Bolivia, Alexander Firfer, hailed the Bolivian government's efforts, gushing that "the Alliance for Progress is being executed better in Bolivia than any other country,"[5] and Assistant Secretary of State Martin dropped by for three days to congratulate Paz Estenssoro for finally having adopted the Alliance's reforms. Stephansky cabled Martin several days later to report, "You were a terrific hit with President Paz, who spent a half-hour after the white tie dinner the day you left, repeating to me how impressed he was with you."[6]

Convinced that its pressure was working, Washington doubled down on Paz's government. On 8 August, Kennedy's 5412 Special Group, in charge of authorizing CIA operations throughout the world, approved a "covert subsidy . . . to take the necessary covert actions to overcome the emergency situation . . . and, once the situation normalized, to enable Paz to consolidate his control." The plan called for the CIA, under the auspices of USAID and the United States Information Service (USIS), to eliminate communist and Movimiento Nacionalista Revolucionario (MNR; Revolutionary Nationalist Movement) Left Sector influence throughout Bolivian society. The Indian peasant confederation was targeted, as was the national labor confederation, and CIA funds were earmarked for the creation of parallel labor organizations, fully subservient to Paz's wing of the governing party.[7]

While Assistant Secretary Martin was still in Bolivia, President Paz presented his annual report to Parliament on 6 August. Showing signs of moderating his former neutralism in foreign policy, the Bolivian president declared that the world was "divided into two great camps" and that Bolivia's alignment was "determined by geography, tradition, and the democratic convictions that inspire us."[8] Paz went on to declare: "Never before have such wide horizons opened before Bolivia, yet never before has our future been so risky. . . . Today we have arrived at the point where we can yield no further. . . . COMIBOL must move forward, or all Bolivia will suffer a disaster."[9] In other speeches that month, President Paz explained that "the mines [must] serve the interest of the Bolivian community,"[10] vowing to "maintain his attitude . . . even at the risk of falling from power."[11] President Paz added ominously that "as long as Pimentel and Escóbar are in Catavi, there will be no solution to the conflict,"[12] and in a private letter to his son, he vowed that he would "not yield, whatever the consequences."[13]

The miners of Siglo XX were running short of options, and when they announced plans to march on the provincial capital of Oruro, Paz vowed to US officials that he would "block their access using whatever degree of force necessary." He then ordered newly promoted commander-in-chief General Ovando to "protect Oruro and cut off [the] Huanuni mine" from Siglo XX. Labor unions in La Paz threatened to call sympathy strikes and, smelling blood, Paz's right-wing opposition encouraged the Left's demands in order to "create a revolutionary situation." With a generous injection of CIA funds, Government Minister Arze Murillo sought to head off urban sympathy strikes by using "sizeable bribes." The tactic was successful, but the Right continued to weigh the benefits of a tactical alliance with the striking miners, whom Stephansky averred to be "reacting aggressively since they find themselves directly threatened and [realize] that their national leaders are impotent to help them."[14]

Bitter negotiations between COMIBOL and the Federación Sindical de Trabajadores Mineros de Bolivia (FSTMB; Union Federation of Bolivian Mine Workers) took place throughout late August and early September. Bedregal responded that he was willing to discuss the timing of the Triangular Plan conditions, not the terms, and the two parties signed an interim agreement, stipulating that they would reach a final accord by 15 September. The major sticking point was the fate of Escóbar and Pimentel, both of whose physical removal was demanded by COMIBOL. Bedregal wrote that "the mere presence" of the two mine union leaders "puts the government and our entity in an impossible situation with respect to exercising any sort of management" over Siglo XX. Bedregal added that unless an agreement was reached that included their removal from the mining camp, Triangular's international financiers would refuse to resume economic assistance.[15]

With the miners rejecting any agreement that removed Escóbar and Pimentel, the Bolivian government announced unilaterally on 15 September that it would "proceed with [the] application [of the] terms [of the] rehabilitation . . . on [its] own authority." Most of the mines were subjected to the labor reforms immediately, but COMIBOL's managers admitted to US officials that Siglo XX would require a "major effort." If they could get Escóbar "out," however, and put Pimentel under "judicial proceedings," Triangular could move ahead.[16]

Ambassador Stephansky reported that Paz's newfound determination represented a "historic change toward moderation in [the] Bolivian Revolution." Only time would tell if this shift could be "consolidated," however, and Stephansky recommended the United States "do all we can to encourage GOB [the Government of Bolivia; to] continue its policy of firmness." He was pleased that the Paz government had taken steps toward "raising productivity and reducing costs" in COMIBOL and that it appeared to be pushing the revolution into its "constructive era." This was "not anti-labor policy," he argued, "but rather policy to restore balance against excessive and anarchical influence as long exercised by labor unions." In order to "maintain very favorable momentum" in this endeavor, Stephansky recommended an additional $1.6 million in economic assistance in late September, funds that would be used to offset the costs of the "increased number [of] layoffs programmed." Stephansky reiterated that "prompt action" was crucial, since the firings were "basically addressed to getting rid of Commies," an enterprise in which the "GOB deserves our fullest support."[17]

Two weeks before Paz left for Washington, Siglo XX once again called for a general strike against the firings. "Furious," President Paz called an emergency cabinet meeting on 5 October to discuss "definitive measures," which included the "use of force to displace [the] miners and [the] arrest of communist mine union leaders." Stephansky expressed satisfaction that the Bolivian president was preparing to take "drastic action" against the leftists, and he requested that Secretary of State Rusk be "alert [to] possible resort [to the] special fund," previously approved by the Special Group.[18] COMIBOL once again froze food shipments, and by 17 October, the US Embassy reported that "there is no meat or bread at Catavi-Siglo XX."[19] Meanwhile, the Bolivian government hired airplanes to drop leaflets over Siglo XX imploring workers to "Free Yourselves from Union Dictatorship! It is the Motto of Free Workers!"[20]

The miners responded to COMIBOL's threat of starvation by sending a delegation of thirty women to La Paz, representing a front for the Partido Comunista de Bolivia (PCB; Communist Party of Bolivia), the Comité de

Amas de Casa, who declared themselves on a hunger strike on 14 October along with almost a hundred children.[21] A week later, the Bolivian government brought criminal charges against Escóbar and Pimentel, accusing them of "attempted murder" for instigating the hunger strike.[22] Demanding they both leave the mining camp immediately, the government announced that "both men have been deprived of legal status, and orders for their arrest have been issued."[23] Escóbar responded that he would leave if his family and Pimentel were allowed to stay, and on the condition that COMIBOL pay for him to travel to Cuba and the Soviet Union. The "retired" Control Obrero vowed that the miners would accept the Triangular conditions, and that he would take up an administration position with the FSTMB in La Paz. The US Embassy scoffed that Escóbar's conditions "virtually preclude [an] agreement."[24]

Ambassador Stephansky planned to accompany Paz to Washington in late October, at which point he would take up a senior position in the State Department's Latin American office. "I was eventually going to get back to academia," he later recalled, adding, "I had not started in the Foreign Service; I had just kind of slithered in." Stephansky also admitted to having clashed with career diplomats in La Paz. "The clubby side of . . . the State Department was really one of . . . its most heinous aspects. . . . They didn't like the lateral entry program at all."[25] According to Embassy Air Attaché Fox, "Stephansky always talked down to you, like he was better than the rest of us. A real superstar."[26]

For the Paz government, this superstar had been a godsend. COMIBOL President Bedregal recalled that Stephansky's departure was "bad news for all of us." Affectionately called *Compañero* Stephansky by members of Paz's inner circle, the economist had battled tirelessly against MNR skepticism in the US foreign policy bureaucracy. Bedregal writes that no other diplomat could possibly boast "the abilities and affections that this short, bald American Jew possessed," adding that, "more than a diplomat, [Stephansky] was an admirer of the Revolution and an intimate friend of the President."[27]

Before bidding La Paz farewell, Ambassador Stephansky singled out one effort by the Alliance for Progress that had been "unusually successful in the fulfillment of its original objectives." According to Stephansky, the military's employment of USAID funds to carry out "civic improvement and development-oriented projects" had made the institution "more acceptable to the people of Bolivia." This program of civic action was a "model for other countries," he declared, before admonishing that without continued US support, the valuable effort "would collapse."[28]

By October 1963, few observers doubted that Víctor Paz Estenssoro was Washington's man. After years of debate regarding the wisdom of US support for revolutionary Bolivia, Kennedy's development-minded appointees had been vindicated. With Paz preparing for his historic White House visit, the Kennedy administration made it abundantly clear that he was a model Latin American leader in the era of the Alliance for Progress. He had demonstrated that he was an authoritarian modernizer, willing to enforce development-oriented reforms, even at the cost of violence.

Víctor Paz Goes to Washington

In late October 1963, President Paz had the bittersweet honor of being the last head of state to meet with President Kennedy before the latter's assassination in Dallas. The visit was accompanied by generous pomp, and Kennedy betrayed effusive sympathy for Paz's modernizing regime. According to one of the foremost historians of the Bolivian revolution, Kennedy saw in Paz "a man after his own heart, a politician capable of substituting for the progressive national bourgeoisie that Bolivia so manifestly lacked for its necessary transformation into a modern state."[29] By the time he arrived in Washington, Paz Estenssoro had fully committed his repressive state apparatus to the anticommunist reforms called for by the Alliance for Progress, and Kennedy had no shortage of praise for his Bolivian ally.

In its previsit White House briefing paper, the State Department stressed the importance of Paz's commitment to development, highlighting specifically the recent US-funded Indian militia operations against the Siglo XX miners. The department wrote that July's bloody showdown at Irupata "indicated [a] determination to enforce the discipline essential to economic development." Continued support was necessary, State reported, in order to frustrate Communist plans to take the country "farther to the left toward instability, continuing economic unreality, and the possible emergence of a Castro-communist type state." The briefing paper explained that Paz had "shown his desire to lead the revolution into a constructive development phase" with the enthusiastic support of Bolivia's "new armed forces," backed heavily by funds from the Alliance for Progress. According to the State Department, "the potential gains are large."[30]

Bolivia offered Washington an opportunity, the State Department continued, to demonstrate "continuing US support for the second profound revolution in Latin America" after Mexico's, and especially for Paz Estenssoro as the "father of this revolution." If the White House could "strengthen the identification of Paz and Bolivia with the United States and the Alliance for Progress," the State Department believed it could demonstrate to the Western Hemisphere that communists were the "enemies of the existing order in Latin America and of the efforts of the Alliance for Progress to accomplish major improvements there." Specifically, the State Department urged President Kennedy to openly "admire and support" President Paz for following through on the Triangular Plan conditions and for moving to undercut communism in the mines. The mine rehabilitation was the "most important single mutual US-Bolivian effort," the State Department explained, since it was designed to "weaken the political opposition to the development programs supported by President Paz." By standing up to "gangster-disruptive elements" who sought to "obstruct our programs in Bolivia," President Paz was well on his way to implementing the rehabilitation plan and making his country's economy "viable for the foreseeable future." In the opinion of the State Department, the most important aspect of the upcoming meeting was to convince Paz to "make a final break with [Vice President] Lechín."[31]

Finally, the State Department recommended that President Kennedy use his meetings to remind the Paz of the "threat of communist subversion in underdeveloped countries." Bolivia was a "logical target because of its unsettled political and economic conditions," the State Department explained, and it was therefore important to pressure Paz to "control Bolivian travel to Cuba . . . and prevent the use of Bolivian territory for the movement of Cuban-trained subversives to neighboring countries." The briefing concluded by warning that Havana was "making a concerted effort to fish in Bolivia's troubled waters," adding that the hundreds of Bolivian students who were studying in Cuba and Soviet bloc countries represented the "largest number from any one Latin American nation."[32]

On 22 October 1963, President Paz opened his first face-to-face meeting with President Kennedy by expressing concern at the growing divide within Bolivian communism. Implicitly referencing the miners, who despised PCB tolerance of the MNR regime, Paz blamed the deepening Sino-Soviet split for encouraging many Latin American leftists to spurn Moscow's policy of "peaceful coexistence" in favor of the "Chinese Communist thesis of violence." Paz warned Kennedy that these adventurers welcomed military coups, even those fomented by Latin American conservatives, because they recognized that the "counter to a military government is not a democratic, progressive government, but a radical one." Finally, Paz explained that his country was susceptible to regional trends, and he expressed concern that the previous year's coups in neighboring Peru and Argentina did not bode well for the MNR. After Kennedy expressed agreement, Paz requested the United States nonetheless continue its military assistance, which "goes into a very effective civic action program."[33]

One portion of their conversation did not make it into the official record. Three weeks earlier, Yugoslav president Josip Broz Tito had spent five days in Bolivia, where he and Paz signed a laundry list of economic agreements, including a $5 million credit for industrial equipment and technical training.[34] Ambassador Stephansky had reported that the embassy was doing everything possible to block the offer,[35] but Kennedy appeared unbothered. According to Kennedy's interpreter, he told Paz, with a "sidelong glance . . . 'Yes, but of course President Tito is a very conservative communist.'"[36]

When the two resumed their talks the following day, it was Kennedy's turn to begin. He expressed concern regarding Bolivian youth who were traveling to Cuba and the Soviet bloc for studies and possibly guerrilla training. Promising to address this "travel problem," Paz explained that his successful liquidation of the Bolivian Right had led the Left to become the new "enemies of the revolution." He vowed therefore to take steps toward "preventing or reducing the movement of students who go to Cuba not for academic study but for subversive guerrilla training." The two presidents concluded their second meeting by considering the Irupata peasant-miner clash in the context of ongoing tension at Siglo XX. Paz confidently agreed that the implementation of the mine rehabilitation program was a "prerequisite to Bolivian development" and boasted that his government was taking decisive steps to "impose its authority on the mine union extremists."[37]

According to Kennedy's interpreter, the two heads of state spoke with "complete frankness—no great beating around the bush—no protocol—two men, both busy men, just saying, 'We have a couple of hours. Let's talk our problems out.'" President Kennedy reportedly listened with "great, vital interest," paying "very close attention" as Paz revealed that "he had been for years waiting till he felt strong enough politically, especially vis-à-vis the mine workers in Bolivia, and Lechín . . . to embark on a new approach to modernizing the mines. . . . And he was sure it would be successful."[38]

At a press conference later that day, Kennedy hailed Paz as a "pioneer of the Alliance for Progress," who had been "engaged in this effort for more than ten years." Kennedy then turned to President Paz, in front of the nation's press, declaring, "What you are attempting to do in your country is what we hope all of us in all of our countries in this hemisphere would try to do for our peoples."[39] The Bolivian Foreign Ministry was thrilled by the result of Paz's White House visit, relishing in Republican senator Barry Goldwater's attacks on President Kennedy for offering the Bolivian president such a generous show of support.[40] Privately, President Paz characterized the trip as "a great success," boasting of having struck up "a true friendship with Kennedy."[41]

Several days after Paz left Washington, Kennedy sent him a glowing letter, which was given wide coverage in Latin America. It read, in part, "Your visit has given me the opportunity to become personally acquainted with you and to appreciate your qualities of leadership in this momentous period of hemispheric development. . . . These days you have spent with us have enabled us to know more intimately and therefore to value more highly than ever the valiant efforts which Bolivia has made in her social revolution and within the Alliance for Progress to accelerate the rate of economic and social advance."[42]

Figure 3. In late October 1963, President Paz had the bittersweet honor of being the last head of state to visit the Kennedy White House. For US liberals, Paz was a model Latin American leader, "a pioneer of the Alliance for Progress," in Kennedy's words. The visit came weeks after a US-equipped peasant militia failed in its mission to assassinate left-wing mine union leaders, but Paz vowed to Kennedy that his government would soon "impose its authority on the mine union extremists." President Paz later confided to his family that the visit enabled him to strike up "true friendship with Kennedy." Photograph courtesy of Carlos Serrate Reich.

During his visit, Paz also met Douglas Henderson, Kennedy's appointee to replace Ambassador Stephansky. A career foreign service officer who had earned kudos for guiding the Lima embassy, as deputy chief of mission, in Washington's opposition to Peru's 1962 military coup d'état, Henderson had a reputation as a political liberal and a military skeptic. The ambassador-designate appeared the perfect choice to promote Kennedy's development-oriented policies in Bolivia without ruffling the feathers of career diplomats. Colonel Fox recalled, "Doug was just great. He'd really listen to you and talk to you like your equal. I felt very much a part of Henderson's team. We shared our opinions in private, and then Henderson came up with a policy, which we supported."[43] Former CIA station chief Larry Sternfield agrees, character-izing Henderson as an "Alliance for Progress ideologue, just like Stephansky, but at least Henderson knew a thing or two about diplomacy."[44] Perhaps most important, Henderson had spent three years in the US Consulate in Cocha-bamba, and unlike Stephansky, "I knew the country well. I liked the people."[45]

At his Senate confirmation hearing in early November, Henderson noted the existence in Washington of "diametrically opposed views" toward Paz Estenssoro. Citing Senator Goldwater's harsh criticism, Henderson conceded that Paz "came to power by violence, and Paz's party is the only political party in Bolivia today that can field a winning candidate." Henderson explained, however, that "since 1952, two presidential elections have been held and power has been transmitted peacefully to the elected successor." This was "without precedent in Bolivia." Henderson praised Paz's developmentalism, noting that "even the armed forces have been engaged in this program through civic action projects." Characterizing Paz as "the rare revolutionary who rec-ognizes the need for construction as well as destruction," Henderson admitted nonetheless that "Bolivia is still a difficult problem, and no bed of roses for any American Ambassador." Revealing the development-oriented approach he would employ as ambassador, Henderson pointed out that Third World masses were becoming a "potent new political force, unpredictable unless care-fully directed." Washington would be unable to influence the course of events "by abstention or negative action," he warned, stressing that "we have no ac-ceptable alternative to making the effort."[46]

On 20 November, just before leaving for La Paz, Henderson held a private meeting with President Kennedy. Praising Paz's "helpful attitude toward the Alliance for Progress," Kennedy revealed his desire to become the first US president to visit Bolivia.[47] According to Henderson, "a good bit of my con-versation with him that day was about Bolivia, about what he could expect, what kind of accommodations were available, what affect the altitude would have, a whole series of things, and it was quite obvious that Kennedy was planning a state visit, a reciprocal state visit, probably in January [1964]."[48] Henderson left to pack his bags. It was Wednesday afternoon. Friday morning, Kennedy was shot dead in Dallas.

When President Paz received news of the Kennedy assassination, he was "deeply grieved," according to COMIBOL president Bedregal. Paz stated ominously that "the assassin's bullet in Dallas could also injure the Bolivian National Revolution, because we have lost a great friend, and the world will never be the same after this dreadful tragedy."[49] Henderson recalls that after Kennedy's death, "I wasn't even sure if my appointment would stand. I was afraid Johnson would want to review all the recent appointments, but my sources told me to go ahead to La Paz."[50]

Four days after the assassination, the State Department circulated a "Bolivia Strategy Statement," in which it strongly recommended the continuation of Kennedy's support for Paz Estenssoro's MNR. Washington's "strategic objective," the department wrote, was to "exploit the existing development potential and improve the political situation" so that the Paz government could "fight off communist threats to its existence . . . [and] make the difficult decisions" necessary to "foster speedier development." The department urged the incoming administration to use Bolivia to "prove to other Alliance countries" that social reform and US economic assistance could together "transform a feudal society without slipping into a communist or military dictatorship." State recommended that USAID continue working with the Pentagon to "utilize military personnel to the maximum extent feasible" in the development process, adding that the Bolivian armed forces should continue to "receive training and commodities to cope better with the threat of dissident armed miners, *campesinos*, and other disruptive elements."[51]

With these goals in mind, President Johnson sent a personal letter to President Paz on 29 November, assuring the Bolivian leader of his commitment to "work with you and your government toward the successful outcome of the plans discussed with President Kennedy." Johnson noted that Paz had been "the last official visitor received" by Kennedy, adding that he had "asked Ambassador Henderson to meet with you to consider further those issues discussed during your visit." Johnson concluded his letter by stressing that his embassy would "cooperate in every way with your government in seeking to achieve the objectives of the Alliance for Progress."[52]

President Kennedy's appointees defended Bolivia's revolutionary regime with tireless devotion, and Paz's White House visit demonstrated that he had succeeded in gaining Washington's nearly unconditional support. Moreover,

Kennedy's appointment of a pro-Paz development-oriented ambassador shortly before his death helped to ensure continued US backing. For President Paz, however, there was work left to be done. He had demonstrated a willingness to attack the leftist miners, but Escóbar and Pimentel still had to be removed from the Siglo XX mining camp. In early December, the Bolivian government arrested the two legendary union leaders, setting off a chain reaction that brought the country to the verge of civil war.

US Hostages at Siglo XX

In Paz Estenssoro's US-backed push to bring the Bolivian mining camps under the authority of the central government, he ran up against the intransigent resistance of the workers at the country's largest mine, Siglo XX. Union leaders Federico Escóbar and Irineo Pimentel were independent-minded communists who refused to respect the PCB's modus vivendi with the Paz government, and they championed an increasingly violent struggle against the labor reforms required by the Alliance for Progress Triangular Plan. The two boasted such enormous influence at Siglo XX that the technocrats who designed the mine rehabilitation program included their physical removal in the list of conditions. In a revolutionary environment governed by popular militias, the communists' removal was easier said than done.

In August 1963, the White House 5412 Special Group had approved several covert operations to battle communist influence in the labor unions, and funds were flowing freely by December. Shortly before Henderson arrived in La Paz, USIS Labor Officer Thomas Martin—"a pioneer in reaching out to the miners"[53]—made contact with union leaders at Catavi-Siglo XX, informing them that $45,000 had been earmarked for two schools in the rebellious region. Martin's contact was Catavi union leader Arturo Crespo, an MNR leftist who subsequently invited Martin to deliver the funds directly to the community. Martin happily accepted, and set off toward the mine region in the company of three other US officials, USAID labor advisers Bernard Rifkin and Michael Kristula and Peace Corps volunteer Robert Fergerstrom. Their trip coincided with the twelfth national miners' congress at Colquiri, which they attended as Crespo's guests.[54]

Vice President Lechín later wrote that the FSTMB's Colquiri conference "was important because it would take a different path: the independence of the labor movement from the MNR right, and therefore from Paz." The miners planned to "repudiate all the programs that the MNR had implemented," including the "Triangular Plan . . . and the construction of a new, repressive army." At Colquiri, the FSTMB proceeded to "denounce the terror used by the government" and announce itself "clearly in favor of a destiny formulated by the workers themselves. . . . It was the break with the MNR."[55] Crespo adds that "like never before," Colquiri managed to bring together "all political currents" behind a "unanimous" proclamation in favor of the miners' "future opposition to all the government's political, economic, and social programs." The federation declared itself in a "head-on struggle . . . until the ultimate consequences" against the Triangular Plan, representing the "workers' definitive break from the MNR."[56] For the first time, anti-MNR rightist parties allied with the miners, and the convention unanimously endorsed Lechín's declaration that it was necessary "to rise in arms to struggle against Paz's 'police state.'"[57]

On Friday, 6 December, the conference adjourned, and USIS Officer Martin departed for Catavi with his three colleagues. Meanwhile, as Escóbar and Pimentel left Colquiri, agents from Paz Estenssoro's Control Político opened fire on their truck. Their driver was injured, and the two union leaders were taken prisoner for the second time since 1961. The news went out on radios throughout the country, and within hours, Communist miners from Siglo XX, armed with rifles and dynamite, burst into neighboring Catavi and kidnapped thirty hostages, including the four Americans.[58] Peace Corps volunteer Robert Fergerstrom, who was taken hostage that night, recalls, "We were having dinner with the boss [of Catavi], and they came in looking for him. They immediately spotted Martin, who was very well known there. They took him and I lay low. A few minutes later, they came back in and took the rest of us. When we got outside there were 150–200 miners yelling, '*Gringos de mierda! Mueran los gringos!*' I could see that they would have killed us.[59]

Gerónima Jaldín de Romero, interim head of the Communist-front Comité de Amas de Casa de Siglo XX (Siglo XX Housewives Committee), recalls rushing to the union building that Friday night when the sirens went off. She was principally worried that something might have happened to her husband on his way back from Colquiri. When she arrived, Gerónima saw that a mass of workers had already gathered in the plaza. Escóbar's wife, Alicia, grabbed Gerónima and told her, "Look, they took our leaders prisoner again, and right now the miners are bringing prisoners from Catavi. Word has it there are a lot of foreigners in the group." Alicia revealed that the Amas de Casa would be taking charge, and she told Gerónima, "You will be responsible for everything that happens over the next few days." With a "bit of fear," Gerónima accepted, asking Escóbar's wife, "What are we supposed to do?" Alicia replied curtly, "We'll see."[60]

The two women went into the union building where the other wives had begun to gather. Before they could call an assembly, the hostages arrived and were sequestered in a second-floor room. Gerónima then explained to the group that the Amas would be "staying here as guards, all of us, as long as there are prisoners in that room," adding that "those men will not come out from inside . . . until they release our union leaders." The women were proud of their leadership role, and responded, "Now we really are going to earn respect as the women we are! These men will not get away! Not a single one of them is going to get out!" At that point, Gerónima's husband arrived back from Colquiri. He asked her somewhat impatiently, "Who is going to cook?" to which she answered, "Well, we'll have to arrange to have someone come to the house and cook." With that, the Communist leader was off the hook; her husband shrugged his shoulders and responded, "Ok. You can stay."[61]

Fergerstrom recalled, "I was really afraid of the women. They had awful, mean looks on their faces."[62] Another hostage, Bernard Rifkin, agreed that "the real hellions were the *Amas de Casa*. . . . These were regular Madame De-farges, and [I] used to kid [my] guards concerning whether they were afraid of the *Amas de Casa*."[63] When Vice President Lechín arrived, the Amas demanded that he declare a general miners' strike "in solidarity with the Siglo XX union" until Escóbar and Pimentel were freed.[64] Crespo recalled that Gerónima and her colleagues "were very heated, and we could see that any talk of liberating the hostages would be futile." He nonetheless tried to explain that the US officials were in the area to provide funding to build schools and that "the treatment they were receiving was not right."[65]

The following afternoon, 7 December, Bolivian Foreign Minister José Fellman Velarde paid a visit to Ambassador Henderson, who had arrived only two days earlier. Fellman assured Henderson that the Bolivian government was "most concerned about the situation and determined [to] take action against [the] kidnappers." Fellman wanted to make it "perfectly clear, however, that [the] government could not consider using Escóbar and Pimentel as exchange for [the] Americans," explaining that the two union leaders faced "criminal charges." Henderson stressed that Martin and his colleagues had been "on legitimate business in [the] area," adding that "their proposed travel plans had been cleared with COMIBOL."[66]

Minister Fellman then outlined President Paz's "three phase operation" to bring the crisis to a head. First, the government would open indirect negotiations with the miners' federation, making the case that the "Americans and COMIBOL technicians have nothing to do with [the] arrest of Escóbar and Pimentel" and warning that the "mine workers and their leaders run grave

Figure 4. In December 1963, the Paz government finally implemented one of the toughest conditions of Alliance for Progress aid funding: the physical removal of left-wing labor leaders from the Siglo XX mining camp. Hours after Paz's agents arrested two union leaders in a shootout, rank-and-file miners took four US officials hostage, holding them for nine tense days in their dynamite-laden union hall. Peering nervously from the window above are, counterclockwise from the far right, USAID labor officers Bernard Rifkin and Michael Kristula, USIS labor officer Thomas Martin, and Peace Corps volunteer Robert Fergerstrom. Photograph by Michael Rougier/ Time & Life Pictures/Getty Images.

risks by keeping hostages." Phase two would begin on Monday, Fellman explained, at which point the air force would drop "ultimatum" leaflets notifying the miners of the "government threat [of] eventual action" after twenty-four hours, and army regiments would "commence [a] show of force directed toward the mining area but without provoking conflict." If these steps did not secure the release of the hostages, phase three would begin on Tuesday, Fellman continued, with military units "mov[ing] in force against Siglo XX, using [a] special para[trooper] company." In his report to Secretary Rusk, Henderson asked if a US Special Forces deployment would be possible, stressing that their mission "would be limited to [the] publicly announced and sole objective [of] protect[ing] American hostages in [a] joint operation with the Bolivian military."[67]

Having presented his credentials to Paz Estenssoro in a brief ceremony just hours earlier, Ambassador Henderson had yet to hold his first policy meeting with the Bolivian president.[68] Henderson cabled Rusk on Saturday night to warn that he would not see Paz again until Monday evening, hours before the ultimatum was set to expire and a "military showdown" would be likely. Henderson wrote that it was "probable" that the situation would disintegrate into "open civil war with unforeseeable consequences." He further predicted that the crisis could lead to the "postponement or cancellation of elections" and the "increased possibility, especially if civil unrest [is] prolonged, of [a] military coup." Henderson expressed concern that Paz's plan to attack Siglo XX also included the "possibility that [the] hostages will be killed, either in deliberate retaliation or as a result of mob action." The ambassador was generally supportive of the Bolivian government's resolve to "remain firm," but he wondered if there were "some intermediate steps available to it, e.g., cutting off shipments [of] food supplies, which might help persuade the miners [to] avoid violence and release the hostages." Henderson concluded by recommending that the US government "avoid . . . any suggestion which Paz might use as rationalization for temporizing and eventually for ineffectual half measures," while still making steps to "cautiously sound out Paz along [the] lines [of] possible intermediate steps."[69]

Before receiving a reply from Washington, Henderson held a secret meeting with several FSTMB leaders, who had been escorted to his house under the cover of darkness by Tom Martin's wife, Mariela.[70] After assuring Henderson that the "American prisoners at Siglo XX were not harmed," the delegation explained that their fellow miners had "taken . . . prisoners without thinking beyond [the] terms [of] their anger over [the] capture [of] Escóbar and Pimentel." The union leaders further described a "public feeling" in Bolivia that the US Embassy "ran" the country and that it could therefore "influence Bolivian government actions." They expressed a conviction that President Paz was "determined to persecute them," revealing that they personally feared arrest, and they asked Henderson to help them set up an indirect line of communication with the Paz government. Ambassador Henderson agreed to try, but he added that "release [of] American hostages could not be related to success or failure of my effort or of negotiations to follow."[71]

Secretary Rusk responded to both of Henderson's cables late that night, ordering him to "see Paz soonest Sunday and inform him USG [US Government;

is] opposed [to the] use of military force as outlined in phases 2 and 3 of Bolivian plan while US citizens [are] held hostage." Rusk explained that the State Department "consider[s] use of Bolivian military [a] very dangerous move not only for GOB (in view [of] pre-revolutionary military-miner clashes) but particularly for [the] safety [of] US personnel." Rusk added that the "same reasoning applies to possible request from GOB re[garding] use [of] any US Special Forces." Coaching the new ambassador through the crisis, Rusk recommended that in his conversations with Paz, Henderson "emphasize the political dangers inherent [in the] use of military force while US hostages remain cause célèbre for action." Rusk expressed doubts that it was possible to carry out military action while simultaneously "prevent[ing] miner retaliation against hostages," and he argued that "high-level, highly competent negotiators" were needed to break the stalemate. Rusk suggested putting pressure on Vice President Lechín, who as *"jefe máximo* of the miners" could be backed into offering a *"quid pro quo"* that might result in the exile of Escóbar and Pimentel in exchange for the hostages' release. Pushing Paz to revoke Lechín's official immunity would "seem to be the first order of business," Rusk concluded.[72]

The next morning, Sunday, 8 December, Secretary Rusk briefed President Johnson on the crisis, explaining that Escóbar and Pimentel were the "ring leaders of elements opposing implementation of the US-supported mine rehabilitation program" and informing the president that the State Department was "opposed to portions of the Bolivian proposal which include the use of force basically because we do not see how the safety of our personnel can be assured." Rusk added that using "Americans as a cause célèbre for military action by the Bolivian army against the miners has deep-rooted political significance and dangers," and he proceeded to inform Johnson that Henderson would meet with Paz later that day. Finally, Rusk detailed his proposal to put maximum pressure on Lechín and to recommend exile for Escóbar and Pimentel "in lieu of trial."[73]

Hours later, Assistant Secretary of Defense William Bundy wrote to his brother, National Security Adviser (NSA) McGeorge Bundy, to report that the Pentagon was readying forces "which might be necessary to respond to Bolivian government call for assistance." Assistant Secretary Bundy explained that US Southern Command in Panama had a thirty-man Special Forces Mobile Training team on six-hour alert, a group that included "specialists of the exact sort which would be needed in a rescue operation of this type." The assistant secretary wrote that Secretary of Defense Robert McNamara believed "the US should use military force only in an extreme emergency not only because of the physical restrictions on military operations in the area, and the great distances involved, but also because of the violent reaction against the military in Bolivia which seems certain to follow." One of the principal aims of the Alliance for Progress had been to "erase the bitter feeling of the peasants and miners against the Bolivian military," William Bundy added, noting that this effort was sure to be frustrated if the crisis developed to a point of armed confrontation.[74]

In an attached memorandum to the Joint Chiefs of Staff, US Southern Command (SOUTHCOM) reported that despite Paz's "past policy of not employing military forces against the miners, it appears that President Paz is prepared to risk the serious domestic violence which would almost certainly follow such a move." SOUTHCOM believed that "in view of lingering anti-army feelings which date back to the 1952 revolution, Bolivian peasants, miners, and armed militiamen would probably react violently to any military move against them," putting the "stability of the government and the lives of the hostages . . . in grave jeopardy." For this reason, the State Department was "strongly opposed to use of Bolivian military as has been proposed by Bolivia, or to possible use of US military Special Forces, as has been mentioned by the US Ambassador in La Paz." As a precautionary measure, however, the Pentagon drafted an action plan outlining precisely "what we could do . . . [and] how long would it take" to carry out "combat operations in conjunction with local government forces."[75]

After receiving the Pentagon report, NSA Bundy submitted a long memorandum to President Johnson on Sunday afternoon, detailing Washington's plan to "support Paz in pressure plus negotiations, pay no blackmail, avoid military action if possible, and try to make Lechín lose ground in the upshot." This policy was supported, Bundy explained, by the State and Defense departments, the Joints Chiefs of Staff, and SOUTHCOM, and it contained only a "low" chance that the hostages would be harmed. Military action should not be encouraged, threatened, or executed, he added, because it "greatly increases danger to hostages, [and] is likely to weaken the government and increase danger of civil war." If Johnson rejected this proposal and the hostages were harmed, Bundy warned that "very heavy criticism, both foreign and domestic, would fall on the new Administration."[76] At Bundy's recommendation, Johnson issued a press release on Sunday evening, condemning the "indefensible seizure of four United States officials in Catavi–Siglo XX, Bolivia." The White House statement, which was interpreted in

Bolivia as the prelude to US intervention, offered "full assistance to President Paz in his actions" to secure the hostages' release, "in line with [Johnson's] determination to protect United States citizens everywhere."[77]

Shortly after the White House statement was made public, Henderson held his first meeting with President Paz. The Bolivian president launched into a soliloquy about how the crisis offered his government an "opportunity . . . [to] impose discipline on [the] miners and take agreed measures [to] increase productivity and efficiency." After repeating "several times and with great emphasis" that he was "determined to take all necessary measures to this end," Paz explained that Lechín had been "falling more obviously under communist influence during recent weeks." Paz relished the fact that Lechín was faced with a dilemma, telling Henderson that "he must either release [the] hostages and face hostility from his erstwhile supporters or accept international and national opprobrium for violation [of] criminal law and international code."[78]

When Paz finished, Henderson expressed some hope that "intermediate steps would be followed" prior to military action, and he relayed the miners' federation offer to negotiate. Paz was adamant, however, expressing confidence that the crisis would be over as soon as his government completed phase two the following day. He categorically rejected negotiations with the FSTMB and made no mention of needing US Special Forces.[79] Using the "Roger Channel" for highly sensitive, limited distribution,[80] Henderson sent a separate cable to Secretary Rusk and the White House, reporting his discomfort in being asked to stand up strongly to Paz's proposal for military action against the miners. Conceding that he could not "give assurance beyond reasonable doubt that any repeat any step which is taken [to] bring pressure on the miners [to] effect release of hostages may not result in retaliation on hostages," the US ambassador believed nonetheless that "GOB must be prepared to use [a] combination of measures [to] assure maximum extent possible [the] safety of [the] hostages." Paz had already authorized covert action without consulting the embassy, Henderson explained, expressing his belief that "any attempt by US now to halt or reverse operation could result at best in such confusion as to increase risk of exposure."[81]

On Monday, 9 December, day four of the hostage crisis, commander-in-chief General Alfredo Ovando informed US officials that phase two was well under way. The Viacha-based Max Toledo First Motorized Infantry Division, created with US funds during Paz's first anticommunist crackdown in June 1961, was on its way to the mine region, along with twenty-one men from the First Airborne Infantry Company in Cochabamba and two hundred police officers from La Paz. The remaining members of the First Airborne had begun a road march from Cochabamba to Sucre, where they would join the Third Infantry Regiment and a police detachment and head northward toward Siglo XX. General Ovando then explained that two Indian peasant militia units from highland Cochabamba, consisting of five hundred and one thousand men, planned to block all the roads surrounding the mine and serve as a "rear guard for the Motorized Battalion if committed." The mobilized men—soldiers, Indian peasants, and police—had been instructed to travel with fifteen days' ration, Ovando explained, adding that the armed forces "will draw 5 million rounds [of] 7.65mm ammunition from [the] La Paz arsenal."[82]

In response to the labor reforms called for by Washington's Triangular Plan, Siglo XX miners took their fight to the heart of the Alliance for Progress. By kidnapping four US officials, they courted possible disaster. Despite his previous reluctance to employ uniformed military force against the miners, President Paz saw the presence of US hostages in the Siglo XX mining camp as useful pretense to invade, and his hesitations gave way to steely resolve. The Johnson administration harbored no desire for American martyrs in the name of Bolivia's economic development, however, and US officials strongly resisted Paz Estenssoro's pleas for approval of large-scale military action. Meanwhile, Paz's shows of force only strengthened determination of the miners and their wives to fight to the death, taking their families and the hostages with them.

A Massacre Approaches

The Johnson administration's approach to the hostage crisis was purposely opaque. On the one hand, the White House's press release created fear among the miners that the US military might intervene. At the same time, there were four American lives on the line, greatly diminishing US officials' previously enthusiastic attitude regarding a mine invasion. Throughout the crisis, State Department officials reminded their colleagues that a principal goal of the Alliance for Progress in Bolivia was to force an open break between President Paz and Vice President Lechín. By placing the blame squarely on Lechín and by pressuring his FSTMB to strike a deal with the government leading to the release of the hostages, US officials hoped to save the lives of their colleagues while delivering a political blow to Lechín. This approach was well served by the Bolivian military, which had little desire to follow Paz's orders to invade but every reason to use the crisis to secure ever-higher levels of US military equipment.

Ambassador Henderson recognized that national mine union leaders were more "rational" than Siglo XX's workers and their wives, who were "more willing [to] run serious risks in defiance of the government." In response to Paz's mobilization of the armed forces and Indian militias, Siglo XX interim leader Nicolás López announced to members of the press that the miners boasted alliances with several anti-Paz Indian communities and were "ready to defend ourselves to the last drop of blood."[83] CIA Director John McCone told Johnson that the situation was "extremely dangerous . . . because the miners in this area were notorious, vicious men who ruled with guns and placed a very low value on human life."[84] The CIA reported on Tuesday, day five of the crisis, that the hostages were being kept on the second floor of the Siglo XX union building, "almost directly" above a "large stock of dynamite," which the miners threatened to discharge if the mining camp came under attack.[85] Secretary Rusk warned President Johnson that the crisis was "coming to a head here in the next day or so."[86]

Siglo XX housewife Gerónima Jaldín recalled that inside the union building, rumors of Indian militias and US Special Forces led the women to become "psychologically ill . . . pale." She adds, however, that she "looked around at every single one of my *compañeras*. They may have been pale but they were unwavering. Not a single one wanted out." One of the women suggested that in the event of an attack, they could escape through the union building basement, but the group resolved to wage a counterattack, regardless of the risks it entailed. "We lived in a constant state of nervous tension in there," Gerónima recalled.[87]

One of the Amas, Domitila Barrios, explains that with the military and Indians approaching, the women decided that "we could not leave our children to suffer at the hands of those people" and that "our duty was to die together with our kids." At that moment, Domitila recounts, "We all moved permanently to the union building with our children and husbands, arranging the sticks of dynamite in such a way that, if it were necessary, we could destroy the entire building, ensuring that no one survived—neither us nor the hostages." She explains that they "put dynamite on the tables, around the doors, on the windows, and also on our bodies, our children's bodies, ready to light them in the event of an attack." The Amas de Casa planned to "light the matches and blow everything away," Domitila recalls, adding, "I am sure that if that moment had arrived, we would have carried it through! There was such certainty!"[88]

On Sunday, day three, when Lechín tried to convince the Amas to permit the hostages to go to the Catavi camp and telephone their families, Gerónima responded, "Mr. Lechín, this is not the first time you have tried to set a trap for the working class. . . . Every time the working class is about to win a battle, you always appear trying to make deals, and you have your talks with the government. And our strikes all come to nothing." She added, "This time, you won't succeed. We want to see our union leaders here first. Only then will we let these hostages go." After a fruitless argument, Lechín complained, "How is it that I can get myself across to thousands of workers, but I can't get myself across to these few dozen women here?" With that, Lechín left for La Paz.[89]

With the Bolivian government's ultimatum hours away, US officials turned their sights squarely on Lechín. Ambassador Henderson phoned him to say that "the crime of kidnapping is viewed with horror and repugnance throughout the civilized world" and that Henderson could not believe that a government official "could for one moment lend his office to the countenancing of such a criminal act." Alliance for Progress Administrator Moscoso followed this up with a two-sentence message: "Juan, you know me well as a friend of Bolivia. If anything happens to my countrymen the miners are holding I will have to consider you personally responsible." US labor legend Victor Reuther piled on, cabling Lechín that he was "deeply shocked by . . . this outrageous effort," which was "an affront to all who respect human dignity." Finally, White House Press Secretary Pierre Salinger expressed to Lechín his "sense of dismay and outrage. . . . That you, as acknowledged leader of the mines, have not yet made any effective move to obtain [the hostages'] release is inexplicable to me."[90]

As Tuesday night's deadline approached, US officials desperately tried to identify the Bolivian government's intentions. They were comforted, therefore, when General Barrientos revealed that he had "no knowledge of any planned attack on Siglo XX today." General Ovando echoed his colleague's views at a Tuesday press conference, "categorically den[ying] that there was any truth to any report of proposed attack by military or *campesino* forces in [the] present situation" and stressing, "We have no offensive plans." Defense Minister General Luis Rodríguez Bidegaín interjected that the government had not ruled out acting forcefully against "those who are trying to take possession of the nation for their own capricious interests," and Labor Minister Anibal Aguilar stated flatly, "Our problem is to bring reason to [the] communists of Siglo XX."[91]

General Rodríguez followed up the press conference with a statement that "if miners at Catavi-Siglo XX do not release the hostages within 48 hours," the Paz government would take "subsequent measures" to assume control of the mining camp. He added that "Lechín, as the leader of the miners, must assume sole responsibility for what happens." Meanwhile, a CIA source revealed that Paz was feverishly attempting to negotiate the release of the four Americans, after which he would order the military to attack the mine "even if other hostages continue in detention."[92]

Still stymied in his pursuit of US approval to attack, President Paz asked Ambassador Henderson late Tuesday night whether he "considered a week long enough to exhaust intermediate steps before undertaking direct military action." Henderson responded that he was "opposed to artificial deadlines" but conceded that the "responsibility for a decision with respect to such action must vest entirely in [the] Bolivian government and that only he could take that responsibility." Paz continued to press, asking "how [the] American government and [the] American people would react to a Bolivian government decision to commit the Army to action." Henderson, who two days earlier revealed his sympathy for Paz's push for military action, responded halfheartedly that his role "would always be to insist to [the] Bolivian government that it must do everything in its power to protect the American citizens involved and that this would certainly be the position of the American government." Receiving the last word, Paz complained that "it should be obvious to any objective observer" that he had "very limited alternatives and almost no room for maneuver." He stressed that "his eventual decision must be to attack in force and take the risk that American citizens might be harmed." Paz concluded the meeting by pointing out that his only alternative was to "resign Bolivia to extremist control" and handed Henderson a long list of military equipment he would need.[93]

Paz's laundry list, most of which received a hearty endorsement from the US military group in La Paz, included 200 rockets, 36 mortars, 12,600 mortar rounds, 5,000 hand grenades, 2,000 tear gas grenades, sixteen 75mm recoilless rifles, 500 M-1 rifles and carbines, 650,000 rounds of ammunition, 3,000 winter coats, 3,000 pairs of combat boots, 9 armed airplanes, an armored car, and a howitzer.[94] The inventory was leaked to the US press, however, prompting substantial embarrassment and the requisite denials by US and Bolivian officials. Henderson drafted a dummy cable—meant to be leaked—which read "no assistance required," but to be sure, he cabled Secretary Rusk a third time to assure him that the original request was "still valid."[95]

The flurry of contradictory cables disoriented Secretary Rusk, who told President Johnson on Tuesday afternoon that "there seems to be some confusion in the Bolivian government about whether . . . asking or not . . . the Foreign Minister has told us . . . given us a note saying that they are not asking for anything, but we are studying the shopping list, and we will probably be . . . if the Bolivian government clarifies that it wants it, we'll send them some ammunition and tear gas and a few things of that sort . . . we'll try and keep you informed." Johnson was unfazed by Rusk's stuttering statement, approving the military shipment with a simple "Alright."[96]

By Wednesday, 11 December, day six of the crisis, Paz's inner circle had grown increasingly impatient with Washington's hesitant attitude toward military action. Government Minister Arze Murillo warned Henderson that Lechín's popularity was on the rise, the Siglo XX miners were successfully stalling for time, and rumors of an impending government capitulation abounded. Arze Murillo believed that the miners would never release the hostages, which "form the barrier of protection [the] miners now have against action by the government," and he warned that soon "it may be necessary to risk [the] lives of hostages by conducting military action to take Siglo XX." The "only thing holding up [the] operation," Arze Murillo complained, "is [the] problem of [the] Americans." Henderson continued to demonstrate sympathy for the Bolivian position, and responded that "while [the] embassy understands [the] minister's position and [the] problem of [the] Bolivian government, and has even considered the possibility that armed action to rescue the hostages may be required, our primary interest [at] this time must be [the] welfare of [the] American citizens . . . being held." Once again, Henderson let the Bolivian government have the last word, which Arze Murillo used to explain that Paz would give the miners forty-eight hours to release the hostages, after which the government would "move in with Armed Forces to affect their release, accepting any necessary risks to [the] hostages."[97]

As Henderson met with Arze Murillo, the First Motorized Infantry was moving from Oruro to the Huanuni mining camp, sixty kilometers from Siglo XX. Simultaneously, "forty truckloads" of pro-government Indian militiamen arrived in Oruro from Achacachi, near La Paz, and 1,500 armed Indians prepared to deploy from Ucureña in the Cochabamba Valley. The US Embassy reported that "*campesinos* throughout the nation are mobilized behind [the] Paz government in crisis," and the Indian peasant federation of Potosí declared it had 120,000 militiamen ready to "crush [the] revolutionary outbreak."[98]

Meanwhile, it was becoming clear that Washington's pressure campaign against Lechín was working. Hostage Thomas Martin smuggled a letter out to his wife on Wednesday, reporting that Lechín appeared to have "been real worried the last couple of days."[99] White House Press Secretary Salinger followed up his previous day's cable with a letter, claiming to Lechín that if Kennedy were still alive, "he would tell you what I tell you—that no matter how difficult the problems . . . the course you now pursue cannot possibly do anything but severely endanger the relations between our two countries and set back the spirit of United States and Latin American friendship and cooperation for which President Kennedy fought so hard."[100] Peace Corps director Sargent Shriver and Secretary Rusk followed this up with similarly worded letters, and that afternoon Lechín agreed to accept any mediator to resolve the standoff. [101]

Late Wednesday night, Paz revealed to Henderson that early negotiations with Lechín through the student federation had been fruitful. The Bolivian president offered to permit Escóbar and Pimentel to stand trial and to withdraw military regiments from the mining areas in exchange for the release of the hostages. Paz explained that Lechín rejected the idea of a trial for the two union leaders and further demanded that the military withdraw before the hostages were released. President Paz asked what the US government would think if he were to offer exile for Escóbar and Pimentel, perhaps to Cuba or Russia. Having already received word from Secretary Rusk that the State Department was amenable to this option, Henderson did not hesitate to respond that this "seemed like [a] plausible initiative which might break [the] deadlock."[102]

Despite his opposition to military action, and his previous approval of exile, Rusk responded that the student-mediated talks appeared to represent "substantial GOB surrender to [a] major illegal challenge to its authority with serious danger for US nationals in Bolivia and elsewhere and to [the] Paz government." Rusk conceded, however, that the breakthrough could work, if "followed promptly by vigorous GOB action to establish its authority in [the] mine areas and bring perpetrators to justice." He stressed that the State Department was not opposed to Paz's proposal, but he urged Henderson to request specific details as to the "likely terms of [the] negotiated release, [the] ability [of] GOB [to] withstand immediate political consequences [of] such [an] agreement, [and the] potential danger to widely dispersed US nationals and prospects for GOB disciplinary action thereafter."[103]

On Thursday, 12 December, day seven, Air Force Commanding General Barrientos decided to pay a visit to US Southern Command in Panama. Using the crisis as justification for bypassing normal diplomatic channels, Barrientos explained that he was planning to go to the "highest military authorities" in the

Pentagon in support of Paz Estenssoro's recent request for emergency military equipment. The general revealed that President Paz had already made the "political decision" to accept whatever "local and international repercussions" accompany the "arrival of US assistance for use against the miners," claiming fancifully that a shipment was "vital since [the] miners are as well [as] if not better equipped than [the] government armed forces."[104] Henderson endorsed the Paz-Barrientos request, reporting to the State Department that materiel such as airplanes, helicopters, and army clothing "should be considered not only from [the] viewpoint of long-range military planning, but also with recognition [of the] importance [of] hav[ing] some immediate impact on the present situation, particularly with respect [to the] morale of the armed forces and their consequent support [for the] Paz government."[105] US Southern Command agreed. Despite the fact that the list was "excessive from the point of view of meeting the immediate situation with respect to the hostages," the regional command believed that "in light of the current situation and the long-range requirements for government stability and increased morale, and a continuing pro-US orientation among the Armed Forces . . . certain equipment should be furnished to the Bolivian Armed Forces at an early date."[106]

On the morning of Friday, 13 December, day eight, Deputy Secretary of Defense Roswell Gilpatric phoned President Johnson about the request for military shipments, explaining that "some things we can get off quite quickly, such as hand grenades, field packs, clothing, and some ammunition. Some things, like vehicles, will take longer, but we are getting back to State this afternoon what can be made quickly, either from the Canal Zone . . . or what can be moved from the Z.I. [Interior Zone]. And the word over here is, unless you direct otherwise, to do as much as we can as quickly as we can." President Johnson replied nonchalantly, "Yeah, that's right. That's what I'd do."[107] Hours later, Secretary of Defense McNamara "directed that an impact shipment of military equipment be made immediately to the Bolivian government for use in the present crisis." The Pentagon demurred on the armored car and the howitzer, but an "impact shipment," paid for through Special Group–approved "contingency funds," was loaded onto five C-47s. The first transport carrier landed in La Paz at 5:00 p.m. on Saturday, 14 December,[108] including 3,000 pairs of combat boots, 3,000 winter coats, 3,000 field packs, 1,000 rockets, 2,250 grenades, 300 M-1 carbines, and 730,000 rounds of ammunition.[109]

On Friday evening, Siglo XX's Amas de Casa issued a dramatic call to arms:

Women of the heroic Bolivian nation, sisters of our social class, sisters in daily miseries and hardship; mothers, wives, and daughters who love your peaceful homes; women who aspire for progress and happiness: We call on you to meditate for a moment on the grave situation that confronts in the country, a situation that has been created by this anti-popular government with its atrocities and repression against labor leaders. . . . We have truth and righteousness on our side, and for that reason we send out this fervent call for mobilization in defense of the rights and liberties we obtained by blood in difficult battles.

The communiqué condemned the Paz government, "sold out to US imperialism," for mobilizing the military, and vowed to "fight until the death if that is what this reactionary government obliges us to do."[110]

Their bellicose declaration notwithstanding, the women of Siglo XX began to seek a more sophisticated plan of defense. With rumors of an impending invasion, Gerónima recalls that "I began to experience a nervous tension, and it wasn't just me." Gerónima looked at the other women. "It was 1 or 2 in the morning. Pale. Every one of them was pale." The committee leader was scared and asked the women what was wrong. "We are frightened because word has it the helicopters are arriving. Word has it they are going to take the prisoners out through the window." Gerónima responded, "Well, what do you think the workers are doing outside? They are obviously armed, as well." The women persisted, asking if she wanted a massacre. "No, no. There will be no massacre," Gerónima responded, "and to make sure there will be no massacre, we will finally move into the interior of the mine," taking the US hostages with them.[111]

With Siglo XX appearing to be on the brink of a massacre, frantic moves were under way to resolve the impasse. On Friday morning, Eugene Victor Rifkin, brother of USAID Labor Officer—and hostage—Bernard, received President Paz's permission to visit Escóbar and Pimentel in prison. Playing up the fact that his namesake was the great US socialist icon Eugene Victor Debs, the desperate American attorney struggled to convince them to avert bloodshed by recording a statement and drafting a letter imploring Siglo XX to release the hostages. Relying on *New York Times* columnist Juan de Onís as his interpreter, Eugene Victor held three separate meetings with Escóbar and Pimentel throughout the day. Escóbar was at first unconvinced, and he offered to remain in prison if Pimentel was released. Government Minister Arze Murillo responded with two words: "No deal." At this, Escóbar finally relented, drafting a public letter after midnight which Pimentel promptly signed.[112] It read:

Deeply penetrated . . . by the revolutionary firmness of the Siglo XX and Catavi working class. . . . In the face of the military mobilization, and desiring to avoid a bloody massacre, leaving aside all sectarian attitudes, thinking in the future of the workers of Siglo XX and Catavi . . . we call and we beg for you to teach a lesson to the "barbarians," granting liberty to the hostages. . . . Your sacrifice, *compañeros* miners, is very well regarded among all the patriotic forces of the country, and they realize that there are great troubles facing the working class, with the cancer of divisionism, rising unemployment, all fomented by the government. . . . Allow us to carry the full weight of these injustices on our backs, here in the national penitentiary.[113]

Figure 5. After Siglo XX miners took four US officials hostage in 1963, the Johnson White House sought to leverage the crisis to undercut the power of Vice President Juan Lechín, who was also head of the Bolivian Workers Central and the national miners' federation. Caught between intense international pressure and the intransigent demands of rank-and-file workers, Lechín spent hours in La Paz's San Pedro penitentiary, attempting to convince detained Siglo XX union leaders Federico Escóbar and Irineo Pimentel to implore their union to release the hostages. Photograph courtesy of Luis Antezana Ergueta.

On Saturday morning, with this powerful letter in hand, Eugene Victor and de Onís rushed to see Vice President Lechín, who immediately declared that the FSTMB would accept all of Paz's conditions and begged to take the letter to Siglo XX.[114] The following afternoon, as Pentagon "impact shipments" began landing in La Paz, Lechín broadcast an urgent statement by radio, pleading with Siglo XX to accept the deal and release the hostages "in order to show that the FSTMB has authority."[115]

On Sunday night, 15 December, Lechín arrived at Siglo XX accompanied by US Embassy officer Charles Thomas and archbishop of La Paz Abel Antezana. They met for two hours with the Amas de Casa, who agreed to call a miners' assembly in the morning to discuss the Escóbar-Pimentel letter.[116] On the morning of Monday, 16 December, the union siren called for an assembly, in front of a banner that read, "The Working Class against the Calamity Known as the Alliance for Progress."[117] Lechín dramatically recounts that, as the miners gathered, "warplanes circled low overhead and then disappeared over the horizon."[118] A small group of intransigents close to the union building balcony began to shout, "We are not afraid of the soldiers, let them come and we will beat the tar out of them! . . . If we have to die, let it be now! . . . Death to Paz Estenssoro! . . . Death to the Army!"[119] According to Lechín's account, an old miner then rose to speak, his granddaughter in his arms. "It has been days since my granddaughter has had a drink of milk, because there is none in the commissary. But that's not so important. What's important is that if this assembly decides that we should fight, I will fight even if my granddaughter dies, by bullet or by starvation, and I will die with her." The crowd went wild, and the old miner continued: "I see that we are armed and resolved to die. I have seen many combats in this area. Given my age, I have seen quite a lot. But, what possibility do we have to win this battle and then the war? Don't you think the imperialists will send more troops, more planes? We need to think, *compañeros*. . . . This is the moment to think, because later there won't be time. Emotions are good when you are in combat, but they do not counsel well before the combat."[120]

Lechín writes that this old miner's speech "changed the direction of the assembly." The vice president then got up to speak, explaining that "we will be able to win these battles once we get weapons, but at this point the enemy is better equipped. . . . What we are facing is more a massacre of miners than a battle." Lechín urged that "the hostages must be freed, and we will continue our struggle for the liberation of the two detained union leaders and for the objectives of the Revolution." The most important thing, he explained, was "to save our lives so we can continue the struggle. . . . If there is a massacre, everything will be over." The labor icon concluded his speech by warning that a massacre of workers is just "what the government wants, and we must not play their game at the cost of our lives."[121] At 2:00 p.m., the assembly voted to release the hostages, having received nothing in return.[122]

US Embassy Officer Thomas then escorted Lechín to the neighboring Catavi mining camp, where the less radical union promptly ratified the hostages' rendition. Lechín suddenly disappeared, and Thomas was confused about what came next. Telephoning the Siglo XX union building, Thomas was surprised to hear Tom Martin's voice on the other end of the line. Martin informed Thomas that the Amas de Casa were gone and that they were thinking of fleeing. Frightened, Thomas rushed to the union building, where he witnessed the four hostages climbing into one of the automobiles he had brought from La Paz. The people surrounding them were "far from being hostile." Instead, they "were cheering and trying to shake hands with the hostages." Thomas scrambled to organize a caravan, and the group sped away in a cloud of dust. At the gate of the camp, guards from the miners' militia stopped them and demanded they take the wives of Escóbar and Pimentel with them. Thomas recalls that "this we were very happy to do . . . to help ensure our safe passage." Once Alicia de Escóbar and Bertha de Pimentel were on board, the caravan hightailed to Oruro. According to Thomas, "The rest of the trip was gay . . . without incident."[123]

The women in the Comité de Amas de Casa were "completely destroyed" by this turn of events. "Our spirits were crushed," Domitila recalls, "as if it was our personal defeat, because all of our efforts had failed to achieve their objective."[124] Gerónima recounts that they were furious, protesting to Juan Lechín, "Every time we are one step away from winning the battle, the Miners' Federation, or the Labor Confederation, or our union leaders, always make a deal with the government. How long must this struggle continue?" Depressed and desperate, Gerónima approached members of the Siglo XX militia, asking them to train her in riflery. "Why would you want to learn how to use these rifles?" they responded, explaining to her that they had no ammunition. "What?" Gerónima replied incredulously, "Then how were we going to defend ourselves all those nights?" Laughing, the militiamen responded, "With nothing more than our dynamite!" Gerónima also laughed, but mostly out of anger and sadness. On leaving the union building, Gerónima began to feel pain in her womb and went straight to the hospital. After eleven days and ten nights guarding the hostages, the pregnant committee leader was bedridden for a week. "I almost lost my daughter," she recalls.

Figure 6. Once detained union leaders Escóbar and Pimentel issued a declaration asking their union to "teach the barbarians a lesson" and release the US hostages, Vice President Lechín rushed to the Siglo XX mining camp to seek ratification from the local union. Lechín hinted that US Special Forces were set to invade, and he warned that they were facing a "massacre." Here, rank-and-file workers vie for a chance to speak as truckloads of miner militiamen stand guard. Photograph by Michael Rougier/Time & Life Pictures/Getty Images.

Three months later, Gerónima de Romero, Communist head of the Siglo XX hostage takers, gave birth to a healthy baby girl.[125]

Meanwhile, Washington celebrated. Without abandoning their commitment to the Alliance for Progress labor reforms that gave rise to the crisis, the Johnson administration had nonetheless done everything it could to protect the lives of the US hostages. Modernization required authority, particularly over rebellious communist miners and their assertive wives. Through a complicated game of cat-and-mouse, Johnson officials sought to raise the specter of US military action while they simultaneously restrained Paz from moving forward with a mine invasion. The delicate balancing act culminated in vague threats and "impact shipments" of US military equipment, enough to break the stalemate and ensure the miners' total capitulation. When asked what convinced Siglo XX to back down, Indian militias or the United States, Catavi union leader Crespo is unequivocal: "It was the US."[126]

Ironically, although they never spoke out publicly, the hostages later demonstrated sympathy for the miners. Days after his release, Bernard Rifkin said in a private interview:

> The situation in the mining camps at Catavi and Siglo XX is a terrible one. . . . Sometimes the workers get no more than $4 a month in cash, the rest being in the form of basic foodstuffs. . . . The whole slant of the United States in dealing with this is wrong. . . . [I am] sick and tired of this economist's way of looking at things. . . . What the government is trying to do, with the urging of the United States, is to break the labor movement as it is now. . . . They are trying to break the independence of the labor movement and the miners in particular and to substitute a labor movement controlled by the government. . . . In the face of this, when Pimentel and Escóbar tell the government that it is not going to fire any of the workers there, the workers rally behind them.

Rifkin added that "Lechín is not as black as he is usually pictured" and complained that US economists pushing Alliance for Progress reforms so aggressively "have no conception what it is like to work in a 15,000 foot altitude, digging coal [*sic*: tin]."[127] When asked about his kidnappers, Fergerstrom said: "I have to say that I am really sympathetic to them. I mean, the army had invaded the mines so many times and would have done it again. From their point of view, they had to do something. It is reasonable, even if it is wrong." Fergerstrom added that "it was all very friendly. We played cards with Escóbar's mom and argued politics. Man, did they love Cuba."[128]

Once the hostages had arrived safely in Oruro, Henderson intimated that the Paz government had no intention of releasing Escóbar and Pimentel. Tom Martin became furious, and according to the story he later told a colleague, he declared, "I'm going to go back and turn myself over as hostage again to my friends. These are my friends. They've been betrayed, and I'm not going to be a part of the betrayal." According to the legend, Henderson then turned to Air Attaché Fox and asked, "Colonel, do you have your .45? . . . If this man leaves the room, shoot him!" Martin later told the same colleague: "The miners had justification for taking [us] hostage; it was the only practical way they could deal with the double dealing their union leaders Escóbar and Pimentel had received from the hands of the government."[129]

Alliance for Progress ideologues were in no mood to listen to former hostages suffering from Stockholm syndrome. *Time* magazine wrote disparagingly of Vice President Lechín, "who is part Arab and part Indian," noting that the real authority in the mines "lies in the primitive breasts" of the "dynamite-laden" Amas de Casa. Reporting that "in Bolivia there was talk of helicopter-equipped US Army Special Forces troops standing by in Panama, ready to fly to Bolivia for a lightning rescue," *Time* gave credit to "an angry President Johnson" for having "immediately offered the Bolivian government 'full assistance'—whatever it wanted, including arms and men—to secure the prisoners' release."[130]

Two weeks after the crisis ended, Kennedy National Security Council hold-over Ralph Dungan cabled Henderson to "congratulate you on your excellent performance." Dungan added that he "had a bit of a chuckle—I have a some-what perverted sense of humor—when I learned that the balloon went up shortly after your arrival." Dungan wrote jokingly that the "sequence of events fits my own conception of executive training," explaining that "I belong to the 'push them off the boat' school, and I must say that you landed in deep water." Dungan told Henderson, "You acquitted yourself with great coolness and cour-age and I offer you my sincere congratulations." Dungan closed his note by mentioning that "perhaps what's more important, your performance was noted well and with approbation in another office in this building."[131]

President Johnson was indeed proud of his administration's response to its first foreign policy crisis. When unrest broke out in Panama in the following month, the US president vowed that "we are not going to get slugged around any more than we did in Bolivia when they captured our men and we told 'em, you better get 'em back or, by God, we'll come and get 'em."[132] In a per-sonal letter to Henderson, Johnson praised "the success of your efforts to re-lease the hostages," complimenting him for "behaving courageously."[133]

If the Indian militia surrounding Siglo XX made the miners' blood run cold, rumors that Washington planned to participate in a Bolivian military in-vasion was enough to force their hand. The Alliance for Progress had reached its apogee in Bolivia, with the Paz government finally able to rid its largest tin mine of Communist union leaders and move forward with the Triangular Plan labor reforms. The event also made an indelible mark on the new US president and his Kennedy-appointed ambassador. If the previous administra-tion saw President Paz as a model of authoritarian modernization it sought for Latin America, the incoming administration's support for Paz Estenssoro had been baptized by crisis.

Chapter 5

Seeds of Revolt

The Making of an Antiauthoritarian Front

With strong backing from Washington, President Víctor Paz set about to drag Bolivia toward his vision of modernity. His authoritarian approach to development was fueling the rapid militarization of the Bolivian countryside, and armed force had been unleashed against recalcitrant miners. Depicted by modernizers in La Paz and Washington as obstacles to economic progress, leftists shed the Movimiento Nacionalista Revolucionario (MNR; Revolutionary Nationalist Movement) in droves, and the revolutionary party atrophied into a hollow redoubt of development technocrats and military officers. As Paz Estenssoro began his constitutionally dubious third term,[1] left-wing miners and right-wing guerrillas agitated to bring him down. Alienated by Paz's newfound anticommunism, his authoritarian approach to labor, and his unabashed alliance with the United States, the Bolivian Left had finally been thrust into the awkward embrace of the MNR's eternal right-wing enemies. Through it all, the Johnson administration never wavered from its predecessor's pro-MNR approach, even as Paz faced widespread popular revolt. By mid-1964, the MNR regime operated exclusively at the pleasure of the armed forces, and military-led development threatened to take on a more literal meaning.

Barrientos's Magic Bullet

When an assassin's bullet ended President Kennedy's life, Bolivia's revolutionary leaders were understandably concerned. Víctor Paz had just received a magnanimous reception at the White House, and his supporters worried that the incoming Johnson administration would be less sympathetic. The Bolivians were soon comforted. Far from abandoning President Paz to his multiplying enemies on the right and left, Washington's new leaders only increased US support for Paz's regime. The December 1963 hostage crisis had forged Paz's reputation as an iron-fisted reformer, and a Kennedy-appointed "Alliance for Progress ideologue"[2] further ensured that development and modernization would continue to guide the US Embassy's approach to Bolivia.[3]

For the incoming Johnson administration, the 1963 hostage crisis provided proof positive that Paz was the only man to guide such a chaotic country. According to Ambassador Henderson, "We never really had any problems of deciding whether Johnson was as good a man as Kennedy. . . . We went immediately into this [hostage] issue and the next eleven days we got thoroughly immersed in it."[4] If Johnson's 1964 presidential contender's criticism that "Cuba is gone, Bolivia is going"[5] had any effect on the White House's approach, it was only to further accentuate Washington's unconditional support for the MNR regime. The Bolivians eventually came to realize that Kennedy appointees continued to control US foreign policy toward Bolivia, and Henderson recalls that "the fact that I was named, nominated, and confirmed under Kennedy, [and] that I was reconfirmed under Johnson, was all that they, the Paz government, needed to know." Even Thomas Mann, Johnson's straight-talking appointee as assistant secretary for Latin America, described the Paz regime as so authoritarian that he "had difficulties in distinguishing politically" between it and the Alfredo Stroessner dictatorship in neighboring Paraguay. He meant that as a compliment.[6]

President Johnson showed no signs of reevaluating US foreign policy toward Bolivia. He wrote Paz days after the hostage crisis that he hoped "we can move ahead with renewed vigor on our many cooperative endeavors," expressing his "earnest desire to continue strengthening the Alliance for Progress."[7] With this White House imprimatur, Ambassador Henderson and local CIA officials issued a joint request for an increase in Washington's covert subsidy, first approved during the Irupata violence of mid-1963, to assist President Paz in his drive "to wrest control of labor organizations away from Juan Lechín Oquendo, the [MNR Left Sector], and the PCB [Partido Comunista de Bolivia (Communist Party of Bolivia)]." Before leaving office, Kennedy appointee Assistant Secretary Martin "agreed that an increase in the subsidy was justified," and the 5412 Special Group promptly approved an expanded covert program at its next meeting on 10 March 1964.[8]

By early 1964, Washington's entire foreign policy bureaucracy saw Paz as sufficiently authoritarian to bring about needed economic reforms and secure US political interests. The State Department reported that the regime's willingness to authorize violence against the miners "had shown a readiness to orient its policies more to development needs and take some of the difficult political decisions required to move that primitive economy forward." President Paz had finally taken steps, long advocated by the Kennedy administration, to "quell forces of anarchism in Bolivia, to foster economic stability, and to marshal resources for development." The State Department expressed unquestioned support for Paz's reelection, which would make it "possible to maintain present gains and accelerate the low rate of development" in Bolivia. "The mine management has gained a dominant position in the struggle with communist elements in the mine unions," State pointed out, a favorable position that meant "more efficient management practices can be carried out." Continuing its predecessor's development-oriented bellicosity, the new administration hoped to "encourage and assist [Paz] to continue and expand attacks on major impediments to stability, self-sufficiency, and development."[9]

Like his predecessor, Ben Stephansky, Ambassador Henderson worried that the Paz government continued to have problems "exercising effective control over Bolivian territory." Despite its efforts, the regime had not yet "established authority over the mine areas, nor have the miners accepted the necessity of measures to make COMIBOL [Corporación Minera de Bolivia (Mining Corporation of Bolivia)] break even." Vice President Lechín and his MNR Left Sector were "committed to continued anarchy in Bolivia," Henderson fretted, warning that if Lechín turned to violent subversion, "the Cuban Embassy, Bolivians trained in guerrilla warfare in Cuba, Communists oriented toward the current Red Chinese activist theories, and even some Trotskyites, would be sorely tempted" to follow his lead.[10]

Henderson acknowledged that Paz's military-led paradigm posed a dilemma. If President Paz demurred in his attempt "to establish his authority throughout the country, particularly in the troublesome mine areas where the crucial mine rehabilitation must be carried out . . . he cannot expect a continued flow of substantial foreign aid on which both his development program and the economy of the country depend." On the other hand, if military attempts to "subdue the mine areas . . . [were] not swift and decisive for lack of adequate planning or lack of equipment and materiel, a failure or prolonged conflict could ensue and the military forces badly mauled." Such an outcome would risk "violence and perhaps a coup," Henderson estimated, recommending therefore the Johnson administration continue its predecessor's policy of "supporting the Bolivian military with training and equipment." The military was "deeply concerned for its prestige and popularity," Henderson noted, gauging that the conditions for a coup d'état had not been reached, "nor [are they] likely to be reached in the near future." To maintain military support for Paz, especially in the mines where resistance to Alliance for Progress programs was fierce, Henderson believed that a higher profile for the armed forces, with their "middle-of-the-road orientation, . . . [is] not necessarily an undesirable development."[11]

Happily riding the coattails of this approach was General Barrientos. During the hostage crisis, Barrientos solicited an increase in military assistance, recognizing that Alliance for Progress reforms were "mak[ing] [the] miners enemies of [the] Paz government." Barrientos explained that Vice President Lechín was sure to "create chaos," and he asked for sufficient equipment to ensure that the armed forces were "stronger to act as deterrent forces." In mid-January 1964, General Barrientos once again approached US officials, concerned that Lechín, "strongly supported by the Cuban Embassy," was in the "planning stage [of a] major effort [to] overthrow [the] Government by violence." Requesting that "military equipment previously requested be hastened," Barrientos also recommended that the US Embassy "keep as close an eye on [the] Cuban Embassy as possible." Barrientos further revealed that Lechín was courting military officials for conspiratorial activity, intimating that he too had been subject to such pressure.[12]

Henderson took the Lechín threat as seriously as had Stephansky, warning Washington that the MNR Left Sector was "more militant, better organized and disciplined, and more willing to fight in the streets for their cause" than either Paz's forces or the MNR's eternal right-wing enemies. The MNR Left also boasted huge numbers, something that could hardly be said for the middle-class Falange Socialista Boliviana (FSB; Bolivian Socialist Falange), or even the Communist Party, whose cadres were principally concentrated in the mines and urban labor unions. To avoid a pro-Lechín coup, Henderson asked Washington to provide "technical assistance to review and recommend measures to improve presidential security."[13] On 28 February, Jacob Jackson, the recently arrived public safety officer for the United States Agency for International Development (USAID), dutifully offered Paz's chief of secret police, Claudio San Román, a "list of Preliminary Recommendations which may assist you in your important responsibility of protecting the Chief of State,"[14] and the new CIA station chief began to work with San Román on a "daily basis."[15]

The January 1964 MNR convention would be a test of the new administration's support for Paz Estenssoro. The State Department feared that "violence may flare" at the convention between Lechín's Left Sector and pro-Paz party bureaucrats, since Paz planned to formally expel Lechín from the party, bringing about a fierce struggle "between two mass-based political forces which have long been united." The department expressed concern that "the right opposition parties are inclined to join with the Left Sector, or with any other group challenging the power of the MNR." Ironically, the possibility of a Lechín alliance with the Right worried US policymakers more than any communist conspiracy. State's intelligence arm believed that the PCB and the Cubans would continue to tread lightly, as "both have something to lose . . . and would wish to avoid giving the Bolivian government an excuse" to crack down on their operations.[16]

On 22 January 1964, the Ninth MNR Party Convention began, five days after it had originally been scheduled.[17] The reason for the delay was a growing rift in the governing party over the vice presidential nomination. Developmentalist MNR bureaucrats, known as the *maquinita*, or "little machinery," coalesced around Senate President Federico Fortún, who was apparently so close to the Bolivian president that "when Paz and Fortún enter an empty room, only one man is there—Víctor Paz."[18] Members of the governing party opposed to Paz's iron grip threw their backing to General Barrientos, who also boasted strong support in his native Cochabamba Valley. Accused by the party machinery of "pressuring the convention delegates" in the days leading up to the convention, Barrientos responded with typical populist flair that "the people are defining this situation." He claimed to be heir to the "tradition of valiant officers who opened the revolutionary horizon," and he vowed to "defend the principles of the revolution at whatever cost, including the sacrifice of my own life."[19]

Unmoved by the general's flowery rhetoric, President Paz told Ambassador Henderson later that day that "Barrientos and Lechín are plotting a coup." Paz was confident that Armed Forces Commanding General Ovando would "remain loyal," but Paz feared Barrientos had become "unpredictable."[20] Seeking to outflank this threat, Paz's supporters closed rank, and on 27 January the convention nominated Fortún for vice president. As expected, General Ovando promptly announced that the military would accept the party decision,[21] but civilian protests immediately exploded in Barrientos's native Cochabamba. Thousands of Quechua Indians, who had benefited most from the general's disbursement of civic action funds, amassed at Cochabamba's air base on 31 January. They were joined by hundreds of urban anti-MNR leftists and rightists, who saw Barrientos as a useful thorn in Paz's side. When the general failed to fly over from La Paz to greet the crowd, thousands marched

to Cochabamba's city center, demanding that local pro-Paz local officials resign in favor of Barrientos supporters.[22] By the end of the day, Paz's secret
police had surrendered Cochabamba's municipal and provincial offices to
Barrientos loyalists, and the general announced coquettishly that he was "still
prepared to be the candidate" if Paz chose to reconsider.[23]

Aside from rejecting General Barrientos, the MNR convention also dramatically expelled Vice President Lechín and his massive Left Sector. Lechín
recalls in his memoirs that "since Paz had lost his influence over the MNR
left, over the unions, he convoked an illegal, rigged MNR convention . . .
with one sole purpose: to expel me from the party." At the convention, Paz
loyalists maintained strict control over the speakers' list, relegating Lechín and
his followers to "hisses and boos" as the expulsion resolution was presented.
Shortly afterward, "at the suggestion of the proletarian rank-and-file," Lechín
writes, "those of us who were expelled founded the Partido Revolucionario
de la Izquierda Nacionalista [PRIN; Revolutionary Party of the Nationalist
Left]. . . . The turnout was massive."[24] The State Department fretted that "for
the first time since [the] MNR seized power in 1952, the party faces the prospect of organized opposition on the left."[25]

In the convention's aftermath, Barrientos became a lightning rod for all
those opposed to Paz, both inside and outside the MNR, and Ambassador
Henderson cabled the State Department on 18 February to warn that Paz's
cabinet was in an "ugly mood" and that the president was "threatening resignation" to regain unity.[26] The following morning, newly appointed Assistant
Secretary of State Thomas Mann warned President Johnson that "we've got
problems in Bolivia right now." Mann agreed completely with the Kennedy
administration view that "Paz is the only man there who can hold things together," and he worried that "his whole cabinet is splintering in all directions
because they want to be president four years from now." Surely recalling the
traumatic December hostage crisis, President Johnson exclaimed, "Well, can
we get in there and do something to help him before it all goes to hell?"
Mann responded, implicitly referencing the expanded pro-Paz covert action
plan under discussion, "We were working on that this morning."[27]

Three weeks after the combative convention, Henderson wrote that "there
has been [a] remarkable acceptance [of] our ideas that military are essentially
servants of [the] people and constitutionally subordinated to civilian authority." Henderson was confident that "US military assistance to Bolivia is not, repeat not, increasing [the] danger [of] military takeovers," and he pointed to Paz's
"complimentary" statements regarding "newly developed military strength." The

armed forces were "conscientiously, even enthusiastically, engaged in civic action programs," one of the cornerstones of the Alliance for Progress.[28]

Henderson failed to grasp the extent to which Bolivians—civilians and military officers—were growing weary of Paz's heavy hand. In the aftermath of the bitter MNR convention, Generals Barrientos and Ovando began to attend secret, late-night lodge meetings, where young military officers complained that "the revolution was off track" with "too much Americanization, too much submission."[29] To be sure, the generals were leading no conspiracy. They were merely aware of unrest in the lower ranks, and they "broke hierarchical barriers to establish direct relations"[30] with junior officers, many of whom had begun to view Barrientos as the "tip of the spear that would weaken the power of [Víctor Paz]."[31] Few junior officers had played a role in the 1952 revolution, and many had suffered the worst years of MNR repression during the mid-1950s.[32]

In their desire to keep restless junior officers close, however, Ovando and Barrientos also appeared reluctant to act. Antonio Arguedas, a strongly anti-MNR air force major, recalls that whenever the young officers brought up the idea of a coup, Barrientos responded angrily: "Don't talk to me about that. . . . We are friends, but I will not tolerate that. I am loyal to my party, the MNR, and to its *Jefe*. What you are saying to me is truly absurd. I am not a coup wager. I want to help the *Jefe*, by being in the party leadership." Arguedas went on to say that "Barrientos was in awe of Dr. Paz," and that even after the coup "he continued to call him *Jefe*!"[33]

After passing over Barrientos's vice presidential bid, President Paz ordered the young general to take up a position in the Bolivian Embassy in London. Barrientos accepted, informing the US Embassy that he would pass through Washington on his way to explain to the Pentagon "that [the] political situation in Bolivia is not as serious as it appears."[34] When Barrientos informed a gathering of officials, young and old, of his decision, Arguedas and several other self-proclaimed anti-Paz *ultras*[35] were "indignant." According to Arguedas, they told him "in no uncertain terms . . . that he had made a grave political error . . . that he should have gone in front of the assembly at that moment and launched a coup d'état." Arguedas recalls that "it was at that moment that we proposed to him the [staged] attack."[36]

When Arguedas and another anti-MNR *ultra*, Air Force Colonel Óscar Quiroga Terán, proposed to General Barrientos that they stage an assassination attempt on the general's life, Barrientos was scandalized. "That's just terrible," Arguedas recalls him responding dismissively, "I've already spoken with the *Jefe* and cannot violate party structure . . . you guys can help me when I get back from England." The two young pilots continued to press, however, and according to Arguedas, Barrientos reluctantly accepted.[37]

At 2:00 a.m. the following morning, hours before General Barrientos was set to leave for London, he was apparently shot in the "right side of the chest" while leaving his sister's house in La Paz's middle-class neighborhood of Miraflores.[38] When Bolivian police arrived, they were met only by the general's "bodyguards," Quiroga and Major Hugo Bozo Alcocer, who explained that Barrientos was undergoing treatment at a nearby clinic, Santa Barbara.[39] At Barrientos's bedside was his good friend US Air Attaché Fox, who called Ambassador Henderson around 3:00 a.m. to request an airlift. At 3:30 a.m., Henderson cabled Secretary Rusk, copying the White House, the CIA, and the Joint Chiefs of Staff,[40] and an hour and a half later, the Pentagon's National Military Command Center gave the go-ahead, despite acknowledging that Barrientos's condition was "good."[41] At 8:00 a.m., Barrientos's stretcher was loaded onto a US Air Force C-54 at the El Alto air base, and flown to Gorgas Military Hospital in the Panama Canal Zone.[42]

Arguedas recalls rushing to the airport to see the general off, only to be told that Barrientos refused to see him.[43] What Arguedas did not realize was that General Barrientos had consciously withheld from US officials—including Colonel Fox—the true nature of the attack. Nevertheless, Fox knew the injuries were minor and that "Barrientos really stretched things out."[44] In the days that followed, the general issued a series of press releases regarding his slow, painful recovery, even declaring that he was resigning from the air force "to dedicate himself to politics."[45] As an added embellishment, General Barrientos gave credit for his miraculous survival to a set of US Air Force wings, gifted by Fox, which he was wearing on his lapel.[46]

Hours after Barrientos left for Panama, the young *ultras* convoked an enormous, armed assembly at the air base,[47] characterized by "hot tempers and violent words," according to Ambassador Henderson. Recognizing that anti-Paz officers were on the verge of provoking mutiny, the High Command attempted to regain control of the meeting, proclaiming "in stern terms that any talk of the military seeking revenge . . . would not be tolerated."[48] In subsequent days, junior officer unrest grew, however, and Ovando finally acquiesced to the formation of a commission that would present Paz with an ultimatum: nullify Fortún's vice presidential nomination and replace him with General Barrientos. Heading the commission was former president Hernán Siles, who had recently arrived from his ambassadorship in Spain with the express purpose of opposing Paz's reelection. The commission members were

General Ovando, Defense Minister General Luis Rodríguez, and two *ultras*, Arguedas and Quiroga. On 4 March, the commission set out for Paz's house. As Arguedas recalls, almost as soon as they arrived, Paz declared that Fortún no longer enjoyed his support. Barrientos would be his new running mate.[49]

The next day, Paz told Henderson that he had been "reluctant [to] accept Barrientos, but felt [the] situation had reached [a] point where he had no other alternative but to dump Fortún." General Barrientos was also hesitant to embrace the alliance until Paz explained that rumors of a possible Lechín-Barrientos ticket abounded, making it "necessary for him to make the announcement at once."[50] Meanwhile, Paz praised the general publicly as "a typical representative of the Armed Forces of the National Revolution; that is to say . . . a soldier identified by his actions with the people . . . determined to contribute to the efforts . . . in favor of economic and social development." Paz added ominously that "the armed forces are inseparable from the revolution."[51] Three weeks later, General Barrientos returned to Bolivia a national hero. During his welcome-back tour through the Cochabamba Valley, one could even hear prescient proclamations of "Barrientos, President!"[52]

By March 1964, Paz Estenssoro was surrounded by military men. His party had bitterly expelled leftists, ignored growing civilian opposition, and placed all its authoritarian hopes on technocratic development. In his attempt to marginalize General Barrientos, however, Paz overstepped. As one young anti-MNR officer recalls, after the so-called "Magic Bullet" catapulted Barrientos into the vice presidential nomination, "Paz was obliged to seek backing increasingly in the armed forces in order to guarantee the stability of his government and the very structure of his own party. A general was his running-mate, another general [Eduardo Rivas Ugalde] was Executive Secretary of his party, generals were governors of the main provinces, likewise with the government's ambassadors abroad. And all of the political decisions now required the previous consent of the High Command."[53]

For more than three years, two US administrations had labored to convince Víctor Paz to make a definite break with his party's left wing and to pursue economic modernization through armed force. The January 1964 MNR convention and its aftermath were therefore the culmination of a piecemeal process whereby the development goals of the national revolution were turned over to the Bolivian armed forces. A uniformed circle was closing in on Víctor Paz, and the beleaguered leader could do little but sit by and hope his generals did not take matters into their own hands. Meanwhile, a unanimous alliance of opposition parties would do everything in its power to spark an uprising.

Civilians and Soldiers

As the 31 May 1964 presidential election approached, civilian opposition to the Paz regime began to coalesce into a united front of right-wing and left-wing parties, whose organized electoral abstention eventually received support from Paz's erstwhile MNR allies, Vice President Juan Lechín and former president Hernán Siles Zuazo. The coalition openly courted military officers, hoping they would move before the third Paz government could be consolidated. Through it all, US liberals never wavered in their ideological commitment to President Paz as the key to order and progress in Bolivia, and they viewed any conspiracy against his government as a backslide away from development toward anarchy and leftism.

Recognizing that the Paz government relied completely on the Bolivian military to guard him against conspiratorial activity on the left and right, the Johnson administration continued Kennedy's policy of generous military assistance. On 4 April, National Security Adviser (NSA) Bundy telephoned Johnson, asking him to "say that are you willing to have us determine in your name a million dollars of special assistance to Colombia and Bolivia." Seeking to move matters along, Bundy added that "this is a perfectly routine thing, but I hate to sign something that says you've determined it unless I mention it to you." Johnson was in no mood to dispense rubber stamps, however, and he interjected to say, "I'm sure slow on determining something on *Bolivia*. . . . What are we doing? . . . Why are we doing it?" Bundy began to explain, "training equipment of $150,000 . . . I don't know . . ." before Johnson interrupted. Stung by the December 1963 hostage situation, he began to inquire, "They're not going to use it to arrest our . . ." but Bundy jumped quickly, saying, "No, sir. These are the goodies, not the baddies." Bundy continued by reminding Johnson that "it was Lechín's crowd who arrested our people in the field," adding that "these are the people working against them." With that, Johnson was satisfied, responding, "Alright. Okay. That's good."[54]

Having received White House approval, two weeks later the Special Group (CI) turned its attention to the "problem of incipient or existing terrorist activities in . . . Bolivia." By sending a new shipment of "soft goods" to the Challapata-based Ranger Battalion that would "operate in the strategic Oruro area" near the mining camps, the Special Group aimed to make a "significantly favorable impact on the morale of the armed forces, and . . . make the troops self-sufficient in the field and allow their deployment to isolated areas." The group also considered the "need for an additional rural adviser to help . . .

counterinsurgency programs for [the] sparsely populated jungle areas of Pando, Beni, and eastern Santa Cruz." The Special Group sought to "prevent [the] development [of] eastern Bolivia as [a] highway and safe-haven for Cuban and other communist-trained guerrillas planning terrorist activities in Bolivia, Peru, and possibly other neighboring countries."[55]

Aside from taking steps to secure Bolivia's highland mining region and its remote Amazonian east, the White House resolved to provide Paz with enhanced personal security detail. The Latin American Policy Committee, made up of representatives from the State and Defense departments, the CIA, USAID, and the United States Information Service (USIS), approved a "Contingency Plan" that sought to prepare for the "distinct possibility" that elements within the growing right-left opposition movement would wage an assassination attempt on Paz's life. Concerned that this would pave "the way for Lechín to the presidency . . . the opening wedge for extremist communist domination of the government," the committee recommended that embassy officials find out "whether President Paz had given thought to preventing Lechín from assuming power in the event of an assassination." The group also drafted an action plan, including possible direct military intervention, for implementation if Lechín took power.[56]

At the end of April, Assistant Secretary Mann reported to the Special Group that the Bolivian "political picture has clarified somewhat." Paz's belated selection of Barrientos as his running mate had "strengthened and consolidated armed forces support for President Paz." According to Mann, it also "lessened somewhat the remote possibility that Vice President Lechín and other extremist forces might obtain some armed forces support for a coup d'état." The central threat, Mann reported, was Lechín's attempt to "form a popular front of rightist and leftist opposition parties," and he noted that there was some evidence that the vice president had begun to seek arms and financial support from the Cuban Embassy. Mann believed, nonetheless, that Paz's security services were "capable of controlling any attempt by Lechín-led forces, as presently constituted, to overthrow it."[57]

Julio Sanjinés Goytia, an inactive Bolivian colonel who headed up USAID's civic action program and La Paz's pro-Barrientos newspaper of record *El Diario*, agreed with Mann's estimation of the Lechín threat, but he also informed embassy officials that Barrientos was not squarely behind Paz. Instead, he reported that the general was in "constant communication with Lechín and former President Siles," both of whose criticism of Paz's reelection had begun to radicalize into conspiratorial activity. More important, Barrientos's personal relationship with Paz was deteriorating, as Barrientos sensed that Paz looked down on him, both politically and intellectually. Sanjinés predicted that "President Paz will not last more than a year," and he urged US officials to consider contingencies to Paz's rule. In Sanjinés's view, Lechín was "promising the workers the sun and the moon" and would pose a significant threat should Paz fall from power.[58]

Lechín's presidential campaign took him first to the Cochabamba Valley in early April, where he attempted to mobilize leftist Indian peasant communities behind his candidacy. To snuff out this challenge, Paz dispatched his running mate, Barrientos, who traveled to the region in the company of the MNR national party leader and former minister of peasant affairs, General Eduardo Rivas Ugalde. Since early 1962, the two *Cochabambino* generals had employed generous sums of civic action funds in the valley, and Paz's strategy to block Lechín's ascent therefore met with significant success. On 9 April 1964, the revolution's twelfth anniversary, Cochabamba's Indian federation signed a historic Military-Peasant Pact at the foot of the Agrarian Reform monument at Ucureña. This pact proclaimed Paz Estenssoro as the undisputed father of the revolution, declared communism anathema to Indian peasant values, and vowed to support the armed forces in putting down threats to MNR rule. For Paz, it was a pyrrhic victory. Despite his name appearing at the top of the document, the anticommunist Military-Peasant Pact demonstrated to the Bolivian public the extent to which Paz relied on the good graces of the armed forces, and it served as a powerful vehicle for the continued militarization of the revolution.[59]

Attempting to deliver Lechín a knockout blow, Paz then sent Barrientos into the mining camps. At the Communist-led Huanuni mine, the swashbuckling general called on the miners to "abandon their extremist leadership," prompting a group of pro-Paz workers from a nearby cooperative to attack the massive Huanuni radio station, killing four in the process. Leftist miners from Huanuni and Siglo XX mounted a counterattack, retook the station, and proceeded to sack the police department, government offices, and private homes of MNR members. A group of leftists captured and beat to death the head of Huanuni's pro-Paz faction, Rafael Montenegro, and the remainder of the town's Paz supporters fled for their lives. Lechín rushed to the district, blamed Paz and Barrientos for having fomented the violence, and called on his supporters to "fight to the death against American imperialism and the tyranny of Víctor Paz." He then warned the government that if it employed fraud in the upcoming elections, his supporters would "resort to armed insurrection."[60]

Paz had the military on his side for now, but civilian opposition was marching apace. In January 1964, Wálter Guevara Arze's middle-class Partido

Revolucionario Auténtico (PRA; Authentic Revolutionary Party), which had broken with Paz four years earlier, joined with the MNR's eternal right-wing nemesis, the FSB, and Bolivia's traditional conservative parties to form the "Bolivian Popular Alliance," whose manifesto condemned Paz for using the "spurious" 1961 constitution to wage an "indescribable attack against the State charter, a reckless challenge against the Bolivian people, in order to submit them to a regime of the Trujillo mold." The alliance's declaration called Paz's reelection bid a "monstrous infraction of basic law," inviting the Left to join their call for electoral abstention. Finally, the Bolivian Popular Alliance vowed to use "any means necessary . . . to prevent the carrying out of this crime against the Homeland."[61]

The national university student federation was the first to join the rightist parties. Led by anti-MNR Falangist Guido Strauss, the federation also boasted strong Communist representation, mirroring the growing coalition against Paz's reelection. "We were enemies of the Communist Party," recalled one FSB student leader, "but early in 1964 we began working together to put forth a stronger, more united front."[62] On 29 January, the student front declared that "re-election violates the spirit of the Republic and is an attack against the most elemental and basic democratic norms."[63] They later added that the Paz government had "failed miserably in its attempt to reestablish the principle of authority in the Nation," adding that "this waning principle of authority has only served in practice to unload responsibility for its failure on the suffering backs of the working people through a political system of terror and intimidation." In the view of the student federation, "this policy, executed slavishly by Dr. Paz, places the country in a situation of full submission to foreign interests."[64]

Leftist political parties were not far behind the rightist and leftist students, and Lechín's newly organized PRIN declared in late February that "the impending dictatorship in Bolivia has not only violated democratic practices, but it has also nullified constitutional liberties using terror and violence as instruments of political struggle." The Cochabamba-based anti-MNR Marxist Partido de la Izquierda Revolucionaria (PIR; Revolutionary Left Party) also acceded to the coalition, denouncing Paz for attempting to "perpetrate in Bolivia a dictatorship that denies the most basic rights" and accusing him of seeking to "consolidate in the country a regime of persecution, terror, starvation, [and] unemployment." In its communiqué opposing reelection, the PCB's regional committee in the mining province of Potosí argued that "the main benefactor of this maneuver is Yankee imperialism, because US monopolies encourage Paz Estenssoro's cult of personality and his dictatorial policies." Predicting that "the Yankee embassy will continue supporting him, as long as they believe he has control," the Communist miners warned that "as soon as they believe he is weak, they will turn their back on him, as that is how the devil pays its servants."[65]

Noting a deafening silence on the part of the Communist Party's national organization, Ambassador Henderson estimated that the PCB leadership had little desire to see Paz fall from power. "Bolivia would not be much of a prize," the ambassador explained, "and a take-over attempt might further alarm Chile, Peru, and Argentina, which are more attractive targets." For this reason, the PCB believed that Bolivian territory was more valuable as a "safe-haven and transit area . . . a point from which to attack those countries." The party hierarchy recognized that "it would be against Communist interests to turn Bolivia into an actively anticommunist state," even if it desired nonetheless to frustrate political stability under Paz's MNR, which would "make their clandestine efforts more difficult." As a result, the PCB leadership sought to encourage Lechín and other leftists whose activities "create discord and chaos, but not to challenge the government too openly or go too far and above all [to] avoid a government crack-down." Henderson believed that Paz recognized this and was therefore basing his tolerant attitude toward the PCB and continued diplomatic relations with Cuba on a "sound instinct for survival."[66]

Many in the Communist rank-and-file, especially in the mining camps, were livid that their party refused to join the anti-Paz alliance. As the US Embassy reported, PCB dissidents argued that "the party should unite with all groups, right and left, to destroy the Paz government, the symbol of imperialism."[67] At the party's Second National Conference in early April, dissident Communists accused the PCB hierarchy of acting as "agents of Paz Estenssoro" and "converting the Party into a parasite of the MNR,"[68] and they began to consider forming a schismatic party along the Maoist Chinese line in favor of armed struggle. During party elections, the anti-Paz faction nominated several mine union leaders, including the head of the hostage-taking Amas de Casa, Norberta de Aguilar, and they proposed imprisoned Siglo XX union leader Federico Escóbar as first secretary. These moves were repeatedly stymied by the party leadership, whom the dissidents condemned as blindly interpreting Moscow's calls for peaceful coexistence as a reason to tolerate Paz Estenssoro. The dissidents left the party conference with a "very profound sense of frustration" and vowed to independently continue the fight against Paz.[69]

Among the many civilians agitating for Paz's downfall, former president Hernán Siles soon became known as the chief conspirator who favored a military solution. Siles's subversive maneuvers drew Washington's wrath, and Henderson complained that Siles was taking advantage of "widespread apathy, the dissidence created within the party by the nominating process, [and] the ineptitude of men like Barrientos . . . who do not recognize Siles is using them as pawns." According to Henderson, Siles hoped to "foment doubt in the ability of Paz to dominate the situation" in the belief that the MNR rank-and-file would abandon Paz "if they thought he is losing the fight to remain in power." By encouraging "chaos and discord," Siles desired to create conditions in which "the military would be forced to take over and would probably look for a civilian leader to head their regime." Henderson doubted that Barrientos had the political skill to depose Paz, however, and believed that if Siles succeeded in "coax[ing] Barrientos into backing a plot," the upheaval would probably result in a military junta led by General Ovando, who was more "capable of navigating Bolivia's Arab-like political world." Ovando would likely frustrate Siles's plans, Henderson added, since he "has sufficient stature and intelligence to achieve and maintain the presidency even as a 'civilian.'"[70]

With three of the four original MNR leaders—Lechín, Siles, and Guevara Arze—agitating for the military to depose President Paz, the right-wing Popular Alliance officially announced that it would follow a policy of organized electoral abstention. The rightists called on all those opposed to the Paz government to "begin an immediate campaign of vigorous civil disobedience which will make the government's electoral machinery impossible."[71] Lechín—still officially vice president—committed his PRIN to the abstention on 23 May, announcing that he was going on a hunger strike against Paz's reelection, and he even challenged Paz to a duel.[72] Lechín was closely followed by Siles,[73] and on the following day, the PCB became the last party to join the abstention.[74] In the face of this astonishingly universal rejection, Paz responded belligerently, "If the opposition takes to the streets, we will be there to meet them."[75]

In the midst of widespread opposition to Paz's reelection, Henderson averred that "a possible Barrientos threat is potentially serious." On 6 May, Henderson reported that embassy officials had "taken every opportunity [to] dispel any belief among Bolivian politicians that [the] USG [US Government] is encouraging military coups or would favor a 'constitutional military coup' that might be possible when Barrientos is Vice President." Sensing a "deep distrust" between Barrientos and Paz, Henderson worried that the general's incessant criticism of the governing party's bureaucratization had succeeded in forming a bloc within the MNR that would oppose the party's "professional politicians . . . [and] support [the] use [of] Barrientos" to foment a military coup.[76]

The following day, Bolivian commander-in-chief General Ovando privately warned Henderson and General Andrew O'Meara, head of US Southern

Command, that Barrientos remained a "possible source of future trouble." Characterizing the young officer as "impulsive and unpredictable," Ovando assured US officials that "if things came to [a] showdown between Paz and Barrientos, Paz could count on [him]." He nonetheless warned that Paz would continue facing unrest, because he was "violating a Bolivian tradition against re-election . . . [and] turning against the extreme left." General Ovando added that Paz was aware of ongoing discussions between Lechín and the Cuban Embassy but that he would "not take action against Cuba soon for fear of turning the left even more against him."[77]

Ovando predicted that during and after the elections, Lechín—with the cooperation of Siles and perhaps Guevara Arze—would try to "draw the armed forces away from La Paz to the mine areas" before proceeding to "mount an attack in La Paz using the labor unions who support him." Ovando reported that he was building up forces in Oruro and in the capital "in order to meet a combined threat from the mine areas and in La Paz." He also began to feel out US officials regarding a preventative coup d'état. Making reference to the Chilean presidential campaign, where Socialist Salvador Allende was making gains, General Ovando asked what Washington would think of a "military takeover in Chile to prevent Allende from assuming power." Henderson responded that this would be a "matter for the Chilean people to decide." Ovando asked the same question in reference to Lechín, receiving the same response.[78]

With the armed forces under growing civilian pressure to remove Paz from office, Henderson provided Washington with a thorough analysis of what he called the "Barrientos threat," beginning by expressing his belief that "Paz and Barrientos are an unequal match." Warning that General Barrientos "injects a new, and in many ways disturbing note into Bolivian politics," Henderson wrote that the general's "unpredictability, egocentricism, ambition, and naiveté are only partly offset by his (present) willingness to listen to US advice." In listing Barrientos's positive qualities, Henderson pointed to his history of praising "the Alliance for Progress, US objectives in Bolivia, and free world ideas." Henderson added that he was "friendly to American officials in Bolivia, and is quick to see how our objectives are useful to Bolivia (and, incidentally, to his own interests)," and he gave Barrientos credit for being "lucky, and usually land[ing] on his feet despite his occasional ineptness or adversity." Finally, Henderson conceded that Barrientos had a "good sense of public relations," and that his speeches, while "usually fatuous, prolix, and sparse in content, move the humble people to whom they are addressed."[79]

On the other hand, Henderson was harshly critical of Barrientos for lacking "the capacity to handle the deviousness, immorality, and byzantine complexity of Bolivian politics." Noting that Barrientos "distrusts all professional politicians," Henderson was concerned therefore that he was "unable to elicit their support." General Barrientos's poor intellect also made him "easy putty to amateur politicians, self-seekers, and opportunists, probably including communists, who use his name or use him for their own purposes." Henderson noted that the general's "egocentricism" caused him to be "apparently incapable of believing that anyone who professes admiration or support could be other than sincere." When US officials criticized Barrientos for maintaining close contact with anti-Paz leftists, especially in Cochabamba, he responded that they were just Marxists who happened to like his speeches. Barrientos even claimed to have "converted" one leftist, Víctor Zannier, who had given refuge to Cuban-trained Peruvian guerrillas in 1963. After viewing Washington's file on Zannier, Barrientos appeared scandalized, replying, "Zannier could not be a communist . . . he intends to become a Trappist monk!" Henderson later joked wryly that Barrientos had even "from time to time unconsciously parroted a communist line to US officials, apparently quoting from some source close to him."[80]

One of Barrientos's Communist confidants conceded that

> many communists, inside and outside the party, wanted to use Barrientos. It was really a thing of friendship. We simply wanted to have influence in his government. Barrientos asked us questions about technical matters. I felt like an advisor, explaining to him the country's problems, especially in the mining industry. Arguedas and Zannier were dying for Barrientos to take power. But in the end, he ended up using them instead of the other way around. Barrientos might have been a simple man, but he was very perceptive.[81]

Henderson was concerned that the general's lack of sophistication made him "an attractive target for this type of communist feeding," and even suggested that Barrientos was "capable of playing a double game with us in the innocent belief that he is being Machiavellian." There was the possibility that Barrientos would "deceive himself into thinking he should risk a 'constitutional military coup' as being in Bolivia's best interest," Henderson continued, stressing, however, that Barrientos was "not foresighted enough nor coldly calculating enough to estimate his chances accurately." If Barrientos took the subversive route, Henderson estimated that "he would have limited civilian and military support" and predicted that "his tenure, if he won, would probably be brief." Expressing his belief that Washington's "best hope" remained Paz, who could "work effectively for our objectives," Henderson recommended that US officials "maintain closest possible relations with Barrientos" to discourage him from engaging in "rash adventures."[82]

Paz Estenssoro was also disdainful toward Barrientos, an attitude that did little to discourage the general's flirtations with the opposition. COMIBOL President Bedregal recalls running into Barrientos waiting patiently in the anteroom of Paz's office in May 1964. When the president sent word through his secretary that he wanted to see Bedregal first, Barrientos's "face appeared distraught with clear signs of degradation." Once inside Paz's office, Bedregal mentioned that the vice presidential candidate was waiting outside, to which Paz replied, "Don't worry, Guillermo, let him wait. Aside from flying his planes and parachute jumping, he doesn't have much work to do."[83]

This treatment was commonplace. Despite harboring an almost devotional respect for Paz, Barrientos was repaid with little more than intellectual disdain. Paz referred without exception to Barrientos as "my cadet," and barely hid his feelings of superiority.[84] According to one Barrientos confidant, Paz believed the general was "of such a low political level that he denigrated the party."[85] Ambassador Henderson later recalled, however, that Barrientos "sandbagged a lot of people who thought he was a clown. They underestimated him and he played up to their underestimation of him. And in a way, he sandbagged Paz, too."[86]

In a meeting with Henderson on 13 May, Barrientos warned that the way in which "Paz has treated Barrientos" was leading to increasing anger in Cochabamba, especially among the region's Indian peasantry. Explaining that the Indians were "ripe for insurgency against Paz," Barrientos added that junior officers were becoming "frantic." Seeking US backing for a coup, Barrientos stressed that he was the only political force that could control the Indians and the military, thereby "keep[ing] them out of the hands of Siles and Lechín." Barrientos complained at length about Paz's attitude of "disloyalty" to him, and he stressed to Henderson that his aim was to continue and deepen the development-oriented "constructive revolution" already under way. Profoundly unsympathetic, Henderson promptly reported to Washington that Barrientos's "unpredictable nature will . . . continue to pose a potential threat to Bolivia's political stability."[87]

General Ovando approached US officials the following day to express his "deep concern" that Barrientos had entered into a conspiracy with Siles and Lechín. Characterizing this as "not healthy," Ovando said Barrientos's "sour grapes attitude" toward Paz had encouraged unrest among Cochabamba military regiments, and he warned of a "possible split between his units there and in La Paz." According to the Ovando, Barrientos was "headstrong, unpredictable, and fighting President Paz rather than cooperating as running mate." At Ovando's request, and with Henderson's approval, US Air Attaché Fox was dispatched to Cochabamba on a mission to bring his friend Barrientos back in line.[88]

Once in Cochabamba, Colonel Fox realized that Ovando's concerns were justified. Fox encountered "considerable unrest among the army officers there," and he believed that the city's anti-MNR rightist and leftist politicians were attempting to use local regiments as a "political football with [the] concerted effort of turning them against Paz and the government of Bolivia." Fox succeeded in convincing Barrientos to return briefly to La Paz, where the general met with President Paz and vowed to cease conspiring with Siles and Lechín. Barrientos also agreed to work closely with General Ovando in a "re-orientation" of the Cochabamba regiments "toward [the] necessity of maintain[ing] [the] unification of [the] Bolivian Armed Forces." Before the two generals departed for Cochabamba, Fox warned Henderson that Ovando would meet with limited success unless he could count on the full acquiescence of Barrientos, whom he characterized as "all powerful" in the area.[89]

Four days after Ovando and Barrientos "re-oriented" Cochabamba's regiments, Barrientos sent an urgent message asking for Fox to return. With Henderson's approval, Fox flew to the Cochabamba air base on 17 May, where he encountered a "very worried" Barrientos. The general asked his friend Fox how he had found out about "it." Having no idea what Barrientos meant, Fox replied nonetheless, "René, you know that I know all that goes on here." Barrientos responded, "Yes, Ed, we know that you know our situation very well, but this is top secret, and the officers here in Cochabamba are frightened and feel that you or your ambassador . . . told the President about our plan to overthrow the government on the 20th of this month." Fox assured Barrientos that neither he nor Henderson had mentioned anything to Paz, suggesting that the information had been passed by some other source, possibly Ovando. Barrientos wanted to know how Fox found out about the plot, to which Fox responded that he had suspected something during his previous week's visit, adding that Ovando likely felt the same way. Barrientos explained that Ovando's visit had played a major role in "settling down the troops and stopping the proposed coup," and he thanked Fox for his "guidance and support." In closing, Fox said that while he was "not about to get into Bolivian politics," Barrientos should "use his head for something other than a hat rack." Barrientos agreed and vowed to "get with the program . . . [and] positively support Paz."[90]

That evening, exactly two weeks before the Bolivian elections, Fox accompanied Barrientos to a meeting of "approximately 500 leading Cochabamba citizens," which he characterized as "without a doubt pro-Barrientos and anti-Paz." When Barrientos revealed his decision to support Paz loyally in the upcoming elections, the anti-MNR crowd screamed angrily, "Paz, no! . . . Only Barrientos can do it!" Fox reported that Barrientos "stuck to his guns and insisted that if the people were his friends they must do as he asks and support Paz for the presidency." After the meeting, Fox expressed concern that "the hysterical crowd looked upon him as a wonder-boy who will solve all their problems at the stroke of a wand." Warning Barrientos that the "myriad problems in Bolivia were very real and complex," Fox asked Barrientos to "appreciate the difficult task that President Paz has had with these very same problems." Barrientos agreed, admitting that his supporters in Cochabamba would be "crying for his head when he cannot solve their problems overnight." He then left to join Paz on the campaign trail.[91]

Three days before the 31 May elections, the White House received a State Department policy statement praising Paz for having taken the Bolivian revolution into "its new, 'constructive,' development phase." Warning that tensions had "intensified" between Paz and former MNR colleagues Lechín, Siles, and Guevara Arze, however, the department worried that matters were reaching a "breaking point." State recognized that the MNR Left Sector had been pushed into opposition by "United States pressure on the government to carry out reforms in the state-owned mines" and worried that Barrientos had been "involved in a plot to overthrow Paz earlier this month." The department felt confident nonetheless that the High Command was "loyal and able to control sporadic violence by the opposition as well as any further attempts by Barrientos or Siles to use middle and junior officers to advance their personal ambition." Stressing that "Paz seems committed to Bolivia's economic and social development under the Alliance for Progress," State believed that his reelection would mean that "our aid policy should be able to show dramatic results in the near future, and forces of political instability will be weakened."[92] Ambassador Henderson agreed, reporting that "Paz's headaches are rapidly disappearing," with Barrientos "no longer causing trouble and Siles evidently impotent."[93]

The Kennedy and Johnson administrations both went to great lengths to ensure that Víctor Paz ran for reelection in 1964. As an authoritarian modernizer, Paz appeared the model Latin American leader to bring the Alliance for Progress to chaotic Bolivia. As political opposition to his government coalesced into a united, conspiratorial movement, US liberals only redoubled support for their beleaguered ally. At no point did Washington consider a coup to be in its best interest, and its officials repeatedly rebuffed conspiratorial entreaties by Bolivian military officers. Paz's MNR represented pro-US stability and progress in one of the most complex countries in the hemisphere, and the Johnson administration had no sympathy for those who wished to open a Pandora's box. With opposition parties taking an increasingly insurrectional posture, however, it was far from certain how much longer Paz's generals would resist the temptation to act.

Communist Miners and Right-Wing Guerrillas

By late May, US officials believed they had headed off the Barrientos threat. Unbothered that all seven opposition parties boycotted the election, the Johnson administration proceeded to offer its full backing as Paz sought to consolidate his third term. His obstacles were significant. The mines had been converted into autonomous soviets, and right-wing guerrillas launched an impressive insurgency in the jungles of Santa Cruz. Through it all, US support for President Paz never wavered. Despite signs that the Bolivian military was growing weary of serving an armed wing of the governing party, Johnson officials adhered strictly to the pro-MNR foreign policy set out by the Kennedy administration. US liberals continued to believe that Paz's authoritarianism remained the key to Bolivia's modernization under the Alliance for Progress.

In mid-1964, civilians were Paz Estenssoro's main threats. When Barrientos informed Siles on 22 May that he was planning to "support Paz and serve as his loyal vice president," Siles responded angrily that Barrientos would "therefore fall along with Paz." The former Bolivian president then declared his support for electoral abstention and joined Lechín in a hunger strike at Oruro's San José mining camp, demanding Paz's resignation. Just as Commander-in-Chief Ovando had predicted the week before, Lechín and Siles planned to foment unrest among the leftist miners, draw the armed forces away from the capital, and then encourage the urban unions and the right-left student alliance to create revolutionary conditions in La Paz. Ovando meanwhile assured US Embassy officials that he doubted the capacity of Siles and Lechín to "rouse adequate enthusiasm for a massive attack on the capital."[94]

As expected, the miners' federation called a nationwide strike on 30 May "in protest against the re-election of Paz," and eight thousand antigovernment miners marched through the streets of Oruro. Meanwhile in La Paz, rightist and leftist university students barricaded the capital's main thorough-fare, announcing they were joining the hunger strike, and two thousand young Falangists marched through the streets, shouting, "Down with Yankee Imperialism!" Responding to accusations of communism, the rightists re-sponded angrily that "the people of Cuba are suffering from the money of the Soviet Union, and the people of Bolivia are suffering from the money of the United States."[95]

Boasting to Ambassador Henderson that he was "probably [the] only presidential candidate to campaign on [the] principles of [the] Alliance for Progress," President Paz was reelected on 31 May in the face of what the em-bassy conceded was "widespread abstentionism in a climate of tension."[96] White House aide Robert Sayre told NSA Bundy that "the only ballots avail-able were the pink ones of the MNR."[97] In the mines, workers "stymied the presidential election . . . by burning MNR ballots publicly, beating up elec-tion officials, and taking hostages," eventually declaring the mining camps "free territories." Henderson fretted that throughout the mining camps there were "no civil authorities."[98] The university students followed suit, declaring their campuses "free territory for all those seeking liberty."[99]

At its first meeting, Paz's cabinet considered the combined threats facing its government. The Bolivian president opened by expressing his desire that Government Minister Fellman take measures "against any disturbance of public order or attack on legal norms," including the "erection of roadblocks on public thoroughfares, destruction of property, or the declaring of free ter-ritories outside the authority of the State." Education Minister Ciro Humbolt agreed with Paz's hard line, explaining that "to avoid anarchy and maintain State authority, energetic measures must be taken." COMIBOL President Bedregal agreed, complaining that "the persistence of Siles and Lechín in the opposition is proof that they seek an insurrection and wish to take advantage of the government's laxity." In Bedregal's view, an "action plan is needed, because excessive tolerance is counterproductive and interpreted as govern-mental weakness." Fellman offered a word of caution, revealing that he was only willing to use "legal recourses and employ ordinary justice," and he urged the rest of the cabinet to avoid "acting against persons in their capacity as politicians . . . [or] taking union leaders prisoner." Vice President-Elect Barrientos agreed with Fellman. Revealing threateningly that Siles and Lechín had offered him the presidency if he launched a coup, Barrientos explained that his refusal, and that of his fellow officers, demonstrated the military's "proven loyalty, its decision not to go against its conscience, and the fact that its position is clearly defined by service to the Homeland and to the National Revolution."[100]

President Paz's principal enemies might have been the miners, but the immediate threat was a right-wing guerrilla effort that broke out in Santa Cruz's Alto Paraguá River region in late May.[101] CIA Agent Nicolas Leondiris (or "Sternfield's assistant," as San Román called him) had arrived in La Paz under the cover of a USAID public safety officer earlier in the year. Leondiris was first tasked with aiding San Román's secret police,[102] but when the right-wing guerrillas began their campaign, he was sent to train Bolivian police units in counterinsurgency, in the company of USAID's chief public safety adviser in Bolivia, Jacob Jackson.[103] Meanwhile, USAID began working on a "shift of SA [Security Assistance] and contingency funds between Bolivia and Vietnam," a move that was "not expected to take much longer."[104]

Washington had poor intelligence on the Paraguá guerrillas, and the Bolivian government had little trouble stoking fears that the group was Communist inspired. Paz Estenssoro's ruse was enabled by the fact that one of the guerrilla leaders, Carlos Valverde, indeed had a Communist past. By the early 1960s, however, Valverde had renounced his previous leftism, joining the right-wing Falange. Meanwhile, the principal organizer of the movement was lifelong Falangist Luis Mayser Ardaya, a wealthy young rancher with extensive holdings in the Paraguá region along Bolivia's northeastern border with Brazil.[105]

Valverde later wrote that "our guerrilla struggle had no relationship with communist guerrillas." In his view, the campaign had one hope: that "the people would follow our example and rise up against the dictatorship." Valverde and the other guerrillas also "believed that members of the army—which had been transformed into an armed wing of the MNR party and were being mistreated—would also follow us." The Falangists were certain that "honorable soldiers remained who would respond and support us in our struggle."[106] Guerrilla leader Óscar Bello echoes Valverde's views, explaining that "there was nothing communist about Valverde. Maybe when he was young. But at that point, no." Bello adds that in the weeks leading up to their campaign, "there was talk everywhere in Santa Cruz about a guerrilla," and he, Valverde, and Mayser all contend that the FSB coordinated the outbreak with Barrientos and Ovando.[107] According to Bello, Barrientos said in one of these meetings, "You start it, I'll finish it." When the Falangists asked, "How can we be so sure?" Barrientos responded, "Assurance arises out of action." Bello recalled, "With that, we believed him."[108]

Mayser later laughed that "the Americans thought guerrilla warfare was a tactic only used by Marxists." He conceded nonetheless that "the incorporation of Valverde in our ranks gave rise to accusations that were believed."[109]

Indeed, Ambassador Henderson wrote in late June that Valverde, "reportedly Cuban-trained, was the leader of one band." A few days later, Henderson again errantly reported that Valverde was a "member of the Bolivian Communist Party." With the Bolivian government laboring to paint the guerrillas red and later claiming they were merely a "gang of about 50 cattle rustlers and horse thieves,"[110] Ambassador Henderson threw up his hands, reporting on 3 August that the "precise political character of [the] guerrillas [was] unknown." He noted, however, that for many Bolivians, Mayser appeared to be a "type of Robin Hood, struggling against government injustice." Henderson warned that the group was "apparently well-armed and well-disciplined."[111]

After the guerrillas captured several sleepy Amazonian villages north of San Ignacio de Velasco in late May, Mayser disappeared on horseback to Brazil, leaving the rest of the column at his hacienda in San Simón. After a few days, a splinter group led by Valverde set its sights on the remote headquarters of the Fifth Army Division in Roboré, four hundred kilometers east of Santa Cruz. Mayser and Bello had been strongly opposed to Valverde's adventure, but many guerrillas were eager. "They wanted to take the garrison right then and there!" Bello recalls.[112] Valverde writes that "the seizure of Roboré was planned . . . to take advantage of the fact that the majority of the youth in Roboré were Falangists, especially those who had presented themselves for military service." Once they reached the outskirts of the town, Valverde's group set up a safe house and made contact with a group of sympathetic young conscriptees. He told them that "their mission on the night of the assault was to lock the [other] soldiers in their barracks with padlocks and open the doors of the garrison to the Falangist guerrillas." Meanwhile, the guerrillas met with an FSB sympathizer, Lieutenant Francisco Monroy, who agreed to disarm his fellow officers and secure the garrison's command headquarters. Once the guerrillas raided the armory, they would have control of the garrison.[113]

On 31 June, the guerrillas returned to their safe house to sleep. The attack would begin the following night. Monroy demurred, and, concerned that he might be responsible for any bloodshed, he notified superior officers. Valverde writes that "at dawn on D-Day, the army surrounded our safe-house and officers entered to arrest us." Once detained, the guerrillas immediately began to plot their escape. Their first plan was to take turns urinating on the wall of their cell and digging a hole with metal spoons. On hearing the racket, one of the officers told them, "You can keep digging, but if you try to sneak out through a hole in the wall, the guards will shoot. . . . Death before escape!"[114]

Two days later, the military permitted journalists to interview the prisoners, and Valverde denounced "the unfortunate error of the United States government, which is setting up and maintaining a counterinsurgency school in our country, as if only communists can be insurgents."[115] FSB leader Mario Gutiérrez ominously declared, from an undisclosed location in southern Santa Cruz, that additional guerrillas remained in Alto Paraguá, adding that they had been ordered to "continue [the] struggle."[116]

After a week at Roboré, the prisoners were transferred to the main civilian jail in the city of Santa Cruz,[117] where they continued to plot their escape with the help of sympathetic *Cruceño* citizens, of which there was no shortage. "The plan was simple, but dangerous," Valverde recalls. "Two rented jeeps were needed . . . and arms had to be smuggled into the jail . . . for our defense and to open a way out for us if needed." From their many visitors, the guerrillas chose a group of young, dedicated Falangists who would organize an assault on the jail. Several revolvers were passed to the prisoners by sympathetic citizens, and on 29 July the assault began. When local Falangists sped up to the jail in two jeeps, police resisted. The assault team shot back, fatally wounding two officers. Meanwhile, the prisoners shot out their locks with the smuggled revolvers, and in a dramatic firefight they made their way to the jeeps. Valverde writes that "the escape lasted no longer than four minutes." Driving through the night, the guerrillas set off in the direction of Mayser's ranch at San Simón.[118]

During the monthlong confinement of Valverde's group, Mayser had returned from Brazil, and the San Simón guerrillas were once again operating in Alto Paraguá. US counterinsurgency efforts were also in high gear. Moving parallel to Valverde's group of escapees was a twenty-five-man Bolivian police contingent, accompanied by CIA Agent Leondiris and USAID Public Safety Officer Jackson. According to Leondiris's subsequent report, they set off northward in two jeeps from San Ignacio de Velasco at daybreak on 2 August, entering the Alto Paraguá at "about 7:30." As they approached the village of San Ramón, which "appeared deserted," the contingent read graffiti on the huts proclaiming, "Long live the FSB!" and "Down with the MNR!" According to Leondiris, "one man was seen running and was fired upon." A few minutes later, "both vehicles [were] ambushed almost simultaneously." Jackson's jeep was "shot to pieces," leaving him "wounded at first fire." After the ambush, in which one Bolivian officer died and five were wounded, the embattled contingent managed to regroup and "march north some 17 kilometers." There they stumbled on the village of Villa Nueva, cleared a field large enough to land a police Cessna, and evacuated Jackson and the wounded Bolivians.[119] The following day, Jackson was airlifted from La Paz to the Panama Canal Zone. He had been paralyzed by a "small caliber slug that entered his back around the

10th vertebrae." Ambassador Henderson reported that Jackson's "prognosis regarding paralysis [is] grave."[120] It was. Jackson would never walk again.[121]

In his report, Jackson explained that the "discipline of [the] attackers [was] impressive, as was their ability to hit and run and to use local terrain to their advantages." He believed reports that the guerrillas were native to the area and "exclusively FSB members." Meanwhile, Leondiris collected shell casings that demonstrated the guerrillas wielded a "heterogeneous collection of old weapons," not unlike hunting rifles and common shotguns.[122] As guerrilla leader Bello described, "Our tactic was to attack and disappear. We didn't stick around for long. It was 13–14 cartridges and *chau*! Our mission was harassment." Mayser agrees: "Our tactic was the surprise attack, so the enemy wouldn't have time to respond."[123]

Despite overwhelming evidence that the guerrillas were local right-wing nationalists, Washington remained supremely confused. NSC member Robert Sayre reported to NSA McGeorge Bundy that, although it was now obvious that the guerrillas were "much more than . . . cattle thieves," their "political orientation is not clear."[124] FSB leader Gonzalo Romero declared adamantly that the guerrillas "had nothing to do with foreign influences," and Government Minister Fellman acknowledged the "surprise blow by the Falangists." But Henderson shrugged, explaining that the "Embassy does not yet have concrete evidence to make [the] assumption" that the guerrillas were not tinged with the red of communism.[125] On the contrary, Henderson still believed that "Mayser's group includes [a] mixed bag of Falangists, nonpolitical adventurers, local *campesinos* irritated by police brutality, communists, and even some MNR members."[126]

Furious at Washington's continued support for the Paz regime, on 10 August the guerrillas sent a threatening note to Gulf Oil's headquarters in Santa Cruz, explaining that they

> are not enemies of the people of the United States . . . but the attitude that some mercenaries of your country have taken . . . at the service of the dictatorship of Paz Estenssoro . . . has obliged us to make the following warning. . . . If the retirement of these mercenaries does not occur within a short time, the groups of the guerrilla command will take reprisals against you, your friends, and your personal belongings. . . . We reiterate that the guerrillas . . . are nationalists and do not have pacts with any foreign power. Therefore, the presence of foreigners in the counterinsurgency means a lack of recognition of freely determined peoples.[127]

Despite this threatening and quite explicit message, the Johnson administration continued to believe the guerrillas included Communists, and it showed
no signs of backing down in its support for the Paz regime. After the ambush, the Bolivian government announced that the armed forces would take
over operations in the guerrilla zone, airlifting ninety troops from La Paz's
Ingavi regiment.[128] Meanwhile, on 3 August, the Bolivian air force unleashed a fierce bombing raid on Mayser's hacienda.[129] The few ranch houses
missed by warplanes were dutifully torched by a large police contingent that
arrived on 9 August. Robbed of their safe houses, the one hundred–strong
guerrilla band fled northward into the rubber plantations and jungles of the
Bajo Paraguá.[130]

Ironically, the militarization of the counterinsurgent campaign was just
what the guerrillas desired.[131] When the guerrillas made contact with the
Fifth Division army commander, Colonel Hugo Banzer Suárez, who assumed
responsibilities in the guerrilla zone in early August, they received encourag-
ingly friendly responses. Banzer, who hailed from the nearby Santa Cruz
countryside, pled with the young Falangists to give up the struggle, writing
mockingly that "Alto Paraguá is by no means the nerve center of the nation."
With Banzer signing his letters as "your warmest friend,"[132] the guerrillas felt
sure that their goal of sparking a coup d'état was nigh. Valverde later wrote,
"We never intended to stop the army advance, much less defeat it. We only
sought to resist long enough to achieve an uprising of junior officers."[133] After
seizing several remote navy garrisons without a shot in August and September, the Falangist guerrillas of Alto Paraguá disappeared across the Brazilian
border, waiting to harvest the seeds of upheaval they had sown. Once Paz fell,
they planned to return to Bolivia as heroes.[134]

For Víctor Paz's enemies on the right and left, Washington's dogged support for the MNR represented arrogant interventionism, backed up cynically
by the language of development and modernization. In order to resist, left-
wing miners declared their camps free territories, prompting rightist and
leftist students to follow suit in the nation's universities. Meanwhile, young
right-wing Falangists took to the hills, vowing to fight to the death. Paz Estenssoro had always responded to unrest with brutal repression, and his third term
was no different. By the middle of the year, civilians had successfully sparked a
revolt. Time would tell whether or not military officers would join in.

Despite the fact that Paz Estenssoro appeared to be an unshakably authoritarian modernizer in the eyes of US officials, multiple nationwide conspiracies

had begun by mid-1964. Paz's decision to expel MNR leftists from the governing party radicalized their opposition to his government, leading them to join a conspiratorial alliance with the MNR's traditional right-wing enemies. Meanwhile, there was a profound restlessness in the junior officer corps, and Ambassador Henderson conceded that young soldiers' "hot-head approach" meant that the "possibility of [a] 'captain and major revolt' attempt remains [a] continuing threat."[135]

Development-oriented liberals like Henderson remained firmly in control of US policy toward Bolivia, however, and there was no sign of wavering. As *Time* magazine reported in the wake of the marred presidential contest, Paz Estenssoro was a "Doctor of Development," one in a new guard of Third World economist-politicians, who were "being called upon to build, revive, or draw together national economies."[136] In *Time*'s view, Paz had "organized a heavy-handed political police and created almost a one-party state." In short, he "gave the country its first taste of competent government."[137]

For his part, President Paz continued to couch his authoritarianism in the rhetoric of development and modernization. In his third inaugural address, he stressed that the "fundamental goal must be to dominate our territory," adding that the "armed forces, with its technical expertise," would be called on to play a central developmental role. By harnessing military "know-how," Paz vowed that his third term would be dedicated to the "construction of a National State." In Paz's words, revolutionary modernization "always causes societal dislocations, and binding elements are needed. The armed forces are this binding element . . . an extremely important element . . . the vanguard of the Bolivian people in the construction of the new society."[138] Within weeks, this people's vanguard would begin to take modernization into its own hands, and Washington would be left with only a consolation prize for its Alliance for Progress efforts: a military junta that offered unstinting praise for the development paradigm that paved its way to power.

Chapter 6

Revolutionary Bolivia Puts On a Uniform

The 1964 Bolivian Coup d'État

With unwavering backing from the liberal Alliance for Progress, President Víctor Paz proceeded to create a development-oriented authoritarian state, dedicated to the transformation of Bolivia into his vision of a modern nation. Left-wing and right-wing conspiracies against his government abounded in mid-1964, but the beleaguered reformer survived thanks in large part to the Johnson administration's fierce resistance to a military coup. Relentless US pressure for the Paz regime to break diplomatic relations with Cuba, however, would pull the rug out from under Paz's Machiavellian modus vivendi with domestic communism. As more factions on the Bolivian Left began warming the anti-Paz conspiracy, the country's military leaders increasingly turned a deaf ear to Washington's injunctions. Facing a society in nearly total rebellion, Paz's generals finally balked. Rather than turn their guns against their countrymen in the name of development, the Bolivian High Command pushed Paz Estenssoro to resign in early November 1964. Dozens of intricate conspiracies failed to bring down Bolivia's Movimiento Nacionalista Revolucionario (MNR; Revolutionary Nationalist Movement) during its twelve years in power. For the country's self-styled revolutionary nationalists, it was cruel irony that they should fall to a halting, haphazard coup waged by one of their own, General René Barrientos.

Bolivia's Break with Cuba

The Johnson administration was deeply frustrated by Bolivia's refusal to break relations with Cuba. After Brazil's new military leaders sent Cuban emissaries packing in April 1964, only four Latin American countries remained immune to US pressure: Chile, Uruguay, Mexico, and Bolivia. As the highest per capita recipient of Alliance for Progress funds, Bolivia's insubordination was embarrassing, and US officials were unsympathetic to Paz's claims that a break with Havana would push the Left further into a conspiratorial alliance with his right-wing enemies. President Paz had long seen his unspoken modi vivendi with Havana and the Bolivian Communist Party as a lynchpin in his survival strategy. His eventual capitulation revealed the extent to which the MNR's revolutionary mysticism had been hollowed out in favor of technocratic ideologies of modernization and economic development. More important, Paz's abrogation of his gentleman's agreement with Havana pushed the remainder of Bolivia's strongly pro-Cuban Left into open confrontation with his government.

Just after Brazil's military government broke relations with Cuba in April 1964, Ambassador Henderson explained to President Paz that sooner or later Paz would "have to face up to [the] anomaly of continued relations while committing himself to the Alliance for Progress." The Bolivian president responded that there was talk in Washington of reconciliation with Castro, and he told Henderson that he did not want to break relations with Havana only to be "faced shortly thereafter with a new US-Cuban rapprochement." Henderson recommended that Johnson write a personal letter to Paz, "correcting any misapprehension about [a] possible new trend in US policy and urging him to consider his position on Cuba in light of" the Brazilian coup d'état. He added that "Paz had responded well in the past to personal letters from US presidents and might be receptive presently to an approach on [the] Cuban issue."[1]

Henderson even provided a draft letter that would highlight what he saw as the importance of economic development over political ideology, recommending that Johnson stress his "unswerving determination to carry forward the policies of the Alliance for Progress, dedicating all the resources we are able to apply to further our common objective." The letter would then stress the "urgent need to take strong, meaningful actions" against Cuba for backing insurgency against Bolivia's anticommunist neighbors. Henderson's draft letter to President Paz went on to warn that, in its "campaign to bring about the overthrow of the governments of this hemisphere, [Cuba was] giving priority to governments that are striving for basic social and economic reforms," and it implored Paz to help Washington "combat the threat of communist subversion so that the partners in the Alliance for Progress may devote even greater resources to the economic development and well being of our peoples."[2]

During a short trip to Washington in mid-July, Henderson held a private meeting with President Johnson in the White House. The first words out of Johnson's mouth were "how Bolivia would vote on the Venezuelan complaint [against Cuba at the Organization for American States (OAS)] . . . and specifically whether Bolivia would be helpful on this issue." Henderson explained that he had just spoken with Bolivia's anticommunist foreign minister Carlos Iturralde, who had "indicated in a general way that, provided the [OAS] conference only recommends a break in diplomatic relations with Cuba, Bolivia would maintain diplomatic relations with that country. If, however, the resolution as passed would make it mandatory under the Rio Treaty to break with Cuba, Bolivia would comply." Realizing that Washington had the votes to make a diplomatic rupture mandatory, Johnson was tepidly pleased, and Henderson returned to La Paz to continue the administration's anti-Cuban crusade.[3]

Despite receiving assurances that Bolivia would respect the will of the OAS, the Johnson administration nonetheless applied unremitting pressure on the Bolivians to vote in favor of the mandatory break. Over lunch two days later, Secretary Rusk convinced Johnson to send a personal telegram to Paz, along the lines of Henderson's previous suggestion, which would "instruct his Foreign Minister to vote with us" at the coming meeting.[4] Rusk followed up with a phone call to Henderson the next day, asking him "to do his very best" with Paz. Rusk believed "this could make quite a lot of difference. . . . We could get [a] very good result if [you are] successful."[5] That afternoon, Henderson had a "two-hour long discussion" with Paz. Citing ongoing diplomatic strife with Chile over the Lauca River dispute, Paz replied that "Bolivia would vote as Chile does on [the] issue of [an] obligatory break in relations with Cuba." He assured Henderson, however, that his country "would vote to condemn Cuban aggression and would break with Cuba if the OAS vote made such a step obligatory." Paz's reasoning was threefold: his government remained disappointed with the OAS's lack of action on the Lauca affair; it did not want the Bolivian public to believe his country enjoyed less foreign policy independence than its neighbor; and finally, any impression that he was taking foreign policy dictates from the United States would "greatly weaken his government domestically."[6]

Henderson was unsympathetic to President Paz's claim that a break with Cuba would radicalize his leftist opposition. He told Paz that it was "extremely difficult for us to understand his position . . . in light of his recently proven strength with an overwhelming majority of voters." Paz defended his contention that, if he broke with Cuba under a nonobligatory situation, "his political opponents would be able to take advantage of a turn-about by him . . . to proclaim that he had turned to the right, that he was a traitor to revolutionary principles, and that he had become a puppet of the US." Henderson continued to press, but he lamented to Washington that Paz had "already made up his mind."[7] In a message to President Johnson, National Security Adviser (NSA) Bundy huffed that "we did not succeed with Paz," missing, however, the significance of Paz's arguments regarding the growing strength of the Bolivian Left. Bundy wrote instead that despite Paz's "good will," he was resisting a break "based on a different issue—a river war with Chile."[8]

Bolivia's OAS delegation voted to condemn Cuban intervention in Venezuela, but it abstained on the question of sanctions against Havana. The vast majority of Latin American states supported Washington's push to make a diplomatic break with Cuba obligatory, however, and Paz told Henderson on 3 August that he would comply soon after his reinauguration, scheduled for the 6th.[9] The following day, however, Foreign Minister Iturralde informed Henderson that Paz was demurring and that he had "decided that Bolivia will not be [the] first country" of the four remaining holdouts to make the break. Iturralde assured the US ambassador that he had "argued with [the] president that his decision [was] not in Bolivia's best interest," but that he had been unable to convince him.[10]

With Bolivia remaining silent on Cuba through Paz's third inauguration, Secretary Rusk cabled Henderson on 7 August that a "prompt GOB [Government of Bolivia] break with Cuba deserves first priority of attention in relations between our two governments." Rusk added that recent statements "led us to suspect that Paz [was] attempting to extricate himself from what we consider his clear commitment to us, made even before [the Foreign Ministers Meeting], to break if sanctions [were] mandatory." Given Paz's previous assurances, personally communicated to Johnson, Rusk characterized this vacillation as "deeply disappointing."[11]

Like most US officials, Rusk was unsympathetic to Paz's argument that a break with Cuba would have serious repercussions for his government's stability. Rusk wrote that Paz had "recently been elected on a pro-Alliance and anticommunist platform, after threats to his government, winning 85 per cent of over a million votes cast, and the opposition [was] in such disarray that it did not offer him an opponent." Rusk failed to mention that opposition abstention was well organized and that an insurgency had already begun. Bolivia's political stability was not Rusk's immediate concern; Cuba was. Placing the importance of isolating Havana at front and center, Rusk asked that Henderson "speak to Paz as soon as possible to request [an] explanation [on] how

he reconciles August 6 statements with previous assurances," adding that
Henderson should "make very clear the importance we attach to Bolivia's
breaking with Cuba."[12] Henderson did just this on 11 August, and Paz once
again pled for patience and understanding, both of which were in short supply. He explained to Henderson that he was waiting for the "opportune moment" to break relations and recommended that Washington instead turn its
attention toward Chile. Henderson, a strong Paz supporter, finally conceded
that Paz's domestic concerns appeared to be "genuine," albeit somewhat "exaggerated." Henderson noted that Paz seemed to be obsessed with the Chilean position, perhaps hoping that Santiago's resistance offered some room for
maneuver.[13]

Unfortunately for Paz Estenssoro, Chile ceded hours later.[14] On 13 August, Paz's cabinet held an emergency meeting to take stock of its difficult
position. Paz explained to his ministers that "the alternative [to breaking with
Cuba] would be to disavow the Rio Treaty, isolating ourselves in the Latin
American community, and losing US aid which, for the moment, is the only
basis upon which to pursue national development." His cabinet reluctantly
agreed, and the decision to break diplomatic relations with Havana passed
tepidly, but "without opposition," leaving Mexico and Uruguay as the only
two Latin American countries left standing in opposition to Washington's
anti–Cuban crusade.[15]

President of the Corporación Minera de Bolivia (COMIBOL; Mining
Corporation of Bolivia) Guillermo Bedregal recalls that when Paz received
Johnson's personal entreaty that Bolivia oust the Cuban embassy, Paz was visibly "angry." Bedregal writes that when he entered the president's office that
day, "in [Paz's] hand he held a cable," which he asked one of his ministers to
read aloud. It was "such an abusive message," Bedregal recounts, and "the next
few days were terrible." Johnson's personal note was followed by pressure
from other Latin American nations, Bedregal recalls, admitting that "given
the Cold War . . . we little Bolivians could expect nothing less." According to
Bedregal, when Chile gave in to US pressure on 11 August, "few times in the
long period of time I got to know Víctor Paz did I see him so pained as I saw
him in the face of that miserable and insupportable situation."[16] Paz's private
secretary Serrate agreed: "After Chile broke relations, Paz had no way out."[17]

Paz's cabinet desired "urgently that the issue become water under the
bridge,"[18] but the opposition was not so amenable. For many Bolivians, the
MNR's break with Cuba grimly demonstrated the technocratization of Paz's
revolutionary government and its submission to the United States, trends
that were both praised in liberal US press outlets.[19] Tiring of Communist Party

reticence to challenge Paz Estenssoro, dissident Communists began a Maoist split that would be formalized the following year, pointing to Paz's capitulation on Cuba as evidence that his government had become "the principal agent of Yankee imperialism"[20] The schismatics declared ominously that "the struggles against Yankee imperialism and the MNR government are inseparable."[21]

In the wake of Bolivia's break with Cuba, Havana also began an all-out propaganda offensive against the MNR government, accusing Paz Estenssoro of "betraying the Indians, who once believed in his promises." Cuba's weekly *Bohemia* excoriated Paz, "yesterday a nationalist, today Washington's peon," accusing the "ex-revolutionary" of "committing abuses against protesters and cutting down university students with bullets." Angrily declaring that President Paz was "copying Rómulo [Betancourt]," Castro's enemy number one, Cuba suddenly characterized his government as "one of the most hostile regimes toward the Latin American people."[22] Havana's *Radio Progreso* put it succinctly: Paz Estenssoro was a "scoundrel" who had "sold out to imperialism."[23]

Clearly, the break with Cuba was "disastrous for Paz's domestic game," in the words of his private secretary, who recalled that "relations with Cuba were the last thread of nationalist clothing he had on."[24] A member of the Partido Comunista de Bolivia (PCB; Communist Party of Bolivia) Central Committee agreed that the break "had an enormous impact" and that for Bolivian leftists, "it determined everything."[25] Seeing the MNR's tacit modus vivendi with Cuba in tatters, many Communists cast aside their doubts and joined the right wing in a rebellion that would soon bring down the Paz regime.

Paz's Last State of Siege

Despite having begun as yet another right-wing anti-MNR revolt, the nationwide rebellion against Paz Estenssoro soon enjoyed enthusiastic left-wing support. Mobilized by the break with Cuba, students and workers throughout the country expressed strong support for guerrilla activity by the Falange Socialista Boliviana (FSB; Bolivian Socialist Falange) in Santa Cruz. As he had so many times before, President Paz relied squarely on political repression, calling on his secret police to harass, intimidate, and attack all threats to his government. Despite his regime being in its death throes, Washington never abandoned its development-oriented ally. Even when Paz invoked his fifth—and final—state of siege in late September, he enjoyed the constant backing of the entire US government, including the Pentagon and the Central Intelligence Agency (CIA). For a time, this well-worn tactic appeared to be working.

On inauguration day, 6 August, outgoing Vice President Lechín's final duty was to place the presidential sash across Paz's breast. As Lechín recalls, "I planned to enter the National Congress and denounce that his election was illegal." Lechín assumed that "Paz's thugs would not have reacted within the parliament, in front of the diplomats and parliamentarians." At noon, however, Lechín was intercepted by agents from Paz's secret police, who gave him what Ambassador Henderson called a "sound beating." Lechín recalls that local residents came to his defense, but "before [the agents] left they took me down with a rifle butt to the kidney. . . . I was bleeding. . . . For one week, I urinated blood." Years later, a Paz colleague revealed to Lechín that Paz had told his secret police chief San Román: "Don't kill him, just leave him paralyzed." According to Henderson, there was "little doubt that security police were instructed to prevent Lechín's attendance at [the] inaugural ceremonies." Control Político did not even bother to hide their role in the attack, utilizing their well-known "covert" jeeps.[26]

In the wake of the attack on Lechín, the labor federation declared a general strike, provoking massive, violent worker demonstrations in league with belligerent students beginning on the 13th.[27] Paz called an emergency cabinet meeting two days later, at which he declared that subversion could not be tolerated, as it was a threat to his government's plans to "execute public works and give a constructive direction to the revolution."[28] During the meeting, the cabinet heard an ominous Labor Ministry report regarding the "serious and frail social situation that confronts the country." The report warned that subversives were preparing to pass from an "intellectual and verbal" approach to an "active, organized, and violent opposition." Normal party debate and democratic structures "are not appropriate for uniquely orienting national development," the report added, criticizing the government for "losing its combativeness and revolutionary mysticism," and thus fighting from a consistently defensive position. "The people do not believe in 'development' due to a lack of adequate propaganda," the report concluded.[29]

Once the report had been read, COMIBOL President Bedregal declared that it was "lamentable to have adopted a democratic path for the Revolution, which is a luxury that demands ironclad discipline to the *Jefe*," that is, to Paz. He added that "democratic centralism is not possible in an underdeveloped country," recommending instead that there be a "political norm fixed by the Party *Jefe*." Bedregal concluded by saying that "we cannot continue to tolerate the existence of division. . . . The opposition must be liquidated and we must create democracy through the Party, dictating a state of siege." Paz agreed, declaring that "subversive action harms the country because it creates a climate of distrust that is not propitious to development." At the meeting, only Vice President Barrientos expressed opposition to martial law.[30]

Two weeks later, Paz's commitment to authoritarianism was put to the test by a nationwide salary strike by the teachers' federation.[31] He did not disappoint. When the student and labor federations took to the streets in support of the teachers on 3 September, Paz responded by closing schools for the remainder of the year,[32] and he ordered secret police chief San Román to deploy CIA-equipped party militias against political gatherings. San Román vowed to "strictly control" travel by suspected subversives,[33] and he called on Barrientos to prove his loyalty by addressing crowds in provincial capitals.[34] This was a dangerous tactic, as Barrientos had already delivered scathing public critique of the "excesses of *Control Político*."[35]

At first, Barrientos agreed to cooperate, ominously declaring to thousands of friendly listeners in Cochabamba and Santa Cruz that order would soon be brought to the country.[36] In private meetings secretly taped by Control Político agents, however, he sat by as citizens "thrashed" the Paz government, waging "open attacks" and threatening to turn Santa Cruz into a "barricaded city."[37] Sensing the pressure rising, Barrientos intimated to members of the press that he might leave the country, prompting twenty-two parliamentarians from various parties to plead for him to stay, declaring that Barrientos's presence in Bolivia "constitutes a guarantee that . . . constitutional liberties will be respected."[38] It was clear that Barrientos had become a figurehead for the resistance, accusations to which he responded, "Nothing is definite, but I have the firm intention of coming to an understanding with [Paz]."[39]

Paz's problems were multiplying. On 6 September, the Siglo XX miners declared themselves in support of the teachers, and a week later the entire miners' federation announced another series of rolling strikes. Paz issued a statement that "in the face of anarchist attitudes," COMIBOL would "tenaciously oppose the climate of violence that prevails."[40] Miners responded to this call to arms by bombing a passenger train on its way from Oruro to La Paz[41] and a pipeline between Oruro and Cochabamba.[42]

Meanwhile, Paz faced violent demonstrations by students in every provincial capital. In Cochabamba on 16 September, students sacked the Bolivian-American cultural center on three separate occasions, destroying all its windows.[43] In Sucre, students marched while chanting slogans declaring that "soon we students and intellectuals will bring down the Paz government." They attacked US installations and stoned several Bolivian government buildings. Students in Tarija issued a statement on 17 September declaring a "state of emergency in the entire student ranks" as a result of the "terrible wave of repression," and they heralded that "the time to liberate the country from the pro-Yankee government is coming." In Potosí, students attacked US government buildings, "causing considerable damage," before moving on to attack private homes of MNR party members.[44]

On 18 September, the teachers rejected a government settlement offer and announced a "Hunger March" to coincide with the upcoming visit of French President Charles de Gaulle to Cochabamba.[45] The following day, MNR Deputy Carmelo Padilla informed Paz's secret police that "there is a coup d'état being arranged between Siles, Guevara [Arze], and Barrientos."[46] Not wanting to be embarrassed in the presence of such an esteemed visitor, at 3:00 a.m. on 20 September, President Paz decreed a ninety-day nationwide state of siege, his fifth since 1961. It would be his last.

Two hours later, San Román's agents snatched sixty opposition figures and labor leaders from their beds. Former president Siles was stuffed onto a plane with thirty members of Lechín's PRIN and dumped unceremoniously in Paraguay. Lechín went into hiding. The detainees who were lucky enough to avoid exile were held in cold, wet Control Político cells, listening intently to radio broadcasts of the ongoing revolt.[47] Press censorship was harshly enforced three days later, and the siege meant "no political gatherings; no parties or drinking; and no sale of liquor."[48] Beginning on 24 September, no newspapers appeared on the streets of La Paz, aside from the MNR daily La Nación.[49]

Meanwhile, Control Político rushed to head off the growing rebellion. In telegrams to San Román, many of them written in code, secret police agents from around the country reported on opposition gatherings, marches, and speeches, using information gathered from their wide network of informants and surreptitious recording devices.[50] On 22 September, Control Político agents in Oruro reported proudly that MNR militias were "breaking up teachers' meetings at this very moment."[51] San Román also distributed generous CIA-funded bribes to labor unions and Indian peasant organizations to secure their support.[52] Far from being bothered by all this, Henderson was bolstered, imploring Paz to reveal if the state of siege would lead to "more civilian controls in the mines," a technocratic euphemism for military invasion.[53]

Regarding San Román, Paz's son recalls that "in 1952, my dad built his entire intelligence team from ex-Nazis, old Gestapos he had met in Argentina" during his period of exile prior to the revolution. "They put together this massive cardex—big, blonde Germans—of everyone in the country. These were very well trained individuals, and they worked closely with San Román. Of course San Román continued these tactics in the second government."[54] According to Paz Estenssoro's private secretary, "San Román was

Paz's [Lavrentiy] Beria," referring to Joseph Stalin's secret police chief. "All of the political, military, and police power was in San Román's hands."[55] When asked if the accusations of San Román's torture and repression were true, Paz cabinet minister Bedregal responded with one word: "Definitely."[56]

In case there was any doubt regarding Paz's warm feelings toward his secret police, he purchased a book on the Nazi Gestapo in early September, joking to the press, "This one is for San Román."[57] Former CIA station chief Stern-field found Paz's humor distasteful but accurate:

> Paz Estenssoro *was* a Nazi. Most of those around him were Nazis. It was like Nazi Germany. Same jails, same brutality. Bolivia was still fighting the war, even though it had ended two decades earlier.
>
> I have served in six countries, and the last days of the Paz regime were the most repressive I ever saw. Claudio San Román, with whom I worked on a daily basis, was the most brutal Latin American I ever met. All San Román ever wanted was guns. He asked me for guns every day. The only thing that kept Paz in power was the United States.

According to Sternfield, "our weapons went to Paz's Control Político and to his MNR militia. All the butchers got weapons. San Román certainly got his share. It was a pretty distasteful task." When asked why the United States supported such brutality, Sternfield wryly answered, "Well, Uncle Sam doesn't put it that way. They say it is in support of democracy and progress, and all that."[58] In fact, it was precisely San Román's brutality that necessitated CIA involvement, since the State Department refused to ship weapons from the United States Agency for International Development (USAID) Office of Public Safety (OPS) to his "harsh and repressive" cadres.[59]

Paz's willingness to rely on political repression to carry out his developmental vision boasted no shortage of support in liberal US press outlets. George Natanson wrote in the *Los Angeles Times* that the "overthrow of the Paz Estenssoro administration would be a severe blow to US policy in Latin America," adding that both Kennedy and Johnson had "made a point of backing moderate, democratic government in answer to Communist charges that it supports only conservative oligarchic regimes."[60] Natanson later added that Paz had been "primarily responsible for the measure of economic development and political stability the country has enjoyed," praising US aid for being "wisely and effectively used."[61]

A *New York Times* editorial opined that "it is a good thing for Bolivia and for the hemisphere as a whole that Mr. Paz Estenssoro continues at the helm."[62] In the *Christian Science Monitor*, James Nelson Goodsell proclaimed that "Bolivia, with massive United States aid, is embarked on a major program of economic and social advancement," praising Paz for his determination to "push Bolivia further along the path of social and economic reform."[63] The following day, Goodsell added US aid had been a "marked success" in Bolivia, thanks to Paz's "firm hand," which was seeking to "keep economic development going at a faster rate than the mounting social pressures," namely, leftists' "snarling mine strikes," which were "a threat to the generally favorable economic climate."[64] Finally, *Time* magazine rushed to Paz's defense, calling him "Latin America's ablest President when it comes to anticipating and disarming trouble before it starts." *Time* hailed Paz for having "once more firmly cinched his authority."[65]

Only the *Chicago Daily News*'s archconservative Georgie Anne Geyer had the gall to question Washington's support for what she called "police rule in Bolivia," where "traffic is closely controlled . . . at roadblocks by 'transit authorities' [who] record who is passing and why." Referencing reports that Paz government agents attacked any press outlet that went too far, Geyer warned that the regime was entering a "new era of toughness" and predicted that Paz's extensive use of "political persecution" harkened "an era of embarrassment" for the United States.[66]

By late September, President Paz faced a nation in revolt. Right-wing guerrillas had sparked the rebellion, but leftist teachers and miners were fueling it. Falangist students had taken to the streets with their Communist classmates throughout the country, demanding political liberties and calling for an end to the Paz government. Never abandoning his ideological and rhetorical commitment to Bolivia's modernization, Paz responded as he always had: with repression. Despite believing that he would ride out the storm once again, there was no shortage of evidence that this revolt was different. For the first time, the Right and the Left were working closely together, and there was growing military reluctance, particularly on the part of Vice President Barrientos, to serve as the MNR's armed wing. For an insurrection to achieve critical mass, however, it often needs martyrs. These were delivered by Paz's Control Político in late October 1964.

October's Martyrs

Paz's implementation of a state of siege in late September 1964 amounted to a welcoming gift to President de Gaulle, and it did provide a semblance of order. This was a mirage. He was facing a nationwide coalition of Communists and Falangists, some of whom were prepared to die to end what they saw as a dictatorship that used economic development to justify brutal police repression. In this environment, Barrientos's October defection spelled trouble, and a series of student and miner deaths at the hands of Paz's security services would symbolize the culmination of the MNR's modernization project. US support never wavered, and on the eve of the coup, Washington approved fresh CIA arms shipments for Paz's militias. The anti-MNR revolt unfolded independent of foreign influence. On the contrary, it was a reaction against US intervention, with Left *and* Right unfurling the anti-imperialist banner.

On 2 October 1964, Víctor Paz celebrated his fifty-seventh birthday. He was given full honors, including protestations of loyalty from the military High Command. According to one minister's account, Commander-in-Chief Ovando declared: "I wish to express my personal devotion to you, and I would like to transmit this personal loyalty to you through a solemn oath. . . . I swear on the Cross of my sword my absolute personal loyalty to the President, Dr. Paz Estenssoro and the constitutional government over which he presides."[67] Barrientos's troubling absence "for health reasons" was somewhat mitigated by a note in which he promised that "your proposals and programs of economic and social liberation will soon be transformed into reality for all Bolivians." Barrientos neglected to mention that he planned to be the one to implement them.[68]

During the coming weeks, Barrientos repeated his demands that Paz lift martial law, condemning the government's belligerent approach to the violent opposition. Instead of repression, Barrientos, in his typical lyrical style, called on Paz to "eradicate the causes" of the insurrection "by procuring for the Bolivian people a closer relationship to the National Revolution." Meanwhile, Cochabamba regiments ominously expressed their "absolute moral and materiel support for the Vice President, General René Barrientos."[69] The CIA fretted on 9 October that "Barrientos is incensed" at Paz, and that a "showdown between" the two "may be imminent."[70]

Barrientos's new wave of criticism sparked fresh demonstrations in Cochabamba. When San Román's agents rounded up right-wing students charged with leading them,[71] "serious rioting developed" on 21 October. After several hours, Paz's security services ran out of tear gas, and students broke through a police cordon and began "moving through the city at will." Police then resorted to their US-supplied M-1 carbines, a decision that left a student by the name of

Jorge Valenzuela dead and another, René Ferrufino, fatally wounded. Ambassador Henderson morosely reported to Washington that that "police restraint shown in repeated clashes with students over [the] last month . . . has come to an end." Recognizing the gravity of the Cochabamba uprising, Henderson wrote that the anti-Paz movement had "apparently achieved its first martyrs."[72]

The following evening, Ferrufino died of his wounds. Funerals were set for 3:00 p.m. on Friday, 23 October, a date marked by simultaneous riots in every major city. The CIA reported that morning that a "battle [is] now taking place at the university of La Paz. Police have forced students back into university grounds, [the] streets [are] full of gas, [and the] students are in an extremely belligerent mood."[73] Paz's announcement that he would lift press censorship only emboldened the nationwide revolt, which Henderson characterized as showing "strong discipline . . . [and] a pattern of conspiracy."[74]

Over the weekend, Paz mobilized Indian and MNR militias to face off with rioters in Santa Cruz and Oruro, and he shipped in "truckloads of armed *campesinos*" to bring La Paz under control. On Monday, 26 October, violence marred a mock funeral by leftist students in Oruro, meant to honor those slain the previous week in Cochabamba. When the dust cleared, four more students lay dead, having clashed with police and military forces throughout the day.[75] Similar riots targeting US and Bolivian government buildings broke out in Sucre, Potosí, and Cobija, and the CIA warned that Paz was "expecting serious trouble in La Paz" in the coming days. Meanwhile, right-wing students in Santa Cruz attacked the regional headquarters of the United States Information Service, burning an American flag in the central plaza for good measure.[76]

On Tuesday, 27 October, Paz's secret police arrested another wave of opposition leaders, and the student federation called for a "Liberty March" to take place in the capital on Thursday. Henderson reported that Paz was facing the "most important test of will to date . . . by Falangist-Communist opposition groups." The ambassador expressed pleasure that Paz was "prepared to take [a] firm stand," and he approved of Paz's use of CIA-equipped Indian militias against students in La Paz, Oruro, and Santa Cruz. Henderson was also encouraged that General Ovando had offered Paz a "completely unqualified statement [of] loyalty," including his assurance that the "military [is] ready [to] carry out any orders [the] president might issue."[77]

Despite Henderson's optimism, the CIA reported on Tuesday evening that "the military has refused to assist in containing riots" in Oruro. The agency also reported that Barrientos was in ongoing conversations with Falangist conspirators, who claimed to have also convinced Ovando that "the FSB should stir up trouble nationally until there is sufficient anarchy . . . that the military would move in." The FSB was warning Ovando that they were "losing control of anti-government agitation to the leftists," and the rightist party was therefore pushing the military to "move quickly."[78] Some civilian conspirators had reportedly proposed that Barrientos "take charge of the government, along with [USAID civic action chief] Julio Sanjinés Goytia, as Vice President."[79]

A few hours later, Barrientos approached US Air Attaché Fox in Cochabamba, asking that Washington evacuate him [on the] basis [of a] medical emergency." When Fox phoned the ambassador that night, Henderson told him that he was "not prepared to respond to this request unless support[ed] by [a] request from [the] President." Henderson reported to Secretary Rusk that Barrientos appeared to be "seeing pressure building up [and] wishes to absent himself during [the] showdown after which he could return as constitutional successor to Paz if [the] opposition manages to overthrow Paz."[80]

Late that night, Tuesday, 27 October, Henderson informed President Paz of Barrientos's request. Paz showed "impatience" and was unequivocally opposed to airlifting Barrientos to Panama. Paz said that he "did not want [the] Vice President running out of [the] country, but rather doing his job in La Paz," and he revealed the dispatch of a commission to Cochabamba that would "bring Barrientos back." Henderson inquired if he could defeat the insurrection, to which Paz replied confidently that he had "more than enough forces to deal with [the] situation, including militia, *campesinos*, and some armed forces upon which he can count on without reservation." Henderson was comforted by these words, reporting that the Bolivian president was "angry, unrattled, and firmly determined to make no more concessions." Washington was backing a winning horse, Henderson stressed, who had "now chosen the ground on which to make a stand, and will if necessary commit maximum forces available to him."[81]

The next day, Paz demanded that Barrientos make himself present in the capital. The vice president obliged, and that night he gave a full report of the meeting to Colonel Fox. Barrientos revealed that Paz had requested him to be at his side for the following day's showdown between pro-Paz Indians and rebellious students. Barrientos told Fox that he had refused, "because he did not want to appear as one of Paz' servants." He added that the meeting had produced "no meeting of the minds and, after mutual recriminations, Paz accused him of planning to overthrow the government and establish a military junta." The CIA reported that "Barrientos personally dislikes Paz and

[says] that he cannot cooperate with him because of what he considers to be the corruption and unpopular attitudes of his regime."[82]

Barrientos then revealed to Fox that the "armed forces would depose Paz within [a] week." He again stressed that that he "wished to be absent from [the] country so [he] could return with clean hands as constitutional successor after Paz [is] deposed." Barrientos believed that his best chance to succeed Paz, and thus guard against a takeover by the leftist Lechín, "required [that] he remain unblemished in [the] crisis."[83] When Colonel Fox stutteringly explained that he had not yet received authorization for the airlift, Barrientos responded wryly, "You're a lousy liar. I know they are opposed to what I'm doing. It doesn't matter. I'll just do this myself."[84] Vice President Barrientos then reiterated that he "definitely broke" with Paz, and that, if necessary, he would remain in the country to "direct the fall of Paz. . . . There is no escape for him." He was waiting to make his move, he explained, because he "feared the communist[s] may try to capitalize on the break between him and Paz, and for that reason would remain 'quiet' for a while in order that it not appear that he was supporting the communists in their fight against Paz."[85]

On receiving this ominous report, the White House solicited a second opinion. Late Wednesday night, Bill Dentzer, head of the State Department's Chile/Bolivia Desk, told National Security Council (NSC) member Gordon Chase that the "present disturbances can be characterized as a popular reaction to a repressive government." The students were a "big factor in this reaction," Dentzer added, explaining that the revolt was being led by an alliance between young right-wing Falangists and their leftist classmates. Dentzer believed that military support for Paz was firm, and he therefore predicted that a coup, while "in the ballpark," was not "highly likely." According to Dentzer, the chances of a takeover by the Communists were "nil," because the military was "violently opposed to them." The main threat existed in the Communists' ability to take advantage of "instability or transition," in which "other parties will be looking around for support." Dentzer concluded by confidently declaring that "there is little likelihood of something happening in Bolivia which we cannot live with." At the same time, "given our druthers . . . we would probably just as soon see the disturbances end with Paz still in the saddle."[86]

As he had previously promised, President Paz ordered the army to retake Oruro on Wednesday, 28 October, in concert with police and Indian militias. A few units complied, clashing throughout the day with students and armed leftist miners from the city's San José mine. Several Indian militiamen were taken hostage in the mining camp, but by nightfall the army had regained control of the city. Four MNR militiamen lay dead, as well as two miners and two police officers.[87]

Receiving word that Oruro had fallen, four truckloads of Siglo XX miners rushed toward the city, but soldiers had already taken up positions on San Pedro Hill overlooking the plains of Sora Sora. With their approach blocked, Siglo XX interim union leader Daniel Ordóñez ordered his men to wait in nearby Huanuni. Meanwhile, he commandeered an ambulance and drove surreptitiously with fellow PCB member Gilberto Bernal to the Machacamarca concentration plant, just short of the roadblock. There, they "mobilized mine workers from Santa Fe, Japo, and Morocala" who would join hundreds of miners from Siglo XX, Catavi, and Huanuni in a "massive demonstration" the following morning. Ordóñez recalls that "we had only dynamite," but they resolved nonetheless to confront the army at daybreak.[88]

Frustrated by the delay and accusing Siglo XX's Communist leadership of "being slow to give orders," a Partido Obrero Revolucionario (POR; Revolutionary Workers' Party [Trotskyist]) contingent opted to go it alone. "The Trotskyists were the only well-armed group," recalls Siglo XX Communist Rosendo Osorio, "and they wanted to take power right away!"[89] POR member Benigno Bastos concedes that "our goal was to take power, and we did not wait for orders from the union." Instead, they loaded into one of the trucks and sped toward the Sora Sora roadblock. The army turned on its floodlights and opened fire, leaving Bastos and fellow POR member Pedro Guzmán gravely injured. Feeling "betrayed by the Communist Party," the Trotskyists were evacuated to the Huanuni hospital just before daybreak by a passing commercial vehicle.[90] Meanwhile, miner radios broadcast false reports that dozens of miners were killed in what they called the "Massacre of Sora Sora."[91]

Several hours later, hundreds of workers from the mines surrounding Oruro descended on the plains of Sora Sora, where they waged what Ambassador Henderson referred to as a "pitched battle with [the] First Ranger Battalion."[92] Siglo XX interim leader Ordóñez recalled arriving with a dump truck full of dynamite. "We cut them into two or three pieces, putting a fuse in each one, and we handed them out to row after row of workers. Every twenty meters, they had orders to launch their dynamite. Imagine the psychological effect of this! So many people and so much dynamite!"[93] By 8:30 p.m., Henderson reported to Washington that the "military fell back on [Oruro] from Sora Sora in [the] face [of] heavy pressure from miners."[94] The following morning, a separate miner contingent from Colquiri converged on Oruro from the north, capturing the town of Caracollo and cutting the road from La Paz to Oruro in the process.[95]

Despite this impressive show of miner force, President Paz assured Henderson that "troop morale [was] high," particularly with the transfer of additional men from the US-built Max Toledo motorized battalion near La Paz. He told the ambassador that "since his forces were brutally and criminally attacked, he [sees] no sense in his not going forward into [the] mines." It was "not going to be nice," Paz warned, but he assured Henderson that the "issue [was] firmly joined."[96] The CIA reported, "This appears to be the long awaited move to take the mines," since the Paz government had "finally found its pretext in the recent violent demonstrations."[97] Hoping to extract maximum support from Washington, President Paz requested an "immediate shipment" of 500,000 rounds of M-1 carbine ammunition. Sensing that the "major scene of conflict [is] now [Oruro,]" Henderson had already released the embassy's remaining stock, just under 100,000 rounds.[98]

It is likely that Assistant Secretary of State Thomas Mann read these Thursday cables together with reports of Barrientos's ominous conversation with Colonel Fox the previous evening. Mann cabled Henderson at 1:30 p.m. to ask that if Henderson had not read the CIA report on Fox's conversation, "you should do so immediately." Mann wrote that the State Department was under the impression that Paz appeared "to have [a] good chance to ride out [the] present disturbances," and he asked the ambassador to confirm this assessment. Then Mann solicited Henderson's views on what a successor government would look like, since the State Department was under the impression that it would be military or noncommunist civilian, adding that "we do not deduce from your reports that there is any possibility at this time of a communist takeover of [the] Bolivian Government." Mann concluded that there appeared to be "no US national purpose to be served by US intervention into [the] present political situation in Bolivia and many disadvantages to intervention by us."[99]

Mann's neutralist proposal would have put Washington in the position of having good relations with whoever came out on top, Paz or Barrientos, and it would require the US Embassy to keep Barrientos at a safe distance while being careful "not [to] become identified at this particular time with Paz' maneuvers." Mann recommended that Henderson call a meeting of "all principal officers on your staff and warn them to refrain from intervening in the next days ahead and suggest that Air Attaché have no further conversations with Barrientos until [the] situation is more stable." During the crisis, all US contacts with Bolivian officials should be "strictly controlled by you," Mann added, reminding Henderson, "Our non-interventionist attitude would of course change if in your estimation there is any substantial risk of a takeover of [the] Bolivian government by communists or pro-communist elements."[100]

Minutes later, Mann gave a similar presentation to the White House Special Group (CI), complaining that Paz "is in trouble because he has not displayed strong leadership" and expressing doubt that Washington should continue to "go all out for Paz as the only one who can control the situation." Mann informed the Special Group that Paz had requested an additional 500,000 rounds of carbine ammunition, adding that the US Embassy had no idea "whether Paz plans to give this ammunition to the army, [to] the *campesinos*, or to the police." According to Mann, it was "an uneasy situation." He agreed that riot gear was appropriate, but he also proposed that the State Department send a special emissary to Bolivia "to evaluate the situation and make an estimate of the loyalty of the army." The Special Group agreed across the board, resolving to take up the issue again the following week, and authorizing Chile/Bolivia Desk Chief Dentzer to leave for La Paz two days later.[101]

While Mann presented his concerns to the Special Group, Henderson cabled a passionate retort to the neutralist argument. With additional regiments rushing to engage the miners at Sora Sora, and with pro-government Indians bringing students to heel in La Paz and Santa Cruz, Henderson wrote that "Paz [is] in control and remains determined in [the] face of [a] difficult situation." While he admitted that some members of the military High Command might be tempted to "step in and remove Paz to stop current bloodshed" or to "forestall [an] extremist takeover," Henderson did not see this as a favorable option, since he did "not believe [that the] armed forces have [a] better chance [of] remaining in power than any group."[102]

Paz's fall would lead to a "highly unstable situation," Henderson explained, in which the right-wing Falange would "drive for power with communist cooperation." Vice President Barrientos might attempt to claim the right of constitutional succession "but would be unable to muster strength," Henderson explained, or Ovando would take power to restore order and "face [the] same oppositional elements now facing Paz." Given the unpredictable contingencies, Henderson recommended that "while it is prudent to look beyond Paz, he and his present backing (including military) appear sufficiently strong to overcome opposition's current challenge." Henderson was confident that "[the] government will maintain control in most of these cities though perhaps [through a] substantial cost of life."[103]

Mann was a career Latin American diplomat, and he trusted his man in the field. Four hours later, he responded that given Henderson's convincing presentation, "and especially in view of [the] possibility that Commie elements might have the maximum chance of take-over in chaos should Paz fall, we believe we have no alternative for [the] time being but to support Paz." Mann recommended that US officials "quietly and orally encourage Ovando and all other key figures currently supporting [the] constitutional government to continue to do so," and he asked that "to [the] extent possible," US officials "avoid our identification in [the] Bolivian public mind with excesses which Paz partisans may commit." If the course of events changed and Paz looked certain to fall, Mann stressed that "we would have to decide quickly on how best to use our considerable influence" in Bolivia to guard against a leftist takeover. In case there was any doubt that Mann had deferred to Henderson, he closed by stressing that "this modifies" his 1:30 p.m. cable.[104]

Late that night, Henderson confirmed receipt of Mann's message. He assured Mann that he would closely "control . . . contacts with political figures personally," adding that he had "repeatedly urged upon political and military leaders [our] position that recognized constitutional government must be upheld by all forces owing allegiance to it." With regard to Bolivian Communists, Henderson wrote that "by themselves . . . [they] cannot and do not intend to overthrow Paz." Instead, the Communist Party was discreetly supporting the FSB and other rightist opposition parties, through which it was able to "use any relatively strong opposition to Paz as [an] instrument through which [to] create maximum disturbances while [they] themselves as a party remain uncommitted." Meanwhile, smarting from Paz's recent diplomatic rupture, Havana issued a communiqué exhorting the students to bring down the Paz government in this "new center of the struggle against imperialism."[105]

When Thursday morning's Liberty March began, the CIA reported that "both rightist and leftist opposition parties are behind the outbreaks, but they have used their followers in the universities and secondary schools to spearhead the demonstrations."[106] The agency added that the PCB had "issued orders to its militants to participate actively" in the march, asking its members to "arm themselves, prepare Molotov cocktails, and to attack United States government installations in La Paz, including the Embassy and the United States Information Service." The CIA reported that "for tactical reasons the Communists have been completely with the FSB in the student field."[107]

On Thursday morning, 29 October, "thirty truckloads" of Indian militiamen from the pro-Paz altiplano stronghold of Achacachi stood ready to defend the Paz regime in the capital.[108] According to Presidency Minister Jaime

Otero, author of the most authoritative firsthand account of the coup, Paz called on his security services to "to cordon opposition forces in the university district" and meanwhile ordered his Indian forces to amass in the confines of the government buildings surrounding La Paz's central plaza. With their citywide march frustrated, the students proceeded to firebomb buildings surrounding the university, including the Health Ministry, the Municipal Library, and the offices of the official government newspaper, *La Nación*.[109]

As evening set in, students were pushed back into the fourteen-story university building by police and MNR militia units in a firefight that left one student dead and three wounded. During an emergency cabinet meeting at 7:30 p.m., Paz phoned Monsignor Andrew Kennedy, a well-respected US-born priest who was secretary of the Bolivian Bishops Conference. Paz asked Kennedy to enter the complex and convince the students that "they must surrender peacefully and deliver their arms," promising no reprisals if they did so.[110] As Otero reports, this was "successfully carried out, as evidenced by the fact that despite an intense firefight (from short distance and with various types of weapons) there was no destruction of the building, and amongst over than 1,000 individuals in the university, there was only one casualty." The Falangist leader of the student federation, Guido Strauss, pled to President Paz for clemency. He received none and was carted away to one of San Román's tiny cells.[111]

Once the students had surrendered "unconditionally," the university rector pled with Paz through Henderson that the government show "mercy" on the students. Paz responded by telling Henderson that he was "not willing to be compassionate to communists," a shockingly misleading characterization of the rightist-led movement, and he announced that the students would "file out of [the] university building one by one, leaving weapons at [the] door." At that point, several of his ministers would "take charge," permitting a "special committee of responsible citizens," Control Político agents and MNR militiamen no doubt, to search the main university building "top to bottom."[112]

By 9:00 p.m., Paz's security services had arrested six hundred students, and Henderson felt confident that the Bolivian regime "require[d] no additional equipment to meet current emergency." Henderson explained that the police and militias had "500,000 rounds [of] ammunition which together with 125,000 rounds we provided [in the] last two days comprises sufficient ammunition [for] several days [at the] present rate of fire."[113] Nonetheless, he asked that Washington move forward with additional tear gas shipments, a request Secretary Rusk promptly fulfilled, cabling Henderson the next day to confirm that USAID was "assembling [a] shipment [of] 4,000 CS tear gas projectiles" from Dover Air Force Base.[114]

With La Paz brought under control, the nation's attention focused on the military's ongoing battle near Oruro, where miners were "mounting [a] major effort to take the city." Paz addressed the nation late Thursday night, announcing that the "subversive effort [in] La Paz [was] overcome" and promising that his government "would soon restore order throughout the country." Barrientos remained conspicuously absent, however,[115] and Paz soon found himself pleading with his reluctant generals to "take charge of the serious situation" in Oruro.[116]

Reeling from Thursday's upheavals, that night the State Department took stock of the delicate situation. Expressing confidence that the Bolivian military had "begun its campaign to take over extremist-controlled mining centers," State believed this demonstrated the armed forces were "willing to support the government when it is threatened by the miners." The department noted, however, that the military would be "far less willing to take action against other elements of society, such as students or peasants." Indian militias were therefore working closely with the police to quell the student-led disturbances, and it seemed that Paz had "overcome the worst of the present crisis." Barrientos remained the wildcard, according to US analysts, since his "ambitions could still lead to serious division of loyalties in military and militia ranks if, with or without the approval of his high-ranking Armed Forces colleagues, he were to challenge the authority of Paz."[117] The following day, Friday, 30 October, NSA Bundy notified President Johnson's top aide, Jack Valenti, that the US Embassy was doing its best to "exert its influence with the Commander-in-Chief of the Army [General Ovando] and all other key Bolivian figures who are accessible to it to urge them to continue to support the Paz government . . . while avoiding public identification of the US with any excesses which partisans of Paz may commit."[118]

Washington had numerous chances to turn its back on Paz's authoritarian development paradigm, which it adopted in early 1961. President Paz was one of Latin America's most unstinting supporters of the Alliance for Progress, however, and the Johnson administration shared its predecessor's view that MNR authority was the key to Bolivia's modernization. Paz had succeeded in implementing the anticommunist labor reforms required by the Alliance for Progress, and with fresh shipments of weaponry from USAID and the CIA, he had unleashed his loyalist militias against rebellious students and workers. The military High Command continued to offer loyal protestations, and US support appeared to be vindicated as Bolivia entered a period of relative calm coinciding with weekend celebrations of All Saints Day and All Souls Day. Vice President Barrientos's absence was disconcerting, and his noisy demands that Paz release hundreds of students was annoying,[119] but he was not yet leading the revolt. A plot was under way, however, and as soon as the holiday weekend concluded, a new uprising began. This time, it would be headed by the armed forces themselves.

The Fall of Víctor Paz

Since early 1961, US liberals were supremely confident in their capacity to guide Bolivia's development under the modernizing regime of Víctor Paz. The Kennedy and Johnson administrations rebuffed numerous coup entreaties by restless generals, and President Paz survived in large part thanks to this unwavering support. Yet US power is not without limits. On Tuesday, 3 November, junior officers led their units to mutiny, one by one. General Barrientos soon joined the revolt, and early the following day, the rest of the High Command convinced Paz Estenssoro to abdicate rather than wage a civil war between his US-equipped civilian militias and a military institution that refused to splinter.

Despite Secretary Rusk's assurance to President Johnson on Friday, 30 October that Paz appeared "now to be ready to stay in office and carry on,"[120] the CIA continued to report unrest in the Bolivian military. That night, Vice President Barrientos met with General Ovando and Army Commanding General Hugo Suárez, and "all agreed that action must be taken to save the country from Víctor Paz Estenssoro." They were hesitant to move, however, because they were "unwilling to join forces" with the FSB, the PCB, or Lechín. According to CIA sources, they considered "fomenting a revolution" but wanted it "to be free of these elements in order that they may form a government more to their liking." During the meeting, Ovando repeatedly complained that "Paz had ordered him to send troops into the Huanuni mining area to pacify the miners." Conceding that he "had not refused," Ovando explained to his fellow generals that he was "stalling for time" because he did not want to "alienate the people towards the army," adding assertively that "army action against [the miners] would be unpatriotic."[121]

In its quest for a more propitious environment in which to launch a coup, the High Command was serendipitously graced with the All Saints Day and All Souls Day weekend, Sunday and Monday, 1–2 November. Paz's Indian militias demobilized and returned to their homes on the altiplano, leaving the capital defenseless. On the eve of the holiday, Saturday, 31 October, Paz once again complained to General Ovando that military units were ignoring his direct order that they march on the mining camps. Paz told Ambassador Henderson on Monday morning that regiments were continuing to throw up a "certain resistance" to his repeated demands that they "take control of key, enemy-controlled mines." As he lost faith in his military, Paz revealed that once the holiday concluded, he would increase the size of his US-equipped Indian militias, putting them under the command of unswervingly loyal pro-Paz generals, many of whom had recently retired. Ever confident in Paz's abilities, Henderson believed that this demonstrated the president was preparing to take decisive action, adding that his decision to remobilize the militias "may foreshadow attempts to deal with military leaders who did not demonstrate complete loyalty to him in the crisis."[122]

Late Sunday night, White House emissary Dentzer arrived in La Paz. The following morning, All Souls Day, he and Henderson visited Paz at his suburban home. The Bolivian president immediately launched into a confident soliloquy, proclaiming that "the agitation had now been conquered, except for the mines near Oruro which were also now quiet." Dentzer misleadingly claimed that his trip was "related to prior plans to visit my area of responsibility," and that it "should not be taken [as] any belief on the part of my government that his government was in great danger." President Paz responded with "gratitude for this attitude," and he once again delivered a "confident and lengthy description" of what had happened, falsely claiming that the "prime cause of the agitation [was] communist-led organization of student activists against a background of uncertainty created by Barrientos's public challenges to his actions." According to Dentzer, the "remainder of the conversation was devoted largely to the second major point I had in mind for the conversation— emphasizing the need for substantial progress on the GOB side of our joint development effort in Bolivia." Dentzer concluded his report by confidently declaring that "Paz has suppressed the recent disturbances in due course, without drawing upon his reserve strength, and appears willing and able to do so for the foreseeable future."[123]

With Paz's approval, Dentzer and Henderson then visited the High Command. The meeting began with US officials praising "the efforts of the Bolivian armed forces in the development of the country" before moving on to an expression of Washington's "opposition to the overthrow of the present government."[124] General Ovando and his men did not beat around the bush. On the contrary, they directly "tested us on [the] idea of coup and found us completely unsympathetic." Henderson reported that he and Dentzer "re-peatedly impressed upon [the] military High Command [the] negative conse-quences of *golpismo* [coup waging]," but Henderson warned that some of the officers, "with characteristic Latin self-delusion, refuse to accept strong prob-ability that once in power they could not remain."[125]

As Henderson and Dentzer held their amicable and supremely confident meeting with President Paz, pro-Barrientos officers had already begun to move. Several junior officers visited US Air Attaché Fox, including the orga-nizers of Barrientos's staged attack in February, Colonel Óscar Quiroga and Major Antonio Arguedas. They were going to launch a coup in the morn-ing. Fox answered as he always had: "I might be in favor of it, but my govern-ment is not, and I have to adhere to what my government says." Fox then added, "assuming it was [in favor], what is it you want? . . . Why do you come to us talking of a coup? If you are so strong and so sure that you have popular backing, why don't you do what you have to do?"[126] As CIA Station Chief Sternfield explained,

> Ed Fox's friendship with Barrientos was an indicator that the US would not *oppose* a Barrientos government. And their friendship would help ameliorate any potential difficulties with the new regime. It was such common knowl-edge in Bolivia at the time that the Air Attaché was a major player in the poli-tics of the country. If Fox had not been Barrientos's friend, it would have been bloody. Because everyone thought, or feared, that the US had been be-hind the coup. That's what kept resistance down. There is no doubt that Fox was a major instigator—*not manipulator*—of Paz's fall by being so close to Barrientos. He didn't have to do anything else. That was enough.[127]

The young officers who were leading the conspiracy apparently felt the same way, because that night, 2 November, they told General Ovando that it was time to act. Ovando responded "in his typical style, expressing his doubts," according to Arguedas. Recognizing their determination, Ovando then asked sheepishly, "Is everything ready?" The decided group responded in unison, "Yes, sir, General!" Ovando then began to ask for specific details, and it appeared to them that he was stalling. As the clock approached mid-night, Colonel Quiroga said, "General, sir. There is no time. In ten minutes the radio will be turned off for the night, and if you don't send the telegram ordering the uprising, I'm out. I will not participate." With that Ovando gave the order, and Quiroga smiled, "Your order will be carried out." Ovando closed the meeting by stating tepidly, "Everyone to your posts." It appeared to

Arguedas that "he didn't do it with much conviction." Arguedas, a Communist Party member, set off for the Milluni mining camp to mobilize its militia in support of any La Paz military units that went through with the mutiny.[128]

Late that night, President Paz received reports from Oruro that miners had "assaulted and sacked" a radio station belonging to government loyalists, prompting him to order additional military units to the region. Two hours later, the army had not made a move, and Paz furiously demanded an explanation for the delay. General Ovando replied stutteringly that his regiments had been "arguing about plans and preparations," and not until 2:00 a.m. on the morning of Tuesday, 3 November, did the military slowly approach Oruro, showing no signs of engaging with the miners.[129]

Five hours later, at 7:00 a.m. on Tuesday, 3 November, both regiments in the General Staff Headquarters, under Colonel Quiroga and Major René Mattos Bustillos, announced they were in revolt. At General Ovando's request, they declared they were holding him and Army Commanding General Suárez hostage. After receiving an 8:00 a.m. phone call from a very worried President Paz, Ambassador Henderson speculated that the High Command's captivity was a ruse that would buy them time to convince their junior officers to abandon their adventure, without appearing to condone the mutiny.[130] Presidency Minister Otero writes that "the imprisonment of both officers was immediately attributed to the government and the armed militias, and the news was sent out over military radio stations throughout the country." At that point, all military regiments in Cochabamba revolted, under pro-Barrientos majors Samuel Gallardo and Simón Sejas.[131]

At 9:40 a.m., Ovando returned "smiling to the Presidential Palace, where [he] was received with a strong, effusive embrace" by President Paz. Ovando asked Paz to consider granting diplomatic asylum to the mutinous junior officers, a solution to which Paz was immediately receptive.[132] Meanwhile, the Waldo Ballivián presidential guard regiment teamed up with police forces to set up roadblocks in the capital, and President Paz told Henderson that he was sending a parliamentary delegation to Cochabamba to "mediate the situation" with Barrientos, who was "attempting to subvert Cochabamba military units." Paz assured Henderson that he was "confident this episode [was] now rapidly being resolved."[133]

Twenty minutes later, however, news arrived that the Cochabamba units had arrested the prefect and taken complete control of the city.[134] Claiming that the Paz government desired to "destroy [the] armed forces" because they "refused [to] employ force against civilians," the Cochabamba garrison declared that it "no longer recognizes Paz government and will fight on [the] side of [the] people."[135] Barrientos cabled Paz shortly afterward, accusing him of using MNR militias to disarm the General Staff Headquarters in La Paz. "The environment is becoming more somber by the minute, and could unravel into a period of pain and mourning," Barrientos wrote, adding that "the Armed Forces will react in defense of the military institution, and this means nothing against the Revolution." Vice President Barrientos closed his cable by recommending that he and Paz both resign to hand over the government to a military junta led by General Ovando, characterizing the offer as "my patriotic and revolutionary proposal, whose aim is to save the Bolivian National Revolution."[136]

The State Department's intelligence arm recognized that Barrientos's call for a military junta represented a "more serious challenge to the authority of President Paz" than the previous week's student and miner disturbances. The situation was "extremely" fluid, the department added, especially since the Bolivian Left had been completely silent on the issue of Barrientos's revolt. The department was confident, nonetheless, that Paz would be able to navigate his way through the crisis, as he had so many times before.[137]

President Paz addressed the nation at 1:00 p.m. on Tuesday, 3 November, calling for the "defense of his revolution and [the] economic development he had brought to the nation." Paz promised that the armed forces "would defend public order," that his Indian militias would "defend revolutionary conquests," and he accused Vice President Barrientos of "playing [the] communist game." Barrientos responded in a nationwide radio broadcast, in which he revealed his proposal that both resign in favor of a military junta that would include neither Paz nor Barrientos.[138] He also called on "all miners to join him in the revolutionary movement," an invitation rapidly accepted by miners' unions throughout the country. The CIA fretted that "the rebellion could take a turn leftward."[139]

At 5:00 p.m., Paz told Henderson that he suspected his military High Command was "playing a double game," leaving him with no choice but to immediately remobilize his Indian militias. Both US-built artillery regiments in Oruro had revolted, and there were rumors that Santa Cruz, Potosi, and Sucre were all in the hands of pro-Barrientos units.[140] The homes of pro-Paz individuals in Cochabamba were being looted, and "all streets leading to the main plaza are jammed with people," attacking with impunity police officers whom they saw as "a symbol of their hatred for Paz."[141] The CIA warned the White House that "armed Ucureña Indians are now marching toward Cochabamba." These were the "most savage fighters in Bolivia" and deeply loyal to General Barrientos.[142] Worst of all, Paz informed Henderson that the General

Staff regiments had not surrendered after all but had instead mobilized and moved to occupy the top floors of the adjacent medical school, where they set up parapets with the acquiescence of the institution's anti-MNR students.[143]

General Ovando called Barrientos from the presidential palace at 7:00 p.m., relating a Paz offer to appoint an exclusively military cabinet headed by Paz Estenssoro. Barrientos rejected the proposal, and President Paz began broadcasting calls throughout the capital for Indian and MNR party militias to mobilize in defense of the revolution.[144] Despite his son's entreaties to "just leave,"[145] Paz remained calm, explaining to Henderson that "as many armed militia and peasants as possible have been ordered to La Paz from the Achacachi area as soon as possible."[146]

That night, Henderson began the "inception of warning phase" of his previously drafted "Escape and Evacuation Plan," asking that his country team begin "warning all resident Americans of possible danger."[147] He then relayed CIA tallies of the armed contingents on each side of the crisis. La Paz, he wrote, remained "quiet with militia on the streets," and Indian reinforcements were en route from Achacachi. Meanwhile, the air base remained loyal and was "supported" by four hundred MNR militiamen who had taken up positions around the airport. In the capital, the president could count on 3,000 police, 900 members of the Waldo Ballivián presidential guard regiment, and "perhaps 800 others in miscellaneous [MNR militia] units." On the other hand, Vice President Barrientos boasted the support of Viacha's 750-strong Max Toledo First Motorized Battalion, 620 men of the Mendez Arcos Ranger Battalion in Challapata, 250 in the Second Division in Oruro, and 800 in various miners' militias. In Cochabamba, Barrientos counted on the loyalty of 500 soldiers in "various units" in addition to "perhaps 2,000" armed Quechua Indians. Most important, La Paz's 400-strong Ingavi Regiment and the Polytechnic Institute, with 300 young officer cadets, had joined the revolt.[148]

With the situation deteriorating, Ambassador Henderson doubled down. At 10:00 p.m., President Paz telephoned to ask the status of an arms shipment that would outfit a "10,000-man [militia] reserve." Henderson told the Bolivian president that a partial shipment was on its way, including one million rounds of .30 Ball ammunition. He then stressed to the State Department the importance of providing a full arms shipment as soon as possible, since "denial to Paz now would in fact signal US withdrawal [of] support of [the] present government to both Paz and Barrientos and would be [a] significant factor [in] unbalancing [the] present odds." Henderson added that Paz's chances were "still better than even," since he controlled the air base and was supported by

"8250 effective armed men in La Paz as against 5900 Barrientos effectives in Cochabamba, Oruro, and elsewhere." Given these odds, "additional weapons in [the] hands [of] even semi-trained personnel which is [the] Paz reserve would increase fire power to [a] degree which could significantly increase [the] odds favoring Paz."[149]

Henderson reiterated to Washington that Barrientos was surrounded by leftist advisers, and he stressed that any post-Paz government would suffer from "inherent instability," leading to the "likelihood of communist influence in [the] chaotic situation." The ambassador expressed that he "would of course prefer [a] position of non-intervention," but he pointed out defiantly that the arms request "comes from [the] head of constitutional government" and that Washington would "not on balance gain by pulling back from Paz now." Finally, Henderson concluded on a firm note: "We wish to reiterate our estimate [that a] Barrientos-led military overthrow [of the] Paz government provides communists [with an] opportunity [to] infiltrate [the] successor government with [a] chance [to] eventually take over, especially since Barrientos has repeatedly demonstrated his inability to discern communists and crypto-communists among his advisors."[150]

Just after midnight on 3 November, President Paz retired to his chambers with his son.[151] The CIA reported that he would "probably resign as President on 4 November 1964," since he "had little confidence in the armed forces and was very pessimistic."[152] There were slivers of hope, however. Paz had recently received reports that Indian forces had remobilized in Oruro and Santa Cruz, and his cabinet appeared to be "maintaining firm behind the president without exception."[153]

Around 1:00 a.m., however, loyalist Generals Eduardo Rivas, Ronant Monje, and Guillermo Ariñez eagerly sought to locate Paz in the presidential palace. First encountering COMIBOL President Bedregal and Mining Minister René Zavaleta on the ground floor, the generals warned them that "all is lost" and that Oruro regiments were "marching rapidly toward La Paz, followed by hundreds of miners." In the company of Bedregal and Zavaleta, the generals ascended to President Paz's chambers, where Rivas explained the situation in Oruro. Bedregal spoke up, urging Paz to "break the supposed truce and attack General Staff Headquarters with all available forces" of militias. Paz responded that additional weaponry would not arrive until 7:00 a.m., and he refused to send them into battle against overwhelming odds. At that moment, word arrived that the Waldo Ballivián presidential guard had joined the uprising, and Paz learned that the miners' militia at nearby Milluni was also marching toward La Paz under the command of Major Arguedas. Paz decided at that moment that there was "no way out," and he ordered the distribution of "the few arms available" to the militias to "avoid a massacre."[154]

Attempting to convince Washington to abandon its support for Paz Estenssoro, Vice President Barrientos sent a message to Ambassador Henderson at 1:00 a.m., promising that "elimination of Communists would be [the] first order [of] business [of] his government." It made no difference. At 6:00 a.m. the High Command confirmed to Paz that it would "not engage armed forces in battle [on] his behalf," forcing the president to "conclude [that] his resignation [was] in [the] best interest of the nation." Not waiting for the two thousand Achacachi Indians to arrive or the US weapons shipment to land, the most powerful Bolivian leader of the twentieth century was on a plane to Lima with his family.[155]

Paz Estenssoro left his last cabinet meeting at 9:30 a.m., after "giving [the] impression that he would return."[156] Indeed, he told one of his advisers that he was "going to inspect his defenses."[157] In fact, he was fleeing for his life.[158] Students and miners never scared Víctor Paz. On the contrary, he believed he had the firepower to enforce his vision of modernity on sectors of Bolivian society who were violently opposed. Days earlier he had successfully headed off student and miner rebellions, but President Paz soon faced a more formidable challenge: the Bolivian military. Some officers had been scheming against the MNR for years. Others simply tired of serving as an armed wing of Paz's repressive, US-backed regime. The High Command had a great deal to lose, however, and junior officers were therefore the ultimate instigators of the coup. When these young soldiers announced their units in mutiny on the morning of 3 November, they forced their generals to take sides. There was no great conspiracy; Paz faced a military uprising from below. Barrientos joined with characteristic impulse, and Ovando deftly converted the revolt into a unified coup d'état.

Meanwhile, Washington was there until the bitter end, doggedly supporting its beleaguered ally. When Henderson received the fateful phone call from the presidential palace at 8:00 a.m. on 4 November, his first question was, "[What] about [the weapons] shipments?" Paz's foreign minister somberly explained to a stunned ambassador that the "shipments requested should not now come forward."[159] As Henderson later explained, "I made up my mind right then that he was probably a goner."[160]

The Johnson administration never vacillated in its support for President Paz, a development-oriented economist and lawyer, over the brash, young Barrientos, and the United States continued to arm Paz's militias, despite the fact that they were set to square off against factions of the Bolivian military. Much to the chagrin of liberal modernizers, the Indian peasants did not arrive in time. Early on 4 November 1964, the highest per capita recipient of Alliance for Progress funding abdicated his position in a most unceremonious fashion, and US officials scrambled to come to terms with the bombshell that had just befallen its foreign policy in Latin America.

Conclusion

Development and Its Discontents

A revolution always causes societal dislocations, and binding
elements are needed. The Armed Forces are this binding
element . . . the vanguard of the Bolivian people in the construction
of the new society.
—President Víctor Paz, 6 August 1964

Was the 1964 coup a revolution or a counterrevolution? As Ambassador
Henderson put it, "In Bolivia, they don't come down so neat."[1] The immediate result of the military takeover was a popular insurrection. Armed students
and workers stormed the national penitentiary and Control Político offices,
freeing hundreds of right-wing and left-wing political prisoners in barrages of
gunfire. At least half a dozen Control Político prisoners were killed by Paz's
agents, who were determined to go down in a blaze.[2] Siglo XX union leaders
Escóbar and Pimentel saw the light of day for the first time in almost a year,
and they returned to the mining camp where Escóbar led a breakaway Maoist
Communist Party officially dedicated to armed struggle.[3] Meanwhile, university students sacked and occupied the home of Control Político chief San
Román, and thousands of his surveillance records were burned in a bonfire in
front of the Justice Ministry. CIA Station Chief Sternfield also visited a few
of San Román's safe houses. "They were the bloodiest things I've ever seen,"
Sternfield recalled, "Skin, blood, arms, legs. Blood on the walls. I was just
sick. San Román was anti-military, pro-Nazi."[4]

If Sternfield was right, and 4 November represented the victory of an antifascist front of rightists, liberals, and communists, what was the new regime

to do with its leftist allies? The answer came swiftly. After Paz fled, thousands of workers took to the streets, assuming that labor leader Juan Lechín would be granted a share of power. They carried Lechín on their shoulders, shouting, "Lechín to the palace!" as they ascended Ayacucho Street to the central plaza. They were too late, as cadets from the Military Academy had already taken control of the plaza, under the command of Captain Luis García Meza, and soldiers from the Ingavi Regiment had occupied the presidential palace. As the demonstrators approached the palace, a military sentry shut the door, prompting the workers to fire their old Mauser rifles into the air and push forward toward the entryway. When the masses pulled back, the soldier fell to the ground. He was only shaken up, but it looked much worse to the cadets who were watching nervously from the other side of the plaza. The soldiers had earlier decided to rely on warning shots above the heads of any trouble-makers, but when Captain García Meza gave the order to fire, at least three workers were fatally shot. In the melee, a bloodstained Juan Lechín fled to General Staff Headquarters, where he lodged a furious complaint with Bolivia's new military leaders. General Ovando characterized the plaza fracas as a mistake, stressing that he and Barrientos hoped to rule with a coalition of civilian parties, including Lechín's left-wing Partido Revolucionario de la Izquierda Nacionalista (PRIN; Revolutionary Party of the Nationalist Left). It was clear, however, that the popular front that brought down Paz Estenssoro was rapidly disintegrating.[5]

Ambassador Henderson would have preferred Ovando, his deal with Lechín notwithstanding, over the unpredictable Barrientos and his Cochabamba leftist friends. The following night, however, when Ovando and Barrientos prepared to address the masses as co-presidents, Ovando was booed off the balcony. Realizing that Barrientos was the popular symbol of the revolt, Ovando resigned his half of the presidency, retaining the powerful position of commander-in-chief.[6] Barrientos gave a rousing speech, peppered with references to social justice and political liberty, declaring that he wished to "restore the revolution." For several weeks, US officials jockeyed with the new president, especially over his left-wing advisers. By early December, the leftists had either been fired or resigned,[7] and Washington finally extended recognition a month after the coup. For the next four years, General Barrientos apparently followed an unwaveringly pro-US line. CIA Station Chief Sternfield boasts that until Barrientos's death in 1969, "nothing happened in Bolivia without our involvement.[8]

Pinning Blame

Aside from Bolivian leftists and rightists, who holds ultimate responsibility for the 1964 coup? Many historians, including James Dunkerley and Kenneth Lehman, contend that US officials, namely, Embassy Air Attaché Edward Fox, gave the green light to General Barrientos. Dunkerley refers to Colonel Fox as "the CIA chief in Bolivia . . . [who] secured such control over the interior ministry that he could act without reference to the [presidential] *Palacio Quemado*."[9] Meanwhile, Lehman writes that US officials "withdrew their support [for the Movimiento Nacionalista Revolucionario (MNR; Revolutionary Nationalist Movement)] . . . [and] in a number of less than subtle ways . . . revealed their waning commitment to civilian democracy."[10] Until now, conspiratorial accounts have also dominated nonspecialist literature on the coup, including popular histories of the CIA and broader Latin American studies.[11]

Similarly, most Bolivian authors pin the blame squarely on Colonel Fox. Former Paz cabinet official Guillermo Bedregal characterizes Fox as the "mentor of the counterrevolutionary regression," the "visible head" of covert action in Bolivia, who channeled Washington's "antidemocratic and militaristic policy . . . of installing military governments that would carry out US dictates."[12] René Zavaleta Mercado, another former Paz minister, writes that the "acquiescence of Fox and CIA agents is so notorious that definite proof is almost unnecessary. . . . Fox was, therefore, the father of 4 November." In Zavaleta's view, "the only person who knows all the aspects of 4 November is Colonel Fox."[13]

On the other hand, historians James Malloy and Herbert Klein describe the Barrientos coup in purely domestic terms, pointing to growing local opposition to Paz's use of repression to carry out his developmentalist vision.[14] Political scientist William Brill also believes the military takeover emerged from within, basing his analysis on dozens of interviews with key actors before and after the coup.[15] A similar line has been taken by Bolivian historian Luis Antezana Ergueta, who argues that MNR dissidents played the central role in their own party's downfall.[16] Military historian Robert Kirkland, the only other scholar to my knowledge who has interviewed Colonel Fox, claims that the air attaché intervened to stop his friend General Barrientos from overthrowing Paz in May 1964, arguing that Fox was eventually disenchanted with Barrientos when the general failed to heed his advice in

November.[17] Finally, at least one CIA memoir suggests that the agency was firmly behind Paz Estenssoro and even tracked Paz's exiled political enemies in Uruguay and Buenos Aires.[18]

The complex process by which the November 1964 coup came to fruition is partially reflected in Paz's own testimony shortly after his overthrow. Conceding that "on 4 November, the coup came from within," the fallen leader cited two other reasons for the military takeover. First, it was "developmentalism, which got us wrapped up in the administrative activity of the government, and we neglected—as a result—politics and the party." Second, Paz claimed that "contractions within US foreign policy" weakened his government and eventually led to his overthrow.[19] A journalist who interviewed Paz in early 1968 reported that the MNR leader "still insists that Fox was behind his ouster. Among Bolivians with an awareness of politics, it is hard to find anyone who disagrees."[20]

Did Colonel Edward Fox single-handedly destroy constitutional government in Bolivia, as many claim? Or were his fervent attempts to defend the Paz government stymied by Barrientos's runaway ambition, as Kirkland recently proposed? In Fox's own words:

> As far as giving Barrientos orders to stop a coup, that's ridiculous. I would never have gotten into Bolivian politics like that, and I certainly wouldn't have treated my friend that way.
>
> Barrientos and I never had a rift. Nothing could be further from the truth. When I arrived back in La Paz [in 1962], I told him, "You do what you have to do, René, and I will try to support you when I can. But we can't bullshit each other."
>
> I always knew Barrientos would go through with it, and I knew he would succeed. That's why I tried to convince [Ambassador Douglas] Henderson to support him. I failed, and was not able to give Barrientos any material support. I didn't agree with Henderson on everything, but it's *normal* to have disagreements. We were friends, though. Hell, we're still friends.
>
> November 4th wasn't our show. They thought they had what they needed, and didn't want to get too many people in on it. Sometimes you get too many people in on these things, and they get all screwed up. They also had pride, and didn't want to be a charity case.[21]

Ambassador Henderson confirmed Fox's recollection: "Ed Fox was the no. 1 freelancer in the world. But he never went rogue."[22] The CIA station chief at the time, Larry Sternfield, agreed: "There was no division in US policy; there were just sentiments. Barrientos was a likeable guy, and a lot of us liked him. But as far as supporting a coup, absolutely not. Henderson was very pro-Paz, and that was the policy of our government. Like Ed Fox, we were being asked to carry out a policy we hated—to support Paz Estenssoro."[23]

It is tempting to search, but an easy villain of 4 November does not exist. As historian Laurence Whitehead writes, "The crucial form of American intervention . . . was not this kind of sinister conspiracy . . . but the increasingly political trend of American pressures over the previous three or four years—pressures which helped create the conditions for a coup, whether it was consciously intended or not."[24] Sergio Almaraz Paz, a Communist who joined the MNR in 1952, agrees that it was precisely US *support* for Paz Estenssoro that undermined his government. Once liberal ambassador Ben Stephansky brought Kennedy's development programs to Bolivia, "the revolution was damned. Its general ideas were lost, its fundamental thrust had been abandoned, and the Americans monopolized all the power: institution by institution, organization by organization, program by program. If economic organizations were under their dependency, those of security were under their complete control." Almaraz adds that the "brutality" of US conservatives, many of whom had long advocated for an end to US aid to revolutionary Bolivia, "would have better preserved the revolution than the liberalism of Stephansky."[25]

If Washington opposed Paz's overthrow, did the Left welcome it? Indeed, one of this book's findings is that many Bolivian leftists actively sought a military coup, in the hope that they could take advantage of the chaos to increase their political influence through sympathetic officers or by filling a vacuum left by the MNR in key Bolivian institutions. The Communist Party was the last leftist party to adopt such a policy, as it interpreted Moscow's call for peaceful coexistence as a reason to tolerate MNR rule, and Paz Estenssoro repaid this tolerance by permitting PCB activity and maintaining diplomatic relations with Cuba and Czechoslovakia. Paz failed in his drive to neutralize Bolivia leftism, however, and under heavy US pressure, Bolivia was the second-to-last Latin American nation to break with Cuba.[26] Communists had already succeeded in infiltrating labor and student organizations, and to a lesser extent the government and military. General Barrientos's endearing tendency to parrot the Communist line to his friends in the US Embassy was testament to the extent to which leftists had achieved powerful positions throughout Bolivian society. Once Paz Estenssoro broke with Cuba in August 1964, dissident Communists—especially in the mining camps—joined with Trotskyists and breakaway MNR leftists to agitate strongly for

Paz's ouster. The Bolivian Right had long conspired against Paz Estenssoro, and throughout September and October, the Left joined them to bring down the regime.

One reason there has been some resistance to the idea that the United States supported Paz to the bitter end, opposing Barrientos's adventure, is that it does not easily square with what came later. As Latin American leftists bitterly recall, General Barrientos governed as a strongly pro–United States president, meted out fierce repression in the mining camps, and presided over the execution of captured Argentine-Cuban guerrilla leader Ernesto "Che" Guevara. None of this was etched in stone in 1964, however, at which time many of General Barrientos's advisers were indeed Marxists. Barrientos conspired against Paz with Washington's chief nemesis, labor federation leader Juan Lechín, and on 3 November he called for the Communist-led miners to join his revolution. Colonel Fox was confident in his friendship with General Barrientos, and he did everything he could to convince Ambassador Henderson that the young, brash pilot was inviolably anticommunist. Many US officials were less convinced, however, worrying that leftists would be able to take advantage of Barrientos's good-natured populism and lack of intellectual sophistication. Washington was correct that the general's youth and impulsivity would require him to seek outside counsel and largely rely on others for day-to-day governance. Rather than benefiting Bolivian communism, however, this played right into the hands of the CIA.

The Decade of Development and the Military Coup

Western developmentalism often has little to do with its stated goals. As James Ferguson suggests in his work on World Bank programs in Lesotho, development is adopted time and again because it invariably produces the same political side effect: an increase in state power.[27] In some cases, it even encourages authoritarianism.[28] In a comparative sense, the Alliance for Progress in Bolivia fits snugly within this rubric. Its ideological makeup was constructed within an anticommunist strategic environment, it justified the growth of a repressive government, and it drove the rapid militarization of Bolivian society. All in the name of development.

The debate that has driven historiography on Kennedy's foreign policy in Latin America falls into two camps. One group of historians contend that Kennedy policymakers genuinely cared about Third World development and that they were frustrated by Latin American elites, the failure of their own ideas, or Kennedy's untimely death.[29] Another group of historians argue that the Kennedy administration was nothing new and that it closely adhered to Washington's perennial drive for political hegemony in the Western Hemisphere, developmentalist rhetoric notwithstanding.[30]

This book suggests that both groups are right. In short, many US liberals cared deeply about Third World development, and that is precisely why they fought so hard against the Bolivian Left. When he resigned from USAID declaring that the agency had "nothing to do with the economic development of Bolivia," Melvin Burke was correct.[31] USAID operated as one political species within a larger strategic ecosystem. If development happened to square with the extension of US power, fine. If not, *tant pis*;[32] there were many other strategies at Washington's disposal.

The benefit of the Bolivian case is that it demonstrates how the Alliance for Progress operated when "development" was perfectly compatible with the extension of US power, where local leaders were fully dedicated to it, where the enterprise got off the ground early, and where there was nothing stopping the program from arriving at its logical apogee before Kennedy passed away. The result was decidedly authoritarian. For Bolivia, the Alliance for Progress hemmed neatly to what Ferguson, Peter Uvin, and James C. Scott have found elsewhere[33]—development as a framework within which states exercise power, sometimes aggressively. Ideological development was the chosen strategy of US liberals, and their ideas were vindicated as the United States achieved unparalleled influence in Bolivian society. As Almaraz writes,

> The absorption of power by the Americans brought with it a more general and imprecise phenomenon: the Bolivians began to feel uncomfortable with themselves. If a foreigner imposes himself as a permanent intermediary; if plans as diverse as electrification, roads, or schools, all depend on him; if he has to tell us how we have to live and how to think . . . finally, if everything that is done, or allowed to be done, depends on the interests of a foreign nation, citizens end up segregating themselves. . . . If it is repulsive to see a member of the bourgeoisie kissing up to an ambassador and smiling with servility to obtain a credit or loan, it is painful to see Indians holding bouquets of flowers as testimony to their gratefulness. . . . Poverty facilitates colonization; men in Bolivia have a lower price. At a certain level, poverty destroys dignity; the Americans have discovered this level, and that is where they work. In their view and for their wallets, a Bolivian costs less than an Argentine or a Chilean.

In Almaraz's view, the Alliance for Progress succeeded in elevating US policy to a higher, development-oriented plane, with deleterious effects for Bolivia: "Under the inspiration of the short, intelligent Ben Stephansky, the methods evolved significantly. . . . Surviving Rooseveltian, friend of writers and professors. . . . He was the creator of a new style. He liked to fancy himself as an unbiased liberal, and perhaps deep down he was. . . . Between smiles and handshakes, he did more damage than all his boorish predecessors: Texans who smelled like cattle, screwballs who collected lighters, and unimaginative bureaucrats."[34]

It would be a mistake, nonetheless, to argue that Stephansky was alone in his authoritarian drive to develop Bolivia, and thus keep it out of communist hands. There are three bodies buried at the Museum of the National Revolution in La Paz, all military generals.[35] Far from being a US export to Bolivia, military-led modernization was an offspring of revolutionary nationalism, which aimed to bring order and authority to a chaotic society and "create out of Bolivia a real Nation."[36] But nation building is inherently political, for the emerging society will bear the image of whoever controls the development process. This book suggests that ideology is a crucial aspect of strategic studies. Liberals in Washington salivated over the opportunity to guide the trajectory of revolutionary Bolivia. Meanwhile, Bolivian nationalists hoped to leverage US aid for their own political ends. Within the framework of a technocratic discourse about economic efficiency, a bloody battle was being waged for the future of the country. As tends to be the case in violent conflict, the better-armed faction won.

Notes

Preface

1. Hunter S. Thompson, "Baffling Bolivia: A Never-Never Land High above the Sea," *National Observer*, 15 April 1963. Thompson wrote of his bourbon-fueled nights in the home of US labor information officer Tom Martin in "Mr. Martin in Bolivia: What the Miners Lost in Taking an Irishman," *National Observer*, 16 December 1963. Confirmed in interviews with Martin's wife, Mariela, and his son Rory.

2. Stephansky to Secretary Rusk, 29 August 1962, "Bolivia, General, 8/62–12/62," box 10, National Security Files—Countries (hereafter NSF-CO), John F. Kennedy Presidential Library (hereafter JFKL); Henderson to Secretary of State Rusk, 7 and 8 May 1964, "Bolivia, Cables, Volume 1, 12/63–7/63," box 7, NSF-CO, Lyndon Baines Johnson Presidential Library (hereafter LBJL); Lansdale to Defense Secretary Robert McNamara, 3 June 1963, "Bolivia, General, 4/63–7/63," box 10A, NSF-CO, JFKL.

3. Unless otherwise noted, all documents cited below are located at NARA. If no record group is specified, the document can be found in record group 59.

4. Barry Goldwater, quoted in "Bolivian Rule of Paz Rapped by Goldwater," *Chicago Tribune*, 25 October 1963.

5. The better-known *Granma* did not begin circulation until 1965.

Introduction

1. Sara Shahriari, "Bolivia's Evo Morales Says 'Adiós' to USAID," *Christian Science Monitor*, 1 May 2013; William Neuman, "U.S. Agency Is Expelled from Bolivia," *New York Times*, 2 May 2013.

2. USAID, "USAID Bolivia," 1 May 2013, http://www.usaid.gov/news-information/fact-sheets/usaid-bolivia, accessed 6 June 2013. Despite claiming to have set up operations only in 1964, USAID-Bolivia has been active since the agency's founding in late 1961. Previously, development operations were carried out by the International Cooperation Administration (ICA). Modern

US development programs in Bolivia are best dated to a 1941 State Department mission led by Merwin Bohan, which called for economic diversification, particularly in the agricultural field. See Lehman, *Bolivia and the United States*, 183.

3. See chapters 3 and 4 in this volume.

4. Kennedy, "Speech before the General Assembly of the United Nations," 25 September 1961, Speeches, Reference Desk, JFKL.

5. Kennedy, "NSAM 88," 5 September 1961; "NSAM 119," 18 December 1961, National Security Action Memoranda, NSF-JFK, JFKL.

6. Westad, *Global Cold War*, 4.

7. Between 1953 and 1965, more than six million hectares of land was redistributed, benefiting more than 170,000 Indian families. A 1950 survey estimated total arable land at just less than thirty-three million hectares. Source: Departamento de Estadística, Servicio Nacional Reforma Agraria (8 February 1966), published in Melvin Burke, "Land Reform in the Lake Titicaca Region," in Malloy and Thorn, *Beyond the Revolution*, 303.

8. Bolivian Foreign Ministry to Embassy (Belgrade), 29 April 1963; RV-4-E-54, Archivo del Ministerio de Relaciones Exteriores y Culto (Archive of the Ministry of Foreign Affairs and Culture), La Paz, Bolivia (hereafter RREE). Regarding the Soviet offer, Juan Lechín, "Comunicado," undated (late 1960), Presidencia de la República (hereafter PR) 945, Archivo y Biblioteca Nacional (National Archive and Library), Sucre, Bolivia (hereafter ABNB). See also "Bolivia Weighing Soviet Aid Offer," *New York Times*, 2 November 1960; "Soviet Assures Bolivia," *New York Times*, 24 December 1960; "US and Soviets Battle over Bolivia's Tin," *New York Times*, 22 January 1961.

9. Between 1953 and 1964, Bolivia received $368 million in US foreign aid, roughly $35 million annually. In 2007 dollars, this represents more than $2 billion, or $187 million annually, the highest per capita amount given to any Latin American nation during that period. Kennedy increased aid to Bolivia from roughly $23 million annually to $51 million. By 1964, Alliance for Progress funds constituted around 20 percent of Bolivian GDP and 40 percent of the nation's public expenditures. Sources: United States Agency for International Development (USAID), *US Overseas Loans and Grants (Greenbook)*, available online at qesdb.usaid.gov/gbk. Bolivia data from USAID, *Economic and Program Statistics,* nos. 5, 11, supplemented by data from Bolivian Development Corporation, to calculate Bolivian government expenditures, and data from Dirección Nacional de Coordinación y Planeamiento, *Bolivia cuentas nacionales*, mimeographed (La Paz, January 1969). The Bolivian data are published in Malloy and Thorn, *Beyond the Revolution*, 370, 380.

10. Said, *Orientalism*, 20, 222; Ferguson, *Anti-Politics Machine*; Uvin, *Aiding Violence*; Scott, *Seeing Like a State*. See also Escobar, *Encountering Development*; Mitchell, *Rule of Experts*.

11. Westad, *Global Cold War*; Cullather, *Hungry World*; Simpson, *Economists with Guns*; Latham, *Right Kind of Revolution*; Latham, *Modernization as Ideology*; Milne, *America's Rasputin*; Gilman, *Mandarins of the Future*; Engerman et al., *Staging Growth*; McVety, *Enlightened Aid*.

12. Simpson, *Economists with Guns*; Cullather, *Hungry World*; Milne, *America's Rasputin*; Latham, *Modernization as Ideology*; Latham, *Right Kind of Revolution*.

13. Despite the fact that revolutionary Bolivia received more per capita US development aid than any other Latin American country during the early 1960s, it has received scant attention from scholars of the Alliance for Progress development program, launched by President Kennedy in 1961. See Rabe, *Most Dangerous Area in the World*; Taffet, *Foreign Aid as Foreign Policy*; Levinson and de Onís, *Alliance That Lost Its Way*. Of diplomatic historians, only three offer more than passing reference to the Alliance for Progress in Bolivia: Siekmeier, *Bolivian Revolution*, 86–102; Lehman, *Bolivia and the United States*, 134–36; and Blasier, *Hovering Giant*, 140–45.

14. Regarding pre-Liberal Bolivia, see Rossana Barragán, "Oppression or Privileged Regions? Some Historical Reflections on the Use of State Resources," in Crabtree and Whitehead, *Unresolved*

Tensions, 86. On *pongeaje* and land tenure, see Herbert Klein, "Prelude to Revolution," in Malloy and Thorn, *Beyond the Revolution*, 27–28. See also Xavier Albó, "The 'Long Memory' of Ethnicity in Bolivia and Some Temporary Oscillations," in Crabtree and Whitehead, *Unresolved Tensions*; Hylton and Thomson, *Revolutionary Horizons*, 50–61; Dunkerley, *Rebellion in the Veins*, 31–32.

15. Klein, "Prelude to Revolution," in Malloy and Thornton, *Beyond the Revolution*, 39.

16. On the lynching of President Villarroel and the *sexenio*, see Dorn, *Truman Administration and Bolivia*; Laurence Whitehead, "Bolivia," in Bethell and Roxborough, *Latin America*, 120–46.

17. For accounts of the revolution, see Dunkerley, *Rebellion in the Veins*, 38–82; Klein, *Bolivia*, 224–45. A theoretical treatment is offered by Trotskyite leader Guillermo Lora, *La Revolución Boliviana*. A less sympathetic narrative is Hugo Roberts Barragán, *La Revolución del 9 de Abril* (La Paz: Cooperativa de Artes Gráficas, 1971). A well-documented, pro-MNR study is Antezana, *Historia secreta del Movimiento Nacionalista Revolucionario, Tomo 7*.

18. For more on Bolivia's success in obtaining US support, see Siekmeier, "Trailblazer Diplomat"; Siekmeier, *Bolivian Revolution and the United States*. See also Lehman, *Bolivia and the United States*; Zondag, *Bolivian Economy, 1952–1965*.

19. Dunkerley, *Rebellion*, 84–93; Lehman, *Bolivia and the United States*, 122–25; Klein, *Bolivia*, 240–42.

20. Prado Salmón, *Poder y fuerzas armadas*, 100–101; Noel, "La génération des jeunes officiers issus du collège militaire Gualberto Villarroel," 27–30.

21. See footnote 8 to this chapter.

22. Paz's trips to Belgrade and Prague provided a foundation upon which Yugoslavia and Czechoslovakia offered economic assistance to Bolivia in the early 1960s. Paz interview, in Trigo, *Conversaciones con Víctor Paz Estenssoro*, 142.

23. Lechín, *El pueblo al poder*, 118.

24. Kennedy, "Address at a White House Reception for Latin American Diplomats and Members of Congress," 13 March 1961, Speeches, Reference Desk, JFKL.

25. Thorpe et al., "Report to the President," 24 March 1961, folder 7, Presidential Office Files (hereafter POF), JFKL, 2 (cover letter) and 2, 22 (report).

26. Rubin to Kennedy, 3 April 1961, "Bolivia, General, 1961," box 10, NSF-CO, JFKL.

27. Webster, "Regimes in Motion."

28. See Juan Lechín, "Comunicado," undated (late 1960), Presidencia de la República (hereafter PR) 945, Archivo y Biblioteca Nacional, Sucre, Bolivia (hereafter ABNB). Alarmed, the US press reportedly extensively the Soviet offer. See "Bolivia Weighing Soviet Aid Offer," *New York Times*, 2 November 1960; "Soviet Assures Bolivia," *New York Times*, 24 December 1960; "US and Soviets Battle over Bolivia's Tin," *New York Times*, 22 January 1961.

29. Simpson, *Economists with Guns*.

30. State Department, "Guidelines for Policy and Operations," March 1963, "Bolivia, 2/63–6/63," box 389A, NSF-Dungan, JFKL, 20.

31. Stephansky to Rusk, 29 September 1962, "Bolivia, General, 8/62–12/62," box 10, NSF-CO, JFKL.

32. State Department, "Bolivia—State-AID Contingency Paper for COMIBOL Crisis," 8 August 1963, "Bolivia, 7/73–6/64," box 389A, NSF-Dungan, JFKL, 3.

1. Modernization's Heavy Hand

1. Pace Piero Gleijeses, who correctly points out that "Fidel Castro was midwife to the Alliance for Progress." Gleijeses, "Book Review: A Sordid Affair," 793.

2. Paz, quoted in Ascarrunz, *La palabra de Paz*, 47.

3. Paz's authoritarianism fell chiefly on the rightist Falange Socialista Boliviana (FSB; Bolivian Socialist Falange). The FSB repaid Paz by organizing a panoply of attempted coups throughout the 1950s. The mysterious death of FSB leader Óscar Unzaga in 1959 temporarily silenced the party and opened space on the right for a new political movement, headed by MNR breakaway Wálter Guevara Arze. When Paz returned from his ambassadorship in London, his main opponent was none other than Guevara, whose Partido Revolucionario Auténtico (PRA; Authentic Revolutionary Party) waged a fiercely anticommunist campaign. For more on Paz's first term and his 1960 electoral battle against the PRA, see Dunkerley, *Rebellion in the Veins*, 38–82, 99–103; Klein, *Bolivia*, 227–41, 243–44; Lehman, *Bolivia and the United States*, 91–123; Malloy, *Bolivia*, 167–242.

4. Interviews with Ramiro Paz.

5. Interviews with Luis Antezana.

6. Sukarno visited 4–7 May 1961, Tito 28 September–4 October 1963, and de Gaulle 28–29 September 1964. See "Arribará Hoy el Presidente de Indonesia," *El Diario*, 4 May 1961; "Protocolar Acogida se Dispensó al Presidente Tito en Cochabamba," *El Diario*, 29 September 1963; "De Gaulle, Halfway through Latin Tour, Arrives in Bolivia," *New York Times*, 29 September 1964.

7. In the early 1940s, Paz strongly advocated for threatening to sell tin to the Axis powers, with an eye toward pressuring the Allies to pay higher prices. In short, Paz believed Bolivia should "take advantage of the circumstances so the country could obtain the maximum benefit possible." Paz interview, in Ascarrunz, *La palabra de Paz*, 40.

8. The US Defense Department noted that Paz's Bolivia was pursuing a "not wholly clear, but nonetheless real, identification with the neutral powers of Africa and Asia." See Special Operations Research Office, *U.S. Army Area Handbook for Bolivia*, 413–14. See also Rakove, *Kennedy, Johnson, and the Nonaligned World*, 222.

9. CIA, Intelligence Bulletin, 3 February 1961, CIA Records Search Tool (hereafter CREST).

10. The Czech visit is reported in Foreign Ministry to Economic Ministry, 13 January 1961, RV-4-E-53, RREE. See also 1961 meetings between Bolivia's chargé in Prague and Czech foreign ministry officials, Inv. č 93, "Relations, Czechoslovakia—Bolivia," *Komunistická strana Československa, Ústřední výbor, Kancelář I, Tajemníka ÚV KSČ Antonína Novotného—II. Č*, *Národní archiv*, Prague, Czech Republic (hereafter KSČ-NA).

11. CIA, Intelligence Bulletin, 13 January 1961, CREST. For more on the Soviet aid offer, see Introduction, footnote 8, in this volume.

12. CIA, Intelligence Bulletin, 3 February 1961, CREST.

13. INR to Secretary of State Rusk, 9 January 1963, "Bolivia, General, 1/63–3/63," box 10A, NSF-CO, JFKL.

14. Mann to Ball, 14 February 1961, "Bolivia, 1961," box 2, lots 62D418 and 64D15, State Department Lot Files (hereafter SDLF).

15. Noel, "La génération des jeunes officiers," 11. Noel bases his doctoral work on interviews with scores of surviving officers, tracing the manner by which the military survived the aftermath of the revolution, going on to rule the country between 1964 and 1982. The 1953 decree reorganizing the armed forces is reprinted in Noel's annex, 473–75. See also Brill, "Military Civic Action in Bolivia," 80.

16. Noel, "La génération des jeunes officiers," 21. For an account based on Bolivian press, see Knudson, *Bolivia*, 295–329.

17. Paz, 1959, *Las Fuerzas Armadas*.

18. MNR, *Programa del Gobierno: Tercer Gobierno*, 118.

19. Paz, 6 August 1960, *Discurso inaugural*, 23. Many thanks to Luis Antezana Ergueta for providing a copy of this document.

20. Yet Paz shunned executions. As one lower-level Paz official explained, his rule was, "It is better to have 100 prisoners than one martyr." Interviews with Antezana. Confirmed by Paz's son Ramiro.

21. "Grupo de 35 Detenidos Será Desterrado Hoy al Paraguay," *El Diario*, 23 February 1961.

22. "Consta de Medidas Estrictas el 'Auto de Buen Gobierno,'" *El Diario*, 22 February 1961.

23. Rivas, "Comunicado," 21 February 1961, PR 945, ABNB.

24. Schlesinger to Kennedy, 10 March 1961, document 7, U.S. Department of State, Foreign Relations of the United States (hereafter *FRUS*), *1961–1963:Volume XII—American Republics*.

25. Schlesinger Journal, 24 February 1961, in Schlesinger and Schlesinger, *Journals, 1952–2000*, 104–6.

26. Ibid.

27. Schlesinger to Kennedy, 3 March 1961, "Bolivia," box WH-3, Schlesinger Papers, JFKL.

28. Williams to Strom, 16 March 1961, "320, General and International Political Relations, 1959–60–61, Vol. III," box 1, Post Files, Record Group (hereafter RG) 84, National Archives and Records Administration (NARA).

29. "Los Presidentes de Bolivia y del BID Firmaron Ayer una Declaración Sobre el Crédito de 10 Millones de Dólares," *El Diario*, 5 March 1961.

30. Strom to Rusk, 5 March 1961, 724.5411/3-161; box 1564, State Department Decimal Files (hereafter SDDF).

31. CIA, Intelligence Bulletin, 7 March 1961, CREST; Strom to Rusk, 5, 6, and 7 March 1961, Williams to State, 6 March 1961, and Rusk to Embassy, 7 March 1961, 724.5411/3-161; box 1564, SDDF.

32. "Comité Nacional de Huelga Suspende la Huelga," *El Diario*, 9 March 1961.

33. Kennedy, News Conference #6, 8 March 1961, Historical Resources, JFKL; Rusk to Embassy, 8 March 1961, 724.5-MSP/3-161, SDDF.

34. Stephansky Oral History, JFKL, 13.

35. Kennedy, "Address at a White House Reception for Members of Congress and for the Diplomatic Corps of the Latin American Republics," 13 March 1961, Speeches, Reference Desk, JFKL.

36. Thorpe et al., "Report to the President," 24 March 1961, folder 7, POF, JFKL, 2–4 (cover letter); 2, 39 (report).

37. Ibid., 5–8, 13, 15–17, 44–49.

38. Rubin to Kennedy, 3 April 1961, "Bolivia, General, 1961," box 10, NSF-CO, JFKL.

39. "After the Ball," *Time*, 14 April 1961.

40. Achilles to Gordon and Berle, 27 March 1961, 724.5-MSP/3-161, box 1563, SDDF.

41. INR, "COMIBOL Problems Considered," 1 March 1961, "Bolivia, 1961," box 7, lot 64D24, SDLF, 1, 3.

42. State Department, "Proposed New Program for Bolivia," 30 March 1961, "Special Mission to Bolivia, 3/9–20/61," box 2, lots 62D418 and 64D15, SDLF, 1, 3, 8–9.

43. Ambassador Strom filed a complaint with the Bolivian Foreign Ministry regarding the attacks. See Strom to Arze Quiroga, 19 April 1961, LE-3-R-340, RREE. Regarding O'Meara's visit and the accompanying riots, see "Llegará hoy Jefe Militar de los EEUU," *El Diario*, 18 April 1961; "Varias banderas Americanas Quemó la Multitud Exaltada," *El Diario*, 19 April 1961; "Existen 370 Voluntarios Para Cuba," *El Diario*, 19 April 1961; "Más de 25 Heridos y Contusos Atendió la Asistencia Pública," *El Diario*, 19 April 1961.

44. Kennedy to Macmillan, "Record of a Meeting Held on President Kennedy's Yacht, 'Honey Fitz,'" 6 April 1961, CAB/129/105, National Archives, Kew, 10T.

45. Bedregal, *De búhos*, 263–65.

46. Bedregal to Paz, 25 April 1961, PR 985, ABNB.

47. Bedregal, *De búhos*, 299. West German participation was Bedregal's idea, as he attended high school there. But bringing Bonn into the program also dovetailed with the Kennedy administration's view that given Washington's balance of payments problems, Bonn's payments surplus was "a bank . . . for our grandiose Third World programs." Undersecretary Ball, quoted in Frank Costigliola, "Nuclear Arms, Dollars, and Berlin," in Paterson, *Kennedy's Quest for Victory*, 36.

48. Salzgitter to Bedregal, undated (April 1961), PR 985, ABNB.

49. IDB documents are dry, technocratic treatises on the urgent need for efficiency in Bolivia's tin mines. It is possible to grasp their significance only through an understanding of the authoritarian process by which the reforms were carried out. "Documents on the Triangular Plan," IDB Archives, Washington, DC. Incidentally, the reforms had their roots in a 1956 study by the US consulting firm Ford, Bacon, & Davis, which argues that "unless the government removes political activities from the management of the mines . . . the entire mineral industry will continue to suffer." It even chides the government for, in an effort to "avoid violence . . . constantly yielding to the demands of irresponsible agitators" and fomenting a "lack of discipline . . . [and] disregard for authority." *Ford, Bacon, & Davis Report: Volume I*, December 1956, Archivo de la Corporación Minera de Bolivia, El Alto, Bolivia, 14, 25, 74.

50. "Workers' Control."

51. Strom to Rusk, 21 and 26 April 1961, Rusk to Embassy, 24 April 1961; Memorandum of Conversation (hereafter MEMCON), 2 May 1961, 724.5-MSP/3-161, box 1563, SDDF.

52. Paz letter to Ramiro, 26 May 1961, published in Ramiro Paz, *Las cartas de Víctor Paz*, 104–5; and in the insert of Ramiro Paz, *En los pasillos del poder.*

53. Lechín, *El pueblo*, 126–27; Williams to Rusk, 8 May 1961, 724.12/8-960, box 1563, SDDF; "'Sólo Soy Agente del Pueblo Boliviano,'" *El Diario*, 9 May 1961.

54. "Borrascosa Sesión Hubo en el Congreso Minero," *El Diario*, 4 May 1961.

55. "US Gives Bolivia 10 Million in Aid," *New York Times*, 15 May 1961; "La Casa Blanca Anunció un Préstamo de Cincuenta Millones de Dólares," *El Diario*, 15 May 1961.

56. The confidential "Accepted Points of View" were leaked to the Bolivian press in June 1961, and embassy officials fretted that papers published were "identical . . . [to the] Accepted Points of View." Embassy to State, 26 July 1961, 824.25/5-961, box 2390, SDDF. See "La Operación Triangular muestra en otros 5 puntos su trágico sello anti-obrero," *El Pueblo*, 24 June 1961; "La Ayuda Norteamericana en Dólares Exigiría que se Cumplan Condiciones," *El Diario*, 23 July 1961. For the entire document, see "Basic Documents on the Triangular Operation," particularly Annex 6 of the "Accepted Points of View," folder "Inter-American Bank & Triangular Operation, 1961," box 9, Records Relating to Bolivia, 1961–1975, SDLF.

57. "Amenazan con Movilización de Mineros Hacia La Paz," *El Diario*, 30 May 1961.

58. Williams to Rusk, 7 June 1961, 724.5/3-460, box 1563, SDDF; State Department, "Report on Current Situation in Bolivia," undated (mid-June); Lane to Coerr, 13 June 1961, "Memoranda, Jan–June 1961," box 1, lots 63D389 and 63D61, SDLF.

59. When asked about these detentions, Bedregal shrugged it off. "I have read the sad tales of the detainees. Give me a break. They were held for a few weeks. No torture, nothing." Bedregal denied that he knew anything of the detentions before they took place. "That was something between Paz and [secret police chief] San Román." Interviews with Bedregal. See also "A San Ignacio de Velasco y Puerto Villarroel Fueron Confinados 50 Comunistas," *El Diario*, 8 June 1961. Trotskyist union leader from Siglo XX Filemón Escóbar recounts his detention at Puerto Villarroel in Escóbar, *De la Revolución al Pachakuti*, 52–61. Confirmed in interviews with Escóbar and fellow Puerto Villarroel detainee José Luís Cueto.

60. Interviews with Bedregal and with San Ignacio de Velasco detainees René Rocabado and Simón Reyes.

61. "Dictóse Estado de Sitio y Auto de Buen Gobierno," *El Diario*, 8 June 1961.

62. Lane to Coerr, 13 June 1961, "Memoranda, Jan–June 1961," box 1, lots 63D389 and 63D61, SDLF; "Los Fabriles no Temen Represiones porque Están Acostumbrados a Derrotar Ejércitos," *El Diario*, 8 June 1961; "Empezó el Paro Universitario con Barricadas de Adoquines," *El Diario*, 14 June 1961.

63. Lane to Coerr, 13 June 1961, "Memoranda, Jan–June 1961," box 1, lots 63D389 and 63D61, SDLF; "Llegaron Ayer Campesinos de Achacachi," *El Diario*, 8 June 1961.

64. These cables can be found in PR 971, ABNB.

65. CIA, Intelligence Bulletin, 13 June 1961, CREST. *Time* magazine was not so wise, parroting the Bolivian line that "Castro agents working out of the Cuban embassy hatched a plot with local Communists to overturn the government of Reformer-President Víctor Paz Estenssoro." "Who's Intervening Where?" *Time*, 16 June 1961.

66. Lane to Coerr, 13 June 1961; State Department, "Report on Current Situation in Bolivia," undated (mid-June 1961), "Memoranda, Jan–June 1961," box 1, lots 63D389 and 63D61, SDLF.

67. Commander-in-Chief Rodríguez to US Embassy, 8 June 1961; Williams to Rusk, 9 June 1961; Bolivian Foreign Ministry to Embassy, 14 July 1961; Rusk to Embassy, 23 June 1961; 724.5411/3-161, box 1564, SDDF.

68. Stephansky to Rusk, 25 June 1961; 724.5411/3-161, box 1564, SDDF.

69. Rusk to Embassy, 30 June 1961; box 1564, SDDF. Confirmation of shipment arrivals can be found in Stephansky to Foreign Minister Arze Quiroga, 14 and 24 July 1961, LE-3-R-340, RREE.

70. Stevenson, "Statement on Arrival at La Paz," 15 June 1961, 5, box 453, Stevenson Papers, Mudd Library, Princeton University, 4–5. See also "La Ayuda Extranjera Hará de Este País un Ejemplo de la Cooperación del Mundo Libre," *El Diario*, 16 June 1961.

71. "Hello, but No Help," *Time*, 23 June 1961; "Tres Horas Conversaron Reservadamente en Calacoto el Presidente y Stevenson," *El Diario*, 16 June 1961; "Cuatro Muertos y Más de Treinta Heridos es el Resultado de las Luchas Callejeras," *El Diario*, 16 June 1961.

72. "Permanecen en la Universidad Alrededor de 80 Estudiantes," *El Diario*, 16 June 1961.

73. Stevenson to Williams, 22 June 1961, folder 5, box 453, Stevenson Papers, Mudd Library, Princeton University. Stevenson did not respond to an FSB letter complaining that Paz was imposing a "dictatorship under the belated cover of anticommunism." See "Al Amparo de Tardía Postura Pretende el MNR Implantar una Dictadura: Carta de Falange al embajador Stevenson," *El Diario*, 17 June 1961.

74. Stevenson to Paz, 17 June 1961, folder 5, box 453, Stevenson Papers, Mudd Library, Princeton University.

75. Williams to Rusk, 18 June 1961; US Embassy (Quito) to Rusk, 18 June 1961; Rusk to Embassies (Quito and La Paz), 19 June 1961, 724.5411/3-161, box 1564, SDDF.

76. Paz to Kennedy, 5 October 1961, "Security, 1961–3," box 112, POF, JFKL; USAID Director Hamilton to Ambassador Andrade, 7 November 1961, "Bolivia, General, 1961," box 10, NSF-CO, JFKL; Weise to Lane, 9 November 1961, "Memoranda, July–December 1961," box 1, lots 63D389 and 63D61, SDLF.

77. Kennedy to Paz, 22 June 1961, "Bolivia, General, 1961," box 112, POF, JFKL.

78. Stephansky Oral History, JFKL, 11.

79. Ibid., 20.

80. Pace Bradley Simpson, whose work on Kennedy's foreign policy of authoritarian development in Indonesia is one of this book's central influences. Simpson, *Economists with Guns*.

81. Thorpe et al., "Report to the President," 15–16; CIA, Current Intelligence Memorandum, 30 July 1963, "Bolivia, General, 3/63–7/63," box 10A, NSF-CO, JFKL, 1–2.

82. Special Operations Research Office, *U.S. Army Area Handbook*, 661.

83. *Juku*, which is Quechua for "owl," reached its apogee in 1964, but it began systematically in the late 1950s. Interviews with PCB members Leónidas Rojas, Víctor Reinaga, Rosendo Osorio, and Daniel Ordóñez; POR members Filemón Escóbar and Benigno Bastos; and MNR leftist Arturo Crespo. For three political groups that rarely agree, their testimony was remarkably similar, particularly regarding POR *juku* activity. See also a 1964 COMIBOL report on *juku*, in Embassy to State, 24 August 1964, INCO Mining, Minerals, and Metals BOL, box 1190, NARA, RG 59, Records of the State Department: Alpha-Numeric Files (hereafter SDANF).

84. The general secretary was Irineo Pimentel, an unaffiliated communist who had previously belonged to the Stalinist *Partido de la Izquierda Revolucionaria* (PIR; Revolutionary Left Party). Meanwhile, the union's Control Obrero was Federico Escóbar, the head of the PCB at Siglo XX. For more on communism in revolutionary Bolivia, see chapter 3 in this volume.

85. Interviews with Lincoln-Castro-Murillo Brigades Vice President Leónidas Rojas, confirmed in interviews with Crespo, Reinaga, Osorio, and Ordóñez. Pedro Domingo Murillo was a martyr for Bolivian independence, executed in 1810 by Spanish authorities in La Paz's central plaza, which today bears his name.

86. Crespo, *El rostro minero de Bolivia*, 295.

87. Ibid.; interviews with Ordóñez, Osorio, Rojas, Reinaga, Bastos, and Filemón Escóbar. For an account of the Trotskyist counterdemonstration, see sections of Filemón Escóbar's unpublished manuscript, cited in Dunkerley, *Rebellion in the Veins*, 106–7.

88. Anthony Freeman, Oral History, Association for Diplomatic Studies and Training.

89. Interviews with Emilse Escóbar, daughter of Federico, and Daniel Ordóñez Plaza, a PCB leader who was chosen to take Escóbar's place as Control Obrero during the latter's confinement. Quotations from Ordóñez. *Moreno*: swarthy.

90. Miners' interviews in López Vigil, *Una mina de coraje*, 55–56. *Campesino*, in the Bolivian context: "Indian peasant."

91. Interviews with Emilse Escóbar.

92. Domitila Barrios de Chungara, quoted in Viezzer, *"Si me permiten hablar . . . ,"* 69.

93. Embassy to State, 26 April 1963, INCO-Mining, Minerals, and Metals BOL, box 3540, SDANF; interviews with PCB miners Ordóñez, Osorio, and Rojas; Escóbar PCB friend Víctor Reinaga; and Emilse Escóbar.

94. Domitila, quoted in Viezzer, *"Si me permiten hablar . . . ,"* 69–72; interviews with Domitila.

95. Filemón Escóbar, *Testimonio de un militante obrero*, unabridged, 41.

96. Interviews with Reinaga.

97. Burke e-mail to author, 9 October 2009.

98. Burke, "Corporación Minera de Bolivia"; Burke, "La crisis de la Corporación Minera de Bolivia," 275, 279.

99. Lechín, *El pueblo al poder*, 123.

100. After retiring from the mines, Crespo spent two decades in COMIBOL and miner archives. His account of the June strike is based on personal memories substantiated by official documents. See Crespo, *El rostro minero*, 284–85. Interviews with Rojas, Reinaga, Ordóñez, Osorio, and Filemón Escóbar were helpful in corroborating Crespo's narrative.

101. "Intento Extremista para un Nuevo Paro Minero en Oruro Rechazaron los Trabajadores," *El Diario*, 17 June 1961; Crespo, *El rostro minero de Bolivia*, 287–89.

102. "Resolución de la Federación Sindical de Trabajadores Mineros de Bolivia (FSTMB)," 25 June 1961, published in Crespo, *El rostro minero de Bolivia*, 289.

103. Bedregal to Paz, 26 June and 1 July 1961, PR 985, ABNB.

104. MEMCON, 21 July 1961, 724.12/8-960, box 1563, SDDF.

105. Stevenson, in "Bolivia Constituye la Situación más Explosiva en América del Sur," *El Diario*, 16 July 1961.

106. "El Presidente Kennedy Envió Nueva Carta al Doctor Paz," *El Diario*, 30 June 1961.

107. Stephansky to Rusk, 26 July 1961, "Bolivia, General, 1961," box 10, NSF-CO, JFKL.

108. Barall to Labouisse, 10 August 1961, 724.12/8-960, box 1563, SDDF.

109. Williams to Rusk, 18 August 1961, in idem.

110. Siglo XX Missionaries, "La situación insostenible de los Católicos en Siglo XX y el campo circundante," 8 December 1961, published in López Vigil, *Una mina de coraje*, 63–65.

111. Escóbar, 2 September 1961, quoted in López Vigil, *Una mina de coraje*, 57–58. Conservative Catholics and orthodox Communists alike were consistently frustrated by Escóbar's declarations that he was "100 percent Catholic . . . [and] 100 percent Communist." Escóbar, quoted in López Vigil, *Una mina de coraje*, 119.

112. Lino to COMIBOL, undated (June 1961), published in Crespo, *El rostro minero*, 288.

113. Miners' interviews, in López Vigil, *Una mina de coraje*, 66–59. See also "Comunistas Promovieron Desórdenes en Siglo XX," *El Diario*, 5 July 1961.

114. Pio XII broadcast, 4 July 1961; miners' interviews, in López Vigil, *Una mina de coraje*, 69, 70–71. One Communist recalled, "Father Lino's Catholic Workers were armed, as well! I know, because we clashed with them many times! Lino was enormous. More like a Marine dressed up like a priest!" Interviews with Reinaga, confirmed by Osorio and Ordóñez.

115. "Laimes y Jucumanis Reiteraron su Adhesión al Gobierno del Presidente Paz Estenssoro," *El Diario*, 6 July 1961.

116. Miners' interviews, in López Vigil, *Una mina de coraje*, 75–89. Lino's afterlife was uncovered by his successor, Father Gregorio Iriarte, who ran into him later in Uruguay. See Gregorio interview, in López Vigil, *Una mina de coraje*, 88–89. See also "Es Grave la Situación en Siglo XX," *El Diario*, 8 July 1961.

117. Dillon to Kennedy, 16 August 1961, document 30, *FRUS, 1961–1963: Volume XII— American Republics*.

118. Rusk to Embassy, 22 August 1961, "Bolivia, General, 1961," box 10, NSF-CO, JFKL.

119. "Creóse Ayer el Primer Batallón Motorizado 'Tnln. M. Toledo,' " *El Diario*, 6 August 1961.

120. Army Attaché Wimert via Williams to Rusk, 19 August 1961, "Bolivia, General, 1961," box 10, NSF-CO, JFKL.

121. Stephansky to Rusk, 24 August 1961, in idem; Stephansky to Rusk, 25 August 1961, 824.25/5-961, box 2390, SDDF.

122. "Tensas Discusiones Motivó la Conservación del Veto Obrero en la Corporación Minera," *El Diario*, 25 August 1961.

123. Prefect-Oruro to Paz, 29 August 1961, PR 975, ABNB. For a US account of this meeting, which is almost identical to Bolivian reports, see Stephansky to Rusk, 29 August 1961, 824.25/5-961, box 2390, SDDF. See also "El Gobierno ha Quedado con las Manos Libres para Firmar y Aprobar hoy el Plan Triangular," *El Diario*, 30 August 1961.

124. "Por decreto supremo se aprobó ayer el plan triangular para la Comibol," *El Diario*, 1 September 1961. Paz's strike-busting vow is referenced in COMIBOL Advisory Group to Paz, 13 July 1962, PR 985, ABNB.

125. Stephansky to Rusk, 4 September 1961, 824.25/5-961, box 2390, SDDF.

126. Prior to 1961, Bolivia had two engineering battalions. These funds went to build the "General Pando" Third Engineering Battalion, and soon afterward, funds of the Alliance for Progress covered the full expenses of the "Alto de la Alianza" Fourth Engineering Battalion. See Noel, "La génération des jeunes officiers," 463.

127. Stephansky to Rusk, 1 and 15 September 1961, 724.12/8-960, box 1563, SDDF. The $7 million package was authorized in late August, but Stephansky withheld this from President Paz until after Triangular had been approved. See Rusk to Embassy, 17 August 1961, same folder.

128. Stephansky was publicly adamant that "the US government has not established any conditions to lending aid." Meanwhile, IDB officials consistently swore that Triangular "has no conditions" and that it "does not contain negative measures for the workers." See "El Gobierno de EEUU no ha Establecido Condiciones para Prestar Ayuda a Nuestro País," El Diario, 31 July 1961; "Afirma el BID que el Plan Triangular para Comibol no Establece Ninguna Condición," El Diario, 29 July 1961.

129. Paz letter to his son Ramiro, 26 May 1961, published in Ramiro Paz, Las cartas de Víctor Paz, 104; and in the insert of Ramiro Paz, En los pasillos del poder.

130. "Gerónima Jaldín de Romero interviews, published in Lagos, Nos hemos forjado así, 37.

131. "White Massacre": mass firings. At first, the Comité was ad hoc. Later, it became a permanent fixture in Siglo XX. Gerónima interviews, in Lagos, Nos hemos forjado así, 37, 43–47. See also "Conmovedor Cuadro Ofrecen 200 Huelguistas en Sede Fabril," El Diario, 17 August 1961; "Hasta Ayer 11 Huelguistas de Hambre se Hallaban Graves y Había 46 Casos de Inanición," El Diario, 19 August 1961.

132. "Recuperaron su Libertad Tres Dirigentes Mineros Confinados," El Diario, 1 September 1961.

133. Gerónima, María Fernández de Valeriano, and Brígida Fernández de Velarde testimony, in Lagos, Nos hemos forjado así, 43–47.

134. CIA, Central Intelligence Weekly Summary (hereafter CIWS), 12 October 1961, CREST.

135. Belcher to Woodward, 29 September 1961, 724.5411/3-161, box 1564, SDDF.

136. Kennedy, "NSAM 88," 5 September 1961, National Security Action Memoranda, National Security Files—John F. Kennedy.

137. Joint Chiefs to Kennedy, 30 November 1961, document 89, FRUS, 1961–1963: Volume XII—American Republics.

138. Stephansky later boasted that he had threatened to "hold back on [USAID] disbursements and programs" when he "required the GOB to increase gasoline prices." MEMCON, 28 May 1963, INCO Mining, Minerals, and Metals BOL, box 3540, SDANF. See also "Fue Develado un Complot!" El Diario, 19 October 1961.

139. CIA, CIWS, 27 October 1961, CREST; "Ha Sido Autorizado la Elevación del Precio de la Gasolina a 700 el Litro," El Diario, 21 October 1961; "Declaróse concluido el año escolar," 22 October 1961," El Diario, 22 October 1961; "Enérgica reacción estudiantil por el aumento de las tarifas de transporte," El Diario, 22 October 1961.

140. Stephansky to Rusk, 26 October 1961, 724.00/6-162, box 1560, SDDF; Stephansky to Rusk, 25 and 26 October 1961; Rusk to Embassy, 27 October 1961, 724.5411/3-161, box 1564, SDDF. State Department cables refer to the airplane as a "private contractor" operated by "Southern Air Transport." The former CIA station chief confirmed that this company "was ours." Interviews with Sternfield.

141. Hilsman to Woodward, 18 July 1961, document 4, FRUS, 1961–1963: Volume XII—American Republics, microfiche supplement.

142. Stephansky to Rusk, 29 August and 4 September 1961, 824.25/5-961, box 2390, SDDF.

143. See Simpson, *Economists with Guns*; Rabe, *U.S. Intervention in British Guiana*.

2. Development as Anticommunism

1. World production was 187,000 tons in 1961. US Geological Survey, *Tin Statistics* (Washington, DC: GPO, 2005), 2.

2. Paz to Kennedy, 16 September 1961, "Bolivia, General, 1961," box 10, NSF-CO; MEMCON, 13 September 1961, PR 985, ABNB; "U.S. Aid Program Undergoes Test," *New York Times*, 20 September 1961.

3. Kennedy to Paz, 6 October 1961, "Bolivia, General, 1961," box 112, POF, JFKL; "No Daré Ningún Paso en Cuanto al Estaño o Cualquier Asunto que Afecte Bolivia," *El Diario*, 7 October 1961.

4. Paz to Kennedy, 5 October 1961, "Security, 1961–3," box 112, POF, JFKL. See also "Fabriles Amenazan con una Huelga a Partir del Día 5," *El Diario*, 30 September 1961.

5. Hamilton to Ambassador Andrade, 7 November 1961, "Bolivia, General, 1961," box 10, NSF-CO, JFKL. See also Weise to Lane, 9 November 1961, "Memoranda, July–December 1961," box 1, lots 63D389 and 63D61, SDLF.

6. Paz to Kennedy, 4 October 1961, "Security, 1961–1963," box 112, POF, JFKL. According to *Time* magazine, as late as August 1962, only Chile, Colombia, and Bolivia had submitted plans. "Troubled Alliance," *Time*, 10 August 1962.

7. Egger to Kennedy, 5 October 1961, "Bolivia, General, 1961," box 10, NSF-CO, JFKL.

8. Schlesinger to Smith, 30 December 1961, "Bolivia, General, 1/62–7/62," box 10, NSF-CO, JFKL; Hansen to Schlesinger, 3 January 1962; Hansen to Moscoso, 3 January 1962, "Bolivia," box WH-3, Schlesinger Papers, JFKL, 1, 3.

9. "Latin American Reds Present Threat to U.S.," *Los Angeles Times*, 10 December 1961; "U.S. Program of Aid Faces a Tough Task with Bolivia Reds," *Chicago Daily Tribune*, 22 January 1961.

10. "Largesse Did Little for Bolivia," *Washington Post, Times Herald*, 5 November 1961; "Bolivia Hunts Funds to Avert Collapse," *New York Times*, 10 January 1962.

11. Drew Pearson, "Bipartisan Plaudits Won by Rusk," *Washington Post, Times Herald*, 7 February 1962.

12. The street battles were recorded by an American eyewitness. See Patch, "Pro and Anti-Catristas in La Paz." See also "Un muerto y 28 hubo ayer," *El Diario*, 24 January 1962.

13. Pearson, "Bipartisan Plaudits."

14. Williams to Fellman, 18 January 1962; Williams to Ambassador Arze Quiroga, 6 February 1962, LE-3-R-357, RREE. When Paz appointed Fellman in early January, the US Embassy was concerned that he was "vigorous and outspoken" in favor of "formalizing relations with the Soviet Union." See Williams to State, 9 January 1962, 724.12/8-960, box 1563, SDDF.

15. Stephansky Oral History, JFKL, 17. The interview transcript incorrectly reads, "shad on," which has been corrected in the text above.

16. Stephansky to Rusk, 13 November 1961, 724.5411/3-161, box 1564; Stephansky to Rusk, 20 December 1961, 824.25/10-161, box 2390, SDDF.

17. "Highlights of the First Meeting of the Working Group on Problems of the Alliance for Progress," 16 January 1962, document 37, *FRUS, 1961–63: Volume XII—American Republics*. For more on Walt Rostow's affinity for bombs as harbingers of economic development, see Milne, *America's Rasputin*.

18. "Report and Recommendations of the Washington Assessment Team on the Internal Security Situation in South America," 10 January 1962, document 90, *FRUS, 1961–63: Volume XII— American Republics*.

19. INR, "Latin American Political Stability and the Alliance for Progress," 17 January 1962, document 38; Hughes to Woodward, 19 January 1962, document 39, in idem.

20. "Highlights of Discussion at the Secretary of State's Policy Planning Committee," 13 February 1962, document 40, in idem; US Southern Command to Rusk, 17 January 1962, 724.5/3-460, box 1563, SDDF.

21. Stephansky to State, 17 March 1962, attached to Osborne to State, 25 April 1962, 724.5411/3-161, box 1564; US Embassy to State, "Annual Politico-Economic Assessment—1962," 8 March 1962, 824.00/1-2362, box 2387, SDDF; Battle to Smith, 20 March 1962, "Bolivia, General, 1/62–7/62," box 10, NSF-CO, JFKL.

22. Stephansky to Rusk, 20 March 1962, "Bolivia, General, 1/62–7/62," box 10, NSF-CO, JFKL. In the original, Stephansky uses the term *Alianza*. For clarity, I have translated this to "Alliance."

23. Goodwin to Rusk, 7 April 1962, "Bolivia, 5/61–12/62," box 389, NSF-Dungan, JFKL; Stephansky to Rusk, 6 and 7 April 1962, "Bolivia, General, 1/62–7/62," box 10, NSF-CO, JFKL.

24. Rubin to Moscoso, Martin, and Schlesinger, 16 April 1962, "Bolivia, 5/61–12/62," box 389, NSF-Dungan, JFKL.

25. While the paper remains classified, much of it is quoted in the embassy response. See Williams to State, 8 May 1962, "Bolivia, 1/62–7/62," box 10, NSF-CO, JFKL.

26. Williams to State, 8 May 1962, in idem. Stephansky was in Washington at the time, so the cable is signed by Williams. It bears Stephansky's indelible stamp, however, and Williams notes at the end that it was largely drafted by the ambassador.

27. Wimert (Army Attaché) to Rusk, 18 April 1962, 724.00/4-262, box 1560, SDDF. See also "Violenta Manifestación Estudiantil Registróse Contra Agresión Chilena," *El Diario*, 17 April 1962.

28. Ball to Embassy, 30 April 1962, 724.5411/3-161, box 1564, SDDF; Stephansky to Rusk, 26 April and 5 May 1962, "Bolivia, General, 1/62–7/62," box 10, NSF-CO, JFKL.

29. Keating (Army), "White House Fact Sheet," 24 April 1962, "Bolivia, General, 1/62–7/62," box 10, NSF-CO, JFKL.

30. MEMCON, 23 April 1962, "Political—General, 1962," box 2, lot 64D518, SDLF; Stephansky to RREE, 24 and 26 April 1962, LE-3-R-357, RREE. These maneuvers took place as a series of war game exercises in late July. President Paz attended approvingly. See "El Capitán General de las FFAA Inspeccionó la Zona de Maniobras," *El Diario*, 31 July 1962.

31. US Embassy (Asunción) to Rusk; Rusk to US Embassy (Asunción), 5 April and 17 August 1962, 724.5/4-562, SDDF.

32. Belcher to Martin and Goodwin, 26 April 1962, "Memoranda, 1962," box 2, lot 64D518, SDLF. In late 1963, USIS labor officer Thomas Martin was taken hostage. For more on Martin, whom this document does not mention by name, see chapter 4 in this volume.

33. "Bolivia: Department of State Guidelines for Policy and Operations," 20 April 1962, "Bolivia, General, 1/62–7/62," box 10, NSF-CO, JFKL.

34. Hilsman to Martin, "Bolivia and the Alliance for Progress," 15 May 1962, "Bolivia, 5/61–12/62," box 389, NSF-Dungan, JFKL, 2–5.

35. For examples of their persistence, see Escóbar to Paz, 11 September and 17 October, 1961, PR 1658; Escóbar to Paz, 21 September 1961; Pimentel to Paz, 16 November 1961, PR 985; Escóbar to Paz, 11 February 1962, PR 1609, ABNB.

36. COMIBOL Advisory Group to Paz, 5 January 1962, PR 985, ABNB.

37. Bedregal, *De búhos*, 302; "Comisionados de Comibol están Detenidos en Calidad de Rehenes en Zona de Catavi," *El Diario*, 1 May 1962.

38. Bedregal, *De búhos*, 306.

39. Ibid., 307; Boggs to State, 15 May 1962, 824.25/1-462, box 2390, SDDF, 1–2, 5–7.

40. Bedregal, *De búhos*, 307.

41. Ibid., 312–13; Boggs to State, 15 May 1962, 824.25/1-462, box 2390, SDDF, 1–2, 5–7. For a miner's version, see Crespo, *El rostro minero*, 329–30.

42. FSTMB to Bedregal, 2 May 1962; Bedregal to FSTMB, 10 May 1962, PR 1609, ABNB.

43. Boggs to State, 25 July 1962, 824.25/6-162, box 2390, SDDF, 1–4; Subprefect-Huanuni to Paz, 12 June 1962; Bedregal to Presidency Minister, 14 June 1962, PR 985, ABNB. See also "Están en Huelga de Hambre 14 Dirigentes Sindicales y Nueve Delegados de Base de Huanuni," *El Diario*, 21 June 1962; "Inició Ayer su Viaje por las Minas la Comisión de Comibol," *El Diario*, 24 June 1962.

44. Boggs to State, 25 July 1962, 824.25/6-162, box 2390, SDDF, 1–4; "Guillermo Bedregal Está Afectado por el Esfuerzo y el Mal Trato de los Mineros," *El Diario*, 28 June 1962; "El Presidente de COMIBOL Logró Burlar la Vigilancia de los Mineros y Fugó de Huanuni," *El Diario*, 29 June 1962.

45. Prefect-Oruro to Paz, 5 July 1962, PR 1019, ABNB; Boggs to State, 2 August 1962, 824.25/6-162, box 2390, SDDF; "Está en Rehenes Parte de la Comisión que fue a Colquiri," *El Diario*, 27 July 1962.

46. Bedregal, *De búhos*, 323–24.

47. Boggs to State, 2 August 1962, 824.25/6-162, box 2390, SDDF.

48. COMIBOL Advisory Group to Paz, 13 July 1962, PR 985, ABNB.

49. Williams to Rusk, 18 May 1962, "Bolivia, General, 1/62–7/62," box 10, NSF-CO, JFKL.

50. Williams to Rusk, 4–6 June 1962; Gavrisheff to State, 16 and 27 June 1962, 1, 8, 11–13; Stephansky to Rusk, 19 June 1962; 724.00/6-162, box 1560, SDDF.

51. Stephansky later recalled that Rusk was "thoroughly pissed off at my appointment." Stephansky Oral History, JFKL, 15.

52. Rusk to Embassy, 10 July 1962, "Bolivia, General, 1/62–7/62," box 10, NSF-CO, JFKL.

53. Stephansky to Rusk, 9 June 1962, in idem.

54. Stephansky to State, "Bolivia and Democratic Processes," 29 August 1962, "Bolivia, 3/61–10/63," box WH-25, Schlesinger Papers, JFKL. Stephansky's "last hope" comment can be found in Stephansky to Rusk, 9 June 1962, "Bolivia, General, 1/62–7/62," box 10, NSF-CO, JFKL.

55. Stephansky to Rusk, 30 June 1962, 724.5/3-460, box 1563, SDDF; Stephansky to Rusk, 15 August 1962, and Stephansky to State, 29 August 1962, "Bolivia, General, 8/62–12/62," box 10, NSF-CO, JFKL.

56. Stephansky to Rusk, 15 August 1962, "Bolivia, General, 8/62–12/62," box 10, NSF-CO, JFKL.

57. Stephansky to State, 29 August 1962, "Bolivia, General, 8/62–12/62," box 10, NSF-CO, JFKL.

58. Martin to Stephansky, 26 September 1962, "Bolivia, 1962," box 4, lots 62D418 and 64D15, SDLF.

59. Topping to Rostow, 30 June 1962, "Bolivia, 7/30/1962," box 213, lot 73D363, SDLF.

60. The ministers' trip was given frequent coverage in Bolivia. See "Enviados bolivianos esperarán a Kennedy para Entrevistarlo," *El Diario*, 1 July 1962; "Debió Ganarse una Dura Batalla para Conseguir el Crédito de 80 Millones," *El Diario*, 22 July 1962.

61. Brubeck to O'Donnell and Bundy, 27 May 1962, "Bolivia, General, 1/61–7/62," box 10, NSF-CO, JFKL.

62. Hamilton to Dungan, 28 June 1962, "Bolivia, 5/61–12/62," box 389, NSF-Dungan, JFKL.

63. Stephansky to Rusk, 10 July 1962, "Bolivia, 1/62–7/62," box 10, NSF-CO, JFKL. Stephansky told the Bolivian press that "if there was a stalemate, I would be informed." See "Dos Ministros Gestionan en Washington la Financiación del Plan de Ingeniería Global," *El Diario*, 11 July 1962.

64. Schlesinger to Dungan, 18 July 1962, "Bolivia, 3/61–10/63," box WH-25, Schlesinger Papers, JFKL.

65. State Department, "Experimental Policy Paper on Bolivia," 19 July 1962, "Bolivia, General, Experimental Policy Paper, 7/19/1962," box 10A, NSF-CO, JFKL, 8–11, 18–23, 30–31, and Annex I, 1–7.

66. Hansen to Dungan, Bundy, and Schlesinger, undated, "Bolivia, 3/61–10/63," box WH-25, Schlesinger Papers, JFKL.

67. State Department, "Experimental Policy Paper on Bolivia," 19 July 1962, "Bolivia, General, Experimental Policy Paper, 7/19/1962," box 10A, NSF-CO, JFKL, 1–3, 16–17.

68. Nor was the liberal allergy to participatory democracy unique to Bolivia. The Alliance for Progress Study Group paradoxically theorized that "the principal task of the democratic movement is to create the skills of politics in the 'emerging elite.'" Alliance Study Group, "Draft Program," 10 December 1962, folder 16, box 3, Professional Activities Files, Alexander Papers, Rutgers, 6.

69. Henderson Oral History, Association of Diplomatic Studies and Training.

70. The tense debate between State Department officials and tin-producing countries makes for surprisingly interesting reading. To witness US officials weeping to unimpressed Bolivian delegates that "we are literally scrounging every way to save $50 million here and $50 million there," see "Meeting between the US and the Delegation from the International Tin Council," 24 July 1962, Collection of the International Tin Council, British Library of Political and Economic Science.

71. Martin to Johnson, 18 July 1962, "Bolivia, 1962," box 4, lots 62D418 and 64D15, SDLF.

72. Ball to Embassy, 28 June 1962; Stephansky to Rusk, 19 and 30 June 1962, "Bolivia, General, 1/62–7/62," box 10, NSF-CO, JFKL.

73. "EEUU Lanzará a la Venta 3 Mil Toneladas de Estaño," *El Diario*, 26 August 1962.

74. Stephansky to Rusk, 13 and 28 August 1962; Ball to Moscoso and Embassy, 23 August 1962, "Bolivia, General, 8/62–12/62," box 10, NSF-CO, JFKL.

75. Rusk to Embassy, 3 September 1962; Stephansky to Rusk, 3 September 1962, in idem. See also "El Primer Mandatario Canceló su Viaje a EEUU Debido a la Venta del 'Stock-Pile,'" *El Diario*, 4 September 1962.

76. This was ostensibly over the Lauca River conflict with Chile, but by removing itself from the OAS, Bolivia also avoided taking a stand in Washington's diplomatic war against Cuba. Fellman denied, however, that the Cuba issue had anything to do with his government's decision. See Stephansky to State, 10 September 1962, "Bolivia, General, 8/62–12/62," box 10, NSF-CO, JFKL; "Bolivia Se Retiró de la OEA," *El Diario*, 4 September 1962.

77. Diputados to Paz, 20 and 29 August 1962, PR 1009, ABNB.

78. Víctor Andrade to Clark Clifford (State Department), 25 March 1963, folder 60, box 9, series E, record group 4, Nelson A. Rockefeller Papers, Rockefeller Archive Center.

79. Stephansky to Rusk, 19 July 1963, "Bolivia, General, 3/62–7/63," box 10A, NSF-CO, JFKL.

80. Stephansky to Rusk, 8 September 1962, "Bolivia, General, 8/62–12/62," box 10, NSF-CO, JFKL.

81. Rusk/Ball and Ball/May, 24 September 1962, "Memoranda of Telephone Conversations," George Ball Papers, JFKL.

82. Kennedy, "National Security Action Memorandum 184," 4 September 1962, "National Security Action Memoranda," NSF-Meetings and Memoranda, JFKL.

83. Kennedy to Rusk, McNamara, and Robert Kennedy, "Establishment of the Special Group (Counter-insurgency)," 18 January 1962, published in US Department of Defense, *The Pentagon Papers: The Defense Department History of United States Decision Making on Vietnam* (Boston: Beacon Press, 1971), 660–61.

84. Embassy to State, "Internal Defense Plan," 31 August 1962, 724.5/3-460, box 1563, SDDF, 1–3, 5.

85. Stephansky to Rusk, 22 and 29 September 1962, "Bolivia, General, 8/62–12/62," box 10, NSF-CO, JFKL.

86. Martin to Rusk, undated (September 1962), "Memoranda, 1962, box 2, lot 64D518, SDLF.

87. Stephansky, cited in interview with Robert Alexander, 8 April 1962, folder 58, Interviews, Alexander Papers, Rutgers.

88. Osborne to State, 6 and 7 October 1962, "Bolivia, General, 8/62–12/62," box 10, NSF-CO, JFKL.

3. "Bitter Medicine"

1. Williams to State, 8 May 1962, "Bolivia, General, 1/62–7/62," box 10, NSF-CO, JFKL.

2. For an analysis of the PCB's vacillating position toward the MNR in the Siles years (1956–1960), see Dunkerley, *Rebellion in the Veins*, 89–92, 98.

3. According to members of Paz's cabinet, "there was definitely an unspoken mutual tolerance" between Paz and the PCB. Interviews with Bedregal, confirmed in interviews with Paz's private secretary, Carlos Serrate.

4. Interviews with Ramiro Otero and José Luis Cueto.

5. In a 1961 letter to his son Ramiro, Paz defended Vice President Lechín as a necessary bulwark against the Communist Party achieving "total control of the unions." The Communists, Paz wrote, "are very adroit, capable, and with a great spirit of sacrifice." Lechín's political removal, he explained, would "create a void into which the Communists would move." Paz letter to Ramiro, 26 May 1961, published in Ramiro Paz, *Las cartas de Víctor Paz*, 104–5; and in the insert of Ramiro Paz, *En los pasillos del poder.*

6. MNR Youth to Paz, 21 July 1961, Wálter Guevara Arze Papers (hereafter WGA), ABNB. See also "Renunciaron al MNR 1964 jóvenes," *El Diario*, 29 June 1961.

7. Diputados to Paz, 25 August 1961, PR 979, ABNB. See also "Dirigentes Sindicales del MNR Desconocen Medidas de Seguridad del Gobierno," *El Diario*, 28 June 1961.

8. CIA, Intelligence Bulletin, 25 April 1963, CREST. MNR Youth leaders Rúa and Muñoz both deny that funds were exchanged, but a former Cuban intelligence official, Juan Benemelis, specifically claims that Havana provided funds to Muñoz. Benemelis was not involved in Latin America, however, so his testimony is not entirely reliable. See Benemelis, *Guerras Secretas de Fidel Castro*, 72.

9. Interviews with Dulfredo Rúa and Alberto Muñoz de la Barra.

10. "Empleado de la Embajada Cubana Reveló la Entrega de Fondos a Elementos Comunistas," *El Diario*, 24 July 1961.

11. This included only materials entering through the US-surveilled postal service. Embassy to State, 7 December 1963, DEF Defense Affairs 6 BOL, box 3432, SDANF.

12. Czech Embassy (La Paz) to Foreign Ministry, 24 July 1962, Inv. č 92, KSČ-NA. My thanks to Petr Stepan for his help translating this document.

13. Stephansky to Rusk, 15 March 1963, INCO Mining, Minerals, and Metals BOL, box 3540, SDANF.

14. CIA, CIWS, 22 March 1963, CREST.

15. State Department, "Policy Paper: Cuban Subversion," 18 October 1963, "Bolivia, Subjects, Paz Visit, Paz Briefing Book, Tabs I–III, 10/22/63–10/24/63," box 11, NSF-CO, JFKL, 3. Bolivians who traveled to Cuba in 1961 and 1962 confirm that their trips were paid for by the Cuban Embassy. Interviews with Rúa, Muñoz, and Simón Reyes.

16. "Back to the Books," Time, 29 March 1963. Time also cites US government sources claiming that one thousand Bolivians visited Cuba in 1962 and that four hundred remained there in March 1963. "The Subversion Airlift," Time, 29 March 1963. While these numbers are exaggerated, many Bolivians visited communist countries in the early 1960s, and a large proportion were MNR members. Interviews with Rúa, Muñoz, and Reyes.

17. Interview with Rúa. Confirmed by Muñoz.

18. Interview with Muñoz.

19. "Bolivia," Bohemia, 2 November 1962; "El estaño, una tragedia boliviana," Bohemia, 4 January 1963.

20. US Embassy (Lima) to Rusk, 19 March 1963; Stephansky to Rusk, 16–19 March 1963, "Bolivia, General, 1/63–4/63," box 10A, NSF-CO, JFKL. Washington's role in the operation was not publicized. For more on the crash, see "Hallaron Ayer los Restos del Avión DC-6B del Lloyd," El Diario, 17 March 1963. The Bolivian press is silent on Cuban and Czech couriers, but Time magazine embellished the story, suggesting the plane went down when the Communists tried to hijack it. "The Subversion Airlift," Time, 29 March 1963.

21. US Embassy (Santiago) to Rusk, 25 March 1963, "Bolivia, 1/63–4/63," box 10A, NSF-CO, JFKL. Working under Ambassador Aja Castro was Cuban intelligence officer Juan Carretero (a.k.a. "Ariel"). See Anderson, Che Guevara, 556.

22. Embassy to Rusk, 1 June 1963, CSM US-BOL 1963, box 3687, SDANF; Embassy to Rusk, 8 June 1963, folder "IPS-1/General/Bolivia, January 1962–June 1963," box 5, USAID OPS files for Bolivia, 1960–1964, RG 286, NARA. Cochabamba police believed these names to be "fictitious." Furthermore, subsequent investigations revealed that the two would-be guerrillas "only had about Bs. two hundred thousand (US $16), but [they] probably had access to substantial funds locally."

23. Embassy to Rusk, 7 June 1963, CSM US-BOL 1963, box 3687, SDANF. Weeks later, Cochabamba's police chief informed the US Consulate, but neither the consul nor the embassy in La Paz appears to have connected the dots.

Zannier later admitted to having been tasked by the Cubans to "help a small group of militants avoid arrest as they prepared themselves in Cochabamba for their departure to Puerto Maldonado." See "Los bolivianos que salvaron los 'tesoros' del Che," Los Tiempos, 12 October 2008. Zannier is most famous for having been the messenger who carried Che Guevara's Bolivian Diary to Havana in 1968. See Ryan, Fall of Che Guevara, 146–53.

24. According to Béjar, "the reason was simple, the Peruvian military junta supported the Bolivian government's enemies number one, the Falange Socialista Boliviana. . . . Falangists received logistic and economic support from the Peruvian military junta, above all in Arequipa, where they had their principal base and along the Peru-Bolivian border." See Béjar interview, published in Vázquez Viaña, Una guerrilla para el Che, 53.

25. Juan Carretero ("Ariel") interview, published in Gálvez, El sueño africano del Che, 49. See also Vázquez Viaña, Una guerrilla para el Che, 59.

26. Interviews with Serrate. Echoed in interviews with Otero Cueto, Reyes, Rocabado, and Soria. Very little has been written on this issue. See, however, Burgos, "L'emprise du castrisme en Bolivie," 83–84; Vázquez Viaña, *Una guerrilla para el Che,* 53–61; Taibo II, *Ernesto Guevara,* 478–79. All three are proponents of the idea that Paz Estenssoro was aware of the operation and that he looked the other way.

27. *Záznam o rozhovoru s prvním tajemníkim KS Bolívie Mario Monjem* (Memorandum of conversation with First Secretary of the Bolivian CP Mario Monje), 21 May 1963, Inv. č 94, KSČ-NA. My thanks to Petr Stepan for his help translating this document.

28. Interviews with Cueto. Confirmed by Otero.

29. Interview with Otero, who adds that Matraca "was Monje's thing" and that it was not official Communist Party business. Confirmed by Cueto, who suspects nonetheless that Matraca was very likely on the meeting agenda of the Communist Party secretariat, even if it was not discussed by the Central Committee.

30. Interviews with Cueto.

31. *Záznam o rozhovoru s prvním tajemníkim KS Bolívie Mario Monjem* (Memorandum of conversation with First Secretary of the Bolivian CP Mario Monje), 21 May 1963, Inv. č 94, KSČ-NA. My thanks to Petr Stepan for his help translating this document.

32. Interviews with Serrate.

33. See Embassy to Rusk, 30 May, 1–2 and 7 June 1963, CSM US-BOL 1963, box 3687, SDANF. It is unlikely that Ambassador Stephansky would have withheld this from Washington. Unlikely, but not impossible. A year earlier, "all of the senior members" of the US Embassy complained to their superiors in the State Department that they were "disturbed about the presentation which the Ambassador makes of the Bolivian situation." In their view, Bolivia was "more delicate and explosive than he indicates." See Topping to Rostow, 30 June 1962, "Bolivia, 7/30/1962," box 213, lot 73D363, SDLF.

34. Interviews with Serrate.

35. Interview with Otero.

36. Interviews with Cueto.

37. Embassy to Rusk, 31 May 1963, CSM Communism BOL 1963, box 3616, SDANF.

38. It was in one of the ensuing shoot-outs that celebrated Peruvian poet Javier Heraud lost his life. In his memoir, guerrilla leader Béjar writes that he "purposely omitted any reference" to Maldonado because "there exist a series of events and circumstances which it is still not time to reveal." Béjar, *Peru 1965.* See, however, Gott, *Guerrilla Movements in Latin America,* 315–20; Americo Pumaruna (Ricardo Letts), "Perú: revolución, insurrección, guerrillas," *Pensamiento Crítico* 1 (February 1967), 81–84. See also Vázquez Viaña, *Una guerrilla para el Che,* 47–61; Taibo II, *Ernesto Guevara,* 478–79; Loveman and Davies Jr., "Peru," 283.

39. Embassy to Rusk, 30 May and 1–2 June 1963, CSM Communism BOL 1963, box 3616, SDANF; Embassy to Rusk, 30 and 31 May 1963, folder "Bolivia, General, 3/63–7/63," box 10A, NSF-CO, JFKL.

40. Ibid. See also "Ya han Sido Capturados Diez Miembros Del Grupo que se Internó en Manuripi," *El Diario,* 31 May 1963. In US documents, Tom Flores is referred to as "Embassy Political Officer," but his true position was revealed in author interviews with his successor as CIA station chief, Larry Sternfield. "*Aprista*" refers to members of the then-repressed Peruvian nationalist party, *Alianza Popular Revolucionaria Americana* (APRA; American Popular Revolutionary Alliance).

41. Embassy to Rusk, 4 July 1963, CSM 9-6 PERU, box 3692, SDANF; Embassy to Rusk, 9 July 1963, CSM US-BOL 1963, box 3687, SDANF; Embassy (Lima) to Rusk, 22 June 1963, CSM 9-6 PERU 1963, box 3692, SDANF. Secretary Rusk complained that the Peruvian would-be

guerrillas were being released under "probably ineffectual Bolivian surveillance." Rusk to Embassies (Lima and La Paz), 5 July 1963, CSM 9-6 PERU, box 3692, SDANF. See also "Serán Sometidos a la Jurisdicción de la Justicia Ordinaria Guerrilleros Peruanos," *El Diario*, 6 June 1963.

42. Interviews with PCB members Loyola Guzmán, Rocabado, Rojas, Reinaga, and Soria and MNR Youth leader Rúa. These sources separately claimed to have helped and housed the Peruvians after the Maldonado disaster. Regarding future Peruvian guerrilla activity, see Béjar, *Peru 1965*. See also Vázquez Viaña, *Una guerrilla para el Che*, 59–61.

43. For more on Operation Sombra, which also ended in failure, including the death of Che Guevara's close friend Jorge Ricardo Masetti, see Vázquez Viaña, *Una guerrilla para el Che*, 61–75; Pilard, *Jorge Ricardo Masetti*; Castañeda, *La vida en rojo*, 407–8; Taibo II, *Ernesto Guevara*, 479–81; Gott, *Guerrilla Movements in Latin America*, 387–90.

44. Interviews with Otero, Cueto, Soria, Rocabado, Reyes, and Guzmán. See also Soria, "La izquierda armada." For more on Papi, see Andrea López et al., eds., *Mártires del MININT: semblanzas biográficas*, vol. 2 (Havana: Editora Política, 1990), 148–54; Mariano Rodríguez Herrera, *Ellos lucharon con el Che* (Havana: Editorial de Ciencias Sociales, 1982), 67–81; both cited in Gleijeses, *Conflicting Missions*, 425. See also Benemelis, *Las Guerras Secretas*, 72.

45. Interview with Soria. Confirmed by Otero and Cueto.

46. Interview with Otero. Confirmed by Cueto.

47. Interviews with Serrate.

48. Paz letter to his son Ramiro, 26 May 1961, published in Ramiro Paz, *Las cartas de Víctor Paz*, 106; and in the insert of Ramiro Paz, *En los pasillos del poder*.

49. Foreign Ministry to Prudencio (Ambassador to Yugoslavia), 29 April 1963; Foreign Ministry to García (Ambassador to Algeria), 17 May 1963, RV-4-E-54, RREE.

50. Former president Enrique Hertzog (1947–49) was one of this argument's foremost proponents. See Hertzog, *Communism in Bolivia* (Buenos Aires: n.p., 1954). My thanks to Pablo Quisbert for sharing this document. See also conversations Hertzog held with US Embassy officials in Buenos Aires, US Embassy (Buenos Aires), 30 October 1964, "Bolivia, Cables, Volume II, 7/64–11/64," box 7, NSF-CO, LBJL.

51. State Department, "Contingency Program for Bolivia," n.d. (1962), folder "Bolivia 1962, Contingency Program for Bolivia," box 10, Records relating to Bolivia, 1961–1975, SDLF.

52. Stephansky to Martin, n.d. (1962), folder "Bolivia 1962, Splitting Paz from Lechín," box 10, Records relating to Bolivia, 1961–1975, SDLF.

53. Stephansky to Rusk, 17 December 1962; Paz to Kennedy, 26 November 1962; Bolivia, "General, 8/62–12/62," box 10, NSF-CO, JFKL.

54. Stephansky to Rusk, 28 October 1962, in idem; Stephansky to Rusk, 24–26 and 29 October 1962, 724.5/3-460, box 1563, SDDF.

55. Stephansky Oral History, JFKL, 33–34.

56. Goodwin to Martin, 2 November 1962; Belcher to Martin, 29 November 1962, "Bolivia, 1962," box 4, lots 62D418 and 64D15, SDLF.

57. Bell, "Bolivian Strategy Statement," 11 February 1963, "Bolivia, 2/63–6/63," box 389A, NSF-Dungan, JFKL, 1–2, 4. *Campesino*, in the Bolivian context: "Indian peasant."

58. Hansen to Bundy and Bell, "The Finances of the Public Sector of Bolivia," 5 March 1963, "Bolivia, General, 1/63–4/63," box 10A, NSF-CO, JFKL.

59. Stephansky to Rusk, 8 April 1963, in idem. Stephansky was later asked about his role in Paz's decision to run for reelection. He replied misleadingly: "The re-election issue didn't come up until late in the game, and it was a rather complicated story . . . the notion that I campaigned for Víctor . . . that I rather favored that he should have a second [*sic*: third] term, you might say that without a doubt I discussed it on several occasions with Paz." Stephansky Oral History, JFKL, 28.

60. State Department, untitled paper (1963), folder "1963 AID Strategy Paper," box 10, Records relating to Bolivia, 1961–1975," SDLF.

61. Foreign embassies were chosen respites for MNR leaders. Paz served as Siles's ambassador to London from 1956 to 1960, and Siles returned the favor by representing Paz's government in Madrid and Montevideo from 1960 to 1964. Lechín had not originally planned to spend his vice presidential years in Rome, but a nervous breakdown resulting from scurrilous accusations of cocaine smuggling convinced him to take a break. Lechín believed this golden exile was a prelude to his 1964 presidential run. See Lechín, *El pueblo al poder*, 137–38; and numerous articles from *El Diario* beginning in late 1961. For more on Bolivia's move to curtail narcotics trafficking during the early 1960s, and accusations against Lechín, see Gootenberg, *Andean Cocaine*, 275–89.

62. Stephansky to Rusk, 22 April 1963, "Bolivia, Subjects, Paz Visit, 10/22/63–10/24/63," box 11, NSF-CO, JFKL; Paz to Kennedy, 24 April 1963, "Bolivia, 1962–3," box 112, POF, JFKL.

63. MEMCON, 10 May 1963, Government POL BOL 1963; Stephansky to Rusk, 7 May 1963, Elections POL BOL 1963, box 3829, SDANF. See "Inicia Mañana Jira Política Vicepresidente Juan Lechín," *El Diario*, 25 May 1963. Barrientos was sly, and Lechín was no doubt flattered by a series of letters from the general calling Lechín the "lighthouse that enlightens the people," among other flowery accolades. See Lechín, *El pueblo al poder*, 159. Barrientos's widow recalls living across the street from Lechín, as well as his frequent visits.

64. MEMCON, 24 April 1963, Elections POL BOL 1963, box 3829, SDANF.

65. MEMCON, 10 May 1963, Government POL BOL 1963, box 3829, SDANF.

66. "Internal Defense Plan for Bolivia," 10 May 1963, "Bolivia, 3/61–10/63," box WH-25, Schlesinger Papers, JFKL, 1–2, 11, 14–15; "Minutes of the Special Group (CI) Meeting," 16 May 1963, CREST.

67. These included the "General Pando" Third Engineering Battalion and the "Alto de la Alianza" Fourth Engineering Battalion. See chapter 1, footnote 126, in this volume.

68. See Shesko, "Constructing Roads," 6–28.

69. Countless Bolivians recount this paradoxical quirk of history. For harder evidence, a documentary by historian Carlos Mesa shows still footage of Barrientos deplaning with Paz on 15 April. Carlos Mesa Gisbert, *Bolivia Siglo XX: Tata Barrientos* (La Paz: Plano Medio, 2009). See also interviews with Arguedas, a latter-day *Barrientista* who served as radio operator on the plane, published in Cuevas, *Arguedas*, 67–70.

70. Anyone who goes to Bolivia asking about Barrientos hears the following legend: In October 1961, during an air show outside La Paz, three airmen lost their lives when their parachutes failed to open. In the face of criticism in the press, Barrientos had journalists accompany him to where the bodies lay. He asked them to pick one parachute among the three that had supposedly failed, and he proceeded to put it on. Barrientos then carried out a dramatic jump, sailing safely to the ground and then being carted away on the shoulders of the masses who had come out to witness the stunt. This is essentially what happened, although Barrientos had the decency to wait until the unfortunate airmen had been buried, and there is little evidence that he used one of the supposedly failed parachutes. See "El Comandante de la Fuerza Aérea se Lanzó en Paracaídas," *El Diario*, 19 October 1961. There is no shortage of Barrientos legends. He is also said to have set up a delicious barbecue in front of hunger strikers to convince them to give up their demands. And in one altercation with a dynamite-wielding miner, Barrientos apparently grabbed the dynamite stick, bear-hugged the miner, and asked around if anyone had a match.

According to Barrientos's friends in Cochabamba, he spoke poor Quechua until 1961. He then began taking lessons from Rocabado and Zannier, both of whom spoke fluently. Interviews with Rocabado and Alberto Iriarte.

Mario Rolón was director of *El Diario* beginning in late 1961, and Víctor Zannier was director of *El Mundo*. Rocabado puts it thus: "Zannier was much closer friends with Barrientos than I was. That's why *El Mundo* took such a pro-Barrientos line." Interviews with Rocabado.

71. Rocabado told Barrientos that, despite the fact that the general gave "such lovely speeches, full of passion and energy," Barrientos was "in big trouble" when the press published transcripts. Rocabado told him: "When you read your speeches verbatim, they are meaningless!" Interviews with Rocabado.

72. "Enérgica Declaración de Legalidad y Apego Constitucional de las FFAA," *El Diario*, 25 July 1962.

73. René Barrientos, *La Unidad de las Fuerzas Armadas*. Many thanks to Luis Antezana E. for providing a copy of this pamphlet.

74. Ibid.

75. Kennedy, NSAM 119, 18 December 1961, National Security Action Memoranda, NSF-JFK, JFKL.

76. Kennedy, "Final Report, 3rd Conference of American Armies," 16–20 July 1962, quoted in Brill, "Military Civic Action," 30.

77. Moscoso, *Lo que he visto*.

78. Gordillo, *Campesinos Revolucionarios en Bolivia*, 131–35. For the backstory of this Cochabamba peasant feuding, see James Kohn's excellent piece "The Cliza and Ucureña War."

79. Interviews with Edward Fox.

80. Interviews with Sternfield.

81. Interviews with Evelyn Fox.

82. Arguedas interviews, published in Cuevas, *Arguedas*, 155–56.

83. Interviews with Edward Fox. Fox's views did not mesh well with the developmentalists, such as Alliance for Progress architect Robert Alexander, who believed Washington's task was "the conversion of the fifteenth-century Indian peasant into a twentieth-century agriculturist and citizen." Alexander, "Nature and Progress of Agrarian Reform," 569–70. For his part, Stephansky told Alexander that "the whole orientation of the country must shift east," away from the Indians' millenary lands on the *altiplano*. Stephansky, interview with Alexander, 8 April 1962, folder 58, Interviews, Alexander Papers, Rutgers.

84. Interviews with Edward Fox. At the time, he was posted in Santiago, Chile.

85. Ibid. With regard to accusations that he worked for the CIA, Colonel Fox was dismissive: "CIA is for civilians!"

86. Fox, "Field Visit—Cliza Valley, October 6–7, 1962," 16 October 1962, 724.5/3-460, box 1563, SDDF.

87. Interviews with Edward Fox.

88. *Chicha* refers to various Latin American drinks. In Bolivia, it is a corn-based intoxicant traditional to Cochabamba.

89. Fox, "Field Visit—Cliza Valley, October 6–7, 1962."

90. Interviews with Rocabado and Iriarte.

91. Fox, "Field Visit—Cliza Valley, October 6–7, 1962."

92. Interviews with Edward Fox.

93. Interviews with Sternfield.

94. For obvious reasons, Lansdale's presence in Bolivia was not revealed to the public. See "Llegó Alto Jefe Militar Norteamericano a Cooperar en Programa Cívico de las FFAA," *El Diario*, 28 May 1963.

95. Lansdale Oral History, JFKL, 39.

96. Lansdale to McNamara, Gilpatric, and Bundy, 3 and 6 June 1963, "Bolivia, General, 4/63–7/63," box 10A, NSF-CO, JFKL, 1–2, 4; interviews with Sanjinés. In a Pentagon-endorsed study of military civic action in Bolivia, William Brill writes that Sanjinés was "a man whose name is indeed inseparable from civic action in Bolivia." Brill, "Military Civic Action," xxxii. In early 1963, Sanjinés took over as interim president of *El Diario*, which further accentuated the paper's pro-Barrientos bias.

97. Interviews with Sanjinés.

98. Lansdale to McNamara, Gilpatric, and Bundy, 3 and 6 June 1963, "Bolivia, General, 4/63–7/63," box 10A, NSF-CO, JFKL, 1–2, 4. The *El Diario* article is indeed dramatic. Indians are quoted, "If the *gringos* help, then we must believe that potable water for Achacachi will be a beautiful reality" and "Our dream has finally been fulfilled . . . I give thanks to the national army." See "Agua Potable en Achacachi: Dentro de Tres Meses," *El Diario*, 26 May 1963. The denouement of the story is less glowing. The Indians saw little use in paying for indoor water when they could get it free from community sources. The inauguration of the water system was marred by a bombing attempt on the pump, which eventually required twenty-four-hour army security. Worse, only 150 families out of 5,000 were willing to pay, and the rest, when asked about the project, "simply shrugged." Brill writes that army units needed to do a better job "to educate the people as to [the pump's] value and induce them to pay for the service." See Brill, "Military Civic Action," 191–95.

99. Lansdale to McNamara, Gilpatric, and Bundy, 3 and 6 June 1963, "Bolivia, General, 4/63–7/63," box 10A, NSF-CO, JFKL, 1–2, 4. According to Brill, these colonization projects were successful only when they recruited landless Indians, "who had little choice but to stay and work." See Brill, "Military Civic Action," 169 (footnote 12).

100. Lansdale to McNamara, Gilpatric, and Bundy, 3 and 6 June 1963, "Bolivia, General, 4/63–7/63," box 10A, NSF-CO, JFKL, 1–2, 4. Regarding CIA civic action programs leading up to the 1958 Lao elections, see William J. Rust, *Before the Quagmire: American Intervention in Laos, 1954–1961* (Lexington: University Press of Kentucky, 2012), 82–92; Seth Jacobs, *The Universe Unraveling: American Foreign Policy in Cold War Laos* (Ithaca, NY: Cornell University Press, 2012), 77–81.

101. Lansdale to McNamara, Gilpatric, and Bundy, 3 and 6 June 1963, "Bolivia, General, 4/63–7/63," box 10A, NSF-CO, JFKL, 1–2, 4. Arze Murillo's offer was made on 30 May. See Stephansky to Rusk, 30 May 1963, "Bolivia, 4/63–7/63," box 10A, NSF-CO, JFKL. Flores is referred to here as "Embassy Political Officer," but his true position was confirmed in interviews with his successor, Larry Sternfield.

102. Interviews with Sternfield. Another former CIA agent writes that Arze Murillo "worked closely with the La Paz station" in support of the agency's "Bolivian operations" in support of Paz. Agee, *Inside the Company*, 385.

103. Brill, "Military Civic Action," 52–53.

104. Colonel Cook, "Prologue," in Sanjinés, *Civic Action*, 1–3.

105. Brill, "Military Civic Action," 90–91, 128–31. Thanks to Colonel Sanjinés, the engineers were even exempt from taking the despised MNR oath of loyalty. Interviews with Sanjinés and army engineer Eduardo Claure.

106. Brill, "Military Civic Action," 103 (footnote 2), 209.

107. USAID, "Briefing Paper," 1963, quoted in Brill, "Military Civic Action," 41.

108. COMIBOL Advisory Group to Paz, 13 July 1962, PR 985, ABNB.

109. Bedregal, *De búhos*, 302, 337, 339.

110. MEMCON, 19 June 1963, "Government," POL BOL 1963, box 3828, SDANF.

111. MEMCON, 25 June 1963, in idem.

112. MEMCONs, 28 May and 7 June 1963, INCO Mining, Minerals, and Metals BOL, box 3540, SDANF.

113. Martin to Latin American Policy Committee, "Contingency Plan for Meeting COMI-BOL Crisis," 8 June 1963, folder "Miscellaneous Bolivia," box 10, Records Relating to Bolivia, 1961–1975," SDLF; State Department, "Contingency Plan for Meeting Possible COMIBOL Crisis," 8 August 1963, "Bolivia, 7/63–5/64 and undated," box 389A, NSF-Dungan, JFKL. See also State Department, "Contingency Plan for Meeting COMIBOL Crisis," 3 June 1963, folder "Miscellaneous Bolivia," box 10, Records Relating to Bolivia, 1961–1975," SDLF.

114. "You had these poor saps in the Kennedy administration . . . going down to Bolivia . . . and deciding that if you just put enough money in aid programs, that the Bolivians would became a new Puerto Rico. Well, they didn't." Stutesman Oral History, Association for Diplomatic Studies and Training.

115. Stutesman to Rusk, 28 June 1963, "Bolivia, 3/61–10/63," box WH-25, Schlesinger Papers, JFKL.

116. "La Huelga de Catavi es una 'Criminalidad sin Paralelo,' " El Diario, 8 July 1963; "A Partir de Hoy la Comibol no Pagará Salario a Ningún Trabajador de Catavi," El Diario, 9 July 1963; "Celebró Ayer Aniversario el Batallón Motorizado 'Toledo,' " El Diario, 9 July 1963; "El gobierno está dispuesto a enfrentar una huelga general de obreros mineros," El Diario, 10 July 1963.

117. Interviews with Serrate.

118. Crespo, El rostro minero de Bolivia, 332.

119. MNR-Llallagua, 1 July 1963, PR 1051, ABNB.

120. Pimentel to Bedregal, 20 June 1963, published in Crespo, El rostro minero, 332.

121. MNR-Uncía to Paz, 18 July 1963, published in idem.

122. Campesinos-North Potosí to Paz, 20 July 1963, published in idem.

123. Harris and Albó, Monteros y Guardatojos, 91–94.

124. Nery to Paz, 24 December 1962, PR 1610, ABNB.

125. Harris and Albó, Monteros y Guardatojos, 91–94.

126. Stephansky to Rusk, 17 July 1963, "Bolivia, General, 4/63–7/63," box 10A, NSF-CO, JFKL. See also MEMCON, 17 July 1963, INCO Mining, Minerals and Metals BOL, box 3540, SDANF.

127. Interviews with Serrate and Bedregal.

128. Stephansky to Rusk, 17 July 1963, "Bolivia, General, 4/63–7/63," box 10A, NSF-CO, JFKL. See also MEMCON, 17 July 1963, INCO Mining, Minerals and Metals BOL, box 3540, SDANF.

129. Throughout the 1963 mine crisis, Ambassador Stephansky filed two sets of cables, some "Confidential" and others "Secret" and addressed only to Rusk, Martin, and Moscoso. The "Confidential" cables bear little connection to reality since they make no mention of Washington's "contingency fund" or its support for Nery's militia.

130. Stephansky to Rusk, 17 July 1963, "Bolivia, General 4/63–7/63," box 10A, NSF-CO, JFKL. US documents suggest that UK-based tin-smelting company Williams Harvey contributed $800,000 to this paramilitary operation. See Stephansky to State, 31 July 1963, INCO Mining, Minerals, and Metals BOL, box 3540, SDANF.

131. Stephansky to Rusk, 19 July 1963, "Bolivia, General, 4/63–7/63," box 10A, NSF-CO, JFKL.

132. CIA, Information Report, 20 July 1963, in idem.

133. Stephansky to Rusk, 20 July 1963, in idem.

134. Stephansky to Rusk, 19 July 1963, in idem.

135. Stephansky to Rusk, 19 July 1963, INCO Mining, Minerals, and Metals BOL, box 3540, SDANF.

136. State Department to Bundy, 20 July 1963; Smith to McHugh, 20 July 1963; "Bolivia, General, 4/63–7/63," box 10A, NSF-CO, JFKL. The bracketed numbers are sanitized in Smith's cable to the White House, but I have filled them in based on the fully declassified State Department memorandum to Bundy.

137. Stephansky to Rusk, Martin, and Moscoso, 23 July 1963; Cook to O'Meara, 24 July 1963, in idem.

138. Rusk to US Embassy (Lima), US Embassy (La Paz), and US Embassy (Panama), 22 July 1963; Stephansky to Rusk, 24 and 26 July 1963; O'Meara to Rusk, 26 July 1963; Joint Chiefs to O'Meara, 26 July 1963, in idem.

139. Rusk to Embassy, 24 July 1963, INCO Mining, Minerals, and Metals BOL, box 3540, SDANF; OPS Technical Services Division to Engle, 31 July 1963; Engle to Bell, 31 July 1963, "Special Group (CI) Meetings—August 1963," box 6, OPS, Numerical File, RG 286.

140. CIA, Information Report, 26 July 1963, "Bolivia, General, 4/63–7/63," box 10A, NSF-CO, JFKL.

141. Paz letter, 22 July 1963; Menacho letter, 25 July 1963; published in Crespo, *El rostro minero de Bolivia*, 336. Miners captured these documents and incorporated them into a Bolivian senate investigation. Some documents can be found in PR 1035, ABNB.

142. CIA, Information Report, 26 July 1963, "Bolivia, General, 4/63–7/63," box 10A, NSF-CO, JFKL.

143. Portugal claims to have been unaware that the purpose of the mission was to "terminate Federico Escobar." According to him, "it was a dispute between Dr. Paz and Federico Escóbar, and Dr. Paz sent Wilge Nery with weapons and money to kill him." Months later, Portugal confronted President Paz in the capital: "Why did you order the death of Federico Escóbar, almost getting me killed in the process? That is wrong." Paz responded, "Portugal, forgive me," after which point Portugal resigned from the MNR. Interview with Fabian Portugal. My thanks to Juan Molina for serving as a Quechua-Spanish interpreter. Shortly after my interviews, Portugal related a similar tale to French anthropologist Claude Le Gouill. See Le Gouill, "Irupata."

144. Interview with Cirilo Jiménez.

145. Interviews with Indian peasant leader Fabián Portugal (Juan Molina interpreting) and miner participants Cirilo Jiménez, Daniel Ordóñez, and Rosendo Osorio. Using official documents captured from Nery's militia, Catavi union leader Crespo reconstructed pieces of the story. See Crespo, *El rostro minero de Bolivia*, 335–36. See also "Mineros de Catavi Atacaron una Población con Armas y Dinamita: Mataron a 6 Personas," *El Diario*, 30 July 1963.

146. Ibid.

147. Harris and Albó, *Monteros y Guardatojos*, 94.

148. Defense Intelligence Agency (hereafter DIA), Intelligence Summary, 31 July 1963; CIA, Intelligence Memorandum, 31 July 1963, in idem.

149. CIA, Intelligence Memorandum, 30 July 1963, "Bolivia, General, 4/63–7/63," box 10A, NSF-CO, JFKL.

150. Stephansky refers to his CIA cable in Stephansky to Rusk, Martin, and Moscoso, 31 July 1963, POL 25 Demonstrations, Protests, Riots BOL, box 3830, SDANF.

151. State Department, Memorandum for the Attorney General, 31 July 1963, "Bolivia, General, 4/63–7/63," box 10A, NSF-CO, JFKL.

152. Cottrell via Harriman to the Special Group (CI), 31 July 1963, in idem.

153. Henry Lee, "Threatened Strike Could Bring Down Bolivian Government," *Washington Post, Times Herald*, 24 July 1963; Juan de Onís, "Bolivia Is Facing Mine Showdown," *New York Times*, 4 August 1963.

154. Dan Kurzman, "Red Labor Leaders in Bolivia Seek Political Showdown," *Washington Post, Times Herald*, 17 August 1963; George Natanson, "A Latin Country Praises the US: Bolivia's President Breaks Rule," *Los Angeles Times*, 11 August 1963.

155. "Solvency and Self-Respect," *Time*, 16 August 1963.

156. State Department, "Bolivia: State-AID Contingency Paper for COMIBOL Crisis," 8 August 1963, "Bolivia, 7/63–6/64, and undated," box 389A, NSF-Dungan, JFKL, 3.

157. Stephansky Oral History, JFKL, 73.

158. Stephansky to Rusk, 30 July 1963, "Bolivia, General, 4/63–7/63," box 10A, NSF-CO, JFKL.

159. US Department of Commerce, "Alliance for Progress," 43.3, RG 43, Moving Images, NARA. My thanks to Senate Historian Donald Richie for identifying the unknown senator as Gale McGee of Wyoming.

4. Development's Detractors

1. Embassy to Rusk, 4 August 1963, "Government," POL BOL 1963, box 3829, SDANF; "Fue Cancelado Ayer el Control Obrero con Derecho a Veto en las Minas Nacionalizadas," *El Diario*, 4 August 1963. *Control Obrero*: "Workers' Control."

2. One miner recalled that leftists, both PCB and POR members, were indeed the first to be fired. He added, however, that with forced retirements at a weekly rate of two hundred, it was not long before noncommunist miners received pink slips. Interviews with Rojas. See Stephansky to Rusk, 9 August 1963, CSM Communism 13 BOL," box 3616, SDANF; Stephansky to Rusk, 24 September 1963, "Bolivia, General, 8/63–1/64," box 11, NSF-CO, JFKL.

3. Stephansky to Rusk, 10 August 1963, INCO Mining, Minerals, and Metals BOL, box 3540, SDANF. See also "Estalló Ayer una Huelga General en Catavi Bajo Inspiración Comunista," *El Diario*, 10 August 1963.

4. Embassy to Rusk, 4 August 1963, "Government," POL BOL 1963, box 3829, SDANF.

5. "La Alianza para el Progreso se Ejecuta en Bolivia Mejor que en Cualquier Otro País," *El Diario*, 9 August 1963.

6. Stephansky to Martin, 9 August 1963, "Travel-Bolivia," box 21, Edwin Martin Papers, JFKL.

7. Excerpts of the minutes from the 5412 Special Group's 8 August meeting, in State Department, Memorandum Prepared for the Special Group, 10 March 1964, document 148, *FRUS 1964–1968: Volume XXXI—South and Central America; Mexico*. Confirmed in interviews with Edward Fox, Henderson, and Sternfield.

8. Osborne to State, 16 August 1963, POL Government BOL 1963, box 3829, SDANF.

9. Stephansky to Rusk, 9 August 1963, INCO Mining, Minerals, and Metals BOL, box 3540, SDANF.

10. One cannot help but imagine that, from the miners' perspective, Paz was saying that the "miners [rather than the 'mines'] must serve the interests of the Bolivian community," meaning the burden of economic development would fall squarely on their backs. Stephansky to Rusk, 23 August 1963, in idem; "Comienza hoy una nueva etapa que tipificará la influencia política," *El Diario*, 23 August 1963.

11. "El Presidente Mantendrá su Actitud Sobre el Problema Minero aun a Riesgo de Caer," *El Diario*, 17 August 1963.

12. "Mientras Estén Pimentel y Escóbar en Catavi no Habrá Solución del Conflicto," *El Diario*, 24 August 1963.

13. Paz letter to Ramiro, 8 September 1963, published in Ramiro Paz, *Las cartas de Víctor Paz*, 117; and in the insert of Ramiro Paz, *En los pasillos del poder.*

14. Stephansky to Rusk, 13 and 24 August 1963, "Bolivia, General, 8/63–1/64," box 11, NSF-CO, JFKL.

15. Stephansky to Rusk, 24 August 1963, in idem; Bedregal to FSTMB, undated, in Crespo, *El rostro minero*, 338; Stephansky to Rusk, 9 September 1963, INCO Mining, Minerals, and Metals BOL, box 3540, SDANF.

16. Stephansky to Rusk, 24 September 1963, "Bolivia, General, 8/63–1/64," box 11, NSF-CO, JFKL.

17. Stephansky to Rusk, 24 September 1963, in idem.

18. Stephansky to Rusk, 4 and 8 October 1963, in idem.

19. Embassy to Rusk, 17 October 1963, INCO Mining, Minerals, and Metals BOL, box 3540, SDANF.

20. Embassy to Rusk, 9 October 1963, in idem.

21. See "A Extremos Deplorables Llegó Ayer la Huelga de Hambre de Mujeres Mineras," *El Diario*, 17 October 1963. Comité de Amas de Casa: "Housewives Committee."

22. Embassy to Rusk, 25 October 1963, INCO Mining, Minerals, and Metals BOL, box 3540, SDANF.

23. Embassy to Rusk, 1 November 1963, in idem.

24. Embassy to Rusk, 5 November 1963, in idem.

25. Stephansky Oral History, JFKL, 37.

26. Interviews with Edward Fox.

27. Bedregal, *De búhos*, 349. *Compañero*, very roughly: "comrade," "colleague," or "fellow party member."

28. Stephansky to State, USAID, and Pentagon, 14 October 1964, "Internal Security," POL BOL 1963, box 3830, SDANF, 1, 3.

29. Dunkerley, *Rebellion in the Veins*, 105.

30. State Department, "Background Paper: Political, Economic, and Social Conditions in Bolivia," 18 October 1963, "Bolivia, Subjects, Paz Visit, Paz Briefing Book, Tabs IV–VII, 10/22/63–10/23/63," box 11, NSF-CO, JFKL, 1–2.

31. Ibid., 7–8; "Policy Paper: The COMIBOL Showdown," 18 October 1963, "Bolivia, Subjects, Paz Briefing Book, Tabs I–III, 10/22/63–10/23/63," 1; Read to Bundy, 18 October 1963, "Bolivia, Subjects, Paz Visit, Briefing Memorandum, 10/18/1963," box 11, NSF-CO, JFKL, 1–3, 8.

32. Read to Bundy, 18 October 1963, "Bolivia, Subjects, Paz Visit, Briefing Memorandum, 10/18/1963," 1–3, 8; "Background Paper: Bloc Aid, Trade, and Diplomatic Relations," 18 October 1963, "Bolivia, Subjects, Paz Visit, Paz Briefing Book, Tabs IV–VII, 10/22/63–10/23/63," 2; "Policy Paper: Cuban Subversion," 18 October 1963, "Bolivia, Subjects, Paz Visit, Paz Briefing Book, Tabs I–III, 10/22/63–10/23/63," box 11, NSF-CO, JFKL, 1, 3.

33. MEMCON, 22 October 1963, "Bolivia, Subjects, Paz Visit, 10/63, MEMCONs," box 11, NSF-CO, JFKL, 2–4 (part I) and 3 (part II).

34. "Otorgará Yugoslavia Crédito de 5 Millones de $US para Plantas y Equipos Industriales," *El Diario*, 3 October 1963.

35. Stephansky rejected the view that "Yugoslavia may not be as bad as USSR or ChiCom. . . . Yugoslavia is admittedly a Communist country and is following a neutralist line." Stephansky to State, 16 August 1963, INCO Mining, Minerals, and Metals BOL," box 3540; CIA, Intelligence Bulletin, 20 August 1963, CREST.

36. Herbert Thompson Oral History, Association for Diplomatic Studies and Training.

37. MEMCON, Department of State, 22 October 1963, "Bolivia, Subjects, Paz Visit, 10/63, MEMCONS," box 11, NSF-CO, JFKL, 2–3 (part III). According to Bolivians who went to Cuba in the early 1960s, most trips were short and included little study and no guerrilla training. Interviews with the Emilse Escóbar; Reyes; Muñoz.

38. Donald Barnes Oral History, JFKL, 98–101.

39. "Kennedy Praises Bolivian President for 'Revolutionary Efforts,'" *Washington Post, Times Herald,* 23 October 1963.

40. Alipaz to Sánchez, 12 November 1963, folio EEUU-2-E-31, RREE. On 24 October, Goldwater called Paz's government a "candy-coated despotism." See "Bolivian Rule of Paz Rapped by Goldwater," *Chicago Tribune,* 25 October 1963.

41. Paz to his son Ramiro, 13 November 1963, published in Ramiro Paz, *Las cartas de Víctor Paz,* 118.

42. Kennedy to Paz, 27 October 1963, POL 15-1 BOL, box 3829, SDANF, RG. See also "Su Visita Nos ha Permitido Apreciar Mejor El Gallardo Esfuerzo que Realiza Bolivia," *El Diario,* 29 October 1963. According to US ambassador to Chile Charles Cole, these words "create almost a sense of shock among other Latin Americans," who could not understand why Washington rewarded a government with policies of "arming the workers, confiscating land without compensation, and taking over mines and other foreign enterprises." Cole to Martin, 29 October 1963, "Travel-Bolivia," box 21, Edwin Martin Papers, JFKL.

43. Interviews with Edward Fox.

44. Interviews with Sternfield.

45. Henderson Oral History, Association for Diplomatic Studies and Training.

46. Henderson, undated, "Amb: Data for Senate Hearings, 1963," box 6, series 2: Subject Files, Henderson Papers, JFKL.

47. MEMCON, 20 November 1963, "Bolivia, General, 8/63–1/64," box 11, NSF-CO, JFKL.

48. Henderson Oral History, JFKL, 70.

49. Bedregal, *De búhos,* 352.

50. Interview with Henderson.

51. "Bolivia Strategy Statement," 26 November 1963, "Bolivia, 7/63–5/64 and undated," box 389A, NSF-Dungan, JFKL, 1, 4. *Campesino,* in the Bolivian context: "Indian peasant."

52. Johnson to Paz, 29 November 1963, "Bolivia, Paz Correspondence," box 8, NSF-CO, LBJL.

53. Anthony Freeman Oral History, Association for Diplomatic Studies and Training. When I mentioned Tom Martin to one Communist miner, he smiled effusively. "Tom Martin was a very good friend of mine. We used to have long theoretical discussions. He would say he was a Kautskyist! Such an interesting guy!" Interviews with Leónidas Rojas. This was confirmed in interviews with Martin's wife, who added that her husband "did not discriminate" against Communists, and that he "worked with all of the workers to make sure things were fair." Interview with Mariela Martin.

54. Crespo, *El rostro minero de Bolivia,* 340; interviews with Fergerstrom.

55. Lechín, *El pueblo al poder,* 141–42. Confirmed in interviews with Reyes.

56. Crespo, *El rostro minero de Bolivia,* 342. Confirmed in interviews with Reyes.

57. Embassy to Rusk, 6 December 1963, INCO Mining, Minerals, and Metals BOL," box 3540, SDANF; "Dramático Rompimiento de Lechín con el Presidente Paz Estenssoro," *El Diario,* 6 December 1963. Confirmed in interviews with Crespo and with Reyes, who admits being troubled by the unabashed enthusiasm demonstrated for the declaration by the small group of right-wing Falangist miners.

58. Lechín, *El pueblo al poder*, 142. Confirmed in interviews with Fergerstrom, who was taken hostage, and in interviews with PCB miner Daniel Ordóñez, who led the assault. Confirmed also in interviews with Reyes, Reinaga, and Rojas. See also "En Rápida Acción Policial se Detuvo a Pimentel y Escóbar," *El Diario*, 7 December 1963. Control Político: "Political Control," Paz's secret police.

59. Interviews with Fergerstrom. *Gringos de Mierda! Muera los Gringos!* translates roughly to: "Fucking gringos! Death to the gringos!"

60. Gerónima interviews, published in Lagos, *Nos hemos forjado así*, 81–85. The committee's secretary general, Norberta de Aguilar, was on leave to accompany her husband in the hospital.

61. Gerónima interviews, published in Lagos, *Nos hemos forjado así*, 81–85.

62. Interviews with Fergerstrom.

63. Rifkin, interview with Robert Alexander, 23 December 1963, folder 51, Interviews, Alexander Papers, Rutgers.

64. Lechín, *El pueblo al poder*, 142.

65. Crespo, *El rostro minero de Bolivia*, 342–43.

66. Henderson to Rusk, 7 December 1963, "Bolivia, US Hostages," box 8, NSF-CO, LBJL.

67. Ibid.

68. "Fue Ovacionado por Miles de Personas el Nuevo Embajador de los Estados Unidos," *El Diario*, 8 December 1963.

69. Henderson to Rusk, 7 December 1963, "Bolivia, US Hostages," box 8, NSF-CO, LBJL.

70. Interview with Mariela Martin.

71. Henderson to Rusk, 8 December, 1963, in idem.

72. Rusk to Henderson, 7 December 1963, in idem.

73. Rusk to Johnson, 8 December 1963, in idem.

74. William Bundy to McGeorge Bundy, 8 December 1963, and attached memorandum, in idem.

75. SOUTHCOM, "Talking Paper for the Joint Chiefs of Staff," 8 December 1963, attached to Bundy to Bundy, 8 December, in idem.

76. Bundy to Kennedy, 8 December 1963, "Chronological File, December 1963," box 1, NSF-McGeorge Bundy, LBJL.

77. White House Press Release, 8 December 1963, in idem; "Plena ayuda ofrece EEUU para conseguir la libertad de los rehenes," *El Diario*, 10 December 1963.

78. Rusk to Henderson, 8 December 1963; Henderson to Rusk, 8 December 1963, "Bolivia, US Hostages," box 8, NSF-CO, LBJL.

79. Henderson to Rusk, 8 December 1963, in idem.

80. State Department, "Captions and Handling Instructions for the Information Management Specialist (IMS)," in *U.S. Department of State Foreign Affairs Manual: Volume 5, Handbook 2—Telecommunications* (Washington, DC: GPO, 2008), 4.

81. Henderson to Rusk and White House, 8 December 1963, "Bolivia, US Hostages," box 8, NSF-CO, LBJL.

82. Henderson to Rusk, 9 December 1963, in idem.

83. Henderson to Rusk (3), 9–10 December 1963, "Bolivia, US Hostages," box 8, NSF-CO, LBJL.

84. MEMCON, 9 December 1963, "Meetings with the President, 23 November—27 December," box 1, John McCone Memoranda, LBJL.

85. CIA, Information Report, 10 December 1963, "Bolivia, US Hostages," box 8, NSF-CO, LBJL.

86. Recording of Telephone Conversation, 10 December 1963, K6312.06, PNO 18, LBJL.

87. Gerónima interviews, published in Lagos, *Nos hemos forjado así*, 88–89.

88. Domitila interviews, published in Viezzer, *"Si me permiten hablar . . . ,"* 85–97. This is not an embellishment. Interviews with Crespo, Reyes, and Fergerstrom and numerous reports in *El Diario*, *The New York Times*, and *Time* magazine.

89. Domitila interviews, published in Viezzer, *"Si me permiten hablar . . . ,"* 91–92.

90. Henderson to Rusk, 9 December 1963; Moscoso via Rusk to Lechín via Henderson, 10 December 1963; Reuther via Rusk to Lechín via Henderson, 10 December 1963, "Bolivia, US Hostages," box 8, NSF-CO, LBJL; Salinger via Rusk to Henderson, 10 December 1963, "Juan Lechín (Bolivia, 1964), Aide Files—Pierre Salinger, LBJL. All these were made public. See "Cables de Personalidades," *El Diario*, 12 December 1963.

91. Henderson to Rusk (2), 10 December 1963, "Bolivia, US Hostages," box 8, NSF-CO, LBJL.

92. Henderson to Rusk, 10 and 11 December 1963, in idem; "Dio Plazo de 48 Horas a Catavi," *El Diario*, 11 December 1963.

93. Henderson to Rusk, 10 December 1963, "Bolivia, US Hostages," box 8, NSF-CO, LBJL.

94. Ibid. The entire list can be found in Military Group to Rusk, Pentagon and Southern Command, 12 December 1963, DEF 12-3 BOL, SDANF.

95. Rusk to Henderson, 11 December 1963; Henderson to Rusk, 11 December 1963, "Bolivia, US Hostages," box 8, NSF-CO, LBJL. The dummy cable is in the same folder.

96. Recording of Telephone Conversation, 11 December 1963, K6312.07, PNO 24, LBJL.

97. Henderson to Rusk, 11 December 1963, "Bolivia, US Hostages," box 8, NSF-CO, LBJL.

98. Henderson to Rusk (2), 11 December 1963, in idem.

99. Henderson to Rusk, 13 December 1963, in idem. According to Martin's wife, these letters were delivered to her by sympathetic national mine union leaders. She recalls that the letters were "personal" but that Martin "would write things between the lines about what was going on" in the union building. Interview with Mariela Martin.

100. Salinger to Lechín, 11 December 1963, "Juan Lechín (Bolivia, 1964)," Aide Files—Pierre Salinger, LBJL.

101. Shriver via Rusk to Lechín via Henderson, 11 December 1963; Rusk to Lechín via Henderson, 11 December 1963, "Bolivia, US Hostages," box 8, NSF-CO, LBJL.

102. Henderson to Rusk, 12 December 1963, in idem.

103. Rusk to Henderson, 12 December 1963, in idem.

104. Southern Command to Joint Chiefs, 12 December 1963, in idem.

105. Henderson to Rusk, 12 December 1963, in idem.

106. Southern Command to Joint Chiefs and White House, 13 December 1963, in idem.

107. Recording of Telephone Conversation, 13 December 1963, K6312.06, PNO 18, LBJL.

108. Southern Command to Military Group, 14 December 1963, DEF 19-3 US-BOL, SDANF.

109. Joint Chiefs to Southern Command, Military Group, and Rusk, 13 December 1963, "Bolivia, US Hostages," box 8, NSF-CO, LBJL.

110. Comité de Amas de Casa de Siglo XX, 13 December 1963, in Lagos, *Nos hemos forjado así*, 90.

111. Gerónima interviews, published in Lagos, *Nos hemos forjado así*, 93–94.

112. Rifkin, interview with Robert Alexander, 23 December 1963, folder 51, Interviews, Alexander Papers, Rutgers; Henderson to Rusk, 14 December 1963, POL 25 BOL, box 3830, SDANF.

113. Escóbar and Pimentel to Siglo XX union, 14 December 1963, published in Lagos, *Nos hemos forjado así*, 95–96. See also "Pimentel y Escóbar Piden Que se Libere a Rehenes," *El Diario*, 14 December 1963.

114. Henderson to Rusk, 14 December 1963, POL 25 BOL, box 3830, SDANF.

115. Henderson to Rusk, 14 December 1963, POL 25 BOL, box 3830, SDANF; Henderson to Rusk, 15 December 1963, folder "Bolivia, US Hostages," box 8, NSF-CO, LBJL.

116. Report of Catavi-Siglo XX Trip of Charles H. Thomas, 6 February 1964, POL 23-8, Demonstrations, Riots BOL, box 1923, SDANF.

117. "Free at Last," *Time*, 27 December 1963.

118. Lechín, *El pueblo al poder*, 145–47. Lechín's memoirs are a mixture of reality and fantasy. He claims, for example, to have been solely responsible for obtaining the Escóbar-Pimentel letter, making no mention of Eugene Victor Rifkin.

119. Ibid.; Report of Catavi-Siglo XX Trip of Charles H. Thomas, 6 February 1964, POL 23-8, Demonstrations, Riots BOL, box 1923, SDANF.

120. Lechín, *El pueblo al poder*, 145–47.

121. Ibid.

122. Ibid.; Report of Catavi–Siglo XX Trip of Charles H. Thomas, 6 February 1964, POL 23-8, Demonstrations, Riots BOL, box 1923, SDANF.

123. Report of Catavi–Siglo XX Trip of Charles H. Thomas, 6 February 1964, POL 23-8, Demonstrations, Riots BOL, box 1923, SDANF.

124. Domitila interviews, published in Viezzer, *"Si me permiten hablar . . . ,"* 85–97; interviews with Domitila.

125. Gerónima interviews, published in Lagos, *Nos hemos forjado así*, 97–98.

126. Interviews with Crespo.

127. Rifkin, interview with Robert Alexander, 23 December 1963, folder 51, Interviews, Alexander Papers, Rutgers.

128. Interviews with Fergerstrom.

129. Anthony Freeman Oral History, Association for Diplomatic Studies and Training.

130. "Free at Last," *Time*, 27 December 1963.

131. Dungan to Henderson, 3 January 1964, "CO-Bolivia," Bolivia, White House Central File, LBJL.

132. Telephone Recording, 31 January 1964, WH6401.26, PNO 25, JFKL.

133. Johnson to Henderson via Rusk, 20 December 1963, "Bolivia, Cables, Volume I, 12/63–7/64," box 7, NSF-CO, LBJL.

5. Seeds of Revolt

1. With Lechín's support, Paz changed the constitution under a state of siege in July 1961 to permit reelection. See "No es Posible Reunir una Asamblea Constituyente Bajo un Estado de Sitio Ilegal, dice FSB," *El Diario*, 2 July 1961.

2. Interviews with Sternfield.

3. Recent scholarship on President Johnson's hands-on approach to public diplomacy in the Third World suggests that he could have found a kindred spirit in General Barrientos, with his man-of-the-people approach to the Indian peasantry. See Lerner, "Big Tree of Peace and Justice," 357–93. Unfortunately for Barrientos, Johnson rarely concerned himself with Bolivia. It seems strange therefore that some historians believe the Johnson administration "squandered whatever promise the Alliance possessed and left behind a heavy-handed policy based on military, narrow

anticommunism, and naked economic exploitation." At least in Bolivia, the heavy hand was Kennedy's. See Mark Lawrence, "Exception to the Rule?" in Lerner, *Looking Back at LBJ*, 20. Lawrence goes on to claim without citation on page 24 that Johnson "supported" the Barrientos coup.

4. Henderson Oral History, JFKL, 78.

5. Goldwater's full statement reads: "Cuba is gone, Bolivia is going, Brazil is on the brink, not to mention the mess in Panama." In "Go-Day," *Time*, 7 February 1964.

6. Thomas Mann, quoted in "US May Abandon Effort to Deter Latin Dictators," *New York Times*, 19 March 1964.

7. Johnson to Paz, 19 December 1963, POL 25 Demonstrations, Protests, Riots BOL, box 3830, SDANF.

8. State Department, Memorandum Prepared for the Special Group, 10 March 1964, document 148, *FRUS, 1964–1968: Volume XXXI—South and Central America; Mexico*. This subsidy is errantly cited by Tim Weiner as coup money in support of General Barrientos. Nothing could be further from the truth. See Weiner, *Legacy of Ashes*, 281.

9. State Department, "Aid and Alliance for Progress, Program and Project Data Related to Proposed Program, 1 of 2," undated (early 1964), box 3, NSF-Agency Files, LBJL, 61–62.

10. Henderson to Rusk, 11 January 1964, "Bolivia, Cables, Volume I, 12/63–7/64," box 7, NSF-CO, LBJL.

11. Ibid.

12. Henderson to Rusk, 14 January 1964, "Bolivia, Cables, Volume I, 12/63–7/64," box 7, NSF-CO, LBJL.

13. Ibid.; Henderson to Rusk, 21 January 1964, in idem.

14. Jackson to San Román, 28 February 1964, "Bolivia, 1 of 2, 1964," box 5, Latin American Branch Country Files, Office of Public Safety, RG 286, NARA.

15. Interviews with Sternfield.

16. Hughes to Rusk, 16 January 1964, "Bolivia, Memos, Volume I, 12/63–7/64," box 7, NSF-CO, LBJL..

17. "Finalmente se Constituyó la Convención del MNR," *El Diario*, 23 January 1964.

18. A commonly heard refrain in La Paz in early 1964, quoted in Brill, "Military Civic Action," 104–5.

19. René Barrientos, *Mensaje a la Nación*. Many thanks to Luis Antezana Ergueta for providing me a copy of this pamphlet.

20. Henderson to Rusk, 22 January 1964, "Bolivia, Cables, Volume I, 12/63–7/64," box 7, NSF-CO, LBJL.

21. "Los militares afirman que acatarán lo que se decida en la convención del MNR," *El Diario*, 28 January 1964.

22. US Consulate (Cochabamba) to State, 15 February 1964, POL 23-8 Demonstrations, Riots BOL, box 1923, SDANF.

23. San Román to Ibañez, 30 January and 1 February, PR 1900, ABNB. My thanks to Eleanor Joyner (codename HONEYBEE) of the American Cryptogram Association for decrypting these telegrams. Quotation from "Jefe de la FAB está aún dispuesto a ser candidato," *El Diario*, 30 January 1964.

24. Lechín, *El pueblo al poder*, 148. See also Henderson to Rusk, 16 January 1964, "Bolivia, Cables, Volume I, 12/63–7/64," box 7, NSF-CO, LBJL; "El MNR expulsó ayer a J. Lechín," *El Diario*, 29 January 1961.

25. Hughes to Rusk, 16 January 1964, "Bolivia, Memos, Volume I, 12/63–7/64," box 7, NSF-CO, LBJL.

26. Henderson to Rusk, 18 February 1964, POL 15-1 Head of State BOL, box 1922, SDANF.

27. Recording of Telephone Conversation, 19 February 1964, WH6401.18, PNO 2, LBJL.

28. Henderson to Rusk, 24 February 1964, "Bolivia, Cables, Volume I, 12/63–7/64," box 7, NSF-CO, LBJL.

29. Interviews with young officers Gary Prado, Edgar Claure, Raúl López, and Simón Sejas. Quotation from Prado. French historian Thierry Noel, who interviewed dozens of military officers, writes, "The staging is important: certain chosen young officers are convoked, in the middle of the night, to a mysterious secret rendezvous during which they are solemnly invited, in the presence of Barrientos and Ovando, to join a secret lodge. A brief ceremony by candlelight, a kiss upon the sword, an oath to die for the cause, and the officer now belongs to an elite group, carefully selected to carry out dangerous missions assigned by direct orders from the institution's two leaders. What honor! What emotion! Something difficult to resist." See Noel, "La génération des jeunes officiers," 35–36, 466–67. See also Prado, *Poder y fuerzas armadas*, 147, 155.

30. Noel, "La génération des jeunes officiers," 35–36. Confirmed in interviews with Claure, Prado, López, and Sejas. See also Prado, *Poder y fuerzas armadas*, 147, 155.

31. Prado, *Poder*, 155.

32. According to Noel, military funding in the mid-1950s was so poor that academy cadets were relegated to parading with batons. Rifles were too hard to come by. See Noel, "La génération des jeunes officiers," 18. Before the revolution, funding for the armed forces hovered around 25 percent. It reached a low point in 1957, at 6.7 percent, but by the early 1960s, it was more than 12 percent. See Wilkie, *Bolivian Revolution and US Aid*, 70–73.

33. Arguedas interviews, published in Cuevas, *Arguedas*, 70, 85. Barrientos's respect for Paz was confirmed in interviews with Rocabado, Iriarte, Antezana, Trigo, Claure, and Sejas. *Jefe* was how MNR *compañeros* referred to Paz. It means, literally, "boss" or "chief."

34. Henderson to Rusk, 25 February 1964, "Bolivia, Cables, Volume I, 12/63–7/64," box 7, NSF-CO, LBJL.

35. "*Ultra*" was Arguedas's term for extreme anti-MNR young officers like himself.

36. Arguedas interviews, published in Cuevas, *Arguedas*, 105. Arguedas's membership in the Communist Party was confirmed by PCB members Otero, Rocabado, and Soria, as well as Cueto, who recalls Arguedas using his position in the air force to transport the Communist weekly, *Unidad*, to every corner of the country.

37. Arguedas interviews, published in Cuevas, *Arguedas*, 106.

38. "Fue herido el General Barrientos con disparo de arma automática," *El Diario*, 26 February 1964. Quotation from Embassy to Rusk, 25 February 1964, folder "IPS-1/Program Cables/Bolivia," box 5, Latin American Branch Country Files, Office of Public Safety, RG286, NARA. See also Rusk to US Embassy, "Report on Attempted Assassination of General Barrientos, February 1964," 6 October 1964, "Bolivia, (1 of 2), 1964," box 5, Latin American Branch Country File, Office of Public Safety, RG 286, NARA.

According to Barrientos's friend Alberto Iriarte, "It was a staged assassination attempt, planned by Arguedas. All of Barrientos's staged attacks helped him tremendously." Barrientos never told Colonel Fox the true origins of the attack, but another close Barrientos associate, General Alberto Guzmán, told Fox's son many times that "Barrientos shot himself." When asked about Arguedas's claims, Fox responded begrudgingly, "It is possible, but more importantly, the attack served its purpose." For his part, Ambassador Henderson responded to this line of inquiry by saying, "That's right! That's exactly right! And in that sense, he was really crazy! It was so Barrientos. There was something weird about his thinking, that he was prepared to shoot himself to get power. More importantly, it worked!" Former CIA station chief Sternfield responded wryly, "I don't know, but it would be perfectly consistent with Barrientos's personality." For her part, Barrientos's widow rejects the accusations. Interviews with Iriarte, Chico Fox, Edward Fox, Henderson, Sternfield, and Rosemarie Galindo.

39. Rusk to US Embassy, "Report on Attempted Assassination of General Barrientos, February 1964," 6 October 1964, "Bolivia" (1 of 2), 1964, box 5, Latin American Branch Country File, Office of Public Safety, RG 286, NARA.

40. Henderson to Rusk, 25 February 1964, POL 23-8 Demonstrations, Riots BOL, box 1923, SDANF.

41. Fahey to Strauss, "Shooting of Gen. Barrientos," 25 February 1964, "Bolivia, Memos, Volume I, 12/63–7/64," box 7, NSF-CO, LBJL.

42. The C-54 was first directed to Lima, where Barrientos was transferred to a C-118. It was not until 6:00 p.m. that evening that the general finally arrived at Gorgas Hospital. See "Unánime repudio de la Fuerza Aérea hubo al conocerse el ataque contra su comandante," *El Diario*, 26 February 1964.

43. Arguedas interviews, published in Cuevas, *Arguedas*, 106.

44. Interviews with Fox, whose sincerity is defended by his son, Chico, who has no doubt, based on close friendships with Barrientos colleagues, that the attack was staged. In Chico's view, his father had difficulty accepting that Barrientos would withhold such information. Interviews with Chico Fox.

45. "René Barrientos dejará el ejército para la política," *El Diario*, 27 February 1964; "René Barrientos estará aún hospitalizado de 5 a 7 días," *El Diario*, 1 March 1964.

46. "Un brevete metálico desvió la trayectoria del proyectil," *El Diario*, 26 February 1964.

47. According to Arguedas, they toted M-1 carbine machine guns, demanding revenge. Arguedas interviews, published in Cuevas, *Arguedas*, 106.

48. Henderson to Rusk, 25 February 1964, POL 23-8 Demonstrations, Riots BOL, box 1923, SDANF.

49. Arguedas interviews, published in Cuevas, *Arguedas*, 106.

50. Henderson to Rusk, 5 March 1964, "Bolivia, Cables, Volume I, 12/63–7/64," box 7, NSF-CO, LBJL. See also "Federico Fortún renunció de candidato a vicepresidencia," *El Diario*, 5 March 1964; "René Barrientos aceptó ser candidato a vicepresidencia," *El Diario*, 8 March 1964.

51. Paz, *Repudio a la contrarrevolución*, 17–19. Many thanks to Luis Antezana Ergueta for providing me with a copy of this document.

52. Gordillo, *Campesinos Revolucionarios*, 143–44. See also "Fue recibido por sus adherentes el nuevo candidato del MNR a la Vicepresidencia," *El Diario*, 25 March 1964.

53. Prado, *Poder y fuerzas armadas*, 141.

54. Recording of Telephone Conversation, 4 April 1964, WH6404.05, PNO 22, LBJL.

55. State to Embassy, "Insurgency in Eastern Bolivia," 17 April 1964, "Bolivia, Cables, Volume I, 12/63–7/64"; Mann to Special Group (CI), 23 April 1964, "Bolivia, Memos, Volume I, 12/63–7/64," box 7, NSF-CO, LBJL.

56. Rusk to Henderson, 21 April 1964, "Bolivia, Cables, Volume I, 12/63–7/64," box 7, NSF-CO, LBJL.

57. Mann to Special Group (CI), 23 April 1964, "Bolivia, Memos, Volume I, 12/63–7/64," box 7, NSF-CO, LBJL.

58. MEMCON, 16 April 1964, "Bolivia, Cables, Volume I, 12/63–7/64," box 7, NSF-CO, LBJL.

59. For Lechín's campaign in the Cochabamba Valley, see Gordillo, *Campesinos Revolucionarios en Bolivia*, 143–44. For the Military-Peasant Pact, see Soto, *Historia del Pacto Militar Campesino*.

60. Henderson to Rusk, 27 April 1964, "Bolivia, Cables, Volume I, 12/63–7/64," box 7, NSF-CO, LBJL; "Refriega en Huanuni arrojó 4 muertos y varios heridos," *El Diario*, 27 April 1964.

61. "Comunicado de la 'Alianza Popular Boliviana,'" 10 January 1964; "Invitación de la Alianza Popular Boliviana," 16 January 1964, WGA 68, ABNB. See also "Alianza Popular incita a la abstención electoral," *El Diario*, 16 February 1964.

62. Interview with Mauro Cuellar. Confirmed in interviews with Communist student leader Loyola Guzmán.

63. "Pronunciamiento de la Confederación Universitaria Boliviana ante la Prorroga Presidencial," 29 January 1964, WGA 68, ABNB.

64. Student Federation, "Pronunciamiento de la Confederación Universitaria Boliviana Ante la Prorroga Presidencial," undated (1964), Arturo Crespo Rodas Papers, Archivo de La Paz (hereafter ALP).

65. PRIN Communiqué, 29 February 1964; PIR Communiqué, 27 February 1964; PCB-Potosí Communiqué, February 1964, WGA 68, ABNB.

66. Henderson to Rusk, 8 May 1964, "Bolivia, Cables, Volume I, 12/63–7/64," box 7, NSF-CO, LBJL.

67. Embassy to State, 27 November 1964, POL 12-6 Membership Leaders BOL, box 1921, SDANF.

68. Partido Comunista de Bolivia, *Documentos*. Confirmed in interviews with Otero and Cueto, who are also the sources of the second quotation.

69. Early the following year, at the festive ceremony in the Siglo XX mining camp, these dissidents formed the Maoist Partido Comunista de Bolivia—Marxista-Leninista (PCB-ML; Communist Party of Bolivia—Marxist-Leninist), appointing Federico Escóbar as First Secretary. See Comité Central del PCMLM, *Historia del Partido Comunista (Marxista-Leninista-Maoista) M-L-M* (La Paz: Liberación, n.d.). Confirmed in interviews with dissidents Víctor Reinaga and Domitila Barrios and nonschismatics Otero, Cueto, Rojas, Soria, Guzmán, Rocabado, and Reyes.

70. Henderson to Rusk, 7 and 8 May 1964, "Bolivia, Cables, Volume I, 12/63–7/64," box 7, NSF-CO, LBJL.

71. "Alianza Popular Boliviana—Prorroga No!" March 1964, WGA 68, ABNB.

72. Lechín's dare was laughed off by the Bolivian president. See "El PRIN Conformó abstención," *El Diario*, 24 May 1964; "Bolivian Chief Spurns Duel Bid," *Washington Post, Times Herald*, 24 May 1964.

73. "Siles anuncia que irá a la huelga de hambre," *El Diario*, 25 May 1964.

74. "Reds in Bolivia Quit Election; Join Lechín in Attacks on Paz," *New York Times*, 24 May 1964.

75. "Si la oposición sale a las calles, allí nos encontraremos," *El Diario*, 22 May 1964.

76. Henderson to Rusk, 6 May 1964, "Bolivia, Cables, Volume I, 12/63–7/64," box 7, NSF-CO, LBJL.

77. Henderson to Rusk, 8 and 14 May 1964; Southern Command to Joint Chiefs, 14 May 1964; in idem.

78. Henderson to Rusk, 8 May 1964, in idem.

79. Henderson to Rusk, 6 and 8 May 1964, in idem.

80. Henderson to Rusk, 8 May 1964, in idem. As Sternfield noted, "Barrientos was always a man of the left, and he was very susceptible to advice." Confirmed in interviews with Barrientos friends Rocabado and Iriarte and with Communist Party leader Cueto, who added, "Barrientos always had leftist friends."

81. Interviews with Rocabado.

82. Henderson to Rusk, 8 May 1964, "Bolivia, Cables, Volume I, 12/63–7/64," box 7, NSF-CO, LBJL.

83. Bedregal, *De búhos*, 360–61, 370.

84. Interviews with Paz confidants Serrate, Bedregal, and Antezana; Barrientos friends Rocabado and Iriarte; Barrientos widow Galindo.

85. Arguedas interviews, published in Cuevas, *Arguedas*, 102.

86. Henderson Oral History, JFKL, 93.

87. Henderson to Rusk, 13 May 1964, "Bolivia, Cables, Volume I, 12/63–7/64," box 7, NSF-CO, LBJL.

88. AIRA and ARMA to RUEAHO/COFS USAF, 14 May 1964, in idem.

89. Ibid.

90. AIRA and ARMA to RUEAHQ COFS USAF, 19 May 1964, "Bolivia, Cables, Volume I, 12/63–7/64," box 7, NSF-CO, LBJL.

91. Ibid.

92. Read to Bundy, 28 May 1964, "Bolivia, Memos, Volume I, 12/63–7/64," box 7, NSF-CO, LBJL.

93. Henderson to Rusk, 20 May 1964, "Bolivia, Cables, Volume I, 12/63–7/64," box 7, NSF-CO, LBJL.

94. Henderson to Rusk, 20 and 29 May 1964, in idem.

95. George Natanson, "Bolivian Miners Call Election-Eve Strike," *Los Angeles Times*, 31 May 1964; Juan de Onís, "Bolivians Stage a Hunger Strike," *New York Times*, 30 May 1964; Juan de Onís, "Bolivians Clash on Election Eve," *New York Times*, 31 May 1964.

96. Henderson to Rusk, 1 June 1964, "Bolivia, Cables, Volume I, 12/63–7/64," box 7, NSF-CO, LBJL.

97. Sayre to Bundy, 1 June 1964, "Bolivia, Memos, Volume I," box 7, NSF-CO, LBJL.

98. Henderson to Rusk, 18 June 1964, INCO Mining, Minerals, and Metals BOL, box 1190, SDANF. Confirmed in interviews with Ordóñez, Osorio, Rojas, and Reinaga. Regis Debray and his partner, Elizabeth Burgos, were on hand, filming the entire thing. Unfortunately, the reels were lost in Paris, never to reappear. E-mail from Elizabeth Burgos to author, 30 August 2010.

99. Henderson to Rusk, 1 June 1964, "Bolivia, Cables, Volume I, 12/63–7/64," box 7, NSF-CO, LBJL.

100. Minutes of Cabinet Meeting, 1 June 1964, PR 1680, ABNB.

101. The Paraguá River flows northward from the Chiquitano village of San Ignacio de Velasco toward the Brazilian border. Alto (Upper) Paraguá refers to the cattle ranching region around San Ramón and San Simón. The Bajo (Lower) Paraguá is a rubber-producing region lying north of the villages of Cafetal and Mateguá.

102. Leondiris's position as a CIA agent was revealed during the Arguedas affair in 1968, something confirmed to this author in interviews with Edward Fox and Sternfield. San Román's characterization of Leondiris as "Sternfield's assistant" can be found in US Embassy (Asunción) to Rusk and US Embassy (La Paz), 7 April 1965, POL 29 Arrests, Detentions, SDANF. With regard to Leondiris's arrival, see Henderson to USAID, 9 January 1964, "Administration, Bolivia, 1962–63," box 5, Latin American Branch Country File, Office of Public Safety, RG 286, NARA.

103. USAID OPS, "Staffing Positions," 29 April 1964, "Public Safety Program/Bolivia—1963," box 5, Latin American Branch Country File, Office of Public Safety, RG 286, NARA.

104. USAID, Public Safety Memorandum for the Record, 11 June 1964, "Bolivia, 1964," box 5, Latin American Branch Country Files, Office of Public Safety, RG 286, NARA.

105. See Valverde, "Guerrillas del Alto y Bajo Paraguá," 1–96; Mayser, *Alto Paraguá*. Confirmed in interviews with Mayser, guerrilla leader Óscar Bello, and FSB student leader Mauro Cuellar.

106. Valverde, "Guerrillas del Alto y Bajo Paraguá," 23.

107. Interviews with Bello and Mayser. See also Valverde, "Guerrillas del Alto y Bajo Paraguá," 48–49.

108. Interviews with Bello.

109. Interviews with Mayser.

110. Henderson to Rusk, 30 June and 2 July 1964, POL 23-7 Subversion, Espionage, Sabotage BOL, box 1923, SDANF. See also "No hay guerrilleros en el oriente," *El Diario*, 1 July 1964.

111. Henderson to Rusk, 3 August 1964, POL 23-9 Rebellions and Coups, SDANF. For their part, the guerrillas claim they possessed only "shotguns, small rifles, hunting weapons." Interviews with Mayser and Bello.

112. Interviews with Bello and Mayser; Valverde, "Guerrillas del Alto y Bajo Paraguá," 21; Mayser, *Alto Paraguá*, 315–16, 327, 333–35, 351–53, 367, 371–72; Henderson to Rusk, 30 May 1964, "Bolivia, Cables, Volume I, 12/63–7/64," box 7, NSF-CO, LBJL.

113. Valverde, "Guerrillas del Alto y Bajo Paraguá," 21.

114. Ibid., 21.

115. Ibid., 58–59; "Cuatro guerrilleros fueron capturados en San Ignacio de Velasco: Versiones contradictorias," *El Diario*, 2 July 1964.

116. Henderson to Rusk, 8 July 1964, POL 23-7 Subversion, Espionage, Sabotage BOL, box 1923, SDANF.

117. Henderson to Rusk, 6 July 1964, in idem.

118. Valverde, "Guerrillas del Alto y Bajo Paraguá," 26–29; "Varios presos a raíz de fuga de guerrilleros falangistas," *El Diario*, 30 July 1964.

119. Leondiris Report, 18 August 1964, POL 23-8 Demonstrations, Riots BOL, box 1923, and Henderson to Rusk, 4 August 1964, POL 23-9 Rebellions and Coups BOL, SDANF; CIA, CIWS, 7 August 1964, CREST. Interviews with Mayser. See also Mayser, *Alto Paraguá*, 333–35, 351–53, 367, 371–72; "Chocan falangistas y fuerzas policiales," *El Diario*, 3 August 1964.

120. Henderson to Rusk, 3 August 1964, POL 23-9 Rebellions and Coups BOL, SDANF.

121. "Sniper's Bullet Couldn't Kill His Courage," *Miami News*, 11 April 1965.

122. Henderson to Rusk, 2 and 3 August 1964, POL 23-9 Rebellions and Coups, SDANF.

123. *Chau*: "Good-bye." Interviews with Bello and Mayser.

124. Sayre to Bundy, 4 August 1964, "Bolivia, Cables, Volume I, 12/63–7/64," box 7, NSF-CO, LBJL.

125. Henderson to Rusk, 4 August 1964, POL 23-7 Subversion, Espionage, Sabotage BOL, box 1923, SDANF.

126. Henderson to Rusk, 7 August 1964, POL 23-9 Rebellions and Coups BOL, SDANF. *Campesino*, in the Bolivian context: Indian peasant.

127. Henderson to Rusk, 13 August 1964, in idem; CIA, CIWS, 21 August 1964, CREST.

128. Henderson to Rusk, 2 and 4 August 1964, POL 23-9 Rebellions and Coups BOL, SDANF; "Ejército remplaza a policía en lucha antiguerrillas," *El Diario*, 13 August 1964.

129. Henderson to Rusk, 5 August 1964, POL 23-9 Rebellions and Coups BOL, SDANF. Interviews with Bello and Mayser.

130. Henderson to Rusk, 10 August 1964, POL 23-9 Rebellions and Coups, SDANF; "La 8z. división anunció la toma de San Simón: Guerrilleros de FSB se retiraron sin oponer resistencia," *El Diario*, 9 August 1964. Interviews with Bello and Mayser.

131. Interviews with Mayser and Bello, and with Falangist student leader Mauro Cuellar, who adds that the FSB "pledged to military officials that we would create problems."

132. Banzer to FSB guerrillas, 23 August 1964, in Valverde, "Guerrillas del Alto y Bajo Paraguá," 37.

133. Valverde, "Guerrillas del Alto y Bajo Paraguá," 47. Interviews with Bello and Mayser.

134. Valverde, "Guerrillas del Alto y Bajo Paraguá," 38–39; interviews with Bello and Mayser. See also Mayser, *Alto Paraguá*, 367, 371–72; "Jefe de guerrillas dice que no desean luchar con FFAA," *El Diario*, 11 September 1964.

135. Henderson to Rusk, 19 May 1964, POL 14 Elections BOL, box 1921, SDANF.

136. "Doctors of Development," *Time*, 26 June 1964.

137. "Progress toward a Third Term," *Time*, 29 May 1964.

138. Paz, "Informe presentado al Congreso Nacional el 6 de agosto de 1964," 191, 197, 199, 206–7.

6. Revolutionary Bolivia Puts On a Uniform

1. Henderson to Rusk, 14 April 1964, "Bolivia, Cables, Volume I, 12/63–7/64," box 7, NSF-CO, LBJL.

2. Ibid.

3. MEMCON, 20 July 1964, "Bolivia, Memos, Volume II, 7/64–11/64," box 7, NSF-CO, LBJL.

The Venezuelans claimed they were "the target of a series of actions sponsored and directed by the Government of Cuba, openly intended to subvert Venezuelan institutions and to overthrow the Government of Venezuela through terrorism, sabotage, assault, and guerrilla warfare." The complaint specifically dealt with a cache of Cuban arms that washed up on a Venezuelan beach in November 1963. See OAS, *Ninth Meeting of Consultation of Ministers of Foreign Affairs* (Washington, DC: Pan American Union, 1964).

4. These words are NSC member Sayre's, who was at the lunch. Sayre to Bundy, 23 July 1964, document 22, *FRUS, 1964–1968: Volume XXXI—South and Central America; Mexico*.

5. Rusk to Henderson, 24 July 1964, 2:50 p.m., Telephone Calls 7/1/64–8/5/64, Rusk Files, lot 72D192, SDLF.

6. Henderson to Rusk, 25 July 1964, 120, "Bolivia, Cables, Volume II, 7/64–11/64," box 7, NSF-CO, LBJL. Regarding the Lauca River dispute, see chapter 2.

7. Ibid.

8. Bundy to Johnson, 25 July 1964, "Bolivia, Cables, Volume II, 7/64–11/64," box 7, NSF-CO, LBJL.

9. Henderson to Rusk, 3 August 1964, in idem.

10. Henderson to Rusk, 4 August 1964, in idem.

11. Rusk to Henderson, 7 August 1964, in idem.

12. Rusk to Henderson, 7 August 1964, in idem.

13. Henderson to Rusk, 11 August 1964, "Bolivia, Cables, Volume I, 12/63–7/64," box 7, NSF-CO, LBJL.

14. Henderson to Rusk, 21 August 1964, in idem.

15. Minutes of Cabinet Meeting, 13 August 1964, PR 1800, ABNB.

16. Bedregal, *De búhos*, 366.

17. Interviews with Serrate.

18. Bedregal, *De búhos*, 366.

19. Acknowledging that the Bolivians were "given no choice" and that "it was a case of conforming or of facing a severe cut in United States aid," the *New York Times* nonetheless believed the break was a good thing. "There is still plenty of tin to be got out of the mines at a price that could be competitive," the paper wrote. With the Cuba issue out of the way, "President Paz Estenssoro can now concentrate on economics." See "Bolivia Gets in Line," *New York Times*, 24 August 1964.

20. "Informe orgánico aprobado por el III Congreso Regional de La Paz del Partido Comunista de Bolivia, 30 November 1964," *Espartaco* 12 (March 1965), 110–12, 117–18. Many thanks to Luis Antezana Ergueta for providing a copy of this publication.

21. Quezada G., "En torno a un artículo," 19. The dissidents further upbraided PCB leadership for "dragging our party along the tail of the MNR government . . . impeding the mass struggle in order to favor Paz's pro-Yankee government." For more on the origins of the Maoist split, see chapter 5. Many thanks to Luis Antezana for providing me a copy of this publication.

22. "El último títere," 28 August 1964; "Bolivia," 16 October 1964; "Bolivia," 30 October 1964; "Bolivia," 6 November 1964; *Bohemia*.

23. "Soliloquio," 31 October 1964, *Radio Progreso*. Transcript in Miami Radio Monitoring Service, Cuban Heritage Collection, University of Miami.

24. Interviews with Serrate.

25. Interviews with Cueto.

26. Lechín, *El pueblo al poder*, 149–50; "Lechín fue agredido ayer en vía pública," *El Diario*, 7 August 1964; Henderson to Rusk, 10 August 1964, INCO Mining, Minerals, and Metals BOL, box 1190, SDANF.

27. Henderson to Rusk, 10 August 1964, INCO Mining, Minerals, and Metals BOL, box 1190, SDANF; "Colegiales promovieron ayer varios incidentes callejeros," *El Diario*, 14 August 1964.

28. Minutes of Cabinet Meeting, 13 August 1964, PR 1800, ABNB, 2–3.

29. Ibid., 3–5.

30. Ibid., 5–7. Paz's personal secretary, former government minister Fellman Velarde, also meekly expressed opposition to a state of siege. He had been removed from his position for this very reason, replaced with hardliner Ciro Humbolt.

31. "Los maestros decretaron huelga general," *El Diario*, 2 September 1964.

32. Referencing the coming presidential elections in Chile, some of the demonstrators carried signs reading "Onward [Salvador] Allende! Tomorrow is your triumph!" Henderson to Rusk, 4 September 1964, POL 23-9 Rebellions and Coups BOL, SDANF; "Incidentes en esta ciudad," *El Diario*, 4 August 1964.

33. Throughout the month of September, there are dozens of telegrams between San Román and his underlings throughout the country. They document the use of MNR militias to attack and intimidate the students and teachers. See telegrams from Menacho, Román, Montenegro, and Blanco, 1–4 September 1964, PR 1894, ABNB. My thanks to Eleanor Joyner (codename HONEYBEE) of the American Cryptogram Association for decrypting the coded telegrams. For more on the CIA connection to San Román, see chapter 5, footnotes 102–104, in this volume, and footnotes 58–59, in this chapter.

34. Román to San Román, 4 September 1964, PR 1894, ABNB.

35. "Barrientos censura al Control," *El Diario*, 11 August 1964; Henderson to Rusk, 10 August 1964, INCO Mining, Minerals, and Metals BOL, box 1190, SDANF.

36. Román to San Román, 7–8 September 1964; Ibañez to San Román, 4 and 7 September 1964; PR 1894, ABNB.

37. Coded message from Menacho to Sán Román, PR 1894, ABNB. Cable decrypted by Eleanor Joyner (codename HONEYBEE) of the American Cryptogram Association.

38. "Veintidós diputados dicen que Barrientos es garantía," *El Diario*, 8 September 1964.

39. "No pudo definir sus relaciones con el presidente," *El Diario*, 7 September 1964.

40. "Mineros de Siglo XX apoyan las demandas del magisterio," *El Diario*, 7 September 1964; "Huelga minera en apoyo a maestros," *El Diario*, 14 September 1964; Presidencia de la República to Cámara de Diputados, 14 September 1964, PR 1661, ABNB.

41. Since the train was moving slowly, no one was injured. The train left the tracks but did not turn over. "Dinamitan ferrovía Estación-El Alto," *El Diario*, 18 September 1964.

42. Prefect-Oruro to Paz, 24 September 1964, PR 1061, ABNB.

43. Henderson to Rusk, 16 September 1964, POL 23-8 Demonstrations, Riots BOL, box 1923, SDANF.

44. Menacho to San Román, 10 September 1964; Montenegro to San Román, 17 September 1964; Blanco to San Román, 18 September 1964, PR 1894, ABNB.

45. "Los maestros realizarán en Cochabamba 'Marcha del Hambre,'" *El Diario*, 19 September 1964.

46. Coded message from Menacho to San Román, 19 September 1964, PR 1894, ABNB. Cable decrypted by Eleanor Joyner (codename HONEYBEE) of the American Cryptogram Association.

47. Henderson to Rusk, 21 September 1964, POL 23-9 Rebellions and Coups, SDANF; Henderson to Rusk, 20 September 1964, "Bolivia, Cables, Volume II, 7/64–11/64," box 7, NSF-CO, LBJL. Interviews with Control Político detainees Cueto, Reyes, Crespo, Sanjinés, and Cuellar.

48. CIA, Information Cable, 20 September 1964, "Bolivia, Volume 2, 7/64–11/64," box 7, NSF-CO, LBJL.

49. Henderson to Rusk, 24 September 1964, POL 23-8 Demonstrations, Riots BOL, box 1923, SDANF.

50. See numerous telegrams in PR 1894, ABNB. My thanks to Eleanor Joyner (codename HONEYBEE) of the American Cryptogram Association, for her work decrypting the coded messages.

51. Ayaviri to San Román, 22 September 1964, PR 1894, ABNB. Throughout the country, Control Político agents were tasked with enforcing the state of siege. See telegrams from General Prado, Ibañez, Menacho, and Montenegro to San Román, 20 September 1964, same folder.

52. San Román gave ten thousand pesos to loyalist labor unions in September, and in early October, he gifted another seven thousand pesos to Indian leaders in Cochabamba. San Román to Hugo Paz Torrez, 27 August 1964; San Román to Reque Terán, 8 September 1964; San Román to Jorge Goméz, 1 October 1964; PR 1676, ABNB.

53. Henderson to Rusk, 21 September 1964, POL 23-9 Rebellions and Coups, SDANF.

54. Interviews with Ramiro Paz.

55. Interviews with Serrate.

56. Interviews with Bedregal.

57. "Un libro para San Román," *El Diario*, 5 September 1964.

58. Interviews with Sternfield.

59. USAID, Briefing Memorandum for the Administrator, 9 April 1964, "Bolivia, 1 of 2, 1964," box 5, Latin American Branch Country Files, Office of Public Safety, RG 286, NARA.

60. George Natanson, "Wounding of Bolivian General May Result in Political Upheaval," *Los Angeles Times*, 3 March 1964.

61. Natanson, "President of Bolivia Begins Second Term," *Los Angeles Times*, 7 August 1964.

62. "The Bolivian Election," *New York Times*, 2 June 1964.

63. James Nelson Goodsell, "Paz Wins Bolivian Elections Easily," *Christian Science Monitor*, 2 June 1964.

64. Goodsell, "Aid, Self-Help Lift Bolivia," *Christian Science Monitor*, 3 June 1964.

65. "Preventing Trouble Before It Starts," *Time*, 2 October 1964.

66. Georgie Anne Geyer, "Police Rule in Bolivia May Embarrass US," *Washington Post, Times Herald*, 27 August 1964.

67. Bedregal, *Víctor Paz Estenssoro*, 544–45.

68. "Réplica del Gral. Monje Roca al Presidente de la República," undated, Arturo Crespo Rodas Papers, ALP.

69. This was quoted in a report by CIA contact Arze Murillo, Paz's former government minister who was serving as ambassador to Uruguay, for the express purpose of keeping tabs on anti-Paz exiles. See Bolivian Embassy (Montevideo) to Foreign Ministry and Paz, 16 October 1964, PR 1065, ABNB. For more on the CIA's role tracking Bolivian exiles on behalf of the Paz government, see Agee, *Inside the Company*, 400.

70. CIA, CIWS, 9 October 1964, CREST.

71. Henderson to Rusk, 22 October 1964, POL 23-8 Demonstrations, Riots BOL, box 1923, SDANF.

72. Henderson to Rusk, 21 October 1964, "Bolivia, Cables, Volume II, 7/64–11/64," box 7, NSF-CO, LBJL. Valenzuela and Ferrufino were immortalized with photographs in a pro-coup pamphlet that circulated the following month. See "El Pueblo ha Triunfado," (n.p., n.d.). Many thanks to Luis Antezana Ergueta for sharing this document with me.

73. CIA, Information Cables (2), 23 October 1964, "Bolivia, Vol. 2, 7/64–11/64," box 7, NSF-CO, LBJL.

74. Henderson to Rusk, 26 October 1964, "Bolivia, Cables, Volume II, 7/64–11/64," box 7, NSF-CO, LBJL.

75. CIA, Information Cables (2), 27 October, "Bolivia, Vol. 2, 7/64–11/64," box 7, NSF-CO, LBJL; Henderson to Rusk, 28 October 1964, "Bolivia, Cables, Volume II, 7/64–11/64," box 7, NSF-CO, LBJL. *Campesino*, in the Bolivian context: "Indian peasant."

76. Ibid.

77. Henderson to Rusk, 27 and 28 October 1964, "Bolivia, Cables, Volume II, 7/64–11/64," box 7, NSF-CO, LBJL.

78. CIA, Information Cables (2), 27 October 1964, "Bolivia, Vol. 2, 7/64–11/64," box 7, NSF-CO, LBJL. Confirmed in interviews with FSB leaders Cuellar, Mayser, and Bello.

79. CIA, Information Cables (2), 27 October 1964, "Bolivia, Vol. 2, 7/64–11/64," box 7, NSF-CO, LBJL. Sanjinés, an inactive army colonel, was also the interim director of *El Diario*. He had been hiding in the home of a pro-Barrientos officer since 20 September, as Control Político sought his arrest. Interviews with Sanjinés.

80. Henderson to Rusk, 27 October 1964, "Bolivia, Cables, Volume II, 7/64–11/64," box 7, NSF-CO, LBJL.

81. Henderson to Rusk, 28 October 1964, in idem.

82. CIA, Information Cables (2), 29 October 1964, "Bolivia, Vol. 2, 7/64–11/64," box 7, NSF-CO, LBJL.

83. Henderson to Rusk, 29 October 1964, "Bolivia, Cables, Volume II, 7/64–11/64," box 7, NSF-CO, LBJL.

84. Interviews with Edward Fox.

85. CIA, Information Cable, 29 October 1964, "Bolivia, Vol. 2, 7/64–11/64," box 7, NSF-CO, JFKL.

86. Chase to Bundy, 28 October 1964, in idem.

87. Henderson to Rusk, 29 October 1964, "Bolivia, Cables, Volume II, 7/64–11/64," box 7, NSF-CO, LBJL. Confirmed in interviews with Leónidas Rojas, who had traveled from Siglo XX to Oruro on 26 October to participate in the mock funerals. When the army retook Oruro late on

28 October, Rojas fell prisoner and was held in a Control Político cell until the government fell seven days later.

88. Interviews with Siglo XX participants, including PCB miners Daniel Ordóñez and Rosendo Osorio; and POR miners Filemón Escóbar, Benigno Bastos, and Cirilo Jiménez. Interview also with Víctor Carrasco, a participating miner from Santa Fe. Quotation from Ordóñez.

89. Interviews with Osorio. Confirmed in interviews with Ordóñez and Trotskyists Bastos and Jiménez, who both added that the Catavi MNR Left contingent carried a few rifles.

90. Interviews with Siglo XX POR members Escóbar and Bastos, who participated in the late-night assault. Quotations from Bastos. Confirmed in interviews with Communist miners Ordóñez and Osorio and POR miner Jiménez, who remained at Huanuni until the following morning. See also Filemón Escóbar, *Testimonio de un militante obrero*, 72.

91. Henderson to Rusk, 29 October 1964, "Bolivia, Cables, Volume II, 7/64–11/64," box 7, NSF-CO, LBJL.

92. Henderson to Rusk, 29 October 1964, "Bolivia, Cables, Volume II, 7/64–11/64," box 7, NSF-CO, LBJL. Confirmed in interviews with Ordóñez, Osorio, Jiménez, and Carrasco.

93. Interviews with Ordóñez, confirmed in interviews with Jiménez and Osorio. Domitila Barrios de Chungara relates a dramatic tale of Siglo XX's Comité de Amas de Casa (Housewives Committee) at Sora Sora, but none of my sources recall their having participated. See Barrios interviews, published in Viezzer, *"Si me permiten hablar . . . ,"* 97–101; and interviews with Barrios.

94. Henderson to Rusk, 29 October 1964, "Bolivia, Cables, Volume II, 7/64–11/64," box 7, NSF-CO, LBJL. Confirmed in interviews with Ordóñez, Osorio, Jiménez, and Carrasco.

95. Henderson to Rusk, 30 October 1964, "Bolivia, Cables, Volume II, 7/64–11/64," box 7, NSF-CO, LBJL.

96. Henderson to Rusk, 29 October 1964, "Bolivia, Cables, Volume II, 7/64–11/64," box 7, NSF-CO, LBJL.

97. CIA, Information Cables, 29 October 1964, "Bolivia, Vol. 2, 7/64–11/64," box 7, NSF-CO, JFKL.

98. Henderson to Rusk, 29 and 30 October 1964, "Bolivia, Cables, Volume II, 7/64–11/64," box 7, NSF-CO, LBJL.

99. Mann via Ball to Henderson, 29 October 1964, 1-Z-322, Mann Papers, Texas Collection at Baylor University.

100. Ibid.

101. Memorandum for the Record, 29 October 1964, "Special Group (CI) Meetings, Oct, Nov, Dec, '64," box 6, Office of the Director, Office of Public Safety, RG 286, NARA.

102. Henderson to Rusk (2), 29 October 1964, "Bolivia, Cables, Volume II, 7/64–11/64," box 7, NSF-CO, LBJL.

103. Ibid.

104. Mann via Ball to Embassy, 29 October 1964, "Bolivia, Cables, Volume II, 7/64–11/64," box 7, NSF-CO, LBJL.

105. Henderson to Rusk, 29 October 1964, in idem; Hughes to State, 29 October 1964, "Bolivia, Cables, Volume II, 7/64–11/64," box 7, NSF-CO, LBJL.

106. CIA, CIWS, 30 October 1964, CREST. Confirmed in interviews with Falangist student leader Cuellar and Communist student leader Guzmán.

107. CIA, Information Cable, 29 October 1964, "Bolivia, Vol. 2, 7/64–11/64," box 7, NSF-CO, LBJL. Confirmed by Cuellar and Guzmán.

108. Henderson to Rusk, 29 October 1964, "Bolivia, Cables, Volume II, 7/64–11/64," box 7, NSF-CO, LBJL.

109. Jaime Otero Calderón, "Dilucidación Histórica," 23 November 1968, Arturo Crespo Rodas Papers, ALP, 1a. According to Paz confidants, Otero's account is spot on. Interviews with Ramiro Paz, Carlos Serrate, and Guillermo Bedregal. See also Henderson to Rusk, 27 and 28 October 1964, "Bolivia, Cables, Volume II, 7/64–11/64," box 7, NSF-CO, LBJL. Events regarding the student march were confirmed by FSB participant Cuellar.

110. Henderson to Rusk, 29 October 1964, "Bolivia, Cables, Volume II, 7/64–11/64," box 7, NSF-CO, LBJL. Confirmed by Cuellar. According to one of Kennedy's colleagues, the monsignor was also an "honorary colonel" and chaplain in the Bolivian army, and therefore "enjoyed relatively open access in the ecclesiastical and military worlds." Monsignor Ratermann e-mail to author, 11 August 2010.

111. Otero, "Dilucidación Histórica," 1b. Confirmed by Cuellar.

112. Henderson to Rusk, 29 October 1964, "Bolivia, Cables, Volume II, 7/64–11/64," box 7, NSF-CO, LBJL. Confirmed by Cuellar.

113. Henderson to Rusk, 29 October 1964, POL 23-9 Rebellions and Coups BOL, SDANF.

114. Rusk to Embassy, 30 October 1964, POL 23-8 Demonstrations, Riots BOL, box 1923, SDANF. The original requests are in Henderson to Rusk, 29 October 1964, POL 23-9 Rebellions, Coups BOL, SDANF.

115. Henderson to Rusk (2), 30 October 1964, POL 23-8 Demonstrations, Riots BOL, box 1923, SDANF.

116. Otero, "Dilucidación Histórica," 1b. Confirmed in interviews with Ramiro Paz, Serrate, and Bedregal.

117. Hughes to State, 29 October 1964, "Bolivia, Cables, Volume II, 7/64–11/64," box 7, NSF-CO, LBJL.

118. Bundy to Valenti, 30 October 1964, "Bolivia, Cables, Volume II, 7/64–11/64," box 7, NSF-CO, LBJL.

119. Henderson to Rusk, 31 October and 3 November 1964, in idem.

120. Recording of Telephone Conversation, 30 October 1964, WH6410.16, PNO 4, LBJL.

121. CIA, Information Report, 30 October 1964, "Bolivia, Vol. 2, 7/64–11/64," box 7, NSF-CO, LBJL.

122. Henderson to Rusk (2), 3 November 1964, "Bolivia, Cables, Volume II, 7/64–11/64," box 7, NSF-CO, LBJL.

123. Dentzer via Henderson to Rusk, 2 November 1964, POL 23-9 Rebellions and Coups BOL, SDANF.

124. Ibid.

125. Henderson to Rusk, 3 November 1964, "Bolivia, Cables, Volume II, 7/64–11/64," box 7, NSF-CO, LBJL.

126. Arguedas interviews, published in Cuevas, *Arguedas*, 157. Confirmed in interviews with Edward Fox.

127. Interviews with Sternfield. Confirmed by young military officers, all of whom presumed the United States was backing Barrientos. Interviews with Sejas, Claure, López, Sánchez, and Prado.

128. Arguedas interviews, published in Cuevas, *Arguedas*, 126–27. This general narrative has been confirmed by López, who was squadron chief in the Ingavi Regiment at General Staff Headquarters. López recalled that "if there was a leader of 4 November, it was Quiroga Terán. He was the most decided." Prado, who was an instructor at the nearby military academy, also finds the narrative convincing: "Our superiors had a stronger commitment to the MNR. We younger officers did not." Interviews with López and Prado.

129. Otero, "Dilucidación Histórica," 1b. Confirmed in interviews with Serrate, Bedregal, and Ramiro Paz.

130. Henderson to Rusk, 3 November 1964, "Bolivia, Cables, Volume II, 7/64–11/64," box 7, NSF-CO, LBJL. Confirmed by López, who recalled that "Ovando and Gúzman had no idea what to do. More or less, their plan was that if this fails, we had nothing to do with it." Interviews with López.

131. Otero, "Dilucidación Histórica," 1b–2a. Confirmed in interview with Sejas, who recalled proudly that "we were the first group to rise up! We took to the streets, and used our control plans to hold each section."

132. Otero, "Dilucidación Histórica," 1b–2a; CIA, Information Cable, 3 November 1964, "Bolivia, Vol. 2, 7/64–11/64," box 7, NSF-CO, LBJL. Confirmed in interviews with Serrate, Bedregal, and Ramiro Paz.

133. Henderson to Rusk (2), 3 November 1964, "Bolivia, Cables, Volume II, 7/64–11/64," box 7, NSF-CO, LBJL.

134. Ibid.; CIA, Information Cable, 3 November 1964, "Bolivia, Vol. 2, 7/64–11/64," box 7, NSF-CO, LBJL. Confirmed in interview with Sejas.

135. Henderson to Rusk (2), 3 November 1964, "Bolivia, Cables, Volume II, 7/64–11/64"; CIA, Information Report, 3 November 1964, "Bolivia, Vol. 2, 7/64–11/64," box 7, NSF-CO, LBJL. Confirmed in interviews with Sejas.

136. Otero, "Dilucidación Histórica," 3a. Confirmed in interviews with Ramiro Paz, Serrate, and Bedregal.

137. Hughes to State, 3 November 1964, "Bolivia, Cables, Volume II, 7/64–11/64," box 7, NSF-CO, LBJL.

138. Henderson to Rusk, 3 November 1964, "Bolivia, Cables, Volume II, 7/64–11/64," box 7, NSF-CO, LBJL.

139. CIA, Information Cable, 3 November 1964, "Bolivia, Vol. 2, 7/64–11/64," box 7, NSF-CO, LBJL.

140. Henderson to Rusk, 3 November 1964, "Bolivia, Cables, Volume II, 7/64–11/64," box 7, NSF-CO, LBJL; CIA, Information Cable, 3 November 1964, "Bolivia, Vol. 2, 7/64–11/64," box 7, NSF-CO, LBJL.

141. CIA, Information Cables (2), 3 November 1964, "Bolivia, Vol. 2, 7/64–11/64," box 7, NSF-CO, LBJL.

142. CIA to White House Situation Room and Joint Chiefs, 3 November 1964, in idem.

143. Henderson to Rusk (2), 3 November 1964, "Bolivia, Cables, Volume II, 7/64–11/64," box 7, NSF-CO, LBJL. Confirmed by López, who recalled that the top floors of the medical school were under construction, thus offering excellent parapets from which to fire.

144. Ibid.

145. Interviews with Ramiro Paz.

146. CIA, Information Cable, 3 November 1964, "Bolivia, Vol. 2, 7/64–11/64," box 7, NSF-CO, LBJL.

147. Henderson to Rusk (2), 3 November 1964, "Bolivia, Cables, Volume II, 7/64–11/64," box 7, NSF-CO, LBJL.

148. Ibid. The original tallies can be found in CIA, Information Cable, 3 November 1964, "Bolivia, Vol. 2, 7/64–11/64," box 7, NSF-CO, LBJL.

149. Henderson to Rusk, 3–4 November 1964, "Bolivia, Cables, Volume II, 7/64–11/64," box 7, NSF-CO, LBJL.

150. Ibid.

151. Otero, "Dilucidación Histórica," 4b–5a. Confirmed in interviews with Serrate, Bedregal, and Ramiro Paz, who recalls, "We couldn't sleep."

152. CIA, Information Cable, 3 November 1964, "Bolivia, Vol. 2, 7/64–11/64," box 7, NSF-CO, LBJL.

153. Otero, "Dilucidación Histórica," 4b–5a. Confirmed in interviews with Serrate and Bedregal.

154. Otero, "Dilucidación Histórica," 4b–5a. Confirmed in interviews with Serrate, Bedregal, and Ramiro Paz.

155. Henderson to Rusk (2), 4 November 1964, "Bolivia, Cables, Volume II, 7/64–11/64," box 7, NSF-CO, LBJL. Confirmed in interviews with Serrate, Bedregal, and Ramiro Paz.

156. Henderson to Rusk, 4 November 1964, POL 23-9 Rebellions and Coups BOL, SDANF. Confirmed in interviews with Serrate and Bedregal.

157. "Paz dejó el palacio diciendo que iba a inspeccionar sus defensas," El Diario, 5 November 1964.

158. There was a plot under way to assassinate Paz Estenssoro as his car climbed the Lourdes curve from Calacoto to the presidential palace downtown. Fortunately for Paz, he slept in the palace that night. See Noel, whose study is based on interviews with dozens of military officers. Noel, "La génération des jeunes officiers," 73. Confirmed in anonymous interviews.

159. Henderson to Rusk, 4 November 1964, POL 23-9 Rebellions and Coups BOL, SDANF. Ambassador Henderson recalled things differently in a 1988 interview. Rather than Paz refusing the shipments as he was set to flee, Henderson recounts that the State Department vetoed the shipment the night before. Henderson's selective memory could have resulted from Washington's fervent attempts after 4 November to hide its previous role in arming Paz's repressive security services. See Henderson Oral History, JFKL, 91, 96.

160. Interview with Henderson.

Conclusion

1. Interviews with Henderson.

2. Interviews with Partido Comunista de Bolivia (PCB; Communist Party of Bolivia) leader José Luís Cueto, a Control Político detainee who was machine-gunned in the back on the morning of 4 November. In his words, "So as to not give San Román the pleasure, I remained alive." For a dramatic account of other Control Político shootouts, see Crespo, El rostro minero de Bolivia, 351–53. Confirmed in interviews with detainees Reyes, Sanjinés, and Cuellar.

3. Gregorio Iriarte, the new head priest of the Siglo XX Oblate mission, was considerably less anticommunist than his predecessors. He accompanied several Communist miners to La Paz on Friday, 30 October, to plead for the liberation of Escóbar and Pimentel. The Paz government told him it was a matter to be discussed with Ambassador Henderson. After the All Saints holiday, Gregorio's miner friends armed themselves and stormed the penitentiary on the morning of 4 November. See Gregorio, in López Vigil, Una mina de coraje, 111–15.

4. Interviews with Sternfield.

5. This is based on Prado, Poder y fuerzas armadas, 151; Lechín, El pueblo al poder, 154–57; "Sangrienta refriega por una confusión," El Diario, 5 November 1964; CIA, Intelligence Cable, 4 November 1964, "Bolivia, Vol. 2, 7/64–11/64," box 7, NSF-CO, LBJL; and interviews with Prado. When he fled the scene, Juan Lechín lost one of his shoes. In a gesture of unwitting symbolism, General Ovando lent him pair of military boots, which Lechín wore for the remainder of the day.

6. Interviews with Claure, who was with Ovando at the time. For more on the events of 5 November, see Antezana, La contrarrevolución del 4 de noviembre, 2538–50.

7. With one exception. Arguedas refused to go away. He submitted himself to a CIA detector test, including truth serum, and became one of Barrientos's ministers who worked for the agency. Sternfield recalled, "We went through the works with him, and he was reliable until the Che Guevara thing." Interviews with Sternfield. See also Ryan, *Fall of Che Guevara*, 146–53.

8. Interviews with Sternfield; "US Agrees to Resume Bolivia Ties Suspended on Overthrow of Paz," *Washington Post, Times Herald*.

9. Dunkerley makes extensive use of memoirs and press reports, both of which highlight Fox's role. See Dunkerley, *Rebellion in the Veins*, 108.

10. Lehman employs a handful of US documents to make this claim, but his study was by no means exhaustive. See Lehman, *Bolivia and the United States*, 141.

11. William Blum cites Dunkerley and extensive press rumors to suggest that Fox was complicit in Barrientos's coup. Tim Weiner goes a step further, glancing at one online State Department document before recklessly concluding that "Barrientos . . . seized power . . . backed by more than $1 million from the CIA." In fact, the document cited by Weiner describes a covert operation (see chapters 3 through 6 in this volume) to support Paz's government and oppose any attempt to depose him. Sadly, Weiner's claim was uncritically cited in Sándor John's otherwise enlightening study of Bolivian Trotskyism. Finally, historian Mark Lawrence apparently feels that the allegation that Washington "supported [a] military coup . . . in Bolivia (1964)" is so obvious that he need not cite anything at all. See Blum, *Killing Hope*, 221–22, 225; Weiner, *Legacy of Ashes*, 281; John, *Bolivia's Radical Tradition*, 183; Lawrence, "Exception to the Rule?" in Lerner, *Looking Back at LBJ*, 20.

12. Bedregal, *De búhos*, 371, 377.

13. Zavaleta, *La caída del MNR*, 112, 150, 178.

14. Malloy, *Bolivia*, 310–14; Klein, *Bolivia*, 244–45.

15. Brill, *Military Intervention in Bolivia*.

16. Ergueta, *La contrarrevolución*.

17. Robert O. Kirkland, "Colonel Edward Fox and the 1964 Bolivian Coup," *International Journal of Intelligence and Counterintelligence* 18 (2005), 473–82.

18. See Agee, *Inside the Company*, 383–85, 400, 601. Another insider CIA history is silent on Barrientos prior to the coup. See Marchetti and Marks, *CIA and the Cult of Intelligence*, 138–45.

19. Paz, interview with Sergio Almaraz Paz, in Ascarrunz, *La palabra de Paz*, 128–29. Ascarrunz served as Paz's campaign manager in 1985 and has since published these interview transcripts.

20. Josh Goskho, "Latins Blame the US for Military Coups," *Washington Post, Times Herald*, 5 May 1968. Quoted in Blum, *Killing Hope*, 225.

21. Interviews with Edward Fox.

22. Interviews with Henderson.

23. Interviews with Sternfield.

24. Whitehead, *United States and Bolivia*, 25.

25. Almaraz Paz, *Réquiem para una república*, 21, 30.

26. Uruguay was the last. Mexico never broke relations with Cuba.

27. Ferguson, *Anti-Politics Machine*.

28. Uvin, *Aiding Violence*.

29. For the first, see Levinson, *Alliance That Lost Its Way*; for the second, Latham, *Modernization as Ideology*; and for the third, Schlesinger, *A Thousand Days*.

30. Rabe, *Most Dangerous Area*; Taffet, *Foreign Aid as Foreign Policy*.

31. Burke e-mail to author.

32. Pace Piero Gleijeses, "Afterward," in Nick Cullather, *Secret History: The CIA's Classified Account of Its Operations in Guatemala, 1952–1954* (Stanford, CA: Stanford University Press, 1999), xxix.

33. Ferguson, *Anti-Politics Machine*; Uvin, *Aiding Violence*; Scott, *Seeing Like a State*.

34. Almaraz Paz, *Réquiem para una república*, 27, 32.

35. In the mausoleum lie former presidents Germán Busch (1937–1939), Gualberto Villarroel (1943–1946), and Juan José Torres (1970–1971).

36. Paz Estenssoro interviews, published in Ascarrunz, *La palabra de Paz*, 47.

Bibliography

Archives

Alexander Library, Rutgers University, New Brunswick, New Jersey
    Robert J. Alexander Papers
Archivo y Biblioteca Nacional de Bolivia, Sucre, Bolivia
    Papers of the Presidencia de la República, 1961–1964
    Wálter Guevara Arze Papers
Archivo de la Corporación Minera de Bolivia, El Alto, Bolivia
Archivo de La Paz, Universidad Mayor de San Andrés, La Paz, Bolivia
    Arturo Crespo Rodas Papers
    Jorge Mercado Papers
Archivo del Ministerio de Relaciones Exteriores y Culto, La Paz, Bolivia
The Association for Diplomatic Studies and Training, Oral History Interviews
    Anthony G. Freeman
    Douglas Henderson
    Robert M. Sayre
    Derek S. Singer
    John Stutesman
    Herbert Thompson
Bibliothèque de documentation internationale contemporaine (BDIC), Nanterre, France
    Inventaire Fonds Movimiento Nacionalista Revolucionario, MNR–Bolivie
    Inventaire du La Central Obrera Bolivia (COB) et syndicats affiliés
British Library of Political and Economic Science
    Collection of the International Tin Council

Hoover Institution, Stanford, California
    Edward Geary Lansdale Papers
    Juan Lechín Oquendo Papers
Library of Congress
    William O. Douglas Papers, Manuscript Division
The Inter-American Development Bank
    Triangular Plan Papers
John F. Kennedy Presidential Library
    George W. Ball Papers
    Donald Barnes Oral History
    Richard Goodwin Papers
    Douglas Henderson Oral History
    Douglas Henderson Papers
    Edward G. Lansdale Oral History
    Thomas Mann Oral History
    Edwin M. Martin Papers
    Teodoro Moscoso Papers
    National Security Files
    Peace Corps Papers
    Presidential Office Files
    Arthur Schlesinger Jr. Papers
    Sargent Shriver Papers
    Ben S. Stephansky Oral History
    Herbert Thompson Oral History
Lyndon Baines Johnson Presidential Library, Austin, Texas
    Aide Files
    George W. Ball Papers
    Gerold F. Baumann Papers
    McGeorge Bundy Papers
    Lyndon B. Johnson Vice Presidential Papers
    John McCone Memoranda
    National Security Files
    Drew Pearson Papers
    Bromley Smith Papers
    Recordings of Telephone Conversations
    White House Central Files
Národní archiv [National Archive], Prague, Czech Republic
    Komunistická strana Československa Ústřední výbor—I
    [Central Committee of the Communist Party of Czechoslovakia—I]
        Tajemníka ÚV KSČ Antonína Novotného—II
        [Secretary of Central Committee Antonín Novotný—II]
            Inv.č 92: Bolivia (policy area)
            Inv.č 92: Relations, Czechoslovakia—Bolivia
            Inv.č 92: Relations, CP Czechoslovakia—CP Bolivia

The National Archives, Kew, Richmond, United Kingdom
  Cabinet Minutes
  Foreign Office Files
National Archives and Records Administration, College Park, Maryland
  Records Group 43, Records of International Conferences, Commissions, and
    Expositions: Motion Picture Films
  Record Group 59, Records of the State Department: Alpha-Numeric Files,
    Subject-Numeric Files, Decimal Files, Lot Files
  Record Group 84, Post Files
  Record Group 111, Records of the Office of the Chief Signal Officer: Moving
    Pictures
  Record Group 263, Central Intelligence Agency Files
  Record Group 286, Records of the Agency for International Development
  Record Group 306, Records of the United States Information Agency
  Central Intelligence Agency Records Search Tool (CREST)
Rockefeller Archive Center, Sleepy Hollow, New York
  Nelson A. Rockefeller Papers
Seeley G. Mudd Manuscript Library, Princeton University, Princeton, New Jersey
  Adlai E. Stevenson Papers
The Texas Collection, Baylor University, Waco, Texas
  Thomas C. Mann Papers

Press

Bohemia, Havana, Cuba, 1961–1964
El Diario, La Paz, Bolivia, 1961–1964
El Mundo, Cochabamba, Bolivia, selected dates
Miami News, April 11, 1965
National Observer, selected dates
ProQuest Historical Newspapers Database, 1961–1964
  Baltimore Sun
  Boston Globe
  Chicago Daily Tribune (1961–1963)
  Chicago Tribune (1963–1964)
  Christian Science Monitor
  Hartford Courant
  Los Angeles Times
  New York Times
  Wall Street Journal
  Washington Post, Times Herald
El Pueblo, La Paz, Bolivia, selected dates
Los Tiempos, Cochabamba, Bolivia, 12 October 2008
Time, 1961–1964

Interviews

Unless otherwise noted, all positions refer to those held on 4 November 1964.

Luis Antezana Ergueta, journalist at MNR daily *La Nación*, numerous interviews between July 2007 and August 2010.

Domitila Barrios de Chungara, PCB member and leader in the Comité de Amas de Casa de Siglo XX, 7 May 2010.

Benigno Bastos, POR member in Siglo XX, 13 October 2010.

Guillermo Bedregal Gutiérrez, president of COMIBOL, minister in Paz government, 1 September 2007, 3 September 2010.

Óscar Bello Marcó, FSB guerrilla leader in Santa Cruz, 31 July 2010.

Javier Campero Paz, nephew of Víctor Paz Estenssoro, 2–3 August 2007.

Raúl Campero Paz, nephew of Víctor Paz Estenssoro, 2–3 August 2007.

Víctor Carrasco Castro, miner at Santa Fe, 19 October 2010.

Edgar Claure Paz, student at Military Engineering Academy, aide to General Ovando on the evening of 4 November, head of military staff for President Siles (1982–1985), 24 and 27 August, 7 September, 4 November 2010, and 20 July 2012.

Arturo Crespo, MNR/PRIN member and Control Obrero for Catavi, 27 April 2010.

Mauro Cuellar Caballero, FSB Youth member and leader in university federation, 10 December 2010.

Marta Cuellar Landívar, wife of General Barrientos (not recognized prior to Barrientos's death), 28 October 2010 and 2 August 2012.

José Luís Cueto Arteaga, PCB Central Committee, editor of PCB daily *Unidad*, 8–9 December 2010 and 29 July 2012.

Father Roberto Durette, parish priest of Catavi mining community, 12 October 2010.

Emilse Escóbar, daughter of Federico Escóbar, head of the PCB in Siglo XX and Control Obrero for Siglo XX, numerous interviews in April 2010.

Filemón Escóbar, leader in the POR at Siglo XX, 26 May 2009.

Robert Fergerstrom, Peace Corps volunteer taken hostage at Siglo XX (December 1963), 16 November 2009.

Chico Fox, son of US Embassy air attaché, 12 December 2008, 1–3 April 2009, 13 January 2010.

Edward Fox, US Embassy air attaché, 12 December 2008, 1–3 April 2009, 13 January 2010.

Evelyn Fox, wife of US Embassy air attaché, 12 December 2008, 1–3 April 2009, 13 January 2010.

Rosemarie Galindo, wife of General Barrientos, May 9, 2013.

Mario Gutiérrez Reese, son of Mario Gutiérrez Gutiérrez, head of FSB, 30 July 2010.

Loyola Guzmán Lara, leader in Juvenil Comunista Boliviana (JCB; Bolivian Communist Youth) in La Paz, 26 August and 6 September 2010.

Douglas Henderson, US ambassador to Bolivia, 13 April 2009.

Guido Humerez, air force officer and friend of General Barrientos, 14 December 2010.

Alberto Iriarte Fiorilo, lifelong friend of Barrientos, member of the Partido de la Izquierda Revolucionaria (PIR; Revolutionary Left Party), and mayor of Tarata, Barrientos's hometown, 25 July 2007 and 4 May 2010.

Cirilo Jiménez, POR leader in Siglo XX, 13 July 2012.

Raúl López Leyton, junior officer at General Staff Headquarters, Barrientos aide-de-camp (1964–1969), 22 November 2010 and 23 July 2012.

Mariela Martin, wife of USIS labor officer Thomas Martin, hostage at Siglo XX, via telephone, 5 June 2013.

Luis Mayser Ardaya, FSB guerrilla organizer and leader, 30–31 July 2010 and 10 July 2012.

Alberto Muñoz de la Barra, leader in MNR Youth breakaway organizations Avanzada Universitaria and Espartaco, 19 July and 16 August 2010.

Daniel Ordóñez Plaza, PCB member and interim Control Obrero in Siglo XX, 25–26 October 2010.

Rosendo Osorio, PCB member in Siglo XX, 11 and 14 October 2010.

Ramiro Otero Lugones, PCB Central Committee, 8 December 2010.

Fernando Paz, close family member and political collaborator of Víctor Paz Estenssoro, 5 July 2012.

Ramiro Paz Cerruto, son of President Víctor Paz Estenssoro, 17 October 2010 and 6 July 2012.

José Pimentel, son of Irineo Pimentel, former member of the PIR and secretary general of Siglo XX miners' union, 4 March and 9 April 2010.

Fabián Portugal, *campesino* leader of North Potosí and Irupata elder, 13 October 2010. (This interview was conducted with Juan Molina present for occasional interpretation from Quechua to Spanish.)

Gary Prado Salmón, instructor at the military academy, 29 October 2010 and 12 July 2012.

David Ratermann, close friend and colleague of Monsignor Andrew Kennedy, chaplain of the Bolivian armed forces and secretary of the Bolivian Bishops Conference, 11 August 2010 (by e-mail).

Víctor Reinaga, leader in PCB at Siglo XX–Llallagua, teacher at Llallagua High School, close friend and colleague of Federico Escóbar, 19 August 2010.

Simón Reyes, leader in PCB and FSTMB, 28 July 2010 and 9 July 2012.

René Rocabado, member of the PCB in Cochabamba, adviser to General Barrientos, and journalist for Cochabamba daily *El Mundo*, 25–26 July 2007 and 5 May 2010.

Leónidas Rojas Navia, leader in JCB in Siglo XX, close friend and colleague of Federico Escóbar, vice president of the Lincoln-Murillo-Castro Brigades, 23 August 2010 and 25 July 2012.

Dulfredo Rúa Bejarano, MNR Youth leader, cofounder of Marxist breakaway groups Espartaco and Avanzada Universitaria, 15 November 2010.

Rubén Sánchez Valdivia, junior officer stationed in Cochabamba, 15 December 2010 and 3 August 2012.

Julio Sanjinés Goytia, founder of Bolivian Army Engineering Corps, founder of Bolivian Army School of Engineering, director of USAID Civic Action, and interim director of opposition daily *El Diario*, ambassador to the United States (1965–1969, 1982–1985), 4 September 2007, 28 November 2008, 17 August 2010.

Simón Sejas Tordoya, head of studies at the military officers' school in Cochabamba, member of Barrientos's conspiratorial group, aide de camp for President Barrientos (1964–1965), head of military staff for President Juan José Torres (1970–1971), and commander-in-chief of the Bolivian armed forces (1984–1985), 23 August 2010.

Carlos Serrate Reich, private secretary to President Paz (1960–1964) and education minister (1964), 17 November and 22 December 2010, 19 July 2012.

Derek Singer, director of the first Peace Corps contingent in Bolivia, 27 June 2009.

Carlos Soria Galvarra, leader in JCB in Cochabamba, 12 April 2010.

Larry Sternfield, CIA station chief in La Paz, 11 July 2009, 10 July 2010 (by phone), 27 June 2011, and 3 January 2012.

Memoirs, Published Documents, and Pamphlets

Agee, Philip. *Inside the Company: CIA Diary*. New York: Stonehill, 1975.

Alexander, Robert J. "Nature and Progress of Agrarian Reform in Latin America." *Journal of American History* 23, no. 4 (December 1963): 559–73.

Almaraz Paz, Sergio. *Réquiem para una república*. La Paz: Universidad Mayor de San Andrés, 1969.

Andrade, Victor. *My Missions for Revolutionary Bolivia, 1944–1962*. Pittsburgh: University of Pittsburgh Press, 1976.

Antezana Ergueta, Luis. *La retirada de Colquiri: El fin del anarco-sindicalismo*. La Paz, n.p., 1964.

Apaza, Maximiliano. "Critica al programa de gobierno del MNR." *Espartaco* 11 (October 1964): 34–39.

Ascarrunz Rodríguez, Eduardo. *La palabra de Paz: Un hombre, un siglo*. La Paz: Plural, 2008.

Barrientos Ortuño, René. *La Unidad de las Fuerzas Armadas de la Revolución Nacional*. La Paz: n.p., 1962.

———. *Mensaje a la Nación del General René Barrientos O. del 22 de enero de 1964*. La Paz: n.p., 1964.

———. *Significado de la Revolución de Noviembre*. La Paz: n.p., 1964.

Bedregal Gutiérrez, Guillermo. *De búhos, políticas, y exilios: Mis memorias*. La Paz: Instituto de Investigación, Formación, y Capacitación Democrática "Carlos Montenegro," 2009.

———. *Víctor Paz Estenssoro, el político: Una semblanza crítica*. Mexico, DF: Fondo de Cultura Económica, 1999.

Béjar, Héctor. *Peru 1965: apuntes sobre una experiencia guerrillera*. New York: Monthly Review Press, 1970.

Benemelis, Juan F. *Las Guerras Secretas de Fidel Castro*. Madrid: Fundación Elena Maderos, 2002.

Bounds, Lieutenant Colonel Malcolm S. "Military Civic Action." *Air University Review* (May–June 1969): 68–73.

Chávez Ortíz, Ñuflo. *Análisis del proceso de la revolución nacional y su proyección hacia el futuro.* La Paz: n.p., 1965.

———. *Carta a los trabajadores de mi patria.* La Paz: Frente de Liberación Nacional, 1964.

Coordinación de la Resistencia Nacionalista. *El nacionalismo revolucionario contra la ocupación norteamericana.* La Paz: n.p., 1967.

Crespo Enríquez, Arturo. *El rostro minero de Bolivia: Los mineros . . . mártires y héroes.* La Paz: Sygnus, 2009.

Cuevas Ramírez, Roberto. *Arguedas.* La Paz: Artes Gráficas Latinas, 2000.

Debray, Régis. *La Guérilla du Che.* Paris: Éditions du Seuil, 1974.

Escóbar, Filemón. *De la Revolución al Pachakuti: El aprendizaje del Respeto Recíproco entre blancos e indianos.* La Paz: Garza Azul, 2008.

———. *Testimonio de un militante obrero.* La Paz: HISBOL, 1984.

———. *Testimonio de un militante obrero: La frustración de la dirección revolucionaria en Bolivia a través de la crisis del POR.* Unabridged, unpublished edition, 1977.

Faum, Nicolás. *El año 1965 en la Revolución Boliviana.* La Paz: Ediciones "Galaxia," 1980. (Nicolás Faum was a pseudonym for breakaway MNR Youth leader Octavio Quisbert.)

Federico Escóbar Zapata: Breve Esbozo Biográfico, vol. 23 of *Cuadernos de Liberación.* La Paz: "Liberación" editores, 2010.

Gálvez, William. *El sueño africano del Che: Qué sucedió en la guerrilla congolesa?* La Habana: Casa de las Américas, 1997.

"Informe orgánico aprobado por el III Congreso Regional de La Paz del Partido Comunista de Bolivia, 30 November 1964." *Espartaco* 12 (March 1965): 108–19.

Iriarte Fiorilo, Alberto. *Tarata: Luz y Sombra.* Cochabamba: n.p., 2000.

Jordán Pando, Roberto. *De Bolívar a la revolución boliviana.* Madrid: Editorial Legasa, 1984.

Kippez Aneiva, Miguel Angel. *René Barrientos Ortuño: El Hombre.* La Paz: Impresiones "Poligraf," 1992.

Lagos, María L., ed. *Nos hemos forjado así: Al rojo vivo y a puro golpe: Historias del Comité de Amas de Casa de Siglo XX.* La Paz: Asociación Alicia "Por Mujeres Nuevas"/Plural, 2006.

Landívar Flores, Hernán. *Infierno en Bolivia.* La Paz: Empresas Talleres Gráficos Bolivianos, 1965.

Lechín Oquendo, Juan. *El pueblo al poder,* 2nd ed. La Paz: La Razón, 2005.

Línea política del Partido Comunista de Bolivia Marxista-Leninista: Aprobado en el Primer Congreso Nacional Extraordinario, Llallagua, Siglo XX, abril 16 de 1965. La Paz: Ediciones "Liberación," 2003.

López Vigil, José Ignacio. *Una mina de coraje.* Quito: Aler/Pío XII, 1984.

Lora, Guillermo. *La Revolución Boliviana: Análisis Crítico.* La Paz: Difusión, 1963.

Marchetti, Victor, and John D. Marks. *The CIA and the Cult of Intelligence.* New York: Dell, 1974.

Mayser Ardaya, Luis J. *Alto Paraguá: Verdaderas Guerrillas Bolivianas.* Santa Cruz de la Sierra: Editorial e Imprenta Universitaria, 2008.

Moscoso, Teodoro. *Lo que he visto hacer las fuerzas armadas en Bolivia es impresionante.* La Paz: USIS, 1963.

——. *Teodoro Moscoso en Bolivia*. La Paz: Alliance for Progress, 1962.

Movimiento Nacionalista Revolucionario. *Programa de Gobierno: Tercer Gobierno de la Revolución Nacional, 1960–1964*. La Paz: n.p., 1960.

——. *Programa de Gobierno, 1964–1968*. La Paz: Dirección Nacional de Informaciones, 1964.

Organization of American States. *Ninth Meeting of Consultation of Ministers of Foreign Affairs*. Washington, DC: Pan American Union, 1964.

——. *Study of the "Diary of 'Che' Guevara in Bolivia*. Washington, DC: Pan American Union, 1968.

Partido Comunista de Bolivia. *Documentos: II Congreso Nacional del PCB*. La Paz: n.p., 1964.

Patch, Richard W. "The Pro and Anti-Castristas in La Paz: An Eyewitness Account of a Political Riot." *West Coast South American Series* 9, no. 2 (February 1962): 1–6.

Paz, Martha, ed. *Diálogos con el P. Gregorio Iriarte*. Cochabamba: Grupo Editorial Kipus, 2010.

Paz, Ramiro V., ed. *Las cartas de Víctor Paz Estenssoro*. La Paz: Producciones Cima, 1994.

Paz, Ramiro V. "El golpe de estado de noviembre de 1964." In *Víctor Paz Estenssoro: Testimonios de sus contemporáneos*, edited by Mariano Baptista Gumucio, 24–35. Cochabamba: Editora Opinión, 2001.

——. *En los pasillos del poder*. Santa Cruz: Editorial Universitaria, 2006.

Paz Estenssoro, Víctor. *Contra la Restauración por la Revolución Nacional*. Lima: n.p., March 1965.

——. *Discurso inaugural dirigido al honorable congreso nacional, 6 de agosto de 1960*. La Paz: Dirección Nacional de Informaciones, 1960.

——. "Informe presentado al Congreso Nacional el 6 de agosto de 1964." In *Pensamiento político de Víctor Paz Estenssoro: Compilación*, edited by Ramiro Antelo León, 187–207. La Paz: Plural, 2003.

——. *Las Fuerzas Armadas y la Revolución Nacional*. La Paz: n.p., 1959.

——. *Mensaje del Presidente de la República Dr. Víctor Paz Estenssoro al H. Congreso Nacional*. La Paz: Dirección Nacional de Informaciones, 1964.

——. *Repudio a la contrarrevolución: Discurso del Jefe Nacional del MNR, Dr. Víctor Paz Estenssoro, en la gigantesca manifestación de reiteración de fe revolucionaria, en La Paz el 11 de Marzo, 1964*. La Paz: Dirección Nacional de Informaciones, 1964.

——. *La Revolución Boliviana: Discurso del Jefe Nacional del MNR, Dr. Víctor Paz Estenssoro, a los Delegados de la IX Convención del Partido el 17 de Enero de 1964*. La Paz: Dirección Nacional de Informaciones, 1964.

Peña Bravo, Raúl. *Hechos y dichos del general Barrientos*. Bolivia: n.p., 1971. (Raúl Peña Bravo was a pseudonym for Luis Antezana Ergueta.)

Peredo, Inti. *Mi Campaña con el "Che."* La Paz: Los Amigos del Libro, 1970.

Posadas, Juan. *Partido Obrero Revolucionario Trotskista (IV International): Alianza Obrero-Campesina, Asamblea Constituyente para imponer el Gobierno Obrero y Campesino frente al caos a que el Capitalismo conduce a Bolivia*. La Paz: Ediciones Lucha Obrera, 1965.

Prado Salmón, Gary. *Defiéndete, Gary Prado: Anecdotario*. Santa Cruz de la Sierra: Reflejos Editores, 1994.

——. *Poder y Fuerzas Armadas, 1949–1982*. La Paz: Editorial Los Amigos del Libro, 1987.

Presidencia de la República. *Informe al Pueblo: Respuesta a una interpelación parlamentaria*. La Paz: Dirección Nacional de Informaciones, 1961.

Quezada G., Guido. "En torno a un artículo 'sobre la pugna comunista.'" *Espartaco* 11 (October 1964): 17–21.

Richards, Allan R. *Administration—Bolivia and the United States*. Albuquerque: University of New Mexico, 1961.

Romualdi, Serafino. *Presidents and Peons: Recollections of a Labor Ambassador in Latin America*. New York: Funk and Wagnalls, 1967.

Rostow, Walt W. *The Stages of Economic Growth: A Non-Communist Manifesto*. London: Cambridge University Press, 1960.

Sanjinés Goytia, Julio. *Civic Action: Role of the Armed Forces in the Social and Economic Development of a Country*. La Paz: Alliance for Progress, 1964.

——. *Ingeniería: 'El Arma del Trabajo.'* La Paz: Centro Boliviano Americano, 2001.

Schlesinger, Andrew, and Stephen Schlesinger, eds. *Journals, 1952–2000: Arthur M. Schlesinger, Jr.* New York: Penguin Press, 2007.

Schlesinger Jr., Arthur M. *A Thousand Days: John F. Kennedy in the White House*. New York: Mariner, 1965.

Senado Nacional. *El Problema de Catavi: Informe de la Comisión Oficial del Senado Nacional*. La Paz: n.p., 1963.

Smith Jr., Major Laun C. "Civic Action: A Weapon for Peace." *Air University Review* (July–August 1968): 97–100.

Soria Galvarra, Carlos. "La izquierda armada." *Barataria* 2 (March–April 2005).

Special Operations Research Office. *U.S. Army Area Handbook for Bolivia*. Washington, DC: American University, 1963.

Suárez Salazar, Luis. *Che Guevara and the Latin American Revolutionary Movements: Manuel Piñeiro ("Red Beard")*. Melbourne: Ocean Press, 2001.

Trigo O'Connor d'Arlach, Eduardo. *Conversaciones con Víctor Paz Estenssoro*. La Paz: Comunicaciones El País, 1999.

U.S. Agency for International Development (USAID). *US Overseas Loans and Grants: Obligations and Loan Authorizations, July 1, 1945–September 30, 2008*. http://www.usaid.gov/policy/greenbook.html (accessed August 2010).

U.S. Department of State. *Foreign Relations of the United States: 1961–1963*. Washington, DC: Government Printing Office, n.d.

——. *Foreign Relations of the United States: 1964–1968*. Washington, DC: GPO, n.d.

Valverde Barbery, Carlos. "Guerrillas del Alto y Bajo Paraguá: Derrocamiento de Víctor Paz Estenssoro." In *Tres hechos históricos narrados por uno de los protagonistas*, 1–96. Santa Cruz de la Sierra: n.p., 2002.

Viezzer, Moema. *"Si me permiten hablar . . ." Testimonio de Domitila, una mujer de las minas en Bolivia*, 3rd ed. Mexico, DF: Siglo Veintiuno Editores, 1977.

Visita del General Barrientos a la Mina de Siglo XX. La Paz: Dirección Nacional de Informaciones de la Presidencia, 1965.

Zavaleta Mercado, René. *La caída del MNR y la conjuración de noviembre: Historia del golpe militar del 4 de noviembre de 1964 en Bolivia*. Cochabamba: Editorial "Los Amigos del Libro," 1995.

Secondary Sources

Alba, Víctor. *Alliance without Allies: The Mythology of Progress in Latin America*. New York: Praeger, 1965.
Alexander, Jeffrey C. "Modern, Anti, Post, and Neo." *New Left Review* 210 (March–April 1995): 63–102.
Alexander, Robert J. *Bolivia: Past, Present, and Future of Its Politics*. New York: Praeger, 1982.
———. *A History of Organized Labor in Bolivia*. Westport, CT: Praeger, 2005.
Anderson, Benedict. *Imagined Communities*. London: Verso, 1983.
Anderson, Jon Lee. *Che Guevara: A Revolutionary Life*. New York: Grove Press, 1997.
Andrew, Christopher, and Vasili Mitrokhin. *The World Was Going Our Way: The KGB and the Battle for the Third World*. New York: Basic Books, 2005.
Antezana Ergueta, Luis. *Historia secreta del Movimiento Nacionalista Revolucionario, Tomo 7: La Revolución del MNR del 9 de Abril*. La Paz: Instituto de Investigación, Formación, y Capacitación Democrática "Carlos Montenegro," 1988.
———. *Historia secreta del Movimiento Nacionalista Revolucionario, Tomo 9: La contrarrevolución del 4 de noviembre de 1964*. La Paz: Instituto de Investigación, Formación, y Capacitación Democrática "Carlos Montenegro," 2006.
———. "La reforma agraria campesina en Bolivia (1956–1960)." *Revista Mexicana de Sociología* 31, no. 2 (April–June 1969): 245–321.
Arthus, Wein Weibert. "L'aide internationale peut ne pas marcher: Évaluation des relations américano-haïtiennes au regard de l'Alliance pour le Progrès (1961–1963)." *Journal of Haitian Studies* 17, no. 1 (April 2011): 155–77.
Beer, Francis A., and Robert Hariman. *Post-Realism: The Rhetorical Turn in International Relations*. East Lansing: Michigan State University Press, 1996.
Bethell, Leslie, and Ian Roxborough, eds. *Latin America between the Second World War and the Cold War: 1944–1948*. Cambridge: Cambridge University Press, 1992.
Blasier, Cole. *The Hovering Giant: U.S. Responses to Revolutionary Change in Latin America, 1910–1985*, rev. ed. Pittsburgh: University of Pittsburgh Press, 1985.
Blum, William. *Killing Hope: US Military and CIA Interventions since World War II*, rev. ed. Monroe, ME: Common Courage Press, 1995.
Borstelmann, Thomas. "'Hedging Our Bets and Buying Time': John Kennedy and Racial Revolution in the American South and Southern Africa." *Diplomatic History* 24, no. 3 (Summer 2000): 435–63.
Brands, H. W., ed. *The Foreign Policies of Lyndon Johnson: Beyond Vietnam*. College Station: Texas A&M University Press, 1999.
Brill, William Handford. "Military Civic Action in Bolivia." PhD dissertation, University of Pennsylvania, 1965.

——. *Military Intervention in Bolivia: The Overthrow of Paz Estenssoro and the MNR.* Washington, DC: Institute for the Comparative Study of Political Systems, 1967.

Brown, Wendy. "Democracy and Bad Dreams." *Theory and Event* 10, no. 1 (2007), https://muse.jhu.edu/journals/theory_and_event/v010/10.1brown02.html.

Bulmer-Thomas, Victor, and James Dunkerley, eds. *The United States and Latin America: The New Agenda.* Cambridge, MA: Harvard University Press, 1999.

Burgos, Elizabeth. " L'emprise du castrisme en Bolivie." *Problèmes d'Amérique Latine* 69 (2008): 79–96.

Burke, Melvin. "The Corporación Minera de Bolivia (COMIBOL) and the Triangular Plan: A Case Study in Dependency." *Latin American Issues* 4 (1987), http://sites.allegheny.edu/latinamericanstudies/latin-american-issues/volume-4/.

——. "La crisis de la Corporación Minera de Bolivia: Un legado del Plan Triangular." In *Estudios Críticas del Neoliberalismo*, by Melvin Burke, 265–300. La Paz: Plural, 2001.

Byrne, Jeffrey James. "Our Own Special Brand of Socialism: Algeria and the Contest of Modernities in the 1960s." *Diplomatic History* 33, no. 3 (June 2009): 427–47.

Calderon, J. *The Bolivian Coup of 1964: A Sociological Analysis.* Buffalo, NY: Council on International Studies, SUNY-Buffalo, 1972.

Carter, William E. "Revolution and the Agrarian Sector." In *Beyond the Revolution: Bolivia Since 1952*, edited by James M. Malloy and Richard S. Thorn, 233–68. Pittsburgh: University of Pittsburgh Press, 1971.

Casteñeda, Jorge G. *La vida en rojo: Todo lo que hay que saber.* Madrid: Punto de Lectura, 2012.

Connelly, Matthew. *A Diplomatic Revolution: Algeria's Fight for Independence and the Origins of the Post–Cold War Era.* Oxford: Oxford University Press, 2002.

——. *Fatal Misconception: The Struggle to Control World Population.* Cambridge, MA: The Belknap Press of Harvard University Press, 2008.

Corbett, Charles D. *The Latin American Military as a Socio-Political Force: Case Studies of Bolivia and Argentina.* Miami: University of Miami, 1972.

——. "Military Institutional Development and Sociopolitical Change." *Journal of Interamerican Studies and World Affairs* 14, no. 4 (November 1972): 399–435.

Crabtree, John, and Lawrence Whitehead, eds. *Unresolved Tensions: Bolivia Past and Present.* Pittsburgh: University of Pittsburgh Press, 2008.

Crespo, Alfonso. *Lydia: Una mujer en la historia.* La Paz: Plural, 1999.

Cullather, Nick. "The Foreign Policy of the Calorie." *American Historical Review* 112, no. 2 (April 2007): 337–64.

——. *The Hungry World: America's Cold War Battle against Poverty in Asia.* Cambridge, MA: Harvard University Press, 2010.

——. *Illusions of Influence: The Political Economy of United States–Philippines Relations, 1942–1960.* Stanford, CA: Stanford University Press, 1994.

——. "The Third Race." *Diplomatic History* 33, no. 3 (June 2009): 507–12.

Cumings, Bruce. "Revising Postrevisionism; or, The Poverty of Theory in Diplomatic History." *Diplomatic History* 17, no. 4 (Fall 1993): 539–70.

Dean, Robert D. "Masculinity as Ideology: John F. Kennedy and the Domestic Politics of Foreign Policy." *Diplomatic History* 22, no. 1 (Winter 1998): 29–62.

Desch, Michael C. "America's Liberal Illiberalism: The Ideological Origins of Over-reaction in US Foreign Policy." *International Security* 32, no. 3 (Winter 2007–8): 7–43.

———. *When the Third World Matters: Latin America and United States Grand Strategy.* Baltimore, MD: Johns Hopkins University Press, 1993.

Diez de Medina, Fernando. *El General del Pueblo: René Barrientos Ortuño, Caudillo Mayor de la Revolución Boliviana,* 3rd ed. La Paz: Los Amigos del Libro, 1972.

Do Alto, Hervé. " 'Cuando el nacionalismo se pone el poncho': Una mirada retrospectiva a la etnicidad y la clase en el movimiento popular boliviano (1952–2007)." In *Bolivia: Memoria, insurgencia y movimientos sociales,* edited by Maristella Svampa and Pablo Stefanoni, 21–53. Buenos Aires: Clacso/OSAL/El Colectivo, 2007.

Dockrill, Saki R., and Geraint Hughes, eds. *Cold War History.* New York: London: Palgrave MacMillan, 2006.

Dodge, Toby. "Coming Face to Face with Bloody Reality: Liberal Common Sense and the Ideological Failure of the Bush Doctrine in Iraq." *International Politics* 46, vol. 2–3 (March 2009): 252–75.

Domínguez, Jorge I. "The Perfect Dictatorship? Comparing Authoritarian Rule in South Korea and in Argentina, Brazil, Chile, and Mexico." Paper presented at the 2002 Annual Meeting of the American Political Science Association (August 29–September 1, 2002).

———. "Samuel Huntington and the Latin American State." In *The Other Mirror: Grand Theory through the Lens of Latin America,* edited by Miguel Angel Centeno and Fernando López-Alves, 219–39. Princeton, NJ: Princeton University Press, 2001.

———. "US–Latin American Relations during the Cold War and Its Aftermath." In *The United States and Latin America: The New Agenda,* edited by Victor Bulmer-Thomas and James Dunkerley, 33–50. Cambridge, MA: Harvard University Press, 1999.

Dorn, Glenn J. *The Truman Administration and Bolivia: Making the World Safe for Liberal Constitutional Oligarchy.* University Park: Pennsylvania State University Press, 2011.

Dunkerley, James. *Bolivia: Revolution and the Power of History in the Present.* London: Institute for the Study of the Americas, 2007.

———. "Evo Morales, the 'Two Bolivias' and the Third Bolivian Revolution." *Journal of Latin American Studies* 39, no. 1 (February 2007): 133–66.

———. *Rebellion in the Veins: Political Struggle in Bolivia, 1952–1982.* London: Verso, 1984.

———. *Warriors and Scribes: Essays on the History and Politics of Latin America.* London: Verso, 2000.

Engerman, David C., Nils Gilman, Mark H. Haefele, and Michael Latham. *Staging Growth: Modernization, Development, and the Global Cold War.* Amherst: University of Massachusetts Press, 2003.

Engerman, David C., and Corinna R. Unger. "Introduction: Toward a Global History of Modernization." *Diplomatic History* 33, no. 3 (June 2009): 375–85.

Escobar, Arturo. *Encountering Development: The Making and Unmaking of the Third World.* Princeton, NJ: Princeton University Press, 1995.

Ferguson, James. *The Anti-Politics Machine: "Development," Depoliticization, and Bureaucratic Power in Lesotho.* Minneapolis: University of Minnesota Press, 1990.

Fish, Howard M. "Bolivia: A First Test of the Alliance for Progress." MA thesis, George Washington University, 1964.

Flores, Edmundo. "Land Reform in Bolivia." *Land Economics* 30, no. 2 (May 1954): 112–24.

Foran, John. *Taking Power: On the Origins of Third World Revolutions.* Cambridge: Cambridge University Press, 2005.

Freedman, Lawrence. *Kennedy's Wars: Berlin, Cuba, Laos, and Vietnam.* Oxford: Oxford University Press, 2000.

Friedman, Max Paul. "Retiring the Puppets, Bringing Latin America Back In: Recent Scholarship on United States–Latin American Relations." *Diplomatic History* 27, no. 5 (November 2003): 621–36.

Gaddis, John Lewis. *The Long Peace: Inquiries into the History of the Cold War.* Oxford: Oxford University Press, 1989.

——. *Strategies of Containment: A Critical Appraisal of Postwar American National Security Policy.* Oxford: Oxford University Press, 1982.

Geertz, Clifford. "Ideology as a Cultural System." In *Ideology and Discontent*, edited by David Ernest Apter, 47–79. New York: Free Press of Glencoe, 1964.

Geidel, Molly. "'Sowing Death in Our Women's Wombs': Modernization and Indigenous Nationalism in the 1960s Peace Corps and Jorge Sanjinés' Yawar Mallku." *American Quarterly* 63, no. 3 (September 2010): 763–86.

Gilman, Nils. *Mandarins of the Future: Modernization Theory in Cold War America.* Baltimore, MD: Johns Hopkins University Press, 2003.

Gleijeses, Piero. "Book Review: A Sordid Affair: The Alliance for Progress in British Guiana." *Diplomatic History* 31, no. 4 (September 2007): 793–96.

——. *Conflicting Missions: Havana, Washington, and Africa, 1959–1976.* Chapel Hill: University of North Carolina Press, 2002.

——. *Shattered Hope: The Guatemalan Revolution and the United States: 1944–1954.* Princeton, NJ: Princeton University Press, 1991.

Goldman, Zachary K. "Ties That Bind: John F. Kennedy and the Foundations of the American-Israeli Alliance." *Cold War History* 9, no. 1 (February 2009): 23–58.

Gootenberg, Paul. *Andean Cocaine: The Making of a Global Drug.* Chapel Hill: University of North Carolina Press, 2008.

Gordillo, José M. *Arando en la Historia: La experiencia campesina en Cochabamba.* La Paz: Plural, 1998.

——. *Campesinos Revolucionarios en Bolivia: Identidad, territorio y sexualidad en el Valle Alto de Cochabamba, 1952–1964.* La Paz: Plural/Universidad de la Cordillera, 2000.

Gott, Richard. *Guerrilla Movements in Latin America.* New York: Seagull Books, 2008.

Grandin, Greg. *The Blood of Guatemala: A History of Race and Nation.* Durham, NC: Duke University Press, 2000.

Grindle, Merilee S., and Pilar Domingo, eds. *Proclaiming Revolution: Bolivia in Comparative Perspective.* Cambridge, MA: Harvard University Press, 2003.

Gusfield, Joseph R. "Tradition and Modernity: Misplaced Polarities in the Study of Social Change." *American Journal of Sociology* 72, no. 4 (January 1967): 351–62.

Hahn, Peter L. "An Ominous Moment: Lyndon Johnson and the Six Day War." In *Looking Back at LBJ: White House Politics in a New Light*, edited by Mitchell Lerner, 78–100. Lawrence: University Press of Kansas, 2005.

Halberstam, David. *The Best and the Brightest*. New York: Ballantine Books, 1969.

Harris, Olivia, and Xavier Albó. *Monteros y Guardatojos: Campesinos y Mineros en el Norte de Potosí en 1974*. La Paz: n.p., 1984.

Hirsch, Fred, and Richard Fletcher. *The CIA and the Labour Movement*. Nottingham: Spokesman Books, 1977.

Hogan, Michael J. "SHAFR Presidential Address: The 'Next Big Thing': The Future of Diplomatic History in a Global Age." *Diplomatic History* 28, no. 1 (January 2004): 1–21.

Hogan, Michael J., and Thomas G. Paterson, eds. *Explaining the History of American Foreign Relations*. Cambridge: Cambridge University Press, 2004.

Holland, James. "Bolivia." In *Latin American Foreign Policies: An Analysis*, edited by Harold Eugene Davis and Larman C. Wilson, 338–59. Baltimore, MD: Johns Hopkins University Press, 1975.

Hove, Mark T. "The Arbenz Factor: Salvador Allende, US-Chilean Relations, and the 1954 US Intervention in Guatemala." *Diplomatic History* 31, no. 4 (September 2007): 623–63.

Hunt, Michael H. *Ideology and US Foreign Policy*. New Haven, CT: Yale University Press, 1987.

——. "The Long Crisis in US Diplomatic History: Coming to a Closure." *Diplomatic History* 16, no. 1 (Winter 1992): 115–40.

Huntington, Samuel P. "Political Development and Political Decay." *World Politics* 17, no. 3 (April 1965): 386–430.

——. *Political Order in Changing Societies*. New Haven, CT: Yale University Press, 1968.

Hylton, Forrest, and Sinclair Thomson. *Revolutionary Horizons: Past and Present in Bolivian Politics*. London: Verso, 2007.

Irwin, Julia F. *Making the World Safe: The American Red Cross and a Nation's Humanitarian Awakening*. Oxford: Oxford University Press, 2013.

Irwin, Ryan M. "A Wind of Change? White Redoubt and the Postcolonial Movement, 1960–1963." *Diplomatic History* 33, no. 5 (November 2009): 897–925.

Jian, Chen. *Mao's China and the Cold War*. Chapel Hill: University of North Carolina Press, 2001.

John, S. Sándor. *Bolivia's Radical Tradition: Permanent Revolution in the Andes*. Tucson: University of Arizona Press, 2009.

Johns, Andrew L. "The Johnson Administration, the Shah of Iran, and the Changing Pattern of US-Iranian Relations, 1965–1967." *Journal of Cold War Studies* 9, no. 2 (Spring 2007): 64–94.

Johnson, Cecil. *Communist China & Latin America, 1959–1967*. New York: Columbia University Press, 1970.

Joseph, Gilbert, and Daniela Spenser, eds. *In from the Cold: Latin America's New Encounter with the Cold War*. Durham, NC: Duke University Press, 2008.

Justo, Liborio. *Bolivia: La revolución derrotada*. Cochabamba: Editorial Serrano, 1967.

Kahin, Audrey R., and George McT. *Subversion as Foreign Policy: The Secret Eisenhower and Dulles Debacle in Indonesia.* Seattle: University of Washington Press, 1997.

Karl, Robert Alexander. *State Formation, Violence, and Cold War in Colombia, 1957–1966.* PhD dissertation, Harvard University, 2009.

Kirkland, Robert O. "Colonel Edward Fox and the 1964 Bolivian Coup." *International Journal of Intelligence and Counterintelligence* 18 (2005): 473–82.

———. *Observing Our Hermanos en Armas: US Military Attachés in Guatemala, Cuba, and Bolivia, 1950–1964.* New York: Routledge, 2003.

Klein, Herbert. *Bolivia: The Evolution of a Multi-Ethnic Society,* 2nd ed. New York: Oxford University Press, 1992.

Knudson, Jerry W. *Bolivia: Press and Revolution, 1932–1964.* Lanham, MD: University Press of America, 1986.

———. "The Impact of the Catavi Massacre of 1942 on Bolivian Politics and Public Opinion." *The Americas* 26, no. 3 (January 1970): 254–76.

———. *The Press and the Bolivian National Revolution.* Lexington, KY: Association for Education in Journalism, 1973.

Kohn, James V. "The Cliza and Ucureña War: Syndical Violence and National Revolution in Bolivia." *Hispanic American Historical Review* 62, no. 4 (November 1982): 607–28.

———. "Peasant and Revolution in Bolivia, April 9, 1952–August 2, 1953." *Hispanic American Historical Review* 58, no. 2 (May 1978): 238–59.

Kuzmarov, Jeremy. *Modernizing Repression: Police Training and Nation Building in the American Century.* Amherst: University of Massachusetts Press, 2012.

Latham, Michael E. "Ideology, Social Science, and Destiny: Modernization and the Kennedy-Era Alliance for Progress." *Diplomatic History* 22, no. 2 (Spring 1998): 199–229.

———. *Modernization as Ideology: American Social Science and 'Nation Building' in the Kennedy Era.* Chapel Hill: University of North Carolina Press, 2000.

———. *The Right Kind of Revolution: Modernization, Development, and U.S. Foreign Policy from the Cold War to the Present.* Ithaca, NY: Cornell University Press, 2011.

Lavaud, Jean-Pierre. "L'art du coup d'état: Les militaires dans la société bolivienne." *Revue française de sociologie* 30, no. 1 (January–March 1989): 107–36.

———. *El Embrollo Boliviano: Turbulencias Sociales y Desplazamientos Políticos, 1952–1982.* La Paz: IFEA, 1998.

Lawrence, Mark Atwood. "Exception to the Rule? The Johnson Administration and the Panama Canal." In *Looking Back at LBJ: White House Politics in a New Light,* edited by Mitchell Lerner, 20–52. Lawrence: University Press of Kansas, 2005.

Le Gouill, Claude, "Irupata: Historia de un pueblo y de líderes desde la revolución de 1952 hasta la Autonomía Indígena Originaria Campesina." Presentation at the 6th Congress of Bolivian Studies, Sucre, Bolivia, June 2011.

Leacock, Ruth. *Requiem for Revolution: The United States and Brazil, 1961–1969.* Kent, OH: Kent State University Press, 1990.

Lehman, Kenneth D. *Bolivia and the United States: A Limited Partnership.* Athens: University of Georgia Press, 1999.

——. "Revolutions and Attributions: Making Sense of Eisenhower Administration Policies in Bolivia and Guatemala." *Diplomatic History* 21, no. 2 (Spring 1997): 185–213.

Lerner, Mitchell. "'A Big Tree of Peace and Justice': The Vice Presidential Travels of Lyndon Johnson." *Diplomatic History* 34, no. 2 (April 2010): 357–93.

——. *Looking Back at LBJ: White House Politics in a New Light*. Lawrence: University of Kansas Press, 2005.

——. "'Trying to Find the Guy Who Invited Them': Lyndon Johnson, Bridge Building, and the End of the Prague Spring." *Diplomatic History* 32, no. 1 (January 2008): 77–103.

Levinson, Jerome, and Juan de Onís. *The Alliance That Lost Its Way: A Critical Report on the Alliance for Progress*. Chicago: Quadrangle Books, 1970.

Lieuwen, Edwin. "The Military: A Revolutionary Force." *Annals of the American Academy of Political and Social Science* 334 (March 1961): 30–40.

Llosa M., José Antonio. *René Barrientos Ortuño: Paladín de la Bolivianidad*. La Paz: Empresa Editorial "Novedades," 1966.

Lora, Guillermo. *A History of the Bolivian Labour Movement, 1848–1971*. New York: Cambridge University Press, 1977.

Loveman, Brian and Thomas M. Davies Jr. "Peru." In *Che Guevara: Guerrilla Warfare*, edited by Loveman and Davies, 269–310. Wilmington, DE: Scholarly Resources, 1997.

Lumbers, Michael. "The Irony of Vietnam: The Johnson Administration's Tentative Bridge Building to China, 1965–1966." *Journal of Cold War Studies* 6, no. 3 (Summer 2004): 68–114.

Malloy, James M. *Bolivia: The Uncompleted Revolution*. Pittsburgh: University of Pittsburgh Press, 1970.

Malloy, James M., and Richard S. Thorn, eds. *Beyond the Revolution: Bolivia since 1952*. Pittsburgh: University of Pittsburgh Press, 1971.

Mamdani, Mahmood. "Lessons of Zimbabwe." *London Review of Books* 30, no. 23 (4 December 2008): 17–21.

Maul, Daniel. "'Help Them Move the ILO Way': The International Labor Organization and the Modernization Discourse in the Era of Decolonization and the Cold War." *Diplomatic History* 33, no. 3 (June 2009): 387–404.

Mayorga, Rene Antonio, and Stephen M. Gorman. "National-Popular State, State Capitalism and Military Dictatorship in Bolivia: 1952–1975." *Latin American Perspectives* 5, no. 2 (Spring 1978): 89–119.

Mazower, Mark. "Mandarins, Guns, and Money." *The Nation*, 17 September 2008.

——. "Violence and the State in the Twentieth Century." *American Historical Review* 107, no. 4 (October 2002): 1158–78.

McAllister, Carlota. "Rural Markets, Revolutionary Souls, and Rebellious Women in Cold War Guatemala." In *In from the Cold: Latin America's New Encounter with the Cold War*, edited by Gilbert Joseph and Daniel Spenser, 350–77. Durham, NC: Duke University Press, 2008.

McPherson, Alan. "Misled by Himself: What the Johnson Tapes Reveal about the Dominican Intervention of 1965." *Latin American Research Review* 38, no. 2 (2003): 127–46.

McVety, Amanda Kay. *Enlightened Aid: U.S. Development Policy as Foreign Policy in Ethiopia*. Oxford: Oxford University Press, 2012.

Miller, Nicola. *Soviet Relations with Latin America, 1959–1987*. Cambridge: Cambridge University Press, 1989.

Milne, David. *America's Rasputin: Walt Rostow and the Vietnam War*. New York: Hill and Wang, 2008.

Mitchell, Christopher. *The Legacy of Populism in Bolivia: From the MNR to Military Rule*. New York: Praeger, 1977.

Mitchell, Timothy. *Rule of Experts: Egypt, Techno-Politics, and Modernity*. Berkeley: University of California Press, 2002.

Molina Céspedes, Tomás. *Triángulo Letal: Paz, Banzer, Lechín*. Cochabamba: Gráfica J.V., 2007.

Muehlenbeck, Philip E. *Betting on the Africans: John F. Kennedy's Courting of African Nationalist Leaders*. Oxford: Oxford University Press, 2012.

Nairn, Tom. "The Modern Janus." *New Left Review* I/94 (November–December 1975): 3–29.

Nash, June. *We Eat the Mines and the Mines Eat Us: Dependency and Exploitation in Bolivian Tin Mines*. New York: Columbia University Press, 1993.

Navia Ribera, Carlos. *Los Estados Unidos y la Revolución Nacional: Entre pragmatismo y el sometimiento*. Cochabamba: CIDRE, 1984.

Needler, Martin C. "The Latin American Military: Predatory Reactionaries or Modernizing Patriots?" *Journal of Inter-American Studies* 11, no. 2 (April 1969): 237–44.

Nemchenok, Victor V. "In Search of Stability amid Chaos: US Policy toward Iran, 1961–63." *Cold War History* 10, no. 3 (August 2010): 341–69.

Nietzsche, Friedrich. *Beyond Good and Evil: Prelude to a Philosophy of the Future*. Leipzig: Druck und Verlag von C. G. Naumann, 1886 (translation by Walter Kaufman, New York: Vintage Books, 1966).

Ninkovich, Frank. *Modernity and Power: A History of the Domino Theory in the Twentieth Century*. Chicago: University of Chicago Press, 1994.

———. *The Wilsonian Century: US Foreign Policy since 1900*. Chicago: University of Chicago Press, 1999.

Noel, Thierry. "La génération des jeunes officiers issus du collège militaire Gualberto Villarroel: L'armée bolivienne, 1952–1985." Thèse de doctorat, Université Paris 7, Diderot, 2007.

Packenham, Robert A. *Liberal America and the Third World: Political Development Ideas in Foreign Aid and Social Science*. Princeton, NJ: Princeton University Press, 1973.

Painter, David S. "Research Note: Explaining US Relations with the Third World." *Diplomatic History* 19, no. 3 (Summer 1995): 525–48.

Patch, Richard W. "Bolivia: The Restrained Revolution." *Annals of the American Academy of Political and Social Science* 334 (March 1961): 123–32.

Paterson, Thomas G., ed. *Kennedy's Quest for Victory: American Foreign Policy, 1961–1963*. New York: Oxford University Press, 1989.

Pilard, Pierre-Olivier. *Jorge Ricardo Masetti: Un révolutionnaire guévarien et guévariste de 1958 à 1964*. Paris: L'Harmattan, 2007.

Power, Margaret. "The Engendering of Anticommunism and Fear in Chile's 1964 Presidential Election." *Diplomatic History* 32, no. 5 (November 2008): 931–53.

Pribilsky, Jason. "Development and the 'Indian Problem' in the Cold War Andes: *Indigenismo*, Science, and Modernization in the Making of the Cornell-Peru Project at Vicos." *Diplomatic History* 33, no. 3 (June 2009): 405–26.

Rabe, Stephen G. *Eisenhower and Latin America: The Foreign Policy of Anticommunism*. Chapel Hill: University of North Carolina Press, 1988.

——. *The Most Dangerous Area in the World: John F. Kennedy Confronts Communist Revolution in Latin America*. Chapel Hill: University of North Carolina Press, 1999.

——. *U.S. Intervention in British Guiana: A Cold War Story*. Chapel Hill: University of North Carolina Press, 2005.

Rakove, Robert B. *Kennedy, Johnson, and the Nonaligned World*. Cambridge: Cambridge University Press, 2013.

Rivera Cusicanqui, Silvia. *Oprimidos pero no vencidos: Luchas del campesinado aymara y quechwa, 1900–1980*. La Paz: HISBOL–CSUTCB, 1984.

Roberts Barragán, Hugo. *La Revolución del 9 de Abril*. La Paz: Cooperativa de Artes Gráficas, 1971.

Rohde, Joy. "Gray Matters: Social Scientists, Military Patronage, and Democracy in the Cold War." *Journal of American History* 96, no. 1 (June 2009): 99–122.

Rotter, Andrew J. "Saidism without Said: Orientalism and US Diplomatic History." *American Historical Review* 105, no. 4 (October 2000): 1205–17.

Ryan, Henry Butterfield. *The Fall of Che Guevara: A Story of Soldiers, Spies, and Diplomats*. New York: Oxford University Press, 1998.

Said, Edward W. *Orientalism*. New York: Vintage Books, 1978.

Sanders, G. Earl. "The Quiet Experiment in American Diplomacy: An Interpretative Essay on United States Aid to the Bolivian Revolution." *The Americas* 33, no. 1 (July 1976): 25–49.

Schelchkov, Andrey. "La Internacional Comunista, Tristán Marof, y Bolivia." *Archipiélago* 2 (January–March 2008): 56–67.

Schweizer, Karl W., and Matt J. Shumann. "The Revitalization of Diplomatic History: Renewed Reflections." *Diplomacy and Statecraft* 19, vol. 2 (June 2008): 149–86.

Scott, James C. *Seeing Like a State: How Certain Schemes to Improve the Human Condition Have Failed*. New Haven, CT: Yale University Press, 1998.

Selser, Gregorio. *La CIA en Bolivia*. Buenos Aires: Hernández Editorial, 1970.

Sewell, Bevan. "A Perfect (Free-Market) World? Economics, the Eisenhower Administration, and the Soviet Economic Offensive in Latin America." *Diplomatic History* 32, no. 5 (November 2008): 841–68.

Shesko, Elizabeth. "Conscript Nation: Negotiating Authority and Belonging in the Bolivian Barracks, 1900–1950." PhD dissertation, Duke University, 2012.

——. "Constructing Roads, Washing Feet, and Cutting Cane for the *Patria*: Building Bolivia with Military Labor, 1900–1975." *International Labor and Working-Class History* 80 (Fall 2011): 6–28.

Siekmeier, James F. *Aid, Nationalism, and Inter-American Relations: Guatemala, Bolivia, and the United States, 1945–1961*. Lewiston, NY: Edwin Mellon Press, 1999.

——. *The Bolivian Revolution and the United States*. University Park: Pennsylvania State University Press, 2011.

——. "Persistent Condor and Predatory Eagle: The Bolivian Revolution and the United States, 1952–1964." In *The Eisenhower Administration, the Third World, and the Globalization of the Cold War*, edited by Kathryn C. Statler and Andrew L. Johns, 197–221. Lanham, MD: Rowman and Littlefield, 2006.

——. "A Sacrificial Llama? The Expulsion of the Peace Corps from Bolivia in 1971." *Pacific Historical Review* 69, no. 1 (February 2000): 65–87.

——. "Trailblazer Diplomat: Bolivian Ambassador Víctor Andrade Uzquiano's Efforts to Influence U.S. Policy, 1944–1962." *Diplomatic History* 28, no. 3 (June 2004): 385–406.

Simpson, Bradley R. *Economists with Guns: Authoritarian Development and US-Indonesian Relations, 1960–1968*. Stanford, CA: Stanford University Press, 2008.

Soto, Cesar. *Historia del Pacto Militar Campesino*. Cochabamba: Centro de Estudios de la Realidad Económica y Social, 1994.

Speich, Daniel. "The Kenyan Style of 'African Socialism': Development Knowledge Claims and the Explanatory Limits of the Cold War." *Diplomatic History* 33, no. 3 (June 2009): 449–66.

Staples, Amy L. S. *The Birth of Development: How the World Bank, Food and Agriculture Organization, and World Health Organization Changed the World, 1945–1965*. Kent, OH: Kent State University Press, 2006.

Stokes, William S. "The Foreign Aid Program in Bolivia." *Western Political Quarterly* 15, no. 3 (September 1962): 28–30.

Suri, Jeremi. "Lyndon Johnson and the Global Disruption of 1968." In *Looking Back at LBJ: White House Politics in a New Light*, edited by Mitchell Lerner, 53–77. Lawrence: University Press of Kansas, 2005.

——. *Power and Protest: Global Revolution and the Rise of Détente*. Cambridge, MA: Harvard University Press, 2003.

Taffet, Jeffrey F. *Foreign Aid as Foreign Policy: The Alliance for Progress in Latin America*. New York: Routledge, 2007.

Taibo II, Paco Ignacio. *Ernesto Guevara: también conocido como el Che*. Mexico, DF: Planeta Editorial, 1996.

Tomasek, Robert D. "The Chilean-Bolivian Lauca River Dispute and the OAS." *Journal of Inter-American Studies* 9, no. 3 (July 1967): 351–66.

Trentin, Massimiliano. "Modernization as State Building: The Two Germanies in Syria, 1963–1972." *Diplomatic History* 33, no. 3 (June 2009): 487–505.

Tulchin, Joseph S. "The United States and Latin America in the 1960s." *Journal of Interamerican Studies and World Affairs* 30, no. 1 (Spring 1988): 1–36.

Uvin, Peter. *Aiding Violence: The Development Enterprise in Rwanda*. West Hartford, CT: Kumarian Press, 1998.

Vázquez Viaña, Humberto. *Una guerrilla para el Che*, 2nd ed. Santa Cruz de la Sierra: El País, 2008.

Walker III, William O. "Mixing the Sweet with the Sour: Kennedy, Johnson, and Latin America." In *The Diplomacy of the Crucial Decade: American Foreign Relations During the*

1960s, edited by Diane B. Kunz, 42–79. New York: Columbia University Press, 1994.

Walter, Richard J. *Peru and the United States, 1960–1975: How Their Ambassadors Managed Foreign Policy in a Turbulent Era*. University Park: Pennsylvania State University Press, 2010.

Webster, David. "Regimes in Motion: The Kennedy Administration and Indonesia's New Frontier, 1960–1962." *Diplomatic History* 33, no. 1 (January 2009): 95–123.

Weiner, Tim. *Legacy of Ashes: The History of the CIA*. New York: Doubleday, 2007.

Weis, Michael W. *Cold Warriors and Coups d'État: Brazilian-American Relations, 1945–1964*. Albuquerque: University of New Mexico Press, 1993.

Westad, Odd Arne. *The Global Cold War: Third World Interventions and the Making of Our Times*. Cambridge: Cambridge University Press, 2005.

——. "The New International History of the Cold War: Three (Possible) Paradigms." *Diplomatic History* 24, no. 4 (Fall 2000): 551–65.

Weston, Charles. "An Ideology of Modernization: The Case of the Bolivian MNR." *Journal of Inter-American Studies* 10, no. 1 (January 1968): 85–101.

Whitehead, Laurence. *The United States and Bolivia: A Case of Neo-Colonialism*. London: Haslemere Group, 1969.

Wickham-Crowley, Timothy P. "Terror and Guerrilla Warfare in Latin America, 1956–1970." *Comparative Studies in Society and History* 32, no. 2 (April 1990): 201–37.

Wilkie, James W. *The Bolivian Revolution and U.S. Aid since 1952: Financial Background and Context of Political Decisions*. Los Angeles: University of California, 1969.

Williams, William Appleman. *The Tragedy of American Diplomacy*. New York: W. W. Norton, 1959.

Wood, Bernard W. "Foreign Aid and Revolutionary Development: The Case of Bolivia, 1952–1964," Occasional Paper 8. Ottawa: School of International Affairs of Carleton University, undated.

Young, Mariliyn. *The Vietnam Wars, 1945–1990*. New York: Harper Perennial, 1991.

Zondag, Cornelius. *The Bolivian Economy, 1952–1965: The Revolution and Its Aftermath*. New York: Praeger, 1966.

Zunes, Stephen. "The United States and Bolivia: The Taming of a Revolution, 1952–1957." *Latin American Perspectives* 28, no. 5 (September 2001): 33–49.

Index